Political Support in Canada:
The Crisis Years

Of related interest

Influence in Parliament: Canada
Allan Kornberg *and* William Mishler

Legislatures in Developmental Perspective
Edited by Allan Kornberg *and* Lloyd D. Musolf

Canada's New Constitution
Edited by Richard H. Leach

The Politics of Canadian Airport Development
Lessons for Federalism
Elliot J. Feldman *and* Jerome Milch

Perspectives on Revolution and Evolution
Edited by Richard A. Preston

The Influence of the United States on Canadian Development
Eleven Case Studies
Edited by Richard A. Preston

Influence in Parliament: Canada was published as part of a series from the Consortium for Comparative Legislative Studies. All other titles were published for the Duke University Center for Commonwealth and Comparative Studies in a series that has been succeeded by the Duke University Center for International Studies Publications.

litical Support in Canada:
The Crisis Years

Essays in Honor of Richard A. Preston

by

E. Donald Briggs   Alan C. Cairns   Harold D. Clarke
Ronald S. Dick   David Falcone   François-Pierre Gingras
Jane Jenson   Allan Kornberg   Ronald G. Landes
Lawrence LeDuc   J. Alex Murray   Neil Nevitte
Douglas C. Nord   Jon Pammett   Ronald Rogowski
Walter I. Romanow   Mildred A. Schwartz   Joel Smith
Walter C. Soderlund   Marianne C. Stewart   Rick Van Loon
Ronald H. Wagenberg   Geoffrey R. Weller   John Wilson

Edited by
Allan Kornberg and Harold D. Clarke

A Duke University Center for International Studies Publication
Duke University Press
Durham, North Carolina   1983

Library of Congress Cataloging in Publication Data

Main entry under title:

Political support in Canada.

(Duke University Center for International Studies
publications)
   Includes bibliographical references and index.
   1. Federal government—Canada—Addresses, essays,
lectures. 2. Allegiance—Canada—Addresses, essays,
lectures. 3. Legitimacy of governments—Canada—
Addresses, essays, lectures. 4. Political participation
—Canada—Addresses, essays, lectures. I. Kornberg,
Allan. II. Clarke, Harold D. III. Series.
JL27.P64   1983   320.971   83-11567
ISBN 0-8223-0546-1

Contents

III. Policies

IV. Crises

Tables

Figures

Acknowledgments

In editing this volume and conducting the conference at which the several papers contained herein were originally presented we received assistance from numerous organizations and individuals. We wish to acknowledge their assistance.

Bringing a group of scholars from widely separated locations in Canada and the United States to Durham, North Carolina, would have been impossible without generous financial aid from Duke University's Canadian Studies Center, the University of Windsor, and the Canadian Department of External Affairs. Conference arrangements and proceedings were greatly facilitated by the efforts of several individuals at Duke including Richard Leach, Chairman of the Canadian Studies Program, A. Kenneth Pye, University Chancellor and Chairman of the Center for International Studies, Marion C. Salinger, Administrative Coordinator of the Center, Joel Smith, Department of Sociology, and R. Taylor Cole, Department of Political Science. Important logistical assistance for conferees was provided by Keith Archer, John Hogan, and David Jackson. The gracious hospitality of Linda Kornberg and Barbara Smith did much to make the conference an enjoyable experience.

During the manuscript preparation phase of our work, Richard Leach and his predecessor as Chairman of Canadian Studies at Duke, Richard Preston, offered us valuable editorial advice. Their sage counsel is appreciated. Thanks also are due to Amy Levine who assumed the burdensome task of preparing an index. Then too, as is always the case in projects of this kind, an abundance of skillful secretarial assistance is vital. In this respect, we thank Dot Weathers (Duke) and Doris Linkous, Debbie Moran, and Jim Parsons (VPI & SU). Their good cheer and patience while typing and retyping the several papers went well beyond the call of duty.

We also wish to acknowledge the generous financial support of the

Social Sciences and Humanities Research Council of Canada and the National Science Foundation. This assistance was absolutely essential. Without it, the research which we report in our papers in this volume would have been impossible.

Finally, we wish to thank the several conferees. Their willingness to share their wisdom and insights with us during the conference, and then to respond promptly and patiently to our questions and requests while we were editing their papers made the entire venture an enjoyable and valuable educational experience for us. Indeed, their involvement was a sine qua non for making this project a reality and we greatly appreciate their efforts.

ALLAN KORNBERG
HAROLD D. CLARKE

Political Supprt in Canada:
The Crisis Years

Introduction: The Crisis of
Political Support in Canada

Allan Kornberg and Harold D. Clarke

> The decline of Canadian nationhood means then that the
> country is denied many of the material benefits of a domestic
> common market, that the central government is decreasingly
> effective as an international actor and as an agent of interper-
> sonal and interprovincial equalization, and that culture rather
> than nationality is increasingly the principle of political orga-
> nization and political allegiance.
>
> D. Smiley, *Canada in Question*, p. 255

A fundamental task of all political leaders is to maintain the viability of
their political systems by generating adequately high levels of support for them. The task is particularly difficult for the leaders of democratic systems such as Canada for two reasons. Unlike their counterparts in authoritarian and totalitarian systems, political leaders in
democracies must eschew relatively continuous or massive applications of coercive measures to secure compliance with state edicts
because such a "politics of coercion" would contravene the very beliefs on which the legitimacy of democratic regimes rest. Relatedly,
leaders cannot make extensive and sustained use of formal institutions such as schools or the mass media to indoctrinate the public to
support their regimes (and themselves) because the use of such institutions for this purpose both would be repugnant to the great majority of citizens and a violation of cherished cultural norms.

Not surprisingly, given the fundamental importance of the problem, the study of the generation and maintenance of political support
has a history that goes back to the Greek polis. It was given renewed

impetus by the end of colonialism and the emergence of a large number of new states in the post-World War II period. Many of the studies of the political development of these states were informed by the concept of support postulated by David Easton.[1] In discussing support Easton made two crucial distinctions. The first focused on objects of political support of which three were particularly important: the community, the regime, and the authorities. The community is "that aspect of a political system that consists of its members seen as a group of persons bound together by a political division of labor."[2] In contrast, the regime, as conceptualized by Easton, includes not only formal structures and constitutionally prescribed procedures, but also encompasses "a broadly defined underlying set of political values and principles, articulated or implicit, which impose constraints on the purposes for which the energies and resources of the system may be committed."[3] The authorities are defined as occupants of political positions who, on the one hand, may "have acquired the primary responsibility for making decisions at the most inclusive level of the system and hold the broadest discretion in doing so."[4] On the other, authorities also include position holders "whose range of discretion is considerably less . . . and the scope of whose authority is considerably narrower."[5]

The second distinction concerns the nature of support. For Easton, support is either *diffuse* or *specific*. The essential feature of diffuse support is its affective character. Support for various political objects is granted or withheld on the basis of powerful feelings of like or dislike—feelings that are grounded in the early socialization experiences of individuals rather than being contingent upon perceptions of and reactions to the day-to-day behavior of political leaders or the performance of political systems.[6] In contrast, the distinguishing feature of specific support is that it is based on people's "rational" cal-

1. The most comprehensive treatment of the concept is by David Easton, *A Systems Analysis of Political Life* (New York: Wiley, 1965). More recent commentaries include Easton, "A Re-Assessment of the Concept of Political Support," *British Journal of Political Science* 5 (1975): 435–57; and Easton, "Theoretical Approaches to Political Support," *Canadian Journal of Political Science* 9 (1976):431–48.
2. Easton, *A Systems Analysis*, p. 177.
3. Ibid., p. 194.
4. Ibid., p. 213.
5. Ibid.
6. Ibid., chap. 17.

culations, their cost-benefit analyses (albeit possibly of a rough-and-ready sort) of the impact of the actions of political leaders and the performance of political institutions.[7]

It has been argued that, over time, such cost-benefit judgments can seriously erode the level of support the publics of western democracies ascribe to their governments. Rose and Peters, for example, contend that during the post–World War II period, western democracies were able to fund their welfare state programs while having their citizens take home ever-larger pay envelopes because of sustained economic expansion. The payoff yielded by this happy conjunction of circumstances was enhanced regime support. Now, however, economic growth in virtually all of these countries has slowed and, in some cases, essentially ceased. The reasons for this need not be labored. Energy, one of the principal motors of economic development, has become extremely expensive. At the same time inflation both has eroded the real value of currencies while simultaneously raising individual and corporate taxes. Rose and Peters argue that as a result of these and related adverse economic conditions, trust in democratic governments, as well as respect for and deference toward political leaders, has declined, while noncompliance with their edicts has increased.[8] In some instances, these trends have been precipitous and dramatic.[9]

Another problem associated with the maintenance of adequate levels of support derives from intergenerational differences in public judgments about governments and their policies. Some scholarly observers such as Ronald Inglehart argue that a well-educated post–World War II generation tends to be concerned with "quality-of-life" issues and the expansion of opportunities to participate directly in a variety of ways in making political decisions that significantly affect their lives. Older generations, in contrast, continue to focus on "bread-and-butter" issues and are content to leave questions of policy for-

7. Ibid.

8. Richard Rose and Guy Peters, *Can Government Go Bankrupt?* (New York: Basic Books, 1978).

9. Perhaps most noteworthy in this regard is the United States where levels of political trust have declined sharply in the last twenty years. Some analysts argue that this decline has been limited to political authorities whereas others maintain that it extends to government more generally. See Arthur H. Miller, "Political Issues and Trust in Government: 1964–1970," *American Political Science Review* 68 (1974): 951–72; Jack Citrin, "Comment: The Political Relevance of Trust in Government," *American Political Science Review* 68 (1974): 973–88.

mulation to duly constituted political authorities, while confining
their own political activities to voting in periodic elections and other
"conventional" forms of political behavior.[10] If "push comes to shove,"
the younger and older generations seem willing to trade off what the
other group regards as the sine qua non of the good life. The erosion
of specific support for democratic regimes that is a consequence of
these economic and social strains in western societies—should it
persist—eventually could threaten the continued viability of the political systems themselves.

Despite the attractiveness of the concepts of diffuse and specific
support for understanding factors conducive to the maintenance of
political systems, the systematic study of the distribution and bases of
support for political communities, regimes, and authorities has suffered because of a number of factors. Three have proved especially
perplexing. First, it has been extremely difficult to devise measures
of diffuse and specific support that are independent of one another.
Indeed, some investigators have argued that the two types of support
are difficult, if not impossible, to distinguish empirically.[11] To the extent that this is true, research on the causes and consequences of political support using Easton's conceptual framework is bound to be of
limited value. Second, and relatedly, attempts to theorize about specific support have been sharply criticized on the grounds that in the
"real world" the great majority of "ordinary" citizens are simply unable to make a cognitive connection between what they want from a
political system and what the system produces, a connection that is
intrinsic to the concept of specific support. Third, investigators employing putative measures of diffuse or specific support as independent variables in analyses have had difficulty in linking differences in
their levels to significant variations in individual political behavior, or
more importantly, to variations in the stability of political systems.[12]

10. The seminal work in this field is Ronald Inglehart, *The Silent Revolution* (Princeton:
Princeton University Press, 1977). See also Samuel Barnes and Max Kaase, eds., *Political Action* (Beverly Hills: Sage Publications, 1979).

11. See, for example, Gerhard Loewenberg, "The Influence of Parliamentary Behavior on
Regime Stability," *Comparative Politics* 3 (1974):184.

12. Perhaps the most thoroughgoing analysis of the behavioral correlates of political support
is Muller and Jukam's work on "aggressive" political behavior in the German Federal Republic.
See Edward N. Muller and Thomas O. Jukam, "On the Meaning of Political Support," *American Political Science Review* 71 (1977):1561–95; and Muller, *Aggressive Political Behavior*
(Princeton: Princeton University Press, 1979).

Despite these and other problems, as Ronald Rogowski points out in his essay in this volume, scholars recognize the potential theoretical importance of the concept of support, and, as a result, they continue to debate the meaning, measurement, and analytic utility of diffuse and specific support and some of their suggested analogues.

Since the problem of maintaining the integrity of the Canadian political community has been and continues to be the single most salient aspect of the country's political life, it is not surprising that students of Canadian politics long have been concerned with the issue of support, even if they have not always labeled it as such. Of particular interest in the matrix of factors affecting the maintenance of the political community and regime have been the structures and processes of federalism. However—and notwithstanding either the outpouring of research on federalism over the years, or the complaints of generations of politicians about the inequities of existing federal arrangements—little of a systematic nature is known about how citizens perceive and react to the federal system, or what consequences such perceptions and evaluations have for the support they ascribe to the Canadian polity.[13]

There has been even less systematic study devoted to the impact other factors have on political support in Canada. A good example is provided by the mass media. Because the acquisition of information and related values pertinent to the generation and maintenance of political support may be, to a substantial extent, a product of exposure to print and, perhaps especially, electronic media, the potential importance of the media is widely recognized. Despite this and the frequency with which they have been subjected to investigation in recent years,[14] the role of the media in either enhancing or eroding support is, at best, only partially comprehended.

13. One study of these phenomena is by Allan Kornberg, Harold D. Clarke, and Marianne C. Stewart, "Federalism and Fragmentation: Political Support in Canada," *Journal of Politics* 41 (1979):889–906. Other studies of support in Canada include Allan Kornberg, Harold D. Clarke, and Lawrence LeDuc, "Some Correlates of Regime Support in Canada," *British Journal of Political Science* 8 (1978):199–216; and Allan Kornberg, Harold D. Clarke, and Marianne C. Stewart, "Public Support for Community and Regime in the Regions of Contemporary Canada," *The American Review of Canadian Studies* 10 (1980):75–93.

14. The most recent major study of the media in Canada is *The Report of the Royal Commission on Newspapers* (Ottawa: Minister of Supply and Services Canada, 1981). See also *Report of the Special Senate Committee on Mass Media*, vols. I and II (Ottawa: Information Canada, 1970).

Of course, relationships among political institutions and processes and system support have not been entirely neglected. Most notably, there have been a number of major studies of political parties and the varying functions they have performed in the Canadian political system. Some of these do contribute to our understanding of the nature of political support. In particular, several studies of the origins of regionally based "third" parties such as the CCF, Social Credit, and Union Nationale suggest that public disaffection with the policies of the national Liberal and Conservative parties entered into cost-benefit calculations which governed public reactions to those parties.[15] During the 1920s and 1930s, especially in the west and Quebec, such calculations resulted in a substantial erosion of electoral support for the old-line parties. More recently, party scholars have criticized the national party system for its failure to integrate the polity by, among other things, offering the public policies that could transcend regionally based economic and cultural particularisms.[16] Further, a series of national election studies conducted in the 1960s and 1970s indicates that the kind of public disaffection with political parties and cynicism about the actions of their leaders that were prevalent in earlier periods of Canadian history are present among substantial segments of more recent electorates. In this regard, it is espe-

15. J. A. Irving, *The Social Credit Movement in Alberta* (Toronto: University of Toronto Press, 1959); C. B. Macpherson, *Democracy in Alberta: Social Credit and the Party System*, 2nd ed. (Toronto: University of Toronto Press, 1962); Herbert F. Quinn, *The Union Nationale* (Toronto: University of Toronto Press, 1963); Seymour Martin Lipset, *Agrarian Socialism: The Cooperative Commonwealth Federation in Saskatchewan* (New York: Doubleday, 1968); Walter D. Young, *The Anatomy of a Party: The National CCF* (Toronto: University of Toronto Press, 1969); Maurice Pinard, *The Rise of a Third Party: A Study of Crisis Politics* (Englewood Cliffs: Prentice-Hall, 1971); and Michael B. Stein, *The Dynamics of Right-Wing Protest: A Political Analysis of Social Credit in Quebec* (Toronto: University of Toronto Press, 1973). For a recent history of the development of Canadian national parties see M. Janine Brodie and Jane Jenson, *Crisis, Challenge and Change: Party and Class in Canada* (Toronto: Methuen, 1980).

16. See, for example, John Meisel, "The Decline of Party in Canada," in Hugh G. Thorburn, ed., *Party Politics in Canada*, 4th ed. (Scarborough: Prentice-Hall, 1979), pp. 121–35. See also Robert W. Jackman, "Political Parties, Voting and National Integration: The Canadian Case," in R. Schultz, O. Kruhlak, and J. Terry, eds., *The Canadian Political Process*, 3rd ed. (Toronto: Holt, Rinehart and Winston, 1979), p. 139; Alan Cairns, "The Electoral System and the Party System in Canada: 1921–1965, *Canadian Journal of Political Science* 1 (1968):55; Gad Horowitz, "Conservatism, Liberalism, and Socialism in Canada: An Interpretation," *Canadian Journal of Economics and Political Science* 32 (1966):144–71; and John Porter, *The Vertical Mosaic* (Toronto: University of Toronto Press, 1965), chap. 12. It is noteworthy that at least some observers have continued to argue that the national parties do perform a unifying function. For a forceful statement to this effect see R. MacGregor Dawson and Norman Ward, *The Government of Canada*, 5th ed. (Toronto: University of Toronto Press, 1970), p. 415.

cially noteworthy that many people lack a strong sense of political efficacy, believing that political authorities are unwilling or unable to respond to their needs and demands.[17]

Widespread discontent with the political system is not confined to the authorities level. Rather, substantial numbers of people in every region are dissatisfied with the operation of the federal system and would favor a redistribution of the powers of the federal and provincial governments.[18] To date, relatively few Canadians have withdrawn their support from the national political community itself, but perhaps particularly ominous in its implications for the future is the fact that negative feelings about the community are concentrated among a substantial cohort of younger Quebecers. They are the same persons who have formed the core support group of the Parti Québécois.[19] The electoral victory of this party in the November 1976 Quebec provincial election was the prime factor that transformed a long-standing pattern of escalating federal-provincial and interprovincial tensions into the widely recognized "Crisis of Confederation."

A general concern with these and other manifold problems associated with the maintenance of the integrity of the Canadian political system, and a desire to evaluate the utility of employing the concept of support to illuminate these problems, brought a group of students

17. Allan Kornberg, Harold D. Clarke, and Arthur Goddard, "Parliament and the Representational Process in Contemporary Canada," in Harold D. Clarke et al., eds., *Parliament, Policy and Representation* (Toronto: Methuen, 1980), chap. 4.

18. Data documenting dissatisfaction with the operation of the federal system are presented in Allan Kornberg, William Mishler, and Harold D. Clarke, *Representative Democracy in the Canadian Provinces* (Scarborough: Prentice-Hall, 1982), chap. 2. See also Kornberg, Clarke, and Stewart "Federalism and Fragmentation," pp. 896–97; and Michael D. Ornstein, H. Michael Stevenson, and A. Paul M. Williams. "The State of Mind: Public Perceptions of the Future of Canada," in R. B. Beyers and Robert W. Reford, eds., *Canada Challenged: The Viability of Confederation* (Toronto: Canadian Institute of International Affairs, 1979), p. 74. On public sentiments re: redistribution of powers in the federal system see *Une question de pays/A Question of Country* (Radio Canada/CBC, April 1980), section 3, p. 56; and Ornstein et al., "The State of Mind," p. 74.

19. Richard Hamilton and Maurice Pinard, "The Bases of Parti Québécois Support in Recent Quebec Elections," *Canadian Journal of Political Science* 9 (1976):3–26; Maurice Pinard and Richard Hamilton, "The Independence Issue and the Polarization of the Electorate: The 1973 Quebec Election," *Canadian Journal of Political Science* 10 (1977):215–60; Maurice Pinard and Richard Hamilton, "The Parti Québécois Comes to Power: An Analysis of the 1976 Quebec Election," *Canadian Journal of Political Science* 11 (1978):739–76; Harold Clarke, "Partisanship and the Parti Québécois: The Impact of the Independence Issue," *The American Review of Canadian Studies* 8 (1978):28–47; and Harold D. Clarke et al., "Partisanship and the Parti Québécois: Losing a Battle But Winning the War," paper presented at the Annual Meeting of the American Sociological Association, Toronto, Aug. 24, 1981.

of Canadian government and politics together at a conference held at Duke University, November 21 and 22, 1980. The great majority of the essays presented at that conference are included in this volume, which is organized in four sections: problems and approaches, agents, policies, and crises.

As indicated by its title, the first section is concerned with questions pertaining to the conceptualization, measurement, determinants, and consequences of political support. In the lead essay in this section, Ronald Rogowski presents a taxonomy of relevant theories. According to Rogowski, theories of political support may be usefully subsumed under five headings: (1) theories that view support as a function of perceptions of fair treatment of citizens by the political system and its duly constituted authorities; (2) theories that focus on the subconscious, symbolic elements underlying supportive sentiments; (3) theories viewing support as a consequence of political participation and the accompanying psychological implication of individuals in ongoing political processes; (4) theories based on citizens' assessments of regime effectiveness; and (5) theories that relate support to variations in the social division of labor. Using evidence from a variety of sources, Rogowski critically evaluates each of these types of theory and concludes that none has been especially fruitful, largely because the concept of political support itself is wanting. Assuming a reconceptualization of support that takes into account its fundamentally contingent nature, he argues that the type of theory holding greatest promise is a "rationalist" variant of the social division of labor explanation.

Mildred Schwartz, like Rogowski, argues the need for a reconceptualization of support. In her view, it is best to think of it in terms of relationships among social groups rather than as an individual-level phenomenon. Moreover, unlike many scholars who have assumed that political authorities invariably try to maximize support for themselves and the systems of which they are a part among *all* elements of a population, Schwartz contends that the representatives of dominant social groups frequently exclude particular minority groups from the social coalition of system "supporters." She argues that the offering of political support can be conceived of as a "privilege" which symbolizes and defines full membership in a political community. Thus, for Schwartz, theories of political support are closely linked to theories of citizenship. Using the example of the treatment of Japanese Canadians prior to and during World War II she observes that a catalytic event such as a war or depression frequently precipitates intergroup support crises. Interestingly, the resolution of such crises often is a prelude to the subsequent integration of a minority group into the larger political community.

The third essay in this section, by Allan Kornberg and Marianne C. Stewart, examines the relationship between national identity and political support. Employing data derived from a 1979 national survey, Kornberg and Stewart find that approximately one-half of those interviewed included an identification with Canada as a component of their self-concept, even though they were not prompted to do so. Further, despite the salience of provinces in Canadian political life, relatively few respondents included an identification with a province or region in their concepts of self. More generally, although the tendency to have a national identity in one's self-concept varied in predictable ways with certain socioeconomic, demographic, and attitudinal characteristics, what was most impressive was the pervasiveness of national identities among significant proportions of every major social group in all parts of the country. Equally important, variations in the frequency with which national identity was a component of the self-concept were positively associated with levels of support for the national political community and other political objects. On the basis of these and related findings the authors argue that there is more support for the overarching political community than either political elites or many scholars and journalists have assumed.

The second section of this volume focuses on some of the principal agents in processes by which political support may be augmented or diminished. In the first essay in this section, Ronald Landes presents an overview of the relevance of existing research on political socialization for understanding political support. Although there is frequently an implicit assumption that early socialization experiences affect political support patterns in later life ("the primacy principle"), Landes notes that this assumption has not been evaluated systematically in the Canadian context using requisite longitudinal analyses. Existing research suggests, however, that the socialization of politically supportive attitudes is relatively haphazard. Perhaps most notably, little systematic use has been made of schools as socialization agencies. Re-

latedly, to the extent that schools do play an influential role in the
political socialization process, the content of what is transmitted varies sharply between anglophone and francophone milieux, and it is at
least plausible that this variation influences the subsequent attitudes
and behavior of the two ethno-linguistic communities. Landes concludes his analysis by underscoring the argument that explicit attempts to "engineer" political support are unlikely to be successful in
a country such as Canada since such endeavors would run contrary to
widely held beliefs about the inappropriateness of using the educational system or other aspects of the state apparatus for political in-
doctrination. However, in a liberal democratic cultural milieu, system performance counts. Accordingly, perhaps the best way to build
support for the Canadian polity is to show that it deserves support by
enhancing its capacity for effective, equitable responses to citizen
needs and demands.

A second important agent of political support is the mass media. In
advanced industrial societies the media have been hypothesized to
have a variety of significant effects.[20] In Canada, their potential for
generating political support has long been assumed. Indeed, as Ronald
Dick notes, whether realistically or not, publicly financed media such
as the CBC and the National Film Board, from their inception, have
been mandated to protect and develop Canadian national consciousness and identity. For an almost equally lengthy period, they have
been castigated for failing to do so adequately.

In his assessment of the validity of such charges, Dick argues that
although the media can affect political (and other) attitudes, they operate within a framework of basic social and political facts that cannot
be ignored. Canada is, in its nature, a very heterogeneous society,
beset by deep-seated, reinforcing ethno-linguistic, religious, and regional cleavages. Unalterable also is the country's geographic proximity to the United States. Cherished liberal democratic values such
as freedom of speech and the press, together with a shared language
and other cultural affinities, make it virtually impossible, and perhaps
even unwise, to attempt to purge Canadian media of all influences of

20. On the nature of media impact on the political process see H. T. Reynolds, *Politics and
the Common Man* (Homewood, Ill.: Dorsey Press, 1974), chap. 4; and James C. Strouse, *The
Mass Media, Public Opinion, and Public Policy Analysis: Linkage Explorations* (Columbus:
Merrill, 1975), chap. 7.

its giant southern neighbor. Again, democratic values, particularly the doctrine of "fairness" in political reporting, make it difficult for the media to avoid having a negative effect on people's attitudes. The many-sided and seemingly endless political disputation presented by the media acting in accordance with this doctrine breeds feelings of frustration and alienation among the public which are very difficult to overcome.

Despite the ponderous, even intractable, problems associated with the above conditions, it is important to recognize that media effects on political support are complex and multifaceted—and hence not easily assessed. As Dick notes, the publicly financed media in Canada have already presented the public with many excellent public affairs programs which have had the potential to enhance significantly citizens' understanding of and pride in their own country and its political system. Moreover, in the future, by giving greater recognition to, rather than struggling against, regional and other cultural diversities in Canadian society, the media may do much to bolster political support.

The complexity of media effects on political support in a liberal democratic state is also a theme pursued by Ronald Wagenberg and his colleagues in their study of media agenda-setting in the 1979 federal election. This investigation of how various electronic media in the two major language communities covered the election suggests that voters in all parts of the country were presented with essentially the same picture of the campaign. Other things being equal, the authors argue, this common agenda has strong integrative potential. Yet, in this respect, it is ironic that the vast bulk of the electronic coverage of parties and their leaders was either neutral or negative in tone in 1979. In such an instance the possible effect may be to encourage widespread disaffection from political authorities, and perhaps even from the electoral process itself.[21] The latter is, of course, a highly salient symbol of the legitimacy of a democratic political system.

More basically, Wagenberg et al. note that there is a fundamental contradiction in expectations regarding the role of the media in a con-

21. Allan Kornberg and Judith Wolfe, "Parliament, the Media and the Polls," and Richard G. Price and Harold D. Clarke, "Television and the House of Commons," both in Clarke et al., eds., *Parliament, Policy and Representation*, chaps. 3, 4.

temporary liberal democracy such as Canada. On the one hand, the media are supposed to serve as unbiased channels of communication between politicians and the public. However, by so serving, they run the risk of becoming the dupes of manipulative political campaigns—reporting nothing but prestaged "media events" and other sorts of vacuous partisan propaganda. On the other hand, the media are charged with the duty of acting as "watchdogs" of the people, that is, with being uncompromising in their efforts to uncover and publicize political incompetence and corruption. Yet, a zealous acceptance of this latter role runs the risk of generating such a pervasively negative image of the political process that, over time, public confidence in the political order may be seriously eroded.

In Canada, the mass media are not the only agents which have been hypothesized to play important roles in processes by which political support is generated or dissipated. Political parties also have been charged with this task. As noted above, it is a popular sport among observers of Canadian party politics to decry the failure of the national party system to serve as a mechanism of national integration. Whereas prescriptions to enhance the ability of parties to perform the integrative role which they have been assigned have varied, most have included the abandonment of "brokerage politics" as an initial step. Rather than conducting essentially issueless election campaigns that focus on the personalities and styles of supposedly "charismatic" leaders, the national parties should develop meaningful, comprehensible, and identifiably different platforms. In particular, several scholars have argued that the parties should stress issues related to social class. By so doing, they would create lines of political cleavage that cross-cut regional and ethno-linguistic divisions. The political effects of nonclass cleavages thereby would be muted and the result would be enhanced national integration.[22]

In a provocative essay, John Wilson advances a contrary argument that such prescriptions are bound to fail because they are based on a false premise. Using a variety of survey and aggregate data in support of his thesis, Wilson maintains that, in fact, there is no national party system in Canada which could perform an integrative role. The forces of regionalism, politically organized in terms of provincial electorates,

22. See, for example, Gad Horowitz, "Toward the Democratic Class Struggle," *Journal of Canadian Studies* 1 (1966):9–10.

are so strong that federal election results represent not the workings of a national party system, but rather the aggregation of the electoral outcomes of several entirely separate provincial systems. Moreover, given that provincial societies are at different levels of socioeconomic development, abandoning the old conventional wisdom of brokerage politics for a newer version based on the purportedly salutary effects of class politics provides no solution to the present crisis of support. A nationwide emphasis on class issues would not work simply because it is incongruent with present socioeconomic realities in several provinces. Rather, what is needed, Wilson argues, is a fundamental re-thinking of the very purposes of a federal society. The presently Hobbesian world of federal-provincial and interprovincial conflict must give way to a system structuring provinces' political environments in a fashion such that interprovincial cooperation will be encouraged. According to this view, a decentralization of federal power to the provinces is a necessary, but hardly undesirable, step.

The third section of this volume, entitled "Policies," contains three chapters which explore relationships among policy-making processes, the substance of policy, and political support. The first essay, by David Falcone and Richard Van Loon, focuses on the policy/support nexus in the area of health programs. In the 1950s and 1960s, the federal and provincial governments developed and implemented comprehensive hospital and medical insurance programs. In their design and implementation these were archetypical examples of the "cooperative federalism" that characterized federal-provincial relations during this period. In return for agreeing that their health insurance programs would meet certain standards set by the federal government (i.e., universality, portability, comprehensiveness, not-for-profit), the provinces received large grants to help defray the costs of such programs.[23]

Falcone and Van Loon argue that this type of conditional grant formula has significant potential to erode support for the federal government while simultaneously enhancing that for provincial governments. This is so because, to the extent that support is proffered or withdrawn on the basis of perceived costs and benefits (i.e., in Easton's terminology, support is specific), the "baroque" nature of federal-

23. The development of Canada's health insurance policy is described in Malcolm G. Taylor, *Health Insurance and Canadian Public Policy* (Montreal: McGill-Queen's University Press, 1979).

provincial fiscal arrangements in the health area obscures from public scrutiny which level of government is really paying the lion's share of the service. Thus, rather than appreciating the federal government for its willingness to pay large portions of health care costs, the public perceives that Ottawa imposes taxes while the provinces distribute benefits. The authors suggest that over a period of several years these perceptions may well have contributed to a shift in the relative balance of public support for the two levels of government.

Douglas Nord and Geoffrey Weller also are concerned with how policy processes and their outcomes affect political support. Conceptualizing these processes as exercises in intergroup bargaining and accommodation, the authors argue that the entry of new issues into the political arena may alter levels and patterns of political support by stimulating previously inactive citizens to band together to affect policy outcomes. In so doing, such groups invariably conflict with groups which currently enjoy access to and exercise influence in policy-making processes. Depending upon how such conflicts are resolved, it is possible that both the new and the established interest groups will become disaffected with political authorities and perhaps even the regime itself. However, such a negative outcome is not inevitable.

To illustrate this latter point, Nord and Weller focus on environmental issues which became increasingly salient in the late 1960s and early 1970s. These issues spawned a host of sometimes ephemeral new interest groups which pressed for access to loci of political influence in order to generate and implement policies that would reduce pollution, and, more generally, guard the environment from what they perceived to be the unjustified and predatory incursions of "developers" unconcerned with the quality of life. The authors' analysis of how the Ontario government responded to the demands of environmental groups documents that by intervening actively in the emerging political conflict in the environmental area, the provincial government was able to use strategies of cooption and incentives to accommodate the competing groups with no discernible net loss of public support. Although the environmental protection policies were not fully satisfactory to either the environmentalists or their developer adversaries, to a large extent the government offset potential losses in support by creatively modifying existing structures and processes. Political support thus depends not only on what policies are implemented but also on how they are generated.

Unlike Falcone and Van Loon or Nord and Weller, LeDuc and Murray treat political support as an *input* to policy processes. To show how support may function as an independent variable, they examine changes in Canada's foreign investment policies since the late 1960s. In the process by which these policies have been formed, attitudes held by the general public have played a discernible, if not easily measured role. In this respect, nationalist sentiments are one consideration. Also relevant, however, are orientations toward entities external to the polity, particularly the United States, as well as perceptions and evaluations of the impact of various aspects of foreign investment policies. LeDuc and Murray argue that recently the latter have assumed increasing importance. In a period when economic considerations are highly salient, calculations regarding the "dollars and cents" aspects of the costs and benefits to be conferred by various policy options can be expected to dominate public thinking about how the government treats questions of foreign investment. Such an essentially pragmatic approach reflects the fact that for many people orientations toward foreign investment are influenced by a mosaic of supportive attitudes and beliefs which are not deeply rooted in or tightly constrained by more general and diffuse nationalist sentiments.

The concluding section of this volume, entitled "Crises," contains four chapters which focus directly on pressing problems of political support in contemporary Canada. Appropriately, all of the chapters are concerned in whole or in part with Quebec and its relationship to the rest of the country. It is there that continued public support for the existence of a Canadian polity is most problematic, and the threat of widespread withdrawal of support for the political community most serious.

The first essay, by François-Pierre Gingras and Neil Nevitte, considers the evolution of Québécois nationalism. In their analysis of the phenomenon, the authors challenge the conventional wisdom that the Quiet Revolution completely transformed the nature of nationalist sentiments in Quebec political culture. Distinguishing between elite and mass culture, Gingras and Nevitte present data and arguments to support the view that at the mass level the Quiet Revolution is incomplete. As a consequence, the older, traditional, nationalist ideology, with its emphases on Roman Catholicism and a politics of accommodation, now coexists with a newer, secular, statist nationalism which views the government of Quebec as the *only* legitimate and effective instrument for protecting and advancing Québécois interests.

Gingras and Nevitte maintain that the unfinished nature of the Quiet Revolution at the level of mass culture has had profound consequences. On the one hand, because it partially replaced one nationalism with another, it provided the basis for a secular nationalist party such as the Parti Québécois to develop and enjoy marked success. Ironically, however, this configuration of old and new nationalist sentiments makes the PQ most successful when it is operating within a "normal politics" framework: that is, when it is contesting provincial elections. In this respect, the PQ becomes the legitimate successor to earlier nationalist parties, particularly the Union Nationale. By the same token, however, the coexistence of the two nationalisms thus far has limited Péquistes' ability to achieve their dream of a sovereign Quebec.

Given the relatively strong support for the PQ, and more important, for sovereignty-association and independence among younger Québécois, some might argue that it is only a matter of time before the party will have the majority support in the Quebec electorate required to effect radical changes in the province's political status. Gingras and Nevitte admit this possibility, but reemphasize that religious and related influences in Québécois cultural life have not been expunged. In consequence, these influences may well help to shape future political expressions of nationalist elements in ways that are difficult to predict.

The arguments of Gingras and Nevitte are not inconsistent with findings of Pammett et al.'s study of forces shaping voting behavior in the May 1980 sovereignty-association referendum. Pammett and his colleagues argue that although the Parti Québécois labored mightily to present the referendum to the electorate as a choice of alternative political *regimes*, or as an even lesser question relating to the desirability of modifying the existing regime, the choices were otherwise perceived by many voters. A sizable segment of the electorate interpreted the referendum as presenting *community-level* options.

Rather than focusing on the nuances of an ill-defined sovereignty-association versus an even more nebulous renewed federalism, these voters were guided by deep-seated feelings about the Canadian political community. Despite considerable dissatisfaction with the operation of the federal system and an accompanying widespread desire for some sort of regime-level change, many voters wanted Quebec to remain a part of Canada and believed that a "oui" majority, rather than leading to a limited constitutional "deblocage," instead would result in the demise of the Canadian political system.

This is not to say that feelings about the political regime and authorities (both provincial and federal) were irrelevant to voting choice in the referendum. The effects of those latter sentiments could be detected. Particularly salient in prompting a "oui" vote were the effects of positive sentiments toward Lévesque and the PQ government. Those effects, however, were not sufficiently strong to offset the more massive influence of community-level sentiments.

In reviewing these findings, it is intriguing to speculate about the ironies of the PQ's position as a provincial government. Specifically, it is conceivable that to the extent that positive feelings about the provincial authorities were based on judgments that the PQ had been a "good government," the party inadvertently had undercut the rationale for Quebec sovereignty. In attempting to bolster the confidence of the electorate in its ability to guide Québécois' political destiny, the PQ may have shown voters that they could "have their cake and eat it too." Why should they risk the unknowns of sovereignty-association when the PQ was capable of governing effectively within the familiar, if not wholly satisfying, confines of Confederation?

Such speculative interpretations aside, in retrospect it is clear that the referendum was widely perceived as an event of potentially great significance for the future of the Canadian state. In this respect, research findings presented in a paper by Joel Smith and Allan Kornberg supplement those of Pammett et al. In their panel study of public attitudes in three cities (Trois Rivières, Peterborough, and Lethbridge) during the period before and immediately after the referendum, Smith and Kornberg find high levels of awareness of and interest in the event. In all three communities, many people perceived its importance for the future of the country and believed that,

regardless of the result, the referendum presaged significant alterations in the structure of the Canadian political system.

Smith and Kornberg argue their data indicate that the ability of
such structural changes to resolve the difficulties besetting the system is, at best, problematic. On the one hand, public support for the
Canadian political community is high and "except for small groups of
strident, dissatisfied people, the images of Canada are largely positive and built in various combinations around themes of social justice
and energetic dynamism."[24] Such images are prevalent not only in
Ontario, but also in Alberta, and most importantly, in Quebec as well.

On the other hand, popular perceptions of and judgments about
the attitudes and behavior of various provinces suggest the potential
for substantial interprovincial conflict. Specifically, in all three cities
many respondents see their own provinces as a "giver" and other
provinces as less productive, less cooperative "takers," unconcerned
with the welfare of the country as a whole. Residents of various provinces also are prone to see other provinces as powerful actors on the
political stage, and presumably, therefore, as potential if not actual
threats. Echoing the judgment of Wilson that the world of interprovincial relations has degenerated into a struggle of "all against all,"
Smith and Kornberg conclude that a principal danger confronting the
Canadian polity stems from "the combination of domestic provincial
chauvinism and other provincial antipathies."[25] This conclusion serves
as an important caveat for those who would view Canada's political
problems exclusively through the lens of federal-provincial conflicts.
In part at least, the problems reflect culturally based patterns of interprovincial suspicions and enmity—patterns that may prove quite insoluble in the face of limited structural reforms to the federal system.

The conflictual character of federal-provincial and interprovincial
relations is also a principal theme pursued by Alan Cairns in his detailed analysis of the positions adopted by some of the key actors—
Ottawa, Quebec, Alberta, and British Columbia—during the protracted negotiations on the subject of a new Canadian constitution.
According to Cairns, the principal motivation of each of the several

24. Joel Smith and Allan Kornberg, "The Quebec Referendum: National or Provincial
Event?" chap. 11 in this volume.
25. Ibid.

participants in the constitutional drama was naked self-interest. In formulating their positions on a constitution, each government appears to have been guided by some version of a "worst possible case" scenario. The common operating principle was to maximize their current power and influence and to minimize the possibility of any subsequent erosion of their constitutional status under future conditions that could not be predicted with certainty. To explain the behavior of first ministers and their principal advisors in the Hobbesian world of federal-provincial negotiations, Cairns points to two factors: the inexorable growth of governments and the electoral imperative.

Regarding the former, Cairns notes that the size and scope of governments, both federal and provincial, have increased rapidly and continuously since the end of World War II. Provincial bureaucracies, in particular, have not been content to maintain a "steady state." Rather, responding to and aided by important interest groups within their respective provinces and the increasing proportions of their populations directly or indirectly dependent upon them for their livelihood, provincial governments have impinged on ever-broader areas of social and economic life.[26] In so doing, they inevitably have come into conflict with other provinces and the federal government which, under the same impetus, have been pursuing similar policy goals. As for the electoral imperative, the several political parties in each province have found it profitable to harvest votes by presenting themselves as the "true" champions of the interests of their provinces vis-à-vis Ottawa and the other provinces. In so doing, they are constantly driven to formulate ever more self-serving demands and to reject compromises that might make them appear weak or vacillating in the eyes of their electorate.

Cairns emphasizes, by way of conclusion, that throughout this drama the protagonists have been political elites, elected officials and senior bureaucrats. The public has been involved only as an object to be manipulated in the ongoing struggle for constitutional advantage. Indeed, even proposals for such seemingly democratic devices as an entrenched bill of rights or the use of referenda in constitutional

26. On the growth of provincial governmental activity see Kornberg, Mishler, and Clarke, *Representative Democracy in the Canadian Provinces*, chap. 8.

amending formulae have been motivated, in large part, by considerations of present and future self-interest and the tactical position these devices might secure for provinces obtaining these advantages.

It may be inferred from Cairns's description of the profoundly elitist character of constitutional negotiations from which the great majority of Canadians have been entirely excluded that the political regime resulting from a new constitution may well experience many of the same support problems that have bedeviled Canada since Confederation. In commenting on the latter, Garth Stevenson has observed that from the outset the new national government lacked legitimacy because it was the creation of the few rather than the many, and because over the years the few—political and socioeconomic elites—have consciously and effectively excluded the general public from participating in most important political decisions.[27] Stevenson's characterization of the nature of the Canadian political process has been seconded, in whole or in part, by a number of other observers.[28]

In thinking about the implications of such an elitist pattern of political decision making, it is important to note that Canada is not unique in this regard. Other liberal democracies characterized by deep-seated and persistent societal cleavages have relied on similar forms of decision making. Some scholars have maintained that this is both necessary and desirable. In such fragmented societies, the active political involvement of large numbers of the general public drawn from conflicting social groups would severely exacerbate intergroup tensions and markedly enhance the likelihood of continuous and profound political instability. To circumvent such a threat to the political order, it is preferable to exchange extensive public participation in political life for a system of sharply limited citizen involvement that brings together elite representatives of key societal groups in an ongoing process of bargaining, negotiation, and mutual accommodation. This process has been labeled consociational democracy, and a number of scholars have argued that it is both empirically and normatively relevant to the Canadian situation.[29]

27. Garth Stevenson, *Unfulfilled Union* (Toronto: Macmillan, 1979), pp. 44–48.

28. See, for example, Porter, *The Vertical Mosaic*, chap. 12; Robert Presthus, *Elite Accommodation in Canadian Politics* (Toronto: Macmillan, 1973), chaps. 1, 2.

29. Analyses of Canada in terms of the consociational democracy model include S. J. R. Noel, "Consociational Democracy and Canadian Federalism," *Canadian Journal of Political Science* 4

A consociational political order is contingent upon the willingness of elites to bargain in good faith with one another. Elites are motivated to do so because they realize that the continuing viability of the polity depends upon the success of their efforts. The election of a PQ government in November 1976 pledged to hold a referendum on sovereignty-association dramatically symbolized that the assumptions of consociational democracy were no longer operative in Canada. In fact, it might be argued that these assumptions have been problematic for at least a generation. However that may be, we may infer that regardless of the nature of any new constitutional arrangements, the problem of achieving and maintaining "adequate" levels of public support for the Canadian political system is likely to persist until a politically involved citizenry makes clear to federal and provincial elites that the continuation of the political community in its current form is a matter of paramount importance. Indeed, elite recognition of widespread support for such a community is a necessary precondition for the construction of political agendas that effectively and fairly address the legitimate needs and demands of Canadians, irrespective of background or region of residence. In turn, the implementation of such an agenda, within a framework of a revised federal system providing for greater citizen representation and participation at all levels of the political process, is, in our view, the best means for generating the kind of support required to transcend the crisis of Confederation.[30]

(1971): 15–18; Presthus, *Elite Accommodation*, passim; and Kenneth McRae, "Consociationalism and the Canadian Political System," in K. McRae, ed., *Consociational Democracy* (Toronto: McClelland and Stewart, 1974), pp. 238–61.

30. For a more detailed exposition of these points see Kornberg, Mishler, and Clarke, *Representative Democracy*, chap. 9.

· I ·

Problems and Approaches

Political Support for Regimes:
A Theoretical Inventory and Critique

Ronald Rogowski

Not the least of the problems associated with the study of political support is a confusion of definitions, which I propose to remedy by a return to origins. With David Easton, I shall mean by *support* for some object either action on its behalf or a favorable orientation toward it. I shall refer to the actions as *overt*, the orientations as *covert*, support.[1] Still following Easton,[2] and indirectly Arthur F. Bentley,[3] I also shall occasionally deploy, as a kind of midpoint, the concept of a "tendency toward," or a "readiness for," overt support. Tocqueville, for example, draws this useful distinction: himself a covert supporter of monarchy, under the Second Republic he was unwilling to act on behalf of a restoration, even should a favorable opportunity arise; others were willing so to act, even though they took no action in the prevailing unfavorable circumstances.[4]

So defined, support for a regime[5] may usefully be distinguished from belief in its legitimacy.[6] While it is hard to see how one could

1. David Easton, *A Systems Analysis of Political Life* (New York: John Wiley & Sons, 1965), p. 159.
2. Ibid., p. 169.
3. *The Process of Government* (Chicago: University of Chicago Press, 1908), pp. 184–89.
4. *The Recollections of Alexis de Tocqueville*, trans. Alexander Teixeira de Mattos, ed. J. P. Mayer (Cleveland and New York: World Publishing Co., Meridian Books, 1959), pp. 223–24.
5. I thus exclude considerations of support for particular incumbents or, except where specifically indicated, of support for a political community.
6. I join Easton in rejecting the view, which informs much of the survey research on support, that diffuse support is "roughly comparable to . . . legitimacy": Edward N. Muller and Thomas O. Jukam, "On the Meaning of Political Support," *American Political Science Review* 71 (1977): 1561–95, 1563. See also Edward N. Muller, "Correlates and Consequences of Beliefs in the Legitimacy of Regime Structures," *Midwest Journal of Political Science* 14 (1970): 329–412, esp. 395–97. For Easton's position, see David Easton, "A Re-Assessment of the Concept of Political Support," *British Journal of Political Science* 5 (1975): 435–57, 453n.

consider a regime legitimate without supporting it at least covertly, belief in legitimacy by no means entails overt support, as the case of Tocqueville (and of many other French monarchists) makes clear; and one can, as Max Weber surely did, extensively support a regime, covertly and overtly, that one does not really consider legitimate.[7]

A Taxonomy of Theories

If we can agree even preliminarily how to define our subject, however, we come at once to the second, and perhaps more obvious, difficulty, namely, the impossible profusion of explanatory theories. When, almost fifteen years ago, members of Harry Eckstein's project on authority patterns undertook to construct an inventory, they easily found over 200 distinct hypotheses about support; and by now the number will surely have swollen even further. I cannot, therefore, be exhaustive. I propose instead, arbitrarily but unavoidably, to group the main theories of support under five heads, namely:

1. theories that connect support with perceptions of *fairness* or of fair treatment;
2. theories that emphasize the *subconscious* and *symbolic* elements of support;
3. theories that relate support to the experience of *participation* or community;
4. theories based on the *effectiveness* of regimes; and
5. theories that stress people's positions in the *social division of labor*, and changes in that division.

These categories are provisional, and the assignment of specific theories to one or another of them will not always be exact. I claim for them only that they are useful as a guide to further research and reflection.

Support as a consequence of fairness. Aristotle's hypothesis, that support depends ultimately on the equal treatment of equals,[8] may be taken as the foundation of this line of explanation; but the theories of

7. Hans H. Gerth and C. Wright Mills, trans. and eds., *From Max Weber: Essays in Sociology* (New York: Oxford University Press, Galaxy Books, 1958), pp. 42–43.
8. *Politics*, p. 1301b.

Rousseau (at least in the *Second Discourse*), of Locke, and of such contemporary students as Ted Robert Gurr, Michael Hechter, Jürg Steiner, and Arend Lijphart, also fall under this general rubric.[9] In essence, it is claimed that A supports, or at least accepts, the rule of B because B generally treats A *fairly* (i.e., as A deserves to be treated). B does not discriminate invidiously against A, does not seek to exploit A, does not allow even the suspicion of unfair treatment to arise. If, on the other hand, A opposes B, it will generally have been because of unfair treatment, usually continued as a discernible pattern over some length of time.

More detailed hypotheses of course specify the standards of "fairness" and equity that people use. Aristotle's is a theory of contributions to the common good; Lijphart emphasizes "proportionality" in the distribution of power, office, and other political benefits; theorists of relative deprivation ordinarily take "reference groups" as determinant—are workers in Scotland, for example, treated worse than comparable workers in England?[10] Nonetheless, two acid tests of the class of "fairness" theories can be readily conceived: if people whom all concede to be equals are treated unequally, does support wane? And if such admitted equals are treated equally, is support guaranteed, or at least strengthened?

Support as a consequence of pre- or subconscious processes. It is principally to the conservative opponents of the French Revolution and to their ideological heirs in nineteenth-century sociology[11] that we owe the hypothesis that support for regimes or, indeed, for political communities, depends principally on association with the symbolic and familiar, in short with what has already been learned. Burke certainly held that support for the artificial and merely intellectual structures of the Revolution could be neither deep nor lasting. Bagehot, Pareto, and Sorel, each in rather different ways, also saw support far more as a product of appearance, or rationalization, and of myth, than of actual fairness or actual performance. In our own time, the whole

9. Except where a specific point is being raised about a generally familiar work, no footnote will appear.

10. Ted Robert Gurr, *Why Men Rebel* (Princeton: Princeton University Press, 1970), pp. 106–9.

11. Leon Bramson, *The Political Context of Sociology* (Princeton: Princeton University Press, 1961). See also Brian M. Barry, *Sociologists, Economists and Democracy* (London: Collier-Macmillan Ltd., 1970), pp. 7–9.

realm of work on political socialization and political culture, beginning really with Merriam and extending through Almond, Verba,
Eckstein, Easton, and their various associates, has been informed
by, or has represented an elaboration on, this perspective. So, to a
great degree, have the main theories of atomization, including those
of Lederer, Arendt, and Kornhauser.

Again, the common theoretical thread is handled differently by different theorists. For Eckstein it is actually experienced authority, for
Easton early overt learning about authority, for at least the early Almond the whole structure of learned political roles[12] that matter
most. To the atomization theorists, on the other hand, it is familiarity
and community in any guise that are essential; and support wanes because familiar groups are weakened or destroyed. Again, however, a
single crucial test of all these theories can be imagined, i.e., none of
them could admit that a radically new regime or a new political community could readily gain support.[13] Even less could they allow that
support in such a case could be as extensive among the already socialized old as among the younger, and presumably more malleable,
members of society.

Support as the product of participation. This theory, whose origins
are in Rousseau's *Social Contract* and whose most radical present-day
exponent is probably Carole Pateman,[14] has many adherents; but
most of them are silent, assuming or implying their hypotheses rather
than stating them. Thus, S. M. Lipset and Stein Rokkan, or Leon
Epstein, take it as obvious that high "thresholds of representation"
for newly mobilized groups must have contributed to their alienation
from regime and community.[15] Where effective participation was
made easier earlier, as in Norway or the United States, support was
higher. Even when formal admission to participation came early, as it

12. Gabriel Almond, "Comparative Political Systems," *Journal of Politics* 18 (1956):391–409.
13. See particularly William Kornhauser's discussion of "discontinuities in authority": *Politics of Mass Society* (Glencoe, Ill.: The Free Press, 1959), chap. 6.
14. See especially her *The Problem of Political Obligation: A Critical Analysis of Liberal The-ory* (New York: John Wiley & Sons, 1979).
15. Seymour Martin Lipset and Stein Rokkan, "Party Systems, Cleavage Structures, and Voter Alignments: An Introduction," in Lipset and Rokkan, eds., *Party Systems and Voter Alignments: Cross-National Perspectives* (New York: The Free Press, 1967), pp. 1–64, esp. pp. 27–33; and Leon D. Epstein, *Political Parties in Western Democracies* (New York: Praeger Publishers, 1967), pp. 135–36 and 144–45.

did for workers in Britain, informal barriers, such as the Liberals' refusal to nominate working-class candidates in the twentieth century,
could vitiate support, albeit to a lesser degree.

The proper test of this theory, while perhaps less clear-cut in its
implications, ought to be fairly straightforward in its general direction: any case in which, by reasonable external criteria, people were
mobilized but denied effective participation, and in which they nonetheless continued to extend support, would be at least a strong challenge to the theory. More particularly, in any comparison of two
equally mobilized and comparable groups, that which was afforded
the greater effective opportunity to participate ought to be the more
allegiant.

Effectiveness as the basis of support. We owe originally to Hobbes,
and in our own time principally to S. M. Lipset, to Easton, and to
Samuel Huntington, the seemingly evident proposition that governments lose support when they fail to govern. Although ineffectiveness
can be partially compensated for by broader sentiments of legitimacy
(Lipset), or by the more comprehensive attitudes of diffuse support
(Easton), if long continued it must prove fatal. Particularly dangerous
for support, according to Huntington's familiar thesis, are those cases
in which mobilization and participation increase while effectiveness
and legitimacy remain low.[16]

One subclass of theories of effectiveness deserves particular mention. What is often called, accurately, "vulgar Marxism" holds that
only the *economic* performance of regimes matters, at least so far as
specific support is concerned. The regime that "delivers the goods,"
in the form of a steadily increasing standard of living, will be supported; the regime that fails to do so will lose support. In at least
some of its interpretations, James Davies's well-known "J-Curve" hypothesis is but a variant of this thesis.[17]

16. Samuel P. Huntington, *Political Order in Changing Societies* (New Haven and London:
Yale University Press, 1968), chap. 1.

17. James C. Davies, "Toward a Theory of Revolution," *American Sociological Review* 27
(1962): 5–19; Davies, "The J-Curve of Rising and Declining Satisfactions as a Cause of Some
Great Revolutions and a Contained Rebellion," in Hugh Davis Graham and Ted Robert Gurr,
eds., *Violence in America: Historical and Comparative Perspectives* (New York: Bantam Books,
1969), pp. 690–730. While Davies himself has frequently warned against (but not always
avoided) reliance solely on economic indicators of satisfaction, see Raymond Tanter and Manus
Midlarski, "A Theory of Revolution," *Journal of Conflict Resolution* 11 (1967): 264–80.

A somewhat complex but clear-cut test of the whole class of theories based on effectiveness can be proposed: to examine all cases of evidently weak legitimacy, low effectiveness (economic or otherwise), and high mobilization and participation. If support remains high in any instance, the theory is substantially disconfirmed.

Support as a function of the social division of labor. To some extent prefigured in the work of Aristotle and Machiavelli, the view that support depends principally on changes in, and on individuals' positions in, the social division of labor is rightly associated most closely with Marx, and with such recent Marxian successors as John Kautsky, Barrington Moore, Jr., and Immanuel Wallerstein,[18] as well as with— an only superficial contradiction—such anti-Marxists as Mosca and Dahrendorf. The essential Marxist theses are too familiar to require detailed explication, but in short: a given division of labor, institutionalized in relations of property and legal control, originally corresponds well to the prevailing material conditions of production: to resources, technology, means of transportation and exchange, population density, etc. The resultant division of wealth, income, status, and power, including political institutions, is regarded generally as fair. Therefore, support, or at least acquiescence, is high. (In this sense the Marxist thesis is a particular variant of the theories based on fairness.) When material conditions change, however, when new trade routes, technology, or demographics appear, and when some other system of social organization shows itself to be more efficient than the previously prevailing one, then a new class or classes arise which cease to support the older order. Eventually their alienation extends to the sphere of politics. In this way the new feudatories of late Roman Europe had come to reject Imperial authority. In this way, too, the nascent capitalist classes, workers and owners alike, had come to reject the feudal or absolutist regimes under which, for the most part, they arose. In each case the old laws came to be seen as impediments and the old distributions of wealth, status, and power as grossly unfair.

18. Wallerstein, however, represents more of a departure from mainstream Marxism, both in his emphasis on the importance of technology and in his hypothesis of a strict relationship between regime and location in the core-periphery continuum, than is sometimes realized. See the important criticism of Robert Brenner, "The Origins of Capitalist Development: A Critique of Neo-Smithian Marxism," *New Left Review* 104 (July–August 1977).

Barrington Moore has extended the thesis domestically; Lipset and Rokkan, in an offhand remark, regionally.[19] For Moore, even under less drastic changes of trade and production, what counts for support is the admittedly rough calculation of the costs and benefits of existing inequalities. If landlords, or bureaucrats, or a regime generally, are seen to deliver real services, for which the payment, in superior wealth, status, and power is roughly proportionate, then the situation will be seen as fair, and support will be forthcoming. If, for whatever reasons of social or economic change, the elite ceases to deliver that service while continuing to receive the old, or greater, rewards, support will necessarily wane. Similarly for Lipset and Rokkan, a previously peripheral region will begin to reject its dependent station and to strive seriously for autonomy only after it ceases to need the core for any essential goods or services. So long as the costs and benefits of the central regime roughly correspond, the region will continue its support.

Mosca, Durkheim, and their sociological successors—and I count my own early work on support in this category[20]—carry the theme of *perceived* fairness of the division of labor and of rewards one step further, and one large step away from Marx. For they claim that people often accept functions as necessary, and the rewards of those who perform them as fair with no objective basis at all. Priests, magicians, most intellectuals in most ages (I, of course, exclude our own, more enlightened one) are, in fact, useless but in popular perception essential. And if, as such cases seem to show, it is not the real but the perceived suitability of the prevailing division of labor that matters, we are back to an emphasis on socialization and on prerational processes, which presumably persuade people of the necessity of such roles.

Corresponding to these two kinds of theory, two sorts of empirical test can be imagined. Both have, within limits, been performed. One can first try to establish whether changes in support generally covary with major changes in the social division of labor and whether they generally involve the conflict of "new" and "old" classes over the proper form of political community or regime. Secondly, and along

19. Barrington Moore, Jr., *Social Origins of Dictatorship and Democracy: Lord and Peasant in the Making of the Modern World* (Boston: Beacon Press, 1966), pp. 470–78; Lipset and Rokkan, "Party Sytems, Cleavage Structures, and Voter Alignments," p. 42.

20. Ronald Rogowski, *Rational Legitimacy: A Theory of Political Support* (Princeton: Princeton University Press, 1974).

the lines of Mosca's more sociological version of the theory, one can survey the extent to which people's support of the existing order depends on their perceptions of the necessity and fairness of the existing distribution of positions and rewards. Alexander Gerschenkron, Barrington Moore, Jr., and Lawrence Stone, among others, have opened a broad field of historical analysis that has attempted the former task; and their path has recently been followed by some extraordinarily fertile young historians, such as Heinrich August Winkler, Jürgen Kocka, and David Schoenbaum.[21] On the second track, survey work on popular perceptions of the division of labor and rewards is a major aspect of the (overwhelmingly British) study of social class. W. G. Runciman's *Relative Deprivation and Social Justice* is the pioneering work in this particular area.[22]

Evidence

I have summarized, admittedly idiosyncratically and arbitrarily, what has been thought about support; but what is known? As is usually the case in the social sciences, our evidence is far less extensive and less conclusive than our theorizing. Moreover, for reasons I shall try to explicate at various points in what follows, much of the survey research that purports to deal directly with support seems to me to be of doubtful validity or generality.[23] I shall, therefore, not hesitate to

21. Alexander Gerschenkron, *Bread and Democracy in Germany* (1943; New York: Howard Fertig, 1966); Moore, *Social Origins of Dictatorship and Democracy*; Lawrence Stone, *Social Change and Revolution in England, 1540–1640* (New York: Barnes & Noble, Inc., 1965); Stone, *The Crisis of the Aristocracy, 1558–1641* (Oxford: Oxford University Press, 1965). Heinrich August Winkler, *Mittelstand, Demokratie und Nationalsozialismus: Die politische Entwicklung von Handwerk und Kleinhandel in der Weimarer Republik* (Cologne: Kiepenheuer & Witsch, 1972); Jürgen Kocka, *Klassengesellschaft im Krieg: Deutsche Sozialgeschichte 1914–1918* (Göttingen: Vandenhoeck and Ruprecht, 1973); and David Schoenbaum, *Hitler's Social Revolution: Class and Status in Nazi Germany 1933–1939* (Garden City, N.Y.: Doubleday and Co., Anchor Books, 1967).

22. W. G. Runciman, *Relative Deprivation and Social Justice* (London and Berkeley: University of California Press, 1966). See also Barrington Moore, Jr., *Injustice: The Social Bases of Obedience and Revolt* (White Plains, N.Y.: M. E. Sharpe, Inc., 1978); and Jennifer L. Hochschild, *What's Fair? American Beliefs about Distributive Justice* (Cambridge: Harvard University Press, 1981).

23. The problem of generality is raised, in my view, by Edward N. Muller's otherwise often admirable work. To assume that Iowa college students, or present-day West Germans, represent, in the ways they link support with discontent or perceptions of efficacy, all humanity in all ages is at least as bold as reliance on traditional historical methods. See particularly Muller,

use historical case studies and analyses of voting for whatever light they can shed.

Two minor subcategories of theory seem to me to be conclusively refuted by the evidence already at hand. Vulgar Marxism, whether taken neat or in its J-curve variant, is contravened at every turn, even allowing for the *ceteris paribus* of convention. Regime support in Ireland evidently grew as economic conditions, owing largely to de Valera's trade war with the British, steadily worsened in the 1930s.[24] To judge by voting evidence, Quebec has traced an exactly opposite path: support for a federal system in which Quebec is merely one of ten provinces has declined as wealth and power have grown. That story is paralleled in Norway, Scotland, and Iran. Individual-level data, moreover, from as far back as the French Revolution and as recently as the Black Revolts of the 1960s in the urban United States demonstrate conclusively that the most disaffected are often precisely those who—both objectively and in their own perception—have been steadily improving economically.[25] *Sic transit* J-curve.

The theory of atomization, as developed by Arendt and others, has shown itself to be similarly infirm. The single case of Weimar Germany suffices to disprove it, either as a necessary or sufficient condition for weak or declining support. Germany was, first of all, an over- rather than an underorganized society. The number of associations, ranging from *Stammtische* to skat clubs to religious, singing, and shooting societies, to which the average German belonged, even

"Correlates and Consequences"; Muller, "The Representation of Citizens by Political Authorities: Consequences for Regime Support," *American Political Science Review* 64 (1970): 1149–66; and Muller, *Aggressive Political Participation* (Princeton: Princeton University Press, 1979). For Muller's well-argued defense of his position, however, see his "Representation of Citizens," pp. 1152–53. Validity of survey work is at issue wherever a public is "reticent" (as Sani has well put it) on a question; and this is especially likely to obtain with respect to support. Giacomo Sani, "The Political Culture of Italy: Continuity and Change," in Gabriel A. Almond and Sidney Verba, eds., *The Civic Culture Revisited* (Boston and Toronto: Little, Brown and Co., 1980), pp. 273–324, esp. pp. 282–91.

24. J. Bowyer Bell, *The Secret Army: A History of the IRA* (Cambridge: MIT Press, 1970), pp. 103–5.

25. Crane Brinton, *The Anatomy of Revolution*, rev. and expanded ed. (New York: Vintage Books, 1965), chap. 4; Bernard N. Grofman and Edward N. Muller, "The Strange Case of Relative Gratification and Potential for Political Violence: The V-Curve Hypothesis," *American Political Science Review* 67 (1973): 514–39, esp. p. 537; and Abraham Miller, Luis H. Bolce, and Mark Haligan, "The J-Curve Theory and the Black Urban Riots: An Empirical Test of Progressive Relative Deprivation Theory," *American Political Science Review* 71 (1977): 964–82. See also Ronald Rogowski, "The *Gauleiter* and the Social Origins of Fascism," *Comparative Studies in Society and History* 19 (1977): 399–430.

in 1932, still causes the American imagination to boggle.[26] The incidence of such organizations, moreover, was greatest among that middle class which sympathized most strongly with the Nazis. Even when the effects of social class[27] were controlled, Nazi votes came disproportionately from the highly organized and inbred smaller towns rather than from the atomized big cities. Atomization, then, can hardly be required for low support. Neither is it sufficient, for the presumably more atomized large cities remained strikingly supportive of the Weimar regime, and industrialized and urban Prussia remained electorally a solid bulwark against the antiregime Right and Left until Papen destroyed its autonomy by decree in 1932.[28]

Nor, incidentally, can either of two variants of the atomization thesis—Lipset's hypothesis of "working-class authoritarianism" or that of Lipset and Verba on the allegedly supportive effects of education[29]—be readily reconciled with the Weimar evidence. Lipset's argument, in brief, is that isolation rather than strict atomization conduces to extremism, and thus to wavering support. Hence, on this claim, isolated small-town Germans, like isolated Norwegian loggers or isolated Welsh miners, might be expected to desert their respective regimes more readily than their more experienced compatriots. Almond and Verba take a similar line, arguing however, on the basis of much comparative evidence, that education by itself instills the necessary sophistication and openness to compromise that are consonant with consistently high support.[30] In Weimar, however, even controlling for relative isolation, it was the middle and not the lower classes, the more educated rather than the less, and above all, the more worldly Protestants and seculars rather than the culturally isolated Catholics,

26. See, for example, William Sheridan Allen, *The Nazi Seizure of Power: The Experience of a Single German Town, 1930–1935* (Chicago: Quadrangle Books, 1965), pp. 16–19.

27. Seymour Martin Lipset, *Political Man: The Social Bases of Politics* (Garden City, N.Y.: Doubleday & Co., Anchor Books, 1963), p. 144.

28. Georges Castellan, *L'Allemagne de Weimar, 1918–1933* (Paris: Librairie Armand Colin, 1969), pp. 57–58; cf. Richard N. Hunt, *German Social Democracy 1918–1933* (Chicago: Quadrangle Books, 1970), pp. 32–33.

29. Lipset, *Political Man*, chap. 4 and p. 137; Gabriel A. Almond and Sidney Verba, *The Civic Culture: Political Attitudes and Democracy in Five Nations* (Princeton: Princeton University Press, 1963), pp. 110–12, 176–77, and 205–9; cf. Sidney Verba, "On Revisiting the Civic Culture: A Personal Postscript," in Almond and Verba, eds., *The Civic Culture Revisited*, pp. 394–410, esp. pp. 407–8.

30. Cf. Carole Pateman, "The Civic Culture: A Philosophic Critique," in Almond and Verba, eds., *Civic Culture Revisited*, pp. 57–102, esp. pp. 86–87.

who, by their electoral support of National Socialism, so signally repudiated support for the existing, democratic, regime.[31] We too often forget, or repress, the fact that the Nazi student league had won absolute majorities of the student vote at nine German-speaking institutions of higher education, and over 40 percent at five others, out of a total of eighteen such institutions, by early 1931, some eighteen months before the German electorate generally took that fateful step.[32] In short, the claim that educational sophistication makes one more supportive of the existing regime cannot be sustained in the Weimar example. Nor is this claim buttressed by other cases. Indeed, studies ranging from historical accounts of support for nineteenth-century national movements to survey-based analyses of socio-demographic correlates of voting for the Parti Québécois all provide additional disconfirmatory evidence.[33]

The status of the remaining theories is less clear-cut. Let us consider these theories in inverse order of their promise as suggested by available evidence.

Fairness. Does unfairness, arbitrary treatment, even extreme corruption necessarily decrease support for a regime? Does fairness necessarily increase it? The terms are nebulous, but A. H. Birch has recently argued,[34] I think persuasively, that many of the national groups now seeking autonomy or independence are precisely those that have been treated most "fairly"—in terms, at least, of the division of power and of offices—at the level of the larger state, while those that have been treated most harshly have shown the least in-

31. On the immunity of Catholics to National Socialism (or to any other political appeal), see among others Castellan, *L'Allemagne de Weimar*, pp. 117–19; and Ralf Dahrendorf, *Gesellschaft und Demokratie in Deutschland* (Munich: R. Piper & Co., 1968), pp. 139–40. On the immunity of the working-class vote, see Hunt, *German Social Democracy 1918–1933*, pp. 116–20; and Thomas Childers, "Social Class and the Nazi Vote," discussion paper, University of Pennsylvania, 1976.

32. Only at the universities of Hanover and Munich had the Nazis failed to win as much as a third of the vote by 1931. Karl Dietrich Bracher, *Die Auflösung der Weimarer Republik*, 2nd improved and expanded ed. (Stuttgart and Düsseldorf: Ring-Verlag, 1957), pp. 146–49.

33. Richard Hamilton and Maurice Pinard, "The Bases of Parti Québécois Support in Recent Quebec Elections," *Canadian Journal of Political Science* 9 (1979):3–26, esp. 13 and 18–19; E. J. Hobsbawm, *The Age of Revolution, 1789–1848* (New York: New American Library, 1962), pp. 166–68.

34. Anthony H. Birch, "Minority Nationalist Movements and Theories of Political Integration," *World Politics* 30 (1978):325–44.

clination to separate: Scotland or Quebec can be usefully contrasted with, say, Brittany or Corsica. Comparing temporally rather than cross-nationally, we have to note that democratic governments that became vastly more arbitrary, particularly in wartime,[35] did not necessarily lose support; while ones that were fairer, or more bound by equity and the rule of law, were often less popular than the more heavy-handed regimes that preceded or followed them: Weimar Germany once again, or Fourth Republic France.

At the individual level of the *Civic Culture* data, there is also ground for doubt. When 65 percent of the West German respondents express confidence that they would be treated equally and fairly by civil servants, and 72 percent express similar confidence with respect to the police, while only 7 percent (as against 85 in the United States and 46 in Britain) express direct regime support, the connection between fairness and support seems to need further specification.[36]

Now, war and civil insurrection, present or recent, are admittedly exceptional circumstances; but partisans of the "fairness" theories of support are obliged to tell us *how* exceptional (for war, as the Czar learned, does not always increase support). Why does fairness sometimes seem to matter for support and sometimes not? I do not mean the question merely rhetorically, and I shall therefore suggest answers later on.

Effectiveness. We have already disposed of the claim that regime support is determined by economic performance. The broader thesis, however, that ineffective governments must always lose support, would seem to be supported by both logic and evidence. There is, however, at least one all but conclusive countercase, that of the French Third Republic. With masses evidently mobilized and participant (France instituted universal manhood suffrage in 1848, thus becoming after the United States the second of the modern democracies), with its legitimacy continually under attack by both the Left (the heirs of the Commune) and the Right (the Church and its allies),

35. To a later generation, some of Franklin Delano Roosevelt's actions in wartime labor disputes, including arrest and imprisonment of strike leaders solely on presidential warrant, are almost as astonishing as the evident popularity of those actions. For a leading example, see James MacGregor Burns, *Roosevelt: The Soldier of Freedom* (New York: Harcourt Brace Jovanovich, 1970), p. 510.

36. Almond and Verba, *The Civic Culture*, pp. 102 and 108.

with its indecisiveness and ineffectiveness a legend among nations, the Republic nonetheless survived for nearly seventy years. Underway it demanded, and received, overt support probably unparalleled in modern history: a higher share of its adult males was killed or maimed in World War I than in any other major belligerent state, and no revolt—indeed, no significant waning of support—seems to have ensued.[37]

Now a single outlier can of course be a fluke. More problematic still for the theory of effectiveness, however, is the evidence that the Third Republic, and for that matter the Fourth, were supported in many quarters precisely *because* they were weak, and thus incapable of endangering powerful interests.[38] Certainly this was the view of the influential Radical thinker Alain, who explicitly favored an ineffectual regime.[39] In this respect France between 1870 and 1960, and perhaps beyond, may have been but one example of a whole class of "stalemate" or "blocked" societies, in which consensus on any policy of action is so thin that only weak governments can hope to gain wide support.[40] If that is true, and even more if such societies are numerous, then the hypothesis that ineffectiveness vitiates support must be wrong.

Participation. From *The Civic Culture* onward, one of the few seemingly secure findings of survey research on support has been that it is strongly related to perceived political efficacy. Those who believe that government is, or would, if need be, responsive to their needs and wishes, are far more likely to express support for the re-

37. In general, see Alfred Cobban, *A History of Modern France*, 3 vols., *France of The Republics, 1871–1962* (Harmondsworth: Penguin Books, 1965), 3: part 1 and part 2, chaps. 1 and 2. French military losses of the Great War totaled 1.25 million dead, out of a 1914 population of 39.5 million; German losses were 1.8 million out of a 1914 population of 67 millon. In addition, France lost half a million civilians and ended the war with more than 700,000 maimed survivors; ibid., p. 119. On the Army mutinies of 1917, whose main importance was that they were quickly quelled and did not spread to any part of civilian life, see Alistair Horne, *The Price of Glory: Verdun 1916* (Harmondsworth: Penguin Books, 1964), pp. 322–24.

38. So argued, for example, Stanley Hoffmann; see the citations in Philip M. Williams, *Crisis and Compromise: Politics in the Fourth Republic* (Garden City, N.Y.: Doubleday & Co., Anchor Books, 1966), pp. 443–44.

39. Williams, *Crisis and Compromise*, p. 5.

40. Zariski argues forcefully that Italy, since unification, has displayed this same trait; there, he contends, the "blocking" is on behalf of the group rather than (even rhetorically) on behalf of the radically idealized individual; Raphael Zariski, *Italy: The Politics of Uneven Development* (Hinsdale, Ill.: The Dryden Press, 1972) , p. 104.

gime than are those who believe the contrary.[41] Substantially less clear, however, is whether *perceived* efficacy has anything to do with *real* participation. As Kornberg, Clarke, and LeDuc have shown, Canadians who actually have participated, to the extent, at least, of contacting a Member of Parliament, are somewhat less likely to express support for the regime.[42]

In general, the mere opportunity to participate (e.g., through the existence of formal democratic institutions) does not ensure support; otherwise France would hardly have developed the second- or third-largest Communist party in the West. And even less does the lack of formal democracy, even among the politically mobilized, seem to weaken support, as the frequent popularity of totalitarian regimes has surely proved. Astonishingly, even where specific religious or ethnic minorities have explicitly been denied participation, they have frequently enough failed to support efforts for autonomy, or for transfer to neighboring states where their influence would have been greater. Thus South German Catholics, even under the persecutions of Bismarck's *Kulturkampf*, showed little enthusiasm for an *Anschluss* with Austria, and Catholics of the Saarland were not tempted by the proximity of France, even when Hitler was the German alternative.[43] The strong relation between perceived efficacy and expressed support, while important, may prove to be a virtual tautology, leaving unanswered the question of what causes people to see themselves as efficacious. On the evidence to date, one can hardly conclude that participation always conduces to support.

Socialization. The essential tests of the claim that support has pre- or nonrational bases were earlier argued to be: (*a*) can a new regime win wide support; and (*b*) can support in such a case be as strong among older as among younger citizens? The experience of the two German Republics is suggestive if not conclusive. In the first elections under universal suffrage in 1919, clearly pro-Republican parties

41. Almond and Verba, *The Civic Culture*, pp. 246–53 (with reservations, duly noted, about the weakness of the relationship in Italy and Germany); Muller, "Representation of Citizens," pp. 1163–66; Allan Kornberg, Harold D. Clarke, and Lawrence LeDuc, "Some Correlates of Regime Support in Canada," *British Journal of Political Science* 8 (1978): 199–216.

42. "Some Correlates of Regime Support," pp. 208–10.

43. In a free plebiscite in 1935, over 90 percent of the Saarländer favored reintegration with Nazi Germany. John Toland, *Adolf Hitler* (New York: Ballantine Books, 1976), p. 501.

won a total of 85 percent of the poll.[44] I know of no reliable breakdown by age of this early support or opposition, but it does seem plain that the subsequent intense enmity toward the Republic, among Communists as well as Fascists, was strongly age-linked: the extreme opponents of the Weimar regime were overwhelmingly young while older citizens, who had not been socialized under the new regime, supported it disproportionately.[45] In contrast, under the Bonn Republic, change in the most direct measures of support or opposition to the regime are substantially unrelated to age.[46]

Perhaps equally unsettling to adherents of the socialization thesis are the extreme fluctuations in support that manifestly occur, even among older persons, with no clear relation to any of the "output" variables that ought to affect specific support. Remarkable fluctuations in regime support characterized the early years of the French Third, the Weimar, and the Bonn republics; and the extent of these was sometimes as great among the old as among the young.[47]

While there is much evidence that socialization can, and often does, instill sentiments of support and even a propensity to supportive action, we must also admit that there are significant anomalies. What appears to be "diffuse" support can, like its analog in the voting

44. The monarchist DNVP received 10.3 percent of the poll, the ambiguous DVP 4.4 percent. On the final vote of approval of the Weimar Constitution in the National Assembly, there were 75 "nays" among the 421 delegates, or 17.8 percent. Castellan, *L'Allemagne de Weimar*, pp. 48 and 117.

45. Hunt, *German Social Democracy 1918–1933*, pp. 89–91 and 106–11; Schoenbaum, *Hitler's Social Revolution*, pp. 28–29, 37, and 40–41; cf. Hans Gerth, "The Nazi Party: Its Leadership and Composition," *American Journal of Sociology* 45 (1940):517–41.

46. Early research is summarized in Rogowski, *Rational Legitimacy*, pp. 8–9. For later work, in which age differences become more manifest but trends among age groups remain very similar, see: G. R. Boynton and Gerhard Loewenberg, "The Development of Public Support for Parliament in Germany, 1951–1959," *British Journal of Political Science* 3 (1973):169–89, esp. 178–80; Boynton and Loewenberg, "The Decay of Support for Monarchy and the Hitler Regime in the Federal Republic of Germany," *British Journal of Political Science* 4 (1974):453–88, esp. 481–85; and M. Kent Jennings, "The Variable Nature of Generational Conflict: Some Examples from West Germany," *Comparative Political Studies* 9 (1976):171–88.

47. Cobban, *History of Modern France*, 3, pp. 11–21, well describes the fluctuations in French voting support for the Republic, made evident also in by-elections, between 1871 and 1877. Castellan, *L'Allemagne de Weimar*, pp. 117–18, notes that the popular vote for parties fundamentally opposed to the Republic (Nationalists, Nazis, and Communists) rose to 38.1 percent (from a 1919 level of 14.7 percent) as early as 1924; then fell by 1928 to 27.4 percent and rose by late 1932 to 58.8 percent. Boynton and Loewenberg, "Public Support for Parliament in Germany," p. 179, find considerable fluctuation over time in the support expressed both by the youngest and by the oldest respondents: the trend reverses four times in nine years among those over sixty, and three times among those under thirty.

literature "party identification," vary wildly over the short term.[48]
When it does so, can it be the product of socialization?

The social division of labor. The strictly Marxist view seems, on
first inspection, simplistic: industrialization, after all, had vastly different effects on the distribution and intensity of regime support in
the United States than it did in France or Germany; the growth of a
world market in the sixteenth century liberalized much of the West
but brought the "second feudalism" to Prussia.[49] Nonetheless, recent
elaborations and empirical applications of the theory, particularly
with respect to the otherwise so intractable problems of (as we have
seen repeatedly) Weimar Germany, and, more recently, of the "new"
nationalisms of the industrialized West seem to me to have shown
great promise. Pi-Sunyer argues that the mysteriously intense and
middle-class-based demands for Catalan autonomy, and the concurrent waning of support for the larger Spanish state in the late nineteenth century, can be closely connected to the loss of Spanish colonial sources of cheap raw materials, the consequent drastic change in
conditions of production in relatively industrialized Catalonia, and
the refusal of the rural and liberal Spanish regime to offer tariff protection to the affected industries.[50] For the Weimar case, Gerschenkron, Winkler, and others have persuasively connected the changing
patterns of support to the effects of world trade patterns and the collapse of world grain prices on prominent groups such as the large-
scale grain farmers, the smaller farmers oriented to an export market,
the export-oriented industrialists, the industrialists oriented predominantly to the domestic market, and the smaller retail merchants
and artisans.[51]

48. For (admittedly disputed) evidence that diffuse support has dropped dramatically even in
the supposedly well-socialized United States, see Arthur H. Miller, "Political Issues and Trust
in Government," *American Political Science Review* 68 (1974):951–72; and Miller, "Rejoinder,"
American Political Science Review 68 (1974):989–1001. The critique is by Jack Citrin, "Comment: The Political Relevance of Trust in Government," *American Political Science Review* 68
(1974):973–88; Citrin, p. 975, brings out with particular clarity the relationship between trust
and support.

49. Immanuel Wallerstein, *The Modern World-System: Capitalist Agriculture and the Origins of the European World-Economy in the Sixteenth Century* (New York: Academic Press,
1974), chap. 2.

50. Oriol Pi-Sunyer, "Ideology and Social Structure: The Case of Catalonia," paper delivered
at Conference on Contemporary Nationalist Movements, Duke University, October, 1980.

51. Ibid., n. 21.

Two related problems however still plague the Marxian explanation of support. As perhaps the German case demonstrates as clearly as any other, it offers no compelling account of the (often religious) "vertical" divisions whose impact is often as important as that of the "horizontal" social divisions of class or sector. And it does not deal, except to treat it as epiphenomenal, with the possibility of "imagined" importance of sectors or occupations. Thus, we must resort to other approaches to understand why Catholics remained loyal to the Weimar Republic, or why Leftist governments hesitated to dismiss bureaucrats of questionable loyalty. These difficulties may however well be overcome, in a rationalist if not a strictly Marxist framework. The approach therefore seems to me—again, perhaps, idiosyncratically—the most helpful of the five examined.

Some Modest Proposals

Fortunately, I have not promised to remedy the failings I have disclosed. I shall, however, venture to suggest that many of the problems discussed above can be traced back to the definition of support. I think, in particular, that Easton's partition of support into the categories of diffuse and specific is inadequate and misleading, and that it is necessary to develop alternatives. In this I am hardly being daring. A chorus of complaints about the conceptual and operational difficulties of the distinction has been heard, *mezzoforte e crescendo*, for years now; and Easton himself has been moved by the clamor to propose emendations and elaborations.[52] "Trust," "alienation," "commitment," and "compliance," among many other concepts, have been proposed as complements or alternatives.[53] If we are not merely to compound confusion, however, we must be clear about the difficulties with the original Eastonian formulation. Four are apparent:

1. Easton assumed that support must be either diffuse or specific; *tertium non datur*. Historically, this seems wrong. Take again the case of the early Third Republic in France. How could so many convinced monarchists have supported it, both covertly and overtly?

---

52. Easton, "Concept of Political Support."
53. Easton summarizes these proposals very lucidly; ibid., pp. 446–57. He proposes to adopt trust and some manifestations of a belief in legitimacy as aspects of diffuse support.

The conventional account of the historians is wholly convincing: the monarchists were hopelessly divided, Legitimists against Orleanists against a surviving minority of Bonapartists, and saw, for this reason and others, no realistic chance of a restoration. One cannot say that their support for monarchy was merely "specific," since it hardly depended on calculations of personal advantage or even on the material benefits that might flow to France as a whole.[54] Indeed, for the Legitimists particularly the question was often literally a religious one. But neither is it correct to designate the monarchists' support strictly "diffuse," when it could be surrendered so readily to considerations of practicality. The two kinds of support evidently do not exhaust the empirical possibilities.

2. Easton's whole analysis seems to assume that regimes are to be regarded in *isolation*: individuals focus only on a particular regime, and decide whether or not to extend support to it. But as the French case suggests, people often have to decide which of two or more contending regimes (or, for that matter, contending "incumbents" or political communities) they will support, and to what degree.[55] In politics no less than in economics, even slight competition is a very different world from pure monopoly. The American driver who "supported" General Motors as tolerable often judged his Chevrolet intolerable once Toyota and Datsun arrived on the scene. Is it surprising that European peasants often reacted similarly when the Napoleonic armies presented an alternative to the old regime?[56]

3. Easton takes as logically given what can only be demonstrated empirically, namely the existence in every stable regime of a high level of diffuse support. In part, this error is a consequence of the assumption that if there is support, and if it is not specific, then it must be diffuse. But the claim is also asserted independently: specific support alone is insufficient for stability; hence every stable regime

54. In his more recent formulations, it should be mentioned, Easton has broadened the concept of specific support: it "may be a *quid pro quo* not only for the satisfaction of specific demands but also for meeting expectations about . . . general performance by the authorities" (ibid., p. 442). However, the Republic was supported by the monarchists neither because it was especially competent nor because its leading officials were especially likeable—the two possibilities that Easton, following Muller, labels "expressive" and "extraneous" performance.

55. See the incisive discussion by John Fraser, "The Impact of Community and Regime Orientations on Choice of Political System," *Midwest Journal of Political Science* 14 (1970):413–33.

56. Hobsbawm, *Age of Revolution*, pp. 115–18.

must enjoy diffuse support.[57] Yet in reality, as we have seen, diffuse support appears to fluctuate wildly.

4. Concepts similar to diffuse support are treated as fixed in their relation to it, or indeed only as "aspects" of diffuse support.[58] Thus legitimacy, or trust, or commitment, are simply assumed to covary, or defined as covarying, with diffuse support.[59] In fact, these relations need to be established empirically; and, as has been shown above, some obstinate evidence speaks against their existence.

An alternative set of definitions and a research agenda may be proposed which will avoid these four failings. Regarding the former, support may be classified as *unconditional, conditional, specific,* or *affective.* Support that is unconditional is unswayed by considerations of alternatives or of practicality; the unconditional Legitimist will offer no succor, under any circumstances, to an Orleanist regime, let alone to a Republic. A monarchist who, like Tocqueville, lets the facts temper his convictions, will be said to offer *conditional* support to monarchy.

Max Weber's categories of social action offer a useful parallel.[60] Like Weber's *traditional* action, which is based on "stupid habit," *unconditional* support is devoid of reflection. *Conditional* support, on the other hand, is clearly a species of what Weber called *value-rational* orientation or action: the value, in this case the preferred regime, is unquestioned, but the achievement of it is subject to the kind of minimal rational calculation that ordinarily prevents even the most ardent patriot from assaulting enemy machine guns single-handedly. Weber's category of *goal-rational* action, which is based solely on the calculation of individual benefit, is an obvious parallel to Easton's *specific* support; while what Weber called purely *affective* action—the response to momentary emotion, informed neither by tradition nor by calculation—has perhaps its parallel in the kind of orgiastic mass support that has horrified students of crowd psychology from LeBon

57. Easton, *A Systems Analysis of Political Life*, pp. 269–74; Easton, "Concept of Political Support," pp. 445–46.
58. I owe this point to Fraser, "Impact of Community and Regime Orientations," p. 433.
59. Easton, "Concept of Political Support," pp. 446–53.
60. Max Weber, *Wirtschaft und Gesellschaft: Grundriß der verstehenden Soziologie*, ed. Johannes Winckelmann (Cologne and Berlin: Kiepenheuer and Witsch, 1964), part 1, chap. 1, para. 2, pp. 17–18.

onward: this we may rightly call affective, or purely emotional, support.[61] I propose, then, essentially to subdivide Easton's category of diffuse support into unconditional and conditional variants; to retain his category of specific support; and to add, following Weber, a category of purely affective, or emotional, support. It is to be hoped that these categories are exhaustive; but no logic guarantees that they are. Moreover, it remains to be established, even under regimes that seem highly stable, that support of any of these four kinds exists. Equally open to empirical investigation is the question of what relation, if any, obtains between any of these kinds of support and such cognate variables as legitimacy and trust.

To the extent that these categories of support seem useful, future research ought, obviously, to employ them, testing and using appropriate operational measures. For survey research, that implies, at a minimum, the introduction of questions that allow the respondent to distinguish between the regime he would support, ignoring all questions of practicality, and the one that, in full view of the prevailing circumstances, he does support. Only in that way can the distinction between conditional and unconditional support be drawn in the world of experience. One also ought to try to ascertain whether the respondent has considered whether he, or his group might be better off—in material goods, status, or power—under some alternative regime and, if so, whether that consideration underlies his pattern of support.[62]

Substantive research could then usefully be focused on three broad areas: *mapping* of patterns and trends in support; *analysis* of relationships between support and stability; and the investigation of questions of *causality*. *Mapping* is straightforward (although tactically problematic) and crucial; fortunately, as has been seen, much useful

61. ". . . [R]ecently in Berchtesgaden crazed females ate the gravel on which [Hitler] had just trod." Friedrich Percyval Reck-Malleczewen, *Tagebuch eines Verzweifelten* (Stuttgart: Henry Goverts Verlag, 1966), entry for August 11, 1936 (p. 23); Cf. William L. Shirer, *Berlin Diary: The Journal of a Foreign Correspondent, 1934–1941* (New York: Alfred A. Knopf, 1941), entry for September 4, 1934 (pp. 16–18).

62. I have intentionally omitted to discuss here ways of discovering affective support. It should probably be regarded as hypothetically likely whenever support is evidently strong but seemingly unmotivated either by considerations of abstract right or of rational calculation. In such circumstances, open-ended or semi-projective techniques might elicit evidence of purely affective support. For an excellent example—a letter from an obviously affectively motivated Young Nazi—see Reck-Malleczewen, *Tagebuch eines Verzweifelten*, pp. 84–88.

work has already been done. Still, we need to know, for example, to what extent unconditional support actually exists or has existed, and whether despite its seeming firmness it can (as Easton has suggested[63]) be weakened or demolished by some sudden shock. We need to know the extent, the grounds, and the degree of variation, in specific support. For example, do people really claim, against much objective evidence, to extend support on the basis of how the regime affects them economically, or does their perceived share of power—their sense of "efficacy"—matter more?[64]

Above all we are ignorant of the mechanisms of conditional and of affective support. If much support for regimes is conditional—and that of course remains to be shown—does it resemble conditional support for candidates in its susceptibility to "bandwagon" effects?[65] Students from Hobbes to Zolberg have advanced reasons, and some evidence, for thinking that it does wherever real competition among regimes arises.[66] Is affective support, as most wisdom on the subject claims, naturally short-lived, requiring constant and perhaps increasing stimulation to sustain it?[67]

Secondly it must be ascertained whether any of these categories of support is necessary or sufficient for the *stability* of regimes. The long, if troubled, history of the Third Republic seems to argue that conditional support can suffice.[68] Easton advanced a priori arguments that specific support could not be enough, but some appar-

63. Easton, "Concept of Political Support," p. 445.
64. The evidence presented by Fraser, "Impact of Community and Regime Orientations," however, suggests strongly that the calculation of immediate advantage, and of regime efficiency, matters more. Whether that finding is an artifact of the specific situation he treats—choice between two local governments—remains to be seen.
65. Donald Collat, Stanley Kelley, Jr., and Ronald Rogowski, "Presidential Bandwagons," paper delivered at the 1976 annual meeting of the American Political Science Association, Chicago; and Collat, Kelley, and Rogowski, "The End Game in Presidential Nominations," *American Political Science Review*, forthcoming.
66. *Leviathan*, I:10; Aristide R. Zolberg, *Creating Political Order* (Chicago: Rand McNally and Co., 1966), pp. 19–25.
67. I have been struck by the frequency which analysts of totalitarian regimes resort to the analogy of narcosis or addiction, not least in trying to account for such governments' typically insatiable appetites for conquest: e.g., Reck-Malleczewen, *Tagebuch eines Verzweifelten*, pp. 22–23.
68. For Eckstein, however, the Third Republic was not a stable regime: Harry Eckstein, "A Theory of Stable Democracy," Research Monograph No. 10, Center of International Studies, Princeton University, 1961, reprinted in Eckstein, *Division and Cohesion in Democracy: A Study of Norway* (Princeton: Princeton University Press, 1966), Appendix B—see esp. pp. 227–28.

ently stable regimes (e.g., the seventeenth-century Netherlands, present-day Singapore) seem in fact to be little more than joint-stock companies. Some evidence, ranging from Savonarola's Florence through sixteenth-century Munster to Nazi Germany, suggests that even affective support may suffice.

Finally, the various putative *causes* of increases and decreases in support must be examined. Does the perception that the regime is fair, or effective, or participatory, in fact tend to bolster the level of any of the main kinds of support (and, if so, which)? Can socialization instill sentiments of unconditional or conditional support, or increase the likelihood that citizens will extend specific or affective support?[69] Do changes in the division of labor, or perceptions of such changes, change patterns of support, regardless of socialization? Here, as I have managed only to suggest in this essay, much historical evidence can be brought to bear.

Those are the elements and the strategy of research that I suggest. Tactics are perhaps even more important. In contrast to much of previous research,[70] I hold that the most promising course is to examine situations in which alternative regimes directly compete for subjects' support. Only where support is tested can its strength be proved. Present-day Canada, or at least present-day Quebec, is obviously such a case; but it is part of a larger universe of highly similar cases from the late nineteenth century down to the present day—Ireland in the United Kingdom, Norway (and even more rural Norway) in the Personal Union with Sweden, the *Jurassiens* in the Swiss Confederation, the relatively quiescent *Brêtons*, the late-arriving Scots, the ever-aggrieved Catalans and Basques. Can we not sensibly "place" Canadian disunity in this larger context of "new" nationalisms and then use that expanded set, according to what Mill called "the joint method of agreement and difference,"[71] as a particularly important test of our concepts and theories of support?

69. Much of the writing on atomization and "mass man," for example, essentially suggests that inadequate enculturation renders people incapable of anything but affective support. Jose Ortega y Gasset, *The Revolt of the Masses*, authorized trans. (New York: W. W. Norton and Co., 1957), chap. 8.

70. There are of course exceptions, including much of the recent work on Canada. For an exemplary treatment of such a situation, in which moreover no survey work was possible, see Samuel Popkin, *The Rational Peasant: The Political Economy of Rural Society in Vietnam* (Berkeley: University of California Press, 1979).

71. John Stuart Mill, *A System of Logic, Ratiocinative and Inductive* (London: Longmans, Green, and Co., 1919), book 3, chap. 8, para. 4, pp. 258–59.

Political Support and Group Dominance

Mildred A. Schwartz

The Problem

A theory of political support is burdened by two apparent paradoxes: in order to assess the political ramifications of support adequately, theory needs to be broadly societal in scope; and to evaluate
individual acts of support, theory must first emphasize their collective manifestations. The resolution of these paradoxes occurs by
treating political support as a reflection of group dominance. In societies with significant economic, territorial, or cultural cleavages, attributions made about differences in political support are often a sur-
rogate characterization of relations among groups. They occur where
dominant groups assert a claim to be recognized as the depository and
guardian of political support. They seek to politicize nonconformity
when they find its existence offensive to their own prerogatives.
Threats to the integrity of the state are presumed to lie as much in the
beliefs and characteristics of nonconforming groups as in their actions. The machinery of government is then called upon to legitimize
these assertions of threat.

Support is not a serious issue to political authorities except when
attention is drawn to instances of low levels or of outright withdrawal
of support, presented in ways that make these threatening to the political system. For the argument presented here, I do not focus on
political support as the link between the individual citizen and government expressed through positive acts and values stressing loyalty
and allegiance. The machinery of the state and its leading political
actors are not necessarily the primary objects of support, nor do they

necessarily act as the primary responders to withdrawal of support. Concentrating on support as the domain of the individual revealed in positive actions leaves the issue at a level of reality that prevents confronting the interactive and contentious character of political life. To capture the latter, it is necessary to consider the ways in which political support is embedded in the relations among critical groups.

When I speak of dominance, it is not simply in terms of political power. Dominance covers actions, values, and characteristics that set communal standards for what is at least acceptable, but more typically, for what is especially desirable. Including the case of foreign domination, membership in dominant groups in a given society is synonymous with full inclusion in the community, that is, with citizenship, as this confers enjoyment of political, civil, and social rights.[1] The tie between dominant group membership and the status of citizen is what gives the former its symbolic monopoly over political support. Conversely, any form of nonconformity that can be tied to collective action has the potential for being translated into a political threat.

While nonconforming groups remain unequal in any power struggle, attacks on them for displaying low levels of support may be a prelude to major social changes. After a period of denial, there is often a broadening process of inclusion, in which the rights of citizenship are redefined and previous bases of exclusion are dismissed as irrelevant. In this process as well, the state becomes the agent which validates new relations among groups, but not its initiator.

Here, the proposition that political support is a reflection of group dominance is examined through five related themes or hypotheses. In three of these, the focus is on nonconforming groups which can be more easily isolated than less clearly differentiated dominant ones. In the first instance, the argument is made that nonconformity is signified by characteristics and values, as well as by actions. This would hardly be a statement meriting attention, except that it reminds us that characteristics and values can be critical in setting the stage for subsequent allegations about low levels of political support, in effect,

1. See T. H. Marshall, *Class, Citizenship, and Social Development* (New York: Doubleday Anchor, 1965), pp. 71–134; Talcott Parsons, "Full Citizenship for the American Negro?" in T. Parsons and K. Clark, eds., *The American Negro* (Boston: Houghton-Mifflin, 1966); Mildred A. Schwartz, "Citizenship in Canada and the United States," *Transactions of the Royal Society of Canada*, Series 4, 14, pp. 83–96.

the second hypothesis. Moreover, these groups may be involved in incidents that initially have no overtly political content, and do not directly challenge the political authorities or the regime. The third hypothesis then considers the conditions under which nonconformity is defined as politically threatening. The next hypothesis considers dominant groups more directly and argues that the accusatory process is set in motion by dominant groups. The state is often the agent which validates definitions of citizenship, responding to changing pressures, rather than the initiator of them. Finally, a hypothesis is offered which takes into account shifts in political relations, and the implications these have for altering the position of nonconforming groups.

The evidence used to assess these hypotheses is oblique, based on negative cases, and selected from a universe with unknown parameters. Two cases are given special prominence, the experiences of Japanese Canadians and of Jehovah's Witnesses, while those of other groups are used in a supplementary fashion. No sharply defined criteria of either dominance or nonconformity are used; rather, critical elements of both are allowed to emerge in the course of the paper. But given these limitations, I am prepared to argue that I have the makings of a theory, and enough case material to attest to its value—a theory that support is neither essentially individualistic nor narrowly political.

Nonconformity in Characteristics and Values

The motivation to achieve in contemporary society is conditioned by the belief that rewards follow from what one does, rather than from who one is. In general terms, this is descriptive of the real world if we compare traditional, relatively static societies with mobile and complex ones. But in no case does the importance of who one is, that is, of ascriptive criteria, ever disappear, or ever become unimportant.

The most general and most broadly applicable theory of ascription in modern society has been developed by Leon Mayhew.[2] Mayhew argues that ascription continues to be important because it is an easy, inexpensive way to channel and allocate human resources. Ascriptive

2. Leon Mayhew, "Ascription in Modern Societies," *Sociological Inquiry* 38 (1968): 105–20.

processes provide shortcuts for finding solutions to such enduring societal problems as filling jobs, ensuring political participation and
support, controlling conflict, and producing loyalty. Ascription then
brings selective benefits to those with the appropriate characteristics.
As the basis of an inexpensive allocative process, tied to existing
structural arrangements, the ascriptive system is difficult to penetrate
and alter. Meanwhile, those without the "correct" characteristics
must face the interpenetrating ways in which ascription leads to exclusion from full membership in the community. These have often
been described in terms of the costs of deliberate discrimination. It
should be emphasized, however, that this is not a discussion of discrimination and intergroup relations. Ascription is introduced to
identify the systemic consequences of social differentiation and conflict.[3] One of those consequences is the theme of this paper: differential judgments about political support and differential treatment of
threatening groups.

What people believe is not of the same order as who they are, but
the two are treated together here and in the remainder of the paper.
It is possible to do so because the pertinent values are those linked
to ascribed characteristics, in the sense that they deal with group
identity. Further references to ascription then should be understood
to be a shorthand way of talking both about characteristics and related values.

The importance of ascription is demonstrated where it is an avenue
for curtailing the participation of nonconforming groups in ways that
permeate the social system. The cases selected in illustration all have
some bearing on the issue of support (that is, they are not only instances of discrimination). In the economic system, ascription has
been the basis for restriction where nonconforming groups have been
viewed as unfair competitors. This was especially true for Japanese
and other Asian workers in British Columbia in the period from the
late nineteenth century until World War II.[4] Where competition has
not been so evident, economic success can still be frustrated if it pro-

3. Gerald Marwell, "Why Ascription? Parts of a More or Less Formal Theory of the Functions
and Dysfunctions of Sex Roles," *American Sociological Review* 40 (1975):445–55.

4. Charles J. Woodworth, *Canada and the Orient* (Toronto: Macmillan, 1941), pp. 45–71;
W. Peter Ward, *White Canada Forever* (Montreal: McGill-Queen's University Press, 1978),
pp. 120–23; Tomoko Makabe, "The Theory of a Split Labor Market: A Comparison of the Japanese Experience in Brazil and Canada," *Social Forces* 3 (1981):786–809.

vides nonconforming groups with unwelcome resources. The most notorious case concerned Frank Roncarelli, a restaurant owner who lost his liquor license because he had been regularly providing bail to his fellow Jehovah's Witnesses in Quebec.[5] Even age and sex have been relevant, as when during the depression, single men, often excluded from benefits provided to unemployed married men, were treated as a social menace. Reviewing the concerns of local and national authorities, Horn sees them asking: "Were these panhandling, sometimes working, freight-car riding adventurers not a menace to law and order? Were they not dangerously subject to the subversive blandishments of wily agitators, Communists and the like?"[6]

Ascription has also provided the means for preventing involvement in the political system. Suffrage restrictions are considered so important, that in the following section, they are treated as the primary mechanism for distinguishing those presumed to be low in political support. Another political right applied differentially is that associated with military service. Ironically, access to this right has been applied in diametrically different ways. Japanese Canadian citizens, eager to demonstrate their loyalty during World War II, were not conscripted and only a small number of enlistees appear to have been accepted for service.[7] Meanwhile, Jehovah's Witnesses, opposed to all military service, even to alternative service acceptable to other conscientious objectors, were forcibly inducted into one or the other of these types of service.[8] Whether proffered support is rejected (Japanese Canadians), or withheld support is coerced (Jehovah's Witnesses), it is the dominant groups that define what is appropriate.

The integrative institutions, particularly those of the legal and religious systems, have interacted to deny full legitimacy to Jehovah's Witnesses and the Sons of Freedom. Jehovah's Witnesses, while rejecting the notion of a separate clergy, were particularly eager to gain recognition as a body of ministers, since in that fashion they would escape military mobilization, but they failed to achieve this goal.[9] The

5. M. James Penton, *Jehovah's Witnesses in Canada: Champions of Freedom of Speech and Worship* (Toronto: Macmillan of Canada, 1976), pp. 220–21.

6. Michael Horn, *The Dirty Thirties* (Toronto: Copp Clark, 1972), p. 306.

7. Forrest E. LaViolette, *The Canadian Japanese and World War II* (Toronto: University of Toronto Press, 1948), pp. 310–13.

8. Penton, *Jehovah's Witnesses*, pp. 166–74.

9. Ibid., pp. 176–77.

Sons of Freedom, a radical fringe of the Doukhobours, who wished to keep their children from school on religious grounds, were judged not to be a religion after all, in the sense of presenting an acceptable body of beliefs.[10] In playing its integrative role, the law for a period effectively excluded Japanese and Jehovah's Witnesses from the political community, interning citizens, stripping them of citizenship, or banning their religious fellowship.

Ascription contributes to the transmission and support of the value system where the loyalty, solidarity, and commitment evoked by smaller social units can be transferred to, or treated synonymously with, attachments to the larger unit. Where the family functions as a reasonably effective arena for the inculcation of values and commitments, the resources of the larger society do not have to be employed toward this end.[11] But ascription may be used in exactly the opposite way, to seriously disrupt the ability of nonconforming families to nurture their cultural values and socialize their children. During the height of the wartime persecution of Jehovah's Witnesses, children were expelled from schools for not participating in patriotic exercises and parents fined for their religious advocacy, and in extreme cases, children were temporarily separated from their parents.[12] But even into the 1970s, children were threatened with expulsion from school for these reasons.[13] The refusal of Witness parents to allow blood transfusions for their children continues to be used to weaken family solidarity when children are made temporary wards of the local Children's Aid Society.[14] Reference has already been made to the Sons of Freedom sect in British Columbia who were forcibly separated from their children.[15] For Japanese Canadians, even forming a family was difficult because of the uneven demographic balance perpetuated by immigration restrictions, and the general lack of exogamy. Efforts made to foster a Japanese cultural identity were always viewed with suspicion, with Japanese language schools feared as centers of militarism and subversion. Those children who attended community schools were subject not only to the normal pressures to assimilate faced by

---

10. *Perepolkin et al. v. Superintendent of Child Welfare*, A. C. (1947) 1 D.L.R., 599–600.
11. Mayhew, "Ascription," p. 116.
12. Penton, *Jehovah's Witnesses*, pp. 140–52.
13. Ibid., p. 225.
14. Ibid., pp. 231–44.
15. S. M. Katz, "The Lost Children of British Columbia," *Macleans* (May 11, 1957).

all immigrants' children, but to overwhelming prejudice as well. The results were to separate the Japanese community from its white neighbors, and to divide the generations who claimed Japanese ancestry.[16]

Nonconformity as an Indicator of Low Support

A comparative perspective on the history of suffrage uncovers how frequently extending the vote to new groups was viewed as a means for preserving, and even strengthening existing structures of power.[17] This occurred as part of the move from feudal to modern society and, as such, might not be particularly germane to North American experience. But the view of suffrage entailed is not entirely misplaced in this context as well. For example, the extension of suffrage to women in the United States first took place in frontier states and regions where the votes of women could be expected to help protect established order.[18] This is not to say that voting rights have not been gained through the efforts of those excluded who held out no promise that they would perpetuate existing authority once they had the capacity to alter it. But in many instances, the franchise has been a reward for presumptions of loyalty and support.

The connection between voting rights and support has a number of manifestations in Canada that bear on the thesis that nonconforming groups are inherently nonsupportive. One such instance involves the passage of the Wartime Elections Act of 1917. The federal government denied the franchise to all naturalized British subjects born in an enemy country and naturalized after 1902, and also to naturalized subjects, regardless of country of birth, whose mother tongue was the language of any enemy power. It gave the vote to women who had participated in any branch of the armed forces or who had a close rela-

16. LaViolette, *The Canadian Japanese*, pp. 8–28; Charles Young, Helen Y. R. Reid, and W. A. Carrothers, *The Japanese Canadians* (Toronto: University of Toronto Press, 1939), pp. 136–39.

17. Emile Willems, "Brazil," in Arnold Rose, ed., *The Institutions of Advanced Societies* (Minneapolis: University of Minnesota Press, 1958), p. 552; Reinhard Bendix, *Nation-Building and Citizenship* (New York: Wiley, 1964), pp. 93–101; Stein Rokkan, *Citizens, Elections, Parties* (New York: Wiley, 1970), pp. 31–32.

18. Allan Grimes, *The Puritan Ethic and Woman Suffrage* (New York: Oxford University Press, 1967).

tive in the armed forces of Canada or Britain. The assumption was clearly that those with ties to enemy powers would not have dissolved these completely, even after fifteen years in Canada, and hence could not be expected to support the war effort, at least not to the extent that this involved conscription. There was, of course, another significant segment of the population known to be opposed to conscription; but French-speaking native Canadians could not be so easily disfranchised. Instead, a major segment of the non-British foreign born was cast in the role of the questionably loyal. This example should not be abandoned, however, without pointing out the partisan implications of the 1917 Act. While an assumption was made about how supportive certain foreign-born citizens would be toward participating in the war effort, there was more information about their partisan proclivities. These were Liberal, and a Union government was not afraid to equate national loyalty with party support, much to the anger of the Liberal Party.[19]

Other instances using voting rights as a reward for political support do not have this same partisan bias and hence are even clearer in revealing how nonconformity is taken as a sign of low support. Nonconformity in religion and race remained barriers to voting much longer than did property qualifications or sex.[20] The reasons for their perpetuation were clearly enunciated by Prime Minister Macdonald, offering an amendment to the Franchise Act of 1885, in a way that would have durable consequences until the middle of this century:

The Chinese are foreigners. If they come to this country, after three years residence, they may, if they choose, be naturalized. But still we know that when the Chinaman comes here he intends to return to his own country; he does not bring his family with him; he is a stranger, a sojourner in a strange land, for his own purposes for a while; he has no common interest with us, and while he gives us his labour and is paid for it, and is valuable, the same as a threshing machine or any other agricultural implement which we may borrow from the United States on hire and return it to the owner on the south side of the line; a Chinaman gives us his labour and gets his money, but the money does not fructify in Canada; he does not invest it here, but takes it with him and returns to China; and if he cannot, his executors or his friends send his body back to the flowery land. But he has not British in-

19. O. D. Skelton, *Life and Letters of Sir Wilfrid Laurier* II (London: Century, 1921).
20. T. H. Qualter, *The Election Process in Canada* (Toronto: McGraw-Hill, 1970).

stincts or British feelings or aspirations, and therefore ought not to have a vote.[21]

The federal government was perhaps not the major culprit in its exclusionary policies, but by permitting the provinces to define the suffrage it followed the lead of British Columbia. In that province Chinese and East Indians were disfranchised until 1945, and Japanese until 1953, when the last racial qualifications were dropped. Independent criteria for voting in federal elections were established earlier than this. Thus, for example, restrictions were removed from Japanese Canadian citizens in 1948. Religious restrictions, removed federally in 1955, had been applied to all those faiths which did (or might) claim refusal to serve in wartime.

Nonconformity as Politically Threatening

Actions or beliefs construed to imply disloyalty or dedication to violent alteration of the political system, as with radical political movements like communists or separatists, pose no problem in tracing the link between nonconformity and political threats. But while, in general, ascription makes it easy to move from characteristics to imputations of behavior, it is more difficult to identify conditions for associating political threat with nonconforming groups when the latter have no overtly political content. My effort to do this involves attention to two avenues through which linkage may occur. One, the more likely, lies in the effects of a precipitating crisis; the other, from direct attacks on dominant groups and values.

A crisis may be defined as "a situation of unanticipated threat to important values in which decision time is short."[22] When a crisis involves external danger, a connection can be easily made with internal enemies of similar characteristics.[23] This connection would be too simple an interpretation for the treatment of Japanese Canadians in

21. House of Commons, *Debates*, 1885, p. 1582.
22. Ole R. Holsti, "Crisis, Stress and Decision-Making," *International Social Sciences Journal* 23 (1971):53–67.
23. David J. Finley, Ole R. Holsti, and Richard J. Fagen, *Enemies in Politics* (Chicago: Rand McNally, 1967), pp. 238–42.

World War II, however. While the war brought restrictions on all enemy aliens, it did not extend to citizens of German and Italian origin in ways that were used against the Japanese. To generalize from that and other experiences in wartime, it is necessary to consider the nature of crises and the kinds of decisions that are made under crisis conditions.[24] A crisis produces uncertainty, confusion, and possibly even panic. To allay these reactions, it raises demands for immediate action. Characteristically, those in authority respond with coercive measures, over which they have most ready control, and whose employment gives the greatest evidence that they are in fact doing something. A crisis gives, as well, an unusual degree of scope for individual actors, who are less restrained than usual because of the silence of competing and countervailing interests.[25] Under these circumstances, there is a particularly good opportunity to interpret past events as directly leading to, or at least bearing on, the crisis.

The ways in which these elements coalesced in the situation of the Japanese is epitomized in a response to the Speech from the Throne in the first session after Pearl Harbor and Canada's declaration of war against the Japanese. Mr. Howard Green, Conservative Member from Vancouver South, began by castigating the government for not paying sufficient attention to the defense of the Pacific coast. Warming up to his main theme, he argued:

Canadians on the Pacific are entitled to and insist on getting complete protection from treachery, protection from being stabbed in the back. The rest of Canada, under successive dominion governments, failed to listen to our representatives from British Columbia when they asked for an end to Japanese immigration. But now what British Columbia members for the last thirty-five years have been telling other members of the house would happen has come to pass, and the rest of Canada must do its part. It must now come to our help. I appeal to private members on the government side of the House to see that the ministry does come to our help in this matter. We have at least 24,000 of Japanese origin in our province, all in the coastal area—fishermen, men working in our woods in the lumbering industry, men farming on both sides of the great Fraser river valley, which means that they

24. Robert Jackson, "Crisis-Management and Policy-Making: An Exploration of Theory and Research," in Richard Rose, ed., *The Dynamics of Public Policy* (Beverly Hills: Sage Publications, 1976), pp. 209–35.
25. Roger Daniels, *The Decision to Relocate the Japanese Americans* (Philadelphia: Lippincott, 1975), p. 35.

are astride both of our transcontinental lines. There has been treachery else-where from Japanese in this war, and we have no reason to hope that there will be none in British Columbia. If we were in a similar position, if we were Canadians in Japan, we might feel much the same; we would be only too willing to assist British troops should they attempt to land on the Japanese coast. The only complete protection we can have from this danger is to re-move the Japanese population from the province.[26]

In a related way, banning Jehovah's Witnesses and groups associ-ated with them as illegal organizations during World War II, as though they were in the same category with fascist and communist organizations, was justified by the dangerous quality of their teach-ings. Explaining why the Witnesses had been banned, Prime Minis-ter King read the reply of his Justice Minister, Ernest Lapointe:

The literature of Jehovah's Witnesses discloses, in effect, that man-made au-thority or law should not be recognized if it conflicts with the Jehovah's Wit-ness interpretation of the Bible; that they refuse to salute the flag or any nation or to hail any man; and, that they oppose war.

The general effect of this literature is, amongst other things, to under-mine the ordinary responsibility of citizens, particularly in time of war.[27]

After the ban was removed in 1943, the effects of crisis remained, and efforts were made to ensure that Jehovah's Witnesses fulfilled re-quirements of military service. Justice Minister Louis St. Laurent re-minded members of the House that ground for banning them in-cluded: ". . . propaganda to the effect that one could be an ordained minister of Jehovah's Witnesses by making an individual compact with the Almighty, that by doing so one became an ordained minister not subject to mobilization regulations. That is something which I look upon as contrary to the policy which this state has to maintain in war time."[28] In other words, what was unacceptable at the outbreak of war would continue to be so throughout the wartime crisis.

Economic dislocations also generate crises that have been used to justify extreme actions against nonconforming groups. Workers who participated in the Winnipeg General Strike of 1919 were viewed by the established business and professional community as potential rev-

26. House of Commons, *Debates*, 1942, pp. 156–57.
27. House of Commons, *Debates*, 1940, p. 1646.
28. House of Commons, *Debates*, 1944, p. 2917.

olutionaries.[29] Convinced by the alarms of local leaders, Justice Minister Arthur Meighen reasoned that a general strike meant the "usurpation of governmental authority" and hence could not be allowed to continue.[30] The government's response included efforts to strip citizenship from the strikers, a crisis-induced policy of the sort which was later applied to the Japanese.

Conditions of war provide a rationale for imposing stringent measures that are welcomed by those who want controlling actions more than they are concerned about protecting basic rights.[31] In wartime, arrests for sedition may be a measure of the community's efforts to control unpopular groups as much as of the danger inherent in their speech. This appears to have been the case in western Canada during World War I, where the largest proportion of non-British immigrants, many from enemy countries, were concentrated. Six cases of sedition are recorded, all apparently of a quite trivial nature.[32] This led to the observation in the Alberta Court of Appeals by Justice Stuart that, "There have been more prosecutions for seditious words in Alberta in the past two years than in all the history of England over a hundred years and England has had numerous and critical wars in that time."[33] World War II as well produced a flurry of sedition cases, most of which appear to have been confined to police courts, and hence not listed in published records.[34]

Charges of sedition in peacetime appear to be the most severe weapon available to dominant groups faced with the provocative flouting of their position and values. Canadian law on seditious libel provides a welcome hunting ground for those searching for legal argumentation. From a layman's perspective, the law implies that words and actions are criminal when they contribute to the disturbance of orderly communal existence, possibly by inciting violence, in ways

29. D. C. Masters, *The Winnipeg General Strike* (Toronto: University of Toronto Press, 1973), pp. 65–66.
30. House of Commons, *Debates*, 1919, pp. 309–3064; Masters, *The Winnipeg General Strike*, pp. 102–3.
31. Herbert Marx, "The Emergency Power and Civil Liberties in Canada," *McGill Law Journal* 16 (1970):73.
32. D. A. Schmeiser, *Civil Liberties in Canada* (London: Oxford University Press, 1964), p. 206.
33. *Rex v. Trainor*, Alberta C.A. (1917) 1 W.W.R. 423.
34. Lester H. Philips, "The Impact of the Defence of Canada Regulations upon Civil Liberties," unpublished Ph.D. dissertation, University of Michigan, 1945; M. P. Straus, "The Con-

that cast disrespect on the state.[35] The earlier version of the law contained reference to "unlawful associations," and figured in two convictions of strikers, one in 1920 and the other in 1924, the first case an aftermath of the Winnipeg General Strike.[36]

The law on sedition was used to control the actions of Jehovah's Witnesses in Quebec up to 1950. In that year the Supreme Court offered an interpretation of the law that virtually ended its potential use as an instrument in group relations.[37] In *Boucher v. The King*, the defendant had been convicted of distributing an inflammatory pamphlet, "Quebec's Burning Hate for God and Christ and Freedom is the Shame of all Canada." In the first hearing of the Supreme Court, Justice Rand offered what became the critical judgment that:

There is no modern authority which holds that the mere effect of tending to create discontent or disaffection among His Majesty's subjects or ill-will or hostility between groups of them, but not tending to issue an illegal conduct, constitutes the crime, and this for obvious reasons. Freedom in thought and speech and disagreement in ideas and beliefs, on every conceivable subject, are of the essence of our life. The clash of critical discussion on political, social and religious subjects has too deeply become the stuff of daily experience to suggest that mere ill-will as a product of controversy can strike down the latter with illegality.[38]

As MacGuigan asks, "is it still open for counsel to argue that the interest of the State in public order is not at stake when the incitement is directed, not against the State itself, but against a social group?"[39] It would appear from the Boucher ruling that, outside of a crisis, efforts to attribute political threat to less than patently political groups will be frustrated by the courts. A still unknown quantity, however, are recent criminal code additions on group defamation and the spread of hate literature. According to one constitutional expert, "Could it be doubted that the literature which was involved in the

trol of Subversive Activities in Canada," unpublished Ph.D. dissertation, University of Illinois-Urbana, 1959, pp. 202–16.

35. Mark R. MacGuigan, "Seditious Libel and Related Offences in England, the United States and Canada," Appendix I in *Report of the Special Committee on Hate Propaganda in Canada* (Ottawa: Queen's Printer, 1966), pp. 119–26.

36. Schmeiser, *Civil Liberties*, pp. 206–7.

37. *Boucher v. The King* (1950) 1 D.L.R. 657; on rehearing (1951) 2 D.L.R. 369.

38. Ibid., (1950) 682.

39. MacGuigan, "Seditious Libel," p. 126.

case of *Boucher v. The King* could be classed as 'hate propaganda'?"[40]
It is probably not accidental that Glen How, the lawyer who has been
most active in defending Jehovah's Witnesses, strongly objected to
the new law.[41]

The Accusatory Process

The initiation of complaints about lack of support comes largely
from dominant groups with a local rather than a national basis of operation. This has already been suggested by many of the preceding examples. The effectiveness with which demands for action are raised is
tied to the multiple channels of access to centers of power available to
dominant groups and to the status they command to have their demands taken seriously.

When war broke out with Japan, community groups and leaders in
British Columbia began an accusatory process. Motions were passed
and a heavy volume of letters and telegrams went to the Honorable
Ian Mackenzie, Minister for Pensions and National Health, and to a
lesser extent to Prime Minister King. Though the former's official jurisdiction did not involve the Japanese, the fact that he was the sole
cabinet member from British Columbia made him the spokesman for
that province, and the major conduit by which interested groups and
individuals could express their opinions to government. Resolutions
in favor of the evacuation and segregation of all Japanese, regardless
of citizenship, were transmitted from local governments, provincial
authorities, businesses, trade unions, service organizations, veterans'
groups, and political parties. As some Japanese attempted to move
inland on their own, opposition grew from agricultural interests, particularly in the Okanagan Valley. LaViolette attributed particular significance to the formation of the Citizens' Defense Committee on
February 23, 1942:

The reason for the importance of the Committee lies in the fact that it did
not come into existence until relatively late, and that it was made up of the
most prominent citizens of British Columbia, particularly of Vancouver, who

40. Walter S. Tarnopolsky, *The Canadian Bill of Rights*, 2nd revised ed. (Toronto: McClelland and Stewart, 1975), pp. 192–93.
    41. Penton, *Jehovah's Witnesses*, p. 226.

felt that immediate action should be taken, as the general situation was getting out of hand. Because of the prestige of its members, it was possible for the Committee to make a deep impression upon Ottawa. It constituted the focal point of organized pressure and assumed the role of the guardian of British Columbia defences and civilian morale and safety.[42]

In parliament, four Conservatives, ten Liberals, and one Independent from British Columbia provided a more or less unified front in the House of Commons, demanding evacuation. Only the lone CCF Member from the province stayed aloof from drastic proposals, although he too was careful to affirm his concern for military security. In Canada's parliamentary system, there is generally little scope for expressing regional interests within party caucus.[43] The demand for regional policies ordinarily comes from cabinet members from a particular region, and rarely from rank and file MPs.[44] Here was an instance where Liberal backbenchers directly attempted to influence policy in caucus, through pressure on the prime minister and "their" cabinet minister, Ian Mackenzie, but also, informally at least, they displayed dedication to local interests that overcame minimal partisan considerations. In the latter, they were aided by the recent creation of a provincial coalition government.

An examination of the House of Commons Debates, Prime Minister King's diaries, the Cabinet on War Committee minutes, and the papers of Ian Mackenzie suggests the existence of two perspectives on the fate of the Japanese which were initially opposed, but soon coalesced. On the one hand, Members of Parliament from British Columbia used the wartime crisis to preach their views of the Japanese as an internal danger and an insurmountable obstacle to the harmony of their province. On the other hand, at least publicly, the government was reluctant to accept this definition of the situation. As late as February 19, 1942, Mr. King was advocating restraint and temperate language.[45] Well into 1943, he refused to make public commitments about what might be done with the Japanese once the war was over.

42. LaViolette, *The Canadian Japanese*, p. 42.

43. Allan Kornberg, "Caucus and Cohesion in Canadian Parties," *American Political Science Review* 68 (1966):84–87.

44. Hugh McD. Clokie, "The Machinery of Government," in George Brown, ed., *Canada* (Berkeley: University of California Press, 1950), p. 307; Leon D. Epstein, "A Comparative Study of Canadian Parties," *American Political Science Review* 58 (1964):48.

45. House of Commons, *Debates*, 1942, p. 706.

But on the same day as he spoke in the House in 1942, urging restraint, he wrote in his diary of other fears: " . . . there is every possibility of riots. Once that occurs, there will be repercussions in the Far East against our own prisoners. Public prejudice is so strong in B.C. that it is going to be difficult to control the situation."[46] Unlike the United States where evacuation was tied more closely to arguments of military necessity, in Canada the need for internal harmony became the primary justification for the evacuation of the Japanese.

The Prime Minister's fears had roots in his own recollections of earlier events, where violent outbursts against Chinese and Japanese over a period of years had culminated in the Vancouver riot of 1907. Coincidentally, dislike of the Liberal government's policies had led to its defeat in the 1908 election.[47] Later hostile acts against East Indians in British Columbia were contained, apparently by the judgment that the Conservative government would be more sympathetic to demands for restrictive immigration policies.[48]

Local initiative was also prominent in presenting Jehovah's Witnesses as politically dangerous. Early during World War II, while Minister of Justice Ernest Lapointe was receiving advice from the press censors not to move against Jehovah's Witnesses, others, outside the government, were urging contrary actions. Most prominent of these were leaders of the Roman Catholic hierarchy in Quebec.[49] Jehovah's Witnesses remained convinced that their wartime ban was the direct result of such pressure.[50] There is evidence that the Anglican Church also attempted to influence the government against the Witnesses,[51] But Witness distrust of the Quebec Catholic Church remained strong, and they felt their suspicions were confirmed by activities after the war. In Joliette, Quebec, where Witnesses had been harassed for proselytizing, a group of prominent citizens presented a petition on behalf of the local Knights of Columbus to the city council, requesting that Witnesses who came as missionaries be "chased forever from Joliette."[52]

46. J. W. Pickersgill, *The Mackenzie King Record: I, 1939–1944* (Toronto: University of Toronto Press, 1960), p. 354.

47. Ward, *White Canada*, pp. 53–76.

48. Ibid., pp. 79–93.

49. Penton, *Jehovah's Witnesses*, p. 134.

50. Ibid., pp. 144, 152, 185.

51. Ibid., p. 133.

52. Ibid., p. 209.

While it may be true that pressure from the Roman Catholic Church was significant in bringing about the wartime ban, it would be erroneous to see it as the only source of opposition. The unwillingness of Witness children to participate in patriotic exercises was considered sufficiently provocative to lead to their expulsion in a number of areas, with the Hamilton, Ontario, Board of Education being especially punitive. Even though the Ontario authorities ruled that it was not necessary for children to participate in such exercises, it chose not to interfere in the local board's decisions.[53] It was also the case that veterans' organizations in western Canada took the lead in opposing the unpatriotic stance of the Witnesses.[54]

To conclude this section, it may be noted that overtly political acts assumed to be threatening are more likely to come directly to the attention of higher-level authorities. Yet even under such circumstances, lower-level initiatives play a role. Brief references to two additional cases will suffice to illustrate the point. Premier Duplessis waged his own battle against communism, for example, with the Quebec Padlock Act, which was finally judged to be unconstitutional. A second and more recent example is produced by the imposition of the War Measures Act of 1970. This, it will be recalled, had been preceded by appeals from Quebec political leaders, asking for emergency measures.[55]

Changing Definitions

It is not an accident that the two cases which have been examined most closely in this paper, treatment of the Japanese and Jehovah's Witnesses, occurred about the same time, during World War II. Assertions about lack of support and threatening behavior were tied to the motor force of wartime crisis. More generally, however, it is significant that the conditions set in motion by such a crisis do not all work in the same direction. For example, labor unrest following World War I and continuing into the depression produced many in-

53. Ibid., p. 53.
54. Ibid., p. 347, n. 53.
55. John Saywell, *Quebec 70* (Toronto: University of Toronto Press, 1971), pp. 84–86; *Le Devoir*, Oct. 27, 1975, p. 1; *Le Devoir*, Oct. 31, 1975, p. 7.

stances where the efforts of workers to organize or to rely on strike actions produced severe reactions—reactions based at least in part on the assumption that economic unrest was the harbinger of political uprising. But these same conditions also contributed to the growth of the trade union movement and the emergence of new political parties which expanded the range of available political options. In a similar vein, Canadian experiences in World War II stimulated a transformation of the society and economy, and set the stage for acquiring greater national autonomy. In turn, among the subsequent changes of relevance were the Canadian Citizenship Act of 1946 and the 1949 Supreme Court Act.

The passage of the Citizenship Act marked the first affirmative definition of citizenship in which the full nature of "Canadianness" was elaborated.[56] The debates on the act were conducted against the backdrop of a postwar solution to the "Japanese problem." Following notice by the Minister of Labour in February 1945, Japanese were informed of the possibility of "voluntary repatriation to Japan." Those not interested in this option were urged to settle east of the Rockies. Many people displaced during the war interpreted the way these alternatives were presented to mean that there would be no opportunity to return to their coastal homes. Of those who saw their options limited, many requested resettlement in Japan.[57] By Order in Council in December, 1946, the government provided for the deportation and denaturalization of Canadian citizens, along with their wives and dependent children, who had not revoked their request for movement to Japan prior to the formal surrender of Japan on September 1, 1945. One month later Members of Parliament debated provisions of the Citizenship Act, and those from British Columbia pressed for assurances that the bill would not affect the deportation order. Though the opposition was not as vigorous in its arguments, it did point out the anomalies created. For its part, the government was no longer prepared to accept some of the more extreme views voiced by British Columbia members: for example, that anyone who had been counted in a census of the Japanese government should not be considered a citizen of Canada, regardless of birthplace.[58] The Citizenship

56. House of Commons, *Debates*, 1947, pp. 131, 503–10.
57. LaViolette, *The Canadian Japanese*, pp. 238–44.
58. Schwartz, "Citizenship in Canada," pp. 90–92.

Act provided new definitions of inclusion, some of which were in sharp conflict with those implicit in previous treatment of the Japanese. It was obvious that the two would not be able to coexist.

Alternation in the status of Jehovah's Witnesses was aided in a similarly indirect fashion by the passage of the Supreme Court Act, making that judicial body the final appeals court and broadening its responsibilities. According to Penton, the major Witness attorneys "were firmly convinced that if they could once get their cases into the Supreme Court of Canada, they could legally establish the right of Jehovah's Witnesses to preach openly in Quebec."[59] Up to that point, they had limited legal recourse, i.e., most of their cases had been heard in Recorder's courts in the province, without recourse to appeal to higher courts.[60] The Witnesses were apparently correct in their expectation of favorable treatment from the Supreme Court. For example, in the case of *Samur v. Quebec*, in which a Witness challenged the barriers to distributing religious pamphlets in the street without a license, the Court's ruling was not only of benefit to Samur, but was believed to have disposed of about seven hundred similar cases in the province.[61]

As far as the nonconforming groups are concerned, the changes described above are indirect in the sense that new legal and political definitions were created independently of actions by the groups, but eventually helped change their status. At the same time, changes also took place as a result of more direct efforts on behalf of the groups. Illustratively, as it became clear that Japan would soon be defeated, the climate of opinion within British Columbia altered, and church groups, the press, and those concerned with civil liberties began to voice opposition to the government's punitive policy. Indicative of the shifting public mood, the Gallup Poll of January 1945 reported that 59 percent of the Canadian population sampled felt that the Japanese should be allowed to remain in Canada; and while no figures are given, it is said that this was true for a similar proportion in British Columbia.[62] In 1943, this had been the sentiment of only about one-quarter of British Columbians.[63] Then, too, in the election of 1944,

59. Penton, *Jehovah's Witnesses*, p. 203.
60. Ibid., pp. 202–6.
61. Ibid., pp. 206–16.
62. Canadian Institute of Public Opinion (January 17, 1945).
63. Canadian Institute of Public Opinion (December 23, 1943).

the CCF added three seats, which increased that party's voice in supporting rights for the Japanese. Moreover, the Japanese themselves were now better organized, and could call on support from the larger community. The Cooperative Committee on Japanese Canadians, an umbrella organization that had been formed in Toronto in 1942, supported the Japanese in their bid to the Supreme Court and the Judicial Committee of the Privy Council to have the offending orders declared *ultra vires*.[64]

As for the Jehovah's Witnesses, justification for banning the group was not really apparent to many people outside of Quebec. A select committee of the House of Commons met in 1942 to consider all of the organizations listed as illegal and recommended that the ban be lifted for Witnesses. No action was taken, however, and the government began to hear considerable criticism in the House. Then, when the USSR became an ally, and arguments were made to permit legalizing communist organizations, it became even more difficult to see why the Witnesses should be excluded.[65]

As Jehovah's Witnesses grew in their experience as litigants, they also became advocates of expanded legal protections. Witnesses were in the forefront of those pressing for a Bill of Rights in the late 1940s and enlisted considerable support from the general community in this effort. When a bill was eventually passed, the significance of their actions for such legislation was recognized.[66] Witnesses also inspired a growing admiration for their defense of civil liberties, and as major social changes altered the climate of Quebec, for their role in stimulating these changes.[67] In other words, they became respectable.

Building a Theory

Several elements are missing from this effort at theory building. For one thing, it is still necessary to relate overtly political groups to

64. *Cooperative Committee on Japanese Canadians v. Attorney General of Canada*, A.C. (1947) 1 D.L.R. 577.

65. Penton, *Jehovah's Witnesses*, pp. 147–52.

66. Edward McWhinney, "The Bill of Rights, the Supreme Court, and Civil Liberties in Canada," *The Canadian Annual Review for 1960* (Toronto: University of Toronto Press, 1961), p. 271.

67. Pierre Elliott Trudeau, *Federalism and the French Canadians* (Toronto: Macmillan of Canada, 1968), pp. 112, 171, 210.

problems of political support and group dominance. Above, the importance of ascribed characteristics was emphasized to broaden the conception of what is considered politically relevant. Such an emphasis is justified on the grounds that political support is an aspect of contention among groups, and not only a link between individual citizens and the state. But in no way was the argument made that one should discount the importance of political actions, and with them *political* groups. It has already been suggested that political authorities, acting on behalf of dominant groups, but without their intervention, will ordinarily take steps to control nonconforming political groups directly. Thus, local initiatives may not be so important for understanding how such groups are treated. This, however, requires further investigation. To the extent that nonconforming political groups fit this theory, they do so where they are clearly radical, with goals that set them apart as advocates of drastic change. This suggests the need to pursue the ways in which all political movements are initially perceived. When are they seen to affect political support and when are they considered political threats?

As the elements of this theory receive more study, the result may be a minor theory, in the sense that it will be useful for explaining relatively infrequent occurrences. A more effective test will require not only a more thorough search of Canadian history, but also the adoption of a comparative perspective. If it still turns out that the theory accounts only for events that are relatively rare, this will not be without significance. Such a theory would provide a way of considering the problematics of political support, not its incidence or general functions. That is, one would be in a position to judge when low political support results in stress on the political system.

Yet even a minor theory of political support is important through its association with theories of citizenship. The primary sociological theory of citizenship is found in the work of T. H. Marshall. It traces a developmental approach to the full incorporation of citizens, but for all of its usefulness, it still seems incomplete. Parsons was even more explicitly evolutionary in his perspective, and more categorical in his prediction that, "Today, more than ever before, we are witnessing an acceleration in the emancipation of individuals in all categories from these diffuse particularistic solidarities."[68] A developmental perspec-

68. Parsons, "Full Citizenship," passim.

tive on the acquisition of citizen rights does not take into account the unstable nature of these rights, or the possibility that they can be withdrawn. Looking at the way in which political support reflects the presence of a dominant framework of political values provides another way to conceptualize citizenship as membership in a political community. The theory of political support outlined here can lead to an alternative perspective on citizenship, one that emphasizes the latter's instability. According to this view, when limits are placed on citizenship, rights may be curtailed or lost, and claims to full membership must be demonstrated.

By relating both demands for support and evaluations of its shortcomings to a broader theory of citizenship, it becomes possible to more fully appreciate those instances where refusal of some rights is not necessarily an explicit judgment of low support, but still impinges on the nature of citizenship. For example, virtually nothing was said about woman suffrage, even though the extension of the franchise was used as the principal indicator of how support was evaluated. This omission was made consciously, since the struggle for woman suffrage was quite low-keyed in Canada, and does not appear to have been tied to issues of support. At the same time, one can still detect the existence of questions about the supportive position of women, and some fears associated with their gaining the vote, especially in Quebec, where women were denied the vote provincially until 1940. Suffrage was opposed by most politicians, and by all levels of the Catholic Church, including Cardinal Villeneuve, who saw it as generally disruptive. According to one opponent of suffrage, "to give women the vote meant overturning the social order, and was against the spirit of Roman Catholic Church, and would bring no advantage."[69] Reluctance to grant the vote to women was then another instance of the assertion of dominant group rights. While it does not qualify as a good example of assertions about low political support, its relation to full rights of citizenship means we must better account for the presence or absence of overlap between support and citizenship.

In another instance of the changing nature of citizenship, examples of labor unrest after the depression were not used because it was im-

---

69. Cited in Catherine L. Cleverdon, *The Woman Suffrage Movement in Canada* (Toronto: University of Toronto Press, 1950), p. 242.

possible to discern the political significance of strikes at later periods. But this too needs to be elaborated. In Marshall's theory of citizenship, rights of association, as well as the conduct of class conflict, all bear on full inclusion into the political community. This implies the need to be alert to those instances where strike actions are treated as incipient political disorders. For example, in the 1949 asbestos workers' strike in Quebec evaluations of the threatening character of the strike were minimized by the broad community support, including that from many elements in the Catholic Church. It was mainly the provincial government that sided with management in what looked like a classic confrontation with workers. But attributions of threat also existed within dominant groups outside of government, as some segments of the Church circulated a document that suggested strikers and their clerical supporters were revolutionary tools of Moscow.[70]

These examples of woman suffrage and strikes suggest another way in which the present theory has a larger importance, through its connection with theories of change. Such a connection was alluded to in discussing the fifth component of the theory on interacting changes in the larger society and in the situation of nonconforming groups. It was stated earlier that no attempt would be made to deal with a theory of racial or ethnic relations, even though the substantive content of present concerns did bear on this. Instead, what is at issue is the character of the social system and the values that support it. In their daily experiences members of a social unit act in ways to preserve what they value; and they expect those who act on their behalf to behave in a similar fashion. This is where the setting of goals for the political system enters. In British Columbia, prior to the end of World War II, the primary motor force was a desire for a homogeneous, white population.[71] For Quebec until somewhat later, it was for a traditional Catholic society. The dominant interests in both societies battled for their goals until the point of exhaustion. The next stage is then not an acceptance of the inevitable, but a reworking at all levels of system and subsystem goals. In this process the situations

70. Pierre Elliott Trudeau, *The Asbestos Strike* (Toronto: James Lewis and Samuel, 1974), pp. 355–65.
71. Ward, *White Canada*, p. 168.

and expectations of both dominant and nonconforming groups are altered. It is the unfolding of this process of change which may turn out to be the most exciting element in the whole equation of what constitutes political support.

National Identification and Political Support

Allan Kornberg and Marianne C. Stewart

Although Alan Cairns's essay in this volume (chapter 14) suggests that the struggle waged by federal and provincial political elites for the hearts and minds of the Canadian people has become particularly intense in the past decade, it can be argued that this struggle has been going on for more than a hundred years. On the one hand, from Macdonald onward, successive federal governments have sought to establish the legitimacy and primacy of the national political regime in Canadian life and to convince Canadians both that they are a nation and that, irrespective of their province of residence, their federal government is capable of dealing fairly and effectively with their problems. On the other hand, provincial political elites (especially those in Ontario and Quebec) have attempted to represent themselves as the custodians and representatives of the values and interests of their respective political communities. They have encouraged their populations to look to and identify with them, and to support their attempts to deal with problems, largely defined in terms of provincial boundaries. That provincial elites have experienced at least a modicum of success is reflected in the title of Edwin Black's book, *Divided Loyalties*. Black's insights subsequently have been supported by a variety of public opinion surveys which indicate that substantial numbers of Canadians in every province have very strong and positive feelings about their provinces. They feel their provincial governments are close to them and are effective in solving what they deem to be particularly important problems.[1]

---

1. Harold D. Clarke et al., *Political Choice in Canada* (Toronto: McGraw-Hill Ryerson, 1979), chap. 3; Canadian Broadcasting Corporation, "Allegiance to Government, A *Question of*

In light of these findings, it is not surprising that Canadian scholars and intellectuals have argued that Canadians do not have a strong sense of national identity and, further, that those who do, structure their identity largely in terms of antipathy toward the United States.[2] Moreover, it has been argued that the lack of a strong national identity, coupled with increasing American control of the economy and polity, are principal causes of the recurring crises associated with the maintenance of the country's unity.[3] Given these considerations, we decided that it would be especially useful to present an analysis that delineates the degree to which Canadians do have a national identity—at least insofar as this is implied by the inclusion of a reference to being Canadian in the individual's concept of self.

Self-Concepts and Theoretical Expectations

The use of reports of self-concept as a basis for revealing personal identities arises from scholarly interest in the latter. Indeed, personal identity has been of more than occasional interest to social scientists for most of this century.[4] The reason for this interest is clear. In discussing the self-concepts of Americans, McLaughlin observed: "Identity, with its implication of uniqueness, self-determination, and personal dignity, is a red, white, and blue term. The Judeo-Christian traditions and American heritage stress the immeasurable worth of

---

Country" (Montreal: Research Services to English Service Division, April 25, 1980, pp. 26–39b; and David J. Elkins, "The Sense of Place," in *Small Worlds: Provinces and Parties in Canadian Political Life*, ed. David J. Elkins and Richard Simeon (Toronto: Methuen, 1980), pp. 16–25.

2. P. E. Corbett, "Anti-Americanism," *Dalhousie Review* 10 (1930–31): 295–300; S. D. Clark, "The Importance of Anti-Americanism in Canadian National Feeling," in *Canada and Her Great Neighbor*, ed. H. F. Angus (Toronto: The Ryerson Press, 1938); Harry Gordon Johnson, *The Canadian Quandary* (Toronto: McGraw-Hill, 1963), passim; M. Brunet, "Continentalism and Quebec Nationalism: A Double Challenge to Canada," *Queen's Quarterly* 76 (1969): 511–27; and Ian Lumsden, ed., *Close the 49th Parallel: The Americanization of Canada* (Toronto: University of Toronto Press, 1970), passim.

3. Joel Smith and David K. Jackson, *Restructuring the Canadian State: Prospects for Three Political Scenarios* (Durham: Duke University, Center for International Studies, Occasional Papers Series, No. 11, 1981).

4. See William James, *Principles of Psychology*, vols. 1 and 2 (New York: Holt, 1890); Charles H. Cooley, *Human Nature and Social Order* (New York: Charles Scribner's Sons, 1902); George H. Mead, *Mind, Self and Society From the Standpoint of a Social Behaviorist* (Chicago: University of Chicago Press, 1934); and E. H. Erikson, "Identity and the Life Cycle," *Psychological Issues* 1 (1959): 1–171.

individual identity. What is more, every person is conscious that he stands at the center of a unique network of relationships, experiences, and influences."[5]

As used in this paper, identity is a detailed structure of self-attitudes that at any point is a self-concept represented by some summary symbol. For research rather than clinical purposes, the self-concept is not an entity that requires sophisticated skills for classification and interpretation. It is employed only in the sense of "self" for the individual actor, arising out of both his or her past experiences and interpretation of the responses of others to him or her in situations where these experiences were recorded. Thus, our concern is with the social self as it is mediated by and derived from human interactions over time. Due to its reflexive character, we think of identity (that is, the self as object) as a kind of psychological "payoff"—a form of recognition earned by an individual for what others judge to be effective and acceptable behavior. Such a perspective assumes that an identity is learned and dynamic: a child develops; passes through a series of statuses, some of them age-related; is exposed to and becomes cognizant of the expectations of others; learns that it is desirable to mediate behavior so as to take the expectations and likely responses of other individuals into account; and, in so doing, becomes a "social" being. In short, through the course of normal development an individual moves from a largely egotistical and selfish orientation to the environment to an orientation in which "significant others" assume predominant relevance in structuring behavior.

"Significant others" include varying combinations and numbers of people who are involved in different salient social situations in which an individual may be placed. For example, early childhood socialization usually occurs in the personal, interactive setting of the family, whereas many of the socializing experiences during later childhood and the adult stage of life transpire in more impersonal, institutionalized settings in which relationships with various socializing agents generally are structured by both formal and informal institutional norms.[6] Therefore, a person's identity ordinarily includes roles

5. Barry McLaughlin, "The WAI Dictionary and Self-Perceived Identity in College Students," in *The General Inquirer: A Computer Approach to Content Analysis*, ed. Philip J. Stone et al. (Cambridge: The M.I.T. Press, 1966), pp. 548–49.

6. See R. F. Winch, *Identification and Its Familial Determinants* (Indianapolis: Bobbs-

and behavior which not only he or she but other individuals have ratified and recognized as salient and crucial. These recognitions shape, confirm, and reinforce an individual's self-image.

These brief comments on the self-concept have been demonstrated empirically in previous research.[7] By way of illustration, in a study of party officials in Minneapolis, Seattle, Vancouver, and Winnipeg, it was found that more highly educated respondents were more likely than others to include a reference to their education in their self-concepts. Those who were successful professionals were more likely to identify themselves, in part, in terms of their professions. Substantial proportions of the women respondents referred to their gender or their status as wife-mother. Further, since the study focused on high-level party officials, the success attained by these people in politics was reflected in a disproportionately large number (in comparison to a cross-section of the population) who mentioned their status as party officials or their involvement in or enjoyment of politics.[8] Thirty-six percent of the Canadian and 25 percent of the American officials also included one or more references to being Canadian or American in their self-concepts. As the authors noted at the time:

The Canadian party officials' more frequent identification in terms of their country stands in contrast to what is supposedly a commonplace in Canadian society; that is, the lack of a specific Canadian identity. The fact that such a substantial proportion of the Canadians did include being Canadian in their self-concepts may be explained, in part, by the fact that most of the Canadian interviews were taken in 1967—Canada's centennial year—when nationalism and the expression of national sentiments were especially appropriate. Or, it may be that the identity crisis is finally being resolved, at least in the minds of elite groups. Alternatively, one may speculate that is precisely because Canadian elites do experience "Angst" over their national

Merrill, 1962); and O. Brim and S. Wheeler, *Socialization After Childhood* (New York: John Wiley & Sons, 1966).

7. See M. H. Kuhn and T. S. McPartland, "An Empirical Investigation of Self-Attitudes," *American Sociological Review* 19 (1954):68–78; T. S. McPartland and J. H. Cumming, "Self-Conception, Social Class, and Mental Health," *Human Organization* 17 (1958):24–29; M. H. Kuhn, "Self-Attitudes by Sex, Age and Professional Training," *Sociological Quarterly* 1 (1960): 39–55; and Joel Smith, "The Narrowing Social World of the Aged," in *Social Aspects of Aging*, ed. Ida H. Simpson and John C. McKinney (Durham: Duke University Press, 1966), pp. 226–42.

8. Allan Kornberg and Joel Smith, "Self-Concepts of American and Canadian Party Officials," *Polity* 3 (1970):70–99; and Joel Smith and Allan Kornberg, "Self-Concepts of American and Canadian Party Officials: Their Development and Consequences," *Social Forces* 49 (1970): 210–26.

identities, or, in the current jargon, because they are "up tight" about their identities, that they may have felt the need to make such references.[9]

The unexpectedly high percentage of party officials who said that they were Canadians in 1967, and public anxiety over and interest in the long awaited Quebec referendum on sovereignty-association, led us to ask a similar question of a national sample of the voting public in 1979. We reasoned that the problematic outcome of the referendum might enhance dramatically the centrality and the importance of their country and their Canadianism to many people.[10] The notion of identity-as-payoff further suggested that the inclusion of a national identi-

9. Kornberg and Smith, "Self-Concepts of American and Canadian Party Officials," p. 89.

10. The literature on national identity in Canada involves several schools of thought and has grown considerably over time. Examples of this literature include Harry Gordon Johnson, "Problems of Canadian Nationalism," *International Journal* 16 (1961):238–49; Peter Russell, ed., *Nationalism in Canada* (Toronto: McGraw-Hill, 1966); Blair Fraser, *The Search for Identity: Canada, 1945–1967* (Toronto: Doubleday, 1967); Mildred A. Schwartz, *Public Opinion and Canadian Identity* (Berkeley: University of California Press, 1967); Donald V. Smiley, *The Canadian Political Nationality* (Toronto: Methuen, 1967); George Grant, *Lament for a Nation: The Defeat of Canadian Nationalism* (Toronto: McClelland and Stewart, 1970); Lumsden, *Close the 49th Parallel*; Ramsay Cook, *The Maple Leaf Forever: Essays on Nationalism and Politics in Canada* (Toronto: Macmillan, 1971); Donald Creighton, "Canadian Nationalism and Its Opponents," in *Towards the Discovery of Canada: Selected Essays*, ed. Donald Creighton (Toronto: Macmillan, 1972), pp. 271–85; W. L. Morton, *The Canadian Identity* (Toronto: University of Toronto Press, 1972); Ted G. Harvey, Susan K. Hunter-Harvey, and W. George Vance, "Nationalist Sentiment Among Canadian Adolescents: The Prevalence and Social Correlates of Nationalist Feelings," in *Socialization and Values in Canadian Society*, vol. 1, ed. Elia Zureik and Robert M. Pike (Toronto: McClelland and Stewart, 1975), pp. 232–62; Stephen Clarkson, "Canadian-American Relations: Anti-Nationalist and Colonial Realities," in *Nationalism, Technology and the Future of Canada*, ed. W. Gagne (Toronto: Macmillan, 1976), pp. 104–22; H. D. Forbes, "Conflicting National Identities Among Canadian Youth," in *Foundation of Political Culture: Political Socialization in Canada*, ed. Jon H. Pammett and Michael S. Whittington (Toronto: Macmillan, 1976), pp. 288–315; Robert Drummond, "Nationalism and Ethnic Demands: Some Speculations on a Congenial Note," *Canadian Journal of Political Science* 10 (1977):375–89; Gad Horowitz, "On the Fear of Nationalism," in *Politics: Canada*, 4th ed., ed. Paul W. Fox (Toronto: McGraw-Hill Ryerson, 1977), pp. 112–15; Bernard Blishen, "Perceptions of National Identity," *Canadian Review of Sociology and Anthropology* 15 (1978):128–32; Dallas Cullen, J. D. Jobson, and Rodney Schneck, "Anti-Americanism and Its Correlates," *Canadian Journal of Sociology* 3 (1978):103–20; and Abraham Rotstein, "Is There an English-Canadian Nationalism?" *Journal of Canadian Studies* 13 (1978):109–18.

11. David Easton, *A Systems Analysis of Political Life* (New York: John Wiley & Sons, 1965), p. 157.

12. This operationalization has been employed in Allan Kornberg, Harold D. Clarke, and Lawrence LeDuc, "Some Correlates of Regime Support in Canada," *British Journal of Political Science* 8 (1978):199–216; Allan Kornberg, Harold D. Clarke, and Marianne C. Stewart, "Federalism and Fragmentation: Political Support in Canada, *Journal of Politics* 41 (1979):889–906; and Allan Kornberg, Harold D. Clarke, and Marianne C. Stewart, "Public Support for Community and Regime in the Regions of Contemporary Canada," *American Review of Canadian Studies* 10 (1980):75–93.

fication in their self-concepts might be associated with greater positive affect for or favorable perceptions of three political "objects": the
political community, the regime, and political authorities. These,
Easton argued, constitute "the domain of support,"[11] and were opera-
tionalized in terms of public support for Canada (the national political
community), support for the government of Canada and for parliament (the national political regime), and support for the leaders of
three of the federal political parties and for members of parliament
(the national political authorities).[12]

A number of additional assumptions regarding possible relationships between national identity and public support also influenced
analyses of the responses to the self-concept question in the 1979
National Election Study. Of these, the following are particularly
important:

1. The historic struggle for the hearts and minds of the public and
findings from almost two decades of survey research, which indicate
that provincial governments, at the very least, are holding their own
in this struggle, suggested that Canadians would be as likely to include their province as their country in their concepts of self.

2. Both the literature on federalism[13] and political events of the past
decade suggested that the people of Ontario (the heartland) and of
the Atlantic provinces (historically, the most dependent on the redistribution of fiscal resources via federal government action) would
be more likely to include Canada in their self-concepts than would
the people of Quebec, the Prairies, or British Columbia. By implication, then, people who were especially conscious of being part of a
particular region of the country would be expected to be less likely to
identify with the nation than those without those feelings.

3. The literature on ethnicity, social class, and the distribution of
power[14] in the context of the conception of identity-as-payoff indi-

13. For example, J. Peter Meekison, ed., *Canadian Federalism: Myth or Reality*, 3rd ed.
(Toronto: Methuen, 1977); Richard Simeon, ed., *Must Canada Fail?* (Montreal: McGill-Queen's
University Press, 1977); Roddick B. Byers and Robert W. Reford, eds., *Canada Challenged:
The Viability of Confederation* (Toronto: Canadian Institute of Foreign Affairs, 1979); Garth Ste-
venson, *Unfulfilled Union* (Toronto: Macmillan, 1979); and Donald V. Smiley, *Canada in Ques-
tion: Federalism in the Eighties*, 3rd ed. (Toronto: McGraw-Hill Ryerson, 1980).

14. For example, John Porter, *The Vertical Mosaic: An Analysis of Social Class and Power in
Canada* (Toronto: University of Toronto Press, 1965); John Berry, Rudolf Kalin, and Donald M.
Taylor, *Multiculturalism and Ethnic Attitudes in Canada* (Ottawa: Supply and Services Canada,
1976); Leo Driedger, ed., *The Canadian Ethnic Mosaic: A Quest for Identity* (Toronto: McClel-

cated, on the one hand, that members of the two charter groups (especially those in the middle and upper-middle classes) would include nation in their self-concepts more often than would other Canadians. On the other hand, cultural nationalism and the presence of a Péquiste government in Quebec suggested that Québécois least often would include Canada and most often include their province in their self-conceptions.

4. The conceptions of identity as behavior learned through positive reinforcement implied that older people and individuals who have achieved a substantial degree of success in life (for example, they were well educated and enjoyed high incomes) would be more likely to identify themselves as Canadians.

5. Our understanding of the mechanisms through which a self-concept arises also made it reasonable to expect that persons who are both psychologically and behaviorally implicated in the operation of the federal political system (for example, who identify psychologically with one of the federal parties, who feel politically efficacious, who are interested in federal politics, who are oriented more to federal than to provincial politics, and who participate politically in addition to voting) would be more likely to include being a Canadian in their self-concepts—as would those who feel that the operation of the federal government has favorably affected their own and their family's personal situations.

6. The claim that national identity in Canada may be structured in terms of antipathy toward the United States suggested that persons professing negative affective feelings about that country most often would identify themselves as Canadian.

7. Finally, due to factors that may lead to identification as a Canadian, we would expect that one consequence of the inclusion of being Canadian as a central and positive component of self would be the ascription of higher levels of support to the national political community, the regime, and some of its authority figures.

There is in these assumptions the beginnings of a causal model that links sequentially such exogenous factors as region of residence, eth-

land and Stewart, 1978); James E. Curtis and William G. Scott, eds., *Social Stratification: Canada*, 2nd ed. (Scarborough: Prentice-Hall, 1979); Jean Leonard Elliott, ed., *Two Nations, Many Cultures: Ethnic Groups in Canada* (Scarborough: Prentice-Hall, 1979); and John Porter, *The Measure of Canadian Society: Education, Equality, and Opportunity* (Agincourt: Gage Publishing, 1979).

nicity, and language to political behavior and attitudes, to feelings about the United States in interaction with possession of an identity with Canada as part of one's self-concept, to support for the nation. Unfortunately, however, the logic of the ordering of these factors is not yet sufficiently clear and the data were not accessible in a form to permit estimations of such a model (although this will be done in the future). Instead, the analyses undertaken and reported here are preliminary and exploratory. First, we examine data that demonstrate the relative centrality of both Canada and one's province in the self-concepts of individuals. Having done this, we consider in a bivariate fashion evidence that any of the social and political factors mentioned above do contribute to the inclusion of country in reports of self-concepts. Finally, having grounded our ideas about national identity in these clarifying analyses, the central issue of its relation to support is addressed.

Measures

Almost all of the data used in this paper derive from the 1979 Canadian National Election and Panel Study.[15] This study involves a multistage, stratified, cluster sample of 2,744 respondents, weighted by province (to permit some oversampling of the smaller provinces) and by age (to allow for adequate representation of individuals between eighteen and twenty-three who entered the electorate since the federal election of 1974). The weighted national sample includes 2,670 respondents.

As noted above, our measure of national identification is based on responses to a question on self-concepts. Self-conception normally is delineated and measured either: (1) with "closed" measures such as rating scales, Q-sorts, and check lists that predefine individual responses; or (2) with open-ended questions that permit an individual to structure his or her reply freely. A three-sentence version of the latter approach was employed because it was thought to combine the best features of both types of measures.[16] The actual question reads:

15. These data were made available by Harold D. Clarke, Jane Jenson, Lawrence LeDuc, and Jon Pammett. In particular, we acknowledge the assistance of Harold D. Clarke.
16. See Kornberg and Smith, "Self-Concepts of American and Canadian Party Officials," p. 78.

"Now here is an interesting question that I think you can enjoy. What would you say about *yourself* in three sentences in answer to the question, 'Who am I?'" A total of 2,552 individuals responded to this question. Their answers were reduced to 267 codes, eight variables that include both content and order of mention, and 8 other variables that include the number of codable details.[17] As appropriate, the codes were subdivided further as positive, neutral, or negative.

"Nation" is one of fifteen general topics[18] under which many codes fell. Since only two respondents made negative references to Canada or to their Canadianism, they were omitted from the analysis and the measure assigned "0" to those not mentioning Canada, "1" to respondents making nondirectional references, and "2" to those making positive references. This measure is employed in the bivariate analyses presented below.

Socioeconomic-demographic variables in the analysis. The socioeconomic-demographic variables include age, education, ethnicity, annual family income, province of residence, region of residence, gender, occupational prestige, and subjective social class.[19] Occupational prestige is measured using the Blishen scale which ranges from 14.4 to 80.0.[20] Subjective social class is based on a series of questions that ask respondents to place themselves in one of five classes. These

17. The coding of responses to the question was informed by recognition of the need for parsimony, content analysis of the responses, and findings from previous research. Although only three statements were requested, the maximum number of mentions is eight, and the number of codable details ranges between one and thirteen.

18. Two of the fifteen general topics are "personality" and "politics." With respect to the former, it has been suggested that respondents who gave their names (for example, "I'm John Smith.") should not have been coded under the general category of "personality" but, rather, as a separate category. As for "politics," a relatively small number of people made specific negative references to current events in the country, especially to the state of the Canadian economy or to the government's role in managing the economy. These remarks were coded under the general category of "politics."

19. The first four of these variables as well as region have five categories, with region being composed of the conventional but recently disputed divisions of the Maritimes, Quebec, Ontario, the Prairies, and British Columbia. For a discussion of regional boundaries, see Clarke et al., *Political Choice in Canada*, pp. 41–43; and Elkins and Simeon, eds., *Small Worlds*, pp. x–xiii, 7–9.

20. Our measure of occupational prestige is constructed by calculating the mean score (43.23) and dividing the range on either side of the mean into two categories. The four categories are low (14.41 to 28.65), moderately low (28.66 to 43.23), moderately high (43.24 to 57.8), and high (57.81 to 80.0). See Bernard R. Blishen and Hugh A. McRoberts, "A Revised Socioeconomic Index for Occupations in Canada," *Canadian Review of Sociology and Anthropology* 13 (1976): 71–79.

classes were recoded into three categories of upper or upper-middle, middle, and working or lower.

Political variables. The political measures included respondents' federal partisanship, levels of political efficacy and political interest, extent of federal political participation, predominant orientation to federal or to provincial politics, regional consciousness and solidarity, feelings about the United States, and perceptions of government's impact on personal well-being. The direction of federal partisanship is ascertained by using a standard question,[21] with the resulting categories being Liberal, Conservative; New Democrat, Social Credit, and Nonidentifier. The measure of political efficacy derives from a question asking respondents whether they agree or disagree with four statements that were found by LeDuc in his analysis of the 1965 and 1968 election studies to form a strong scale of efficacy.[22] The measure of political interest is based on responses to the question: "We would also like to know whether you pay much attention to politics generally. I mean from day to day, when there isn't a big election campaign going on. Would you say that you follow politics very closely, fairly closely, or not much at all?"[23] Our measure of political participation is based on an index developed by Burke, Clarke, and LeDuc using data from the 1974 election study.[24] Orientations to federal or provin-

21. The question reads: "Thinking of federal politics, do you usually think of yourself as a Liberal, Conservative, NDP, Social Credit, or what? (If 'no') Still thinking of federal politics, do you generally think of yourself as being a little closer to one of the parties than to the others? (If 'yes') Which party is that?"

22. The four statements are: (1) "I don't think that government cares much what people like me think"; (2) "Sometimes politics and government seem so complicated that a person like me can't really understand what's going on"; (3) "People like me don't have any say about what the government does"; and (4) "Generally, those elected to Parliament soon lose touch with the people." Each of the efficacious, that is "disagree," responses is scored 1, and the scores are summed to generate a five-point index ranging from 0 to 4. See Lawrence LeDuc, "Measuring the Sense of Political Efficacy in Canada," *Comparative Political Studies* 8 (1976):490–99.

23. Political interest recently has been constructed with two questions, one on general interest and another on electoral interest. See Clarke et al., *Political Choice in Canada*, pp. 400–401. We omitted electoral interest from our index because we assumed that national identity is a relatively long-term sentiment that would be affected by a general expression of interest in politics, rather than by an expression of interest in a particular election.

24. The index of political participation is cumulative, involving the act of voting together with some other form of electoral participation such as discussing politics, trying to convince friends how to vote, attending political meetings, and engaging in campaign activity. See Mike Burke, Harold D. Clarke, and Lawrence LeDuc, "Federal and Provincial Political Participation in Canada: Some Methodological and Substantive Considerations," *Canadian Review of Sociology and Anthropology* 15 (1978):61–75.

cial politics are derived from responses to queries about the level of government to which respondents were most attentive and felt closest.[25] Judgments about regional consciousness and solidarity are based on answers to the questions: "People often think of Canada as being divided into regions, but they don't always agree on what the appropriate regional divisions are. We would like to know if you think of Canada as being divided into regions. (If yes) Do you feel that you have a lot in common, or not much in common, with other people in this region?"[26] Feelings about the United States are ascertained through a question that asked respondents to place that country on a 100-point thermometer scale.[27] Another measure involves respondents' perceptions of government's impact on their personal well-being. It consists of two indices, one on perceptions of government's impact on economic satisfaction, and the other on perceptions of government's impact on general life satisfaction.[28]

25. The questions are: "Would you say that you pay more attention to *federal* politics, *provincial* politics, or *local* politics? As far as you are concerned personally, which government is more important in affecting how you and your family get on, the one in Ottawa, the provincial government here in _____, or the local government here in _____? When you think of *your* government, which government comes to mind, the government of Canada or the government of (province)?" For each of these questions, federal responses were scored +1, provincial responses were scored −1, and other responses (both, local, etc.) were scored 0. These scores were summed to create a seven-point index ranging from −3 (all provincial responses) to +3 (all federal responses).

26. Responses to this question are used to build a four-category variable of perceptions that the country is not divided into regions or the country is divided into regions, and the respondent has little in common, some things in common, or a lot in common with people in his or her region.

27. On the thermometer scale, 50° is the neutral point with scores below and above it reflecting negative and positive feelings. In the bivariate analysis, feelings about the United States are divided into five categories. They are very negative (1° through 25°), negative (36° through 49°), neutral (50°), positive (51° through 75°), and very positive (76° through 99°).

28. The index of perceptions of government's impact on economic satisfaction is based on the questions: "Now I'd like to ask you how you and your family are doing these days. First, let's think about the material side of your life—the things that you can buy and do—all the things that make up your material standard of living. Would you say that you are very satisfied, fairly satisfied, a little dissatisfied, or very dissatisfied with the material side of your life right now? Do you think that government has had a great deal, something, or not much at all to do with this?" To construct the index, answers were scored such that very satisfied = +2, fairly satisifed = +1, a little dissatisfied = −1, and very dissatisfied = −2; and a great deal = 2, something = 1, and not much = 0. These scores for the two questions were multiplied together, with the resulting index ranging from −4 to +4. The questions for the index of perceptions of government's impact on general life satisfaction are: "Now let's think about your *life as a whole*. Would you say that you are very satisfied, fairly satisfied, a little dissatisfied, or very dissatisfied with your life as a whole right now? Do you think that government has had a great deal, something, or not much at all to do with this?" This index was built in a manner identical to that for the index of perceptions of government's impact on economic satisfaction. Scores for the two indices were

Political support variables. Support for Canada, the government of Canada, parliament, and the several party leaders is ascertained from a series of questions in which respondents were asked to place each of them on a 100-point thermometer scale.[29] The measure of support for party leaders was constructed by averaging the scores assigned to them by each respondent. There also are two indices of the public's perceptions of MPs. The first delineates the perceived responsiveness of MPs and is based on replies to a single question asking how likely MPs would be to perform four tasks.[30] The second is based on a question asking respondents to evaluate the actual performance of MPs.[31]

Findings

Table 3.1 presents responses to the question of "Who am I?" in terms of the fifteen general topics and the order of their mention. There are several noteworthy aspects of these responses. First, consistent with the findings of previous research, there were substantial

summed to create an overall index of perceptions of government's impact on personal well-being with values ranging from −8 to +8.

29. On the thermometer scale, 50° is the neutral point with scores below and above it reflecting negative and positive feelings. The three national party leaders are Pierre Trudeau, leader of the Liberal party, Joe Clark, leader of the Progressive Conservative party, and Edward Broadbent, leader of the New Democratic party. The leader of the Social Credit party was not included in the measure of support for party leaders because the question about affect for him was asked in Quebec only.

30. The question is: "Still thinking about the *federal* government in general, how likely is it, in your opinion, that a Member of Parliament would do the following: (a) Take into consideration the opinions of people like yourself when making up his or her mind on an important issue, if he or she knew your feelings on it. (b) Try hard to do or get something for his riding if people like yourself asked him or her for something or needed something. (c) Try hard to do something about a specific proposal or family problem that a person like yourself approached him or her with. (d) Make himself or herself available at home in his or her constituency office and in Ottawa to people like yourself if they should need to call on him or her." Responses to each statement were scored as very likely = 2, somewhat likely = 1, and not very likely = 0. These scores were added so that the index ranges from 0 to 8.

31. The question reads: "Generally speaking, what kind of job do you think your Members of Parliament, the one that you have now and those you've had in the past, have done in the following areas. As I mention these different areas, would you tell me if they have done a very good job, a good job, a bad job, or a very bad job: (a) Being available to people of the riding. (b) Explaining to the people what kinds of things the federal government is thinking about doing. (c) Taking part in parliamentary debates, question period, and committee work and so forth. (d)

variations in the breadth (the number of topics covered) of individual responses. Second, a large number of respondents included nation in their conceptions of self. Indeed, 45 percent made reference to some aspect of their Canadianism. Moreover, since order of mention may indicate the relative salience of the components included in a self-concept, it is noteworthy that 67 percent of those who alluded to Canada mentioned it first. Third, contrary to the expectation that respondents would more or less divide their references between nation and province, in fact, they did not. Only 10 percent mentioned their province and, *of them*, only 30 percent mentioned it first. These differences between nation and province are particularly impressive because a large part of the 1979 election study consisted of questions on the provinces, provincial politics, and provincial authorities. Thus, the paucity of provincial identifications cannot be attributed to an absence of provincial cues in the interview. If respondents' answers to "Who am I?" were being cued by the contextual material, there were almost as many provincial as federal cues. Fourth, respondents' references range from brief and simple comments to extended, multifaceted, and highly charged expressions. Illustrative of such variations are the following:

I'm a Canadian. (a respondent from Nova Scotia)

I'm a heck of a good guy! I'm just a regular Joe, that's all I can say. Who am I?—a Canadian definitely. (a respondent from Ontario)

I am a young Canadian with a young family trying hard to find my niche in life. Trying to find a better way of life for myself and my children in Canada. Above everything, I'm proud to be a Canadian and I think Canada has more to offer a person like myself than any other country in the world. (a respondent from Manitoba)

I am the son of immigrant parents who have used the opportunities that this country has provided to achieve through hard work many of the benefits this country has to offer. I am a federalist by political nature who believes that the long-term success of our country is based on a strong federal government. I am very much concerned about the country and its future so that my

Helping people in the riding who have problems with the federal government to solve them. (e) Getting projects and other things the riding needs." The responses for each statement were assigned scores of a very good job = +2, a good job = +1, a bad job = −1, and a very bad job = −2. These scores were aggregated to produce an index varying from −10 to +10.

Table 3.1. *Distribution of Self-Concepts*

General topics	Percent who mentioned topic	Percent who mentioned topic and mentioned it first
Personality	50	43
National identification	45	67
Family and sex roles	33	45
Occupation	30	32
Politics	22	16
Provincial identification	10	30
Social class	10	52
Leisure and recreation	6	8
Values and beliefs	6	10
Personal traits	5	45
Ethnicity	5	50
Religion	4	26
Local identification	3	9
Education	3	19
Transcendental concerns	1	50
(Weighted N = 2552)		

children will have at least the same opportunities as I had—if not more. (a respondent from Ontario)

Finally, although not displayed in table 3.1, references to Canada divide almost equally into those that are merely neutral and those that are positive. The frequency, depth, and affective character of responses that indicate a national component to the self-concepts of Canadians' identification are gratifying because they permit us to construct a viable measure of national identification that can be used to pursue the other questions that we have raised.

Our initial use of this measure is in the data displayed in table 3.2. Its purpose is to obtain a first approximation of the direction and strength of any associations between the several measures proposed as relating to national mentions and the actual occurrences of such mentions. Although no single relationship is especially robust, the direction of several of the relationships tends to confirm some of our expectations. For example, younger people expressed a national identification less frequently than older people and, when they did, their references less often were positive. That younger Canadians were more reluctant to think of themselves as Canadians probably reflects more infrequent exposures to identity-building socializing experiences. The pattern of the relationships with education reveals that less-educated people included Canada in their self-concepts less frequently than did better-educated respondents. The latter gave both neutral and positive mentions more often.

With respect to ethnicity, the expectation that a national identity more often would be a component of the self-concepts of the economically favored members of the two charter groups was fulfilled only partially. Among respondents of Anglo-Celtic ethnic origins, mentions of Canada did vary with self-perceived social class status; 64 percent of upper- and upper-middle-class, 51 percent of middle-class, and 44 percent of lower- and working-class persons included a reference to nation in their answers. However, variations among French-Canadian members of these three classes were trivial: 38 percent, 35 percent, and 35 percent, respectively (data not shown in tabular form). Given the historic antagonisms that have characterized relationships between the two groups and the dominance of the English, the relative paucity of French-Canadians of any class identifying with Canada is not especially surprising. Illustrations of these antagonisms are provided by the responses of three French-Canadians:

I am an unemployed professor who is by nationality French-Canadian. I am an unconditional Québécois nationalist.

I am a Québécois. I do not consider myself to be a Canadian. I am more French Québécois than bilingual Canadian.

I am a Québécois citizen who believes that our people have begun to be aware of their reality in federalism and cannot regress. If independence is not achieved by René Lévesque, it will be by Claude Ryan.

As groups, excluding the French and Anglo-Celtics, the respondents who most often included Canada in their self-concepts derived from Western, Northern, or Eastern European backgrounds. Perhaps these respondents did not take their Canadianism for granted whereas persons of Anglo-Celtic origins did. Illustrative of responses that suggest such an interpretation is this observation by a German-born resident of Alberta: "I feel that Canada is my adopted country. I am lucky to be living here and bringing up my three children here. I

Table 3.2. *Placement on the Index of National Identification by Socioeconomic-Demographic Variables (row percentages)*

Socioeconomic-demographic variables	Index of national identification			
	No mention	Neutral mentions	Positive mentions	(N)
Age				
18–25	61	25	14	(647)
26–35	55	26	19	(463)
36–45	47	29	24	(399)
46–55	49	25	26	(450)
56 and over	48	29	23	(591)
Cramer's V = 0.09[a]				
Education				
Elementary or less	63	22	16	(523)
Some high school	54	28	18	(625)
Completed high school	49	27	24	(490)
Some college or university	47	29	24	(380)
Completed college or university	50	28	22	(533)
Cramer's V = 0.08[a]				
Ethnicity				
Anglo-Celtic	50	29	21	(1108)
French	64	18	18	(596)
Western or Northern European	43	33	24	(392)
Eastern European	41	34	25	(187)
Other	47	32	21	(118)
Cramer's V = 0.11[a]				
Income				
Under $10,000	57	24	19	(511)
$10,000–$14,999	54	26	20	(315)
$15,000–$19,999	57	23	20	(483)
$20,000–$24,999	53	27	20	(343)
$25,000 and over	47	30	23	(823)
Cramer's V = 0.06[b]				
Region				
Atlantic	58	26	16	(235)
Quebec	68	15	17	(711)
Ontario	49	28	23	(897)
Prairies	41	37	22	(433)
British Columbia	40	36	24	(276)
Cramer's V = 0.16[a]				
Province				
Newfoundland	63	26	11	(56)
Prince Edward Island	62	27	11	(13)

Table 3.2. *(continued)*

Socioeconomic-demographic variables	Index of national identification			
	No mention	Neutral mentions	Positive mentions	(N)
Nova Scotia	49	32	19	(99)
New Brunswick	64	18	18	(66)
Quebec	68	15	17	(711)
Ontario	49	28	23	(897)
Manitoba	56	28	16	(111)
Saskatchewan	45	29	26	(107)
Alberta	31	46	23	(216)
British Columbia	40	36	24	(276)
Cramer's V = 0.18[a]				
Gender				
Female	55	25	20	(1345)
Male	50	28	22	(1206)
Cramer's V = 0.03				
Objective social class (Blishen score)				
Low	62	23	15	(607)
Moderately low	56	26	18	(747)
Moderately high	50	27	23	(673)
High	40	31	29	(511)
Cramer's V = 0.11[a]				
Subjective social class				
Working or lower	56	26	18	(842)
Middle	53	26	21	(1237)
Upper-middle or upper	46	25	29	(266)
Cramer's V = 0.06[a]				

a. $p \leq 0.001$
b. $p \leq 0.01$

feel that Canadians on the whole should have more pride in their country. I would like to see unity in Canada. We don't advertise or stick up for our country."

Of the remaining socioeconomic-demographic factors, province, region, and social class also were related significantly to the frequency with which nation is a part of personal identity. Residents of Quebec least often thought of themselves as Canadians. Although it might be argued that this is simply another reflection of ethnicity, this is not the case. The difference in the frequency with which Québécois[32] and other residents of Quebec included a reference to nation was minimal (30 percent versus 31 percent, respectively; data not shown in tabular form). Equally surprising is the fact that neither the residents of Ontario (the "linchpin" of the Confederation) nor of the Atlantic provinces most often viewed themselves as Canadians. Rather, it was the residents of Alberta, British Columbia, and Saskatchewan who did so. Given that the regions are amalgams of the provinces, patterns for the regions are similar to those of the provinces.

These patterns lend themselves to several interpretations. One is that the relative paucity of national identifications among Quebecers reflects both the strength of nationalist sentiments and the widespread feeling that the province has been disadvantaged over the years by the way in which the federal system operates.[33] A second interpretation is that Ontarians, like English-Canadians generally, may take their Canadian identification as so self-evident that it does not occur to them to mention it. As for inhabitants of the western provinces, their sense of identification may reflect satisfaction with their country and with the prosperity resulting from the economic boom and the increasing political power of the West. For example, one Albertan stated: "I'm a Canadian . . . part of Canada's growing West. I'm proud to be an Albertan and allowed to voice my opinions freely." Obviously, however, not all Westerners, felt this way. Indeed, one resident of Manitoba claimed: "I'm a Canadian nationalist. I'm proud of our country's past but I resent the central Canada view of the West as a colony for exploitation." Another person living in Saskatchewan declared: "I'm a western Canadian. Government is letting the railway run the country. I think the Quebec issue is political blackmail. Let them separate. If the western provinces separated, we would be the richest country in the world." Finally, the relative infrequency of mention of Canada by residents of the Atlantic provinces may mirror their frustration at not having profited as much as other Canadians from the political and social arrangements of federalism. Although other Canadians may feel that the residents of Atlantic provinces

32. A respondent is a Québécois if he or she is of French ancestry and resides in Quebec.
33. See Kornberg, Clarke, and Stewart, "Federalism and Fragmentation," pp. 896–97, 902–3.

have benefited disproportionately from Confederation, apparently they do not.[34] For example, one Newfoundland respondent observed: "I am proud to be a Canadian and to be a resident of Newfoundland, but conditions are such that you have to go to a richer province to seek employment. The federal government is not doing a good job for things in general. They favour other provinces regarding where they spend their budget."

As for the expectation that the more favored members of the public would be those more likely to identify with the country that provided opportunities for achievements, we find income levels to be associated positively with inclusion of Canada in the self-concept. Also, as anticipated by the discussion above, both occupation and social class were related to national identification. Working- and lower-class persons less often incorporated Canada in their self-concepts than did respondents in more favored groups.

Overall, then, the data in table 3.2, and particularly the relationships involving ethnicity, province, region, and social class—those factors conventionally regarded as the major social cleavages in Canadian society—suggest that members of certain social groups are more prone to identify with Canada than are other Canadians. More generally, however, the dominant feature of these data is relatively weak relationships because substantial numbers of people, irrespective of category, include being Canadian in their self-concepts. The significance of this finding is discussed in the concluding section of this paper.

Table 3.3 presents exploratory data on relationships between political factors and the inclusion of Canada in the self-concept. The first such factor is direction of federal partisanship, a psychological attachment to a political party that is capable of influencing perceptions and actions beyond the realm of electoral politics.[35] Both the people who identified with Social Credit, and those who did not identify with any party, mentioned Canada less often than did those who thought of themselves as Liberals, Conservatives, or New Democrats. Of the three latter groups, those who consider themselves to be Conserva-

34. Ibid., p. 896.
35. Angus Campbell, Philip E. Converse, Warren E. Miller, and Donald E. Stokes, *The American Voter* (New York: John Wiley & Sons, 1970), chaps. 4, 6, and 7.

Table 3.3. *Placement on the Index of National Identification by Political Variables (row percentages)*

	Index of national identification			
Political variables	No mention	Neutral mentions	Positive mentions	(N)
Federal partisanship				
Liberal	52	24	24	(1053)
Progressive Conservative	46	32	22	(706)
New Democrat	55	27	18	(327)
Social Credit	72	18	10	(69)
Nonidentifier	62	24	14	(352)
Cramer's V = 0.10[a]				
Political efficacy				
0 (low)	60	23	17	(351)
1	54	26	20	(299)
2	51	29	20	(281)
3	53	28	19	(218)
4 (high)	45	31	24	(107)
Cramer's V = 0.07				
Political interest				
Not much at all	60	25	15	(964)
Fairly closely	49	28	23	(1214)
Very closely	45	25	30	(365)
Cramer's V = 0.11[a]				
Federal political participation scale				
Inactive	67	22	11	(74)
Vote +	58	25	17	(373)
Discuss politics +	53	28	19	(452)
Convince friends or attend meetings +	49	29	22	(271)
Campaign activity	48	27	25	(86)
Cramer's V = 0.07				
Orientations to federal or provincial politics				
−3 (provincial)	65	18	17	(230)
−2	61	23	16	(231)
−1	57	24	19	(359)
0	52	27	21	(382)
+1	44	30	26	(462)
+2	47	32	21	(358)
+3 (federal)	47	29	24	(343)
Cramer's V = 0.10[a]				
Regional consciousness and solidarity				
Country not divided into regions	56	25	19	(1176)

Table 3.3. *(continued)*

Political variables	Index of national identification			
	No mention	Neutral mentions	Positive mentions	(N)
Country divided into regions and				
Little in common	58	24	18	(160)
Some things in common	52	31	17	(301)
A lot in common	48	27	25	(915)
Cramer's V = 0.06[b]				
Feelings about the United States				
Very negative	60	27	13	(232)
Negative	52	29	19	(287)
Neutral	57	24	19	(750)
Positive	50	28	22	(696)
Very positive	45	28	27	(452)
Cramer's V = 0.08[a]				
Perceptions of government's impact on personal well-being				
−8−−4 (negative impact)	63	24	13	(111)
−3−−1	58	23	19	(280)
0	52	29	19	(787)
+1−+3	53	26	21	(889)
+4−+8 (positive impact)	44	29	27	(394)
Cramer's V = 0.07[a]				

a. $p \leq 0.001$
b. $p \leq 0.01$

tives mentioned Canada most frequently. This also was true of people who had high scores on an index measuring the extent of politically efficacious feelings. Conversely, people who rarely followed politics or were politically inactive also less often identified with Canada. With regard to the predominance of orientations as between federal or provincial politics, those respondents who paid attention to federal politics, who felt that the government in Ottawa most affects how they and their families get on, and who thought of the government of Canada as *their* government more often had a Canadian component in their identities than had those with provincial orientations. In addition, the federally oriented more often made positive statements about their Canadianism. Feelings of regional consciousness and solidarity manifest a rather unexpectedly complex association with national identification. People who saw the country in regional terms but felt that they had little in common with others in their region mentioned Canada less often than either people who did not view the country in regional terms, or who recognized the existence of regional divisions, but felt that they had something in common with their coregionalists.

Finally, the cross-tabulations between national identity and feelings about the United States, and between national identity and perceptions of the federal government's impact on their personal well-being, in the first instance contradict and in the second confirm a priori expectations. That is, the arguments made by some scholarly observers that an important (perhaps the most important) dimension of Canadianism is anti-Americanism are not supported. To the contrary, these data indicate that the more positive are people's feelings about the United States, the greater the likelihood of mentioning Canada and of doing so positively in delineating a self-concept. However, the data do support the assumption that those who feel the federal government affects their current status, and that it does so in a positive manner, more often include an identification with Canada than do people who believe the opposite. In summary, then, table 3.3 demonstrates that people who were psychologically and behaviorally implicated in the national political system tended to identify with Canada more often than did those who were not so involved.

A perusal of the data in figure 3.1 on the distribution of public support for Canada, the government of Canada, and the leaders of the Liberal, Conservative, and New Democratic parties, reveals a hierarchical pattern. Support for Canada is the highest, support for leaders is the lowest, and support for the government of Canada falls between. As the figure indicates, this characterizes the distribution of public support for these political objects in each of the three survey years. These data also reveal that support for the government of Canada is somewhat more volatile over time than is support for either political authorities or the Canadian political community, perhaps because support for the former is affected by the partisanship of respondents.[36]

36. See for example, Kornberg, Clarke, and LeDuc, "Some Correlates of Regime Support in Canada"; and Kornberg, Clarke, and Stewart, "Federalism and Fragmentation."

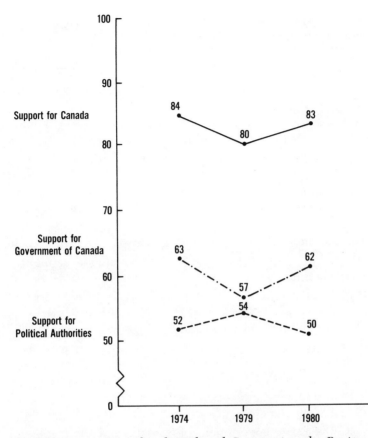

Figure 3.1. *Support for the Political Community, the Regime, and Authorities, 1974, 1979, 1980 (mean scores)*

Table 3.4 addresses the issue of the importance in 1979 of identifying with Canada for national support. It presents relationships between national identity and support for Canada, the government of Canada, Parliament, three national party leaders, and members of Parliament. We find that those who include the nation in their self-concepts have a greater tendency also to ascribe more support to each of these highly salient political objects as well as to have favorable perceptions of MPs. Several of these relationships, although diminished, persist even when the effects of partisanship are controlled.

Table 3.4. *Support for the Political Community, the Regime, and Authorities by the Index of National Identification*

	Index of national identification		
	No mention	Neutral mentions	Positive mentions
X̄ Support for Canada	77	83	86
F = 58.23[a]			
eta = 0.21			
X̄ Support for Government of Canada	53	55	55
Liberals			
F = 0.76			
eta = 0.04			
Progressive Conservatives	65	66	68
F = 2.23			
eta = 0.08			
New Democrats	50	51	50
F = 0.03			
eta = 0.01			
Social Crediters	52	63	42
F = 1.78			
eta = 0.23			
X̄ Support for Parliament			
Liberals	57	61	61
F = 5.23[b]			
eta = 0.10			
Progressive Conservatives	59	62	64
F = 3.01[b]			
eta = 0.10			
New Democrats	51	53	53
F = 0.32			
eta = 0.05			
Social Crediters	49	61	38
F = 2.43			
eta = 0.27			
X̄ Support for Party Leaders			
Liberals	56	58	59
F = 6.92[a]			
eta = 0.12			
Progressive Conservatives	52	53	51
F = 1.00			
eta = 0.06			
New Democrats	54	54	57
F = 1.13			
eta = 0.08			
Social Crediters	46	47	48
F = 0.04			
eta = 0.04			

Table 3.4. (continued)

	Index of national identification		
	No mention	Neutral mentions	Positive mentions
Perceived responsiveness of MPs F = 18.73[a] eta = 0.13	3.48	3.99	4.13
Evaluations of MPs' performance F = 8.20[a] eta = 0.08	2.91	3.45	3.50

a. $p \leq 0.001$
b. $p \leq 0.01$

Summary and Discussion

We began this paper by observing that the components of a self-concept reflect the experiences and behavior which an individual has found to be gratifying and rewarding over time. In part, the underlying mechanism presumed is that they have been reinforced by favorable reactions and recognition from significant others in the person's environment. If this common interpretation of personal identity is valid, it would appear that people find the experience of being Canadian a richly gratifying one. Almost one-half of a national sample of the voting public responded to the "Who am I?" question in terms of: "I am a Canadian." Smith and Jackson have suggested that if most citizens do not feel that they are members of a Canadian nation, if their country is unimportant to them, and if being Canadian is not a positive and important component of self, it may be increasingly difficult to maintain either the political integrity of the country or the present structure of its major political institutions.[37] Our data supplement their analyses based on earlier data by indicating—contrary to laments regarding the absence of a Canadian identity—that *being Canadian is a central and positive component of people's identities*. Also supportive of an argument made by Smith and Jackson is the ab-

37. Smith and Jackson, *Restructuring the Canadian State.*

sence of an inverse relationship between Canadian identity and negative feelings about the United States. If, as has been contended,[38] Canadian identity partly is a response to antipathy toward that country,
the impact is through some highly complex chain that our data do
not reveal.

The inclusion of Canada in one's identity is not a random phenomenon. For example, it tends to vary with factors such as age; younger
respondents less often refer to their Canadianism and, when they
do, their references are less often positive. If, on the one hand, this
is a cohort effect, the implication is that almost one-half of the population (those thirty-five and under) have a weaker sense of national
identity and that they will continue to be more weakly identified as
they grow older. If, on the other hand, the association merely reflects
an aging effect, the inference to be drawn is that as this group of Canadians ages, they also will tend to become more strongly and positively identified with the country.   •

National identity also varies with social status factors. Between 40
and 50 percent of the population—those who are less educated, earn
less, and enjoy less prestigious occupations—less frequently include
Canada in their self-concepts than do the remaining more favored
half. When taken in combination with the findings that: (*a*) respondents less often identify positively with the nation if they feel that government's impact on their personal well-being has not been a salutary
one; and (*b*) the inclusion of nation in the self-concept is associated
positively with support, the implication is that the regime's ability to
maintain an adequately high level of specific support will depend
upon its ability to manage the economy effectively, no easy task under
current conditions let alone those in the uncertain future. For the
same reasons, there may be increasing pressure on political elites to
conduct their affairs in ways that increase both people's interest and
participation in national politics and their sense of political competence. In concluding an earlier paper on political support, we speculated that, ultimately, the cement holding a democratic political system together is a politically implicated and participant citizenry.[39]

38. John T. Woods, "A Cultural Approach to Canadian Independence," in *Nationalism, Technology and the Future of Canada*, ed. W. Gagne (Toronto: Macmillan, 1976), pp. 75–103, and
Cullen, Jobson, and Schneck, "Anti-Americanism and Its Correlates."

39. Kornberg, Clarke, and Stewart, "Public Support for Community and Regime in the Regions of Contemporary Canada," pp. 87–90.

The patterns of the relationships between people's levels of political efficacy, interest, and participation, and the presence of a Canadian identity, and of the positive correlations between a national identity and support for Canada as a political community suggest that the speculation is well grounded. The relatively small proportions of highly politically efficacious (9 percent), interested (14 percent), and active (7 percent) individuals in the population further imply that if even a moderate increase in their numbers could be achieved, it might yield rich dividends to authorities concerned with enhancing their "domain of support."

In conclusion, notwithstanding the aforementioned variations in the frequency with which Canadian identity is a component of the self-concept, and assuming that cognizance is taken of and responses made to the concerns just stated, the relative *similarity* in the frequency with which respondents in the several social and political categories make such references is impressive. Equally striking are the findings that approximately five times as many people include nation than province in their self-concepts and that, among these respondents, more than twice as many mention nation first. These data indicate—despite survey findings regarding people's positive feelings about their provinces—that many Canadians, regardless of where they live or what their status is, want their country to remain united and whole. Taken together with the resounding "non" vote to the sovereignty-association proposal in the Quebec Referendum, they provide evidence that the average Canadian has more faith in the future of the country and is more willing to take the steps required to maintain its integrity than many political leaders appear to assume. In the pull-and-tug of federal-provincial relations, political leaders representing the federal and provincial political communities may have overlooked this simple but critically important fact.

· II ·

Agents

· 4 ·

The Political Socialization of
Political Support

Ronald G. Landes

The apparently intrinsic thrust of the Canadian polity toward self-destruction, or perhaps the interminable century-long discussion of such a possibility, combined with the ongoing separatist challenge in Quebec, has made the study of political support in Canada not only academically salient but politically necessary in the 1980s. Concern for the continued viability of Confederation has led to recent investigations of the causes, correlates, and consequences of political support in the Canadian context.[1] While short-term problems of political support necessitate a focus on the current attitudes and behavior of Canadian citizens, a political socialization perspective on the development of political support argues that support patterns are longer-term processes that must be studied in longitudinal perspective.

If political socialization is "the process whereby we acquire our political values, attitudes, and opinions,"[2] then political support is also a result, or at least in part a reflection, of the more general acquisition of political beliefs by the individual. A fundamental assumption of political socialization research is that political values and behavior pat-

1. Allan Kornberg, Harold D. Clarke, and Lawrence LeDuc, "Some Correlates of Regime Support in Canada," *British Journal of Political Science* 8 (1978):199–216; Allan Kornberg, Harold D. Clarke, and Marianne C. Stewart, "Federalism and Fragmentation: Political Support in Canada," *Journal of Politics* 41 (1979):889–906; Allan Kornberg, Harold D. Clarke, and Marianne C. Stewart, "Public Support for Community and Regime in the Regions of Contemporary Canada," *American Review of Canadian Studies* 10 (1980):75–93; Michael M. Atkinson, William D. Coleman, and Thomas J. Lewis, "Studying Political Support in Canada: An Evaluation of Indicators," paper presented at the annual meeting of the Canadian Political Science Association, Montreal, Quebec, June 1980.
2. Richard Van Loon and Michael S. Whittington, *The Canadian Political System*, 2nd ed. (Toronto: McGraw-Hill Ryerson, 1976), p. 94.

terns are an outgrowth of the learning process: people are not born political animals, but may become so as a result of their socialization experiences. Thus, politically supportive orientations are a consequence of the learning process, a process which begins well before the individual becomes formally eligible to participate in the political arena: "political ideas—like the consumption of cigarettes and hard liquor—do not suddenly begin with one's eighteenth birthday."[3] Therefore, a political socialization perspective on the origin, development, and nature of support for a political community and regime assumes that the initial learning of supportive orientations in childhood and adolescence influences, to a greater or lesser extent, the later political values and behavior patterns of adult members of the polity.[4]

Several key characteristics of the political socialization process in Canada have important implications for the generation of support for the political community and regime. First, for many citizens political matters are not particularly salient: politics is not a "central concern to most people."[5] Canada is probably not unlike other liberal democracies in which "politics is a sideshow in the great circus of life."[6] As a result, the acquisition of supportive orientations is likely to be both indirect (i.e., not specifically taught by the socialization agencies) and implicit (i.e., a consequence of the more general pattern of values learned by the child). Second, political learning begins early in the Canadian context, at least by the elementary school years for a wide variety of political concerns.[7] Third, political learning is continuous throughout a person's life. Even when supportive views are acquired

3. Richard G. Niemi, "Political Socialization," in *Handbook of Political Psychology*, ed. Jeanne N. Knutson (San Francisco: Josey-Bass Publishers, 1973), p. 117.

4. For several challenges to this assumption see the following articles: Donald D. Searing, Joel L. Schwartz, and Alden E. Lind, "The Structuring Principle: Political Socialization and Belief Systems," *American Political Science Review* 67 (1973):415–32; Donald Searing, Gerald Wright, and George Rabinowitz, "The Primacy Principle: Attitude Change and Political Socialization," *British Journal of Political Science* 6 (1976):83–113. A defense of this basic assumption of political socialization research can be found in Niemi, "Political Socialization," pp. 134–36. For a recent study which demonstrates the importance of early political socialization experiences for the later recruitment of Canadian party officials, see Allan Kornberg, Joel Smith, and Harold D. Clarke, *Citizen Politicians—Canada: Party Officials in a Democratic Society* (Durham, N.C.: Carolina Academic Press, 1979), pp. 31–56.

5. Jon H. Pammett and Michael S. Whittington, eds., *Foundations of Political Culture: Political Socialization in Canada* (Toronto: Macmillan, 1976), p. 5.

6. Robert A. Dahl, *Who Governs?* (New Haven: Yale University Press, 1961), p. 305.

7. For a survey of recent research on the political socialization process in Canada, see Ronald G. Landes, "The Political Socialization of Canadian Youth," in *The Canadian Family*, 3rd ed., ed. K. Ishwaran (Toronto: Holt, Rinehart and Winston, forthcoming).

early, they do not necessarily remain untempered by experience. Concern with the linkage between the early-life acquisition of political beliefs and later-life political values and behavior is crucially important in the study of political support. Fourth, for most people the political socialization process is cumulative: political orientations learned in childhood and adolescence serve as the basis for the acquisition of adult belief and behavior patterns. Fifth, the structure and relative influence of the various agents in the political socialization process help to determine the content of the political beliefs acquired. Several major agents of the political socialization process, in particular the schools and the mass media, operate in such a way as to inhibit the generation of political support for the national political community and regime. Moreover, although adequate evidence is unavailable, these agents may well perpetuate and enhance regional and ethno-linguistic differences in support for these political objects and their provincial counterparts.

Finally, even if one were willing to discount the ethical questions raised by such a possibility, the ability of the schools, media, and other agents of socialization to "engineer" higher levels of support for the existing political system appears limited. Rather, bolstering support for the national political community and regime can perhaps best be achieved by enhancing governmental responsiveness to the legitimate needs and demands of citizens in various parts of the country.

The Socialization of Political Support: A Survey of Current Research

The importance of support for a political community and regime stems from the fact that high levels of support allow the political system to adapt more easily to changing circumstances, and, in particular, to survive both demand-input and output stress on the system's essential variables. Support refers to the "feelings of trust, confidence, or affection, and their opposites, that persons may direct to some object."[8] The important political objects are threefold: the political community ("that aspect of a political system that we can iden-

8. David Easton and Jack Dennis, *Children in the Political System: Origins of Political Legitimacy* (New York: McGraw-Hill, 1969), p. 57.

tify as a collection of persons who share a division of political labor"),[9] the political regime ("that part of the political system that we may call its constitutional order in the very broadest sense of the term"),[10] and finally, the political authorities ("those members of a system in whom the primary responsibility is lodged for taking care of the daily routines of a political system").[11] Two basic types of political support (specific and diffuse) may be directed toward each of these three political objects. Specific support concerns quid pro quo relationships between support and satisfaction with the political system based on how the individual evaluates the outputs of the system. Diffuse support, on the other hand, is support that is offered unconditionally: "the generalized trust and confidence that members invest in the various objects as ends in themselves."[12] From a political socialization perspective, "diffuse rather than specific support is likely to be particularly relevant in the study of childhood socialization."[13]

A number of problems exist in applying such concepts to the existing literature on the political socialization process in Canada. First, although a growing body of research is developing on the political learning process, most available studies focus primarily on the content of that process and secondarily on the agents of socialization.[14] Little explicit use of Easton's concepts of political support has been incorporated at the design stage of most research projects. As a result it is difficult to apply retrospectively such concepts to the existing literature. Thus, we will first present an overview of the content of the political learning process in Canada using the general concept of political support, and only then will we speculate on the implications of such findings for the types of support for the three primary political objects. Second, the important conceptual and methodological problems of establishing linkages between early and later learning, be-

9. Ibid., p. 58.
10. Ibid., p. 59.
11. Ibid., p. 60.
12. Ibid., pp. 62–63.
13. Ibid., p. 67. For possible alternatives to the Eastonian definitions, see Ronald Rogowski, "Political Support for Regimes: A Theoretical Inventory and Critique," chap. 1 in this volume.
14. See the collections by Pammett and Whittington, *Foundations of Political Culture*; and Elia Zureik and Robert M. Pike, eds., *Socialization and Values in Canadian Society*, 2 vols. (Toronto: McClelland and Stewart, 1975). For discussions of the role of the mass media in Canada as an important socialization agency, see the essays in this book by R. H. Wagenberg et al., chap. 6, and Ronald S. Dick, chap. 5.

tween types of support, and among the various objects of support have not been dealt with, except in the most tangential way. Existing Canadian research has followed a "summative" approach in investigating the socialization of political support, which has disaggregated the process into views of particular leaders, roles, or levels of government. However, if political support is indeed "holistic in character," then future research must deal with the various problems of linkage and alternative models to the dominant summative perspective.[15] Third, the concept of political support contains both an attitudinal and a behavioral component.[16] Political socialization research has focused on the acquisition of orientations and attitudes rather than on the behavioral consequences of such beliefs. An obvious reason for this is the fact that children and adolescents are not yet members of the electorate. However, the behavioral manifestations of supportive attitudes may be more significant for the persistence of political systems than the attitudes in and of themselves.

Finally, existing research on the political socialization process in Canada has been an outgrowth of either an examination of the general process of socialization ("a general theory of socialization") or an investigation into the learning of specifically political attitudes ("a theory of political socialization"). Concern with the origin and development of political support, however, focuses our attention on the need for a "political theory of political socialization." Such a theory would seek to "demonstrate the relevance of socializing phenomena for the operations of political systems."[17] By providing an explanation of possible variations in patterns of political support, a "political theory of political socialization" would thus aid in making projections about future support systems that might develop for the Canadian political community and regime.

Our survey of existing research efforts on the development of political support will focus on the content of the political socialization process with respect to the following major areas: political cognition, political affect, partisan attachment, and several group identifications

15. David Easton, "Theoretical Approaches to Political Support," *Canadian Journal of Political Science* 9 (1976): 431–48.

16. David Easton, "A Reassessment of the Concept of Political Support," *British Journal of Political Science* 5 (1975): 436.

17. For a discussion of these various theories of socialization, see Easton and Dennis, *Children in the Political System*, p. 18.

(i.e., regional, ethnic, and continental attachments). The implications of these findings for the nature of political support in Canada and for future research efforts will be examined.

Political cognition. The acquisition of political information begins early in the elementary school years and is focused primarily on political leaders rather than on political institutions.[18] A majority of students can correctly name the prime minister by the time they reach the fifth grade, with more than 90 percent able to make a correct identification by grade eight. However, other political leaders rank considerably lower in the child's developing perceptions of the political system: provincial premiers and mayors are less well recognized.[19] The ability to name the occupants of the formal executive positions (i.e., governor general and lieutenant governor) falls well below the recognition of the political executives (i.e., prime minister and premier). For example, among Nova Scotian adolescents in grade twelve only 22 percent and 14 percent could correctly name the governor general of Canada and the lieutenant governor of Nova Scotia, respectively, while 99 percent and 89 percent correctly identified the prime minister of Canada and the premier of Nova Scotia.[20]

If we consider more complicated aspects of political understanding, such as the child's perception of roles rather than simply the ability to name political leaders, we discover that the level of knowledge is minimal. For example, Pammett found that while 74 percent of the Kingston, Ontario, students could correctly name the prime minister by grade eight, only 13 percent had a reasonably accurate understanding of his role in the Canadian political system.[21] A similar pattern was discovered among Nova Scotian adolescents in their ability to name and to describe the role or functions of various political lead-

18. Ronald G. Landes, "The Use of Role Theory in Political Socialization Research: A Review, Critique, and Modest Proposal," *International Journal of Comparative Sociology* 17 (1976): 59–72.

19. Jon H. Pammett, "The Development of Political Orientations in Canadian School Children," *Canadian Journal of Political Science* 4 (1971):132–41; Ronald G. Landes, "Political Socialization Among Youth: A Comparative Study of English-Canadian and American School Children," *International Journal of Comparative Sociology* 18 (1977):63–80; Elia T. Zureik, "Children and Political Socialization," in *The Canadian Family*, ed. K. Ishwaran (Toronto: Holt, Rinehart and Winston, 1971), pp. 186–99.

20. Joseph G. Jabbra and Ronald G. Landes, "Political Orientations Among Adolescents in Nova Scotia: An Exploratory Study of a Regional Political Culture in Canada," *Indian Journal of Political Science* 37 (1976):75–96.

21. Pammett, "The Development of Political Orientations," p. 135.

ers.[22] Such data are consistent with the results of the Canadian Student Awareness Survey which found that 68 percent of high school seniors were unable to name the governor general, 61 percent were unable to name the British North America Act as Canada's constitution, and 70 percent had little or no understanding of what percentage of the population was French Canadian.[23] Thus, many adolescents would appear to have a rather low level of political knowledge by the time they become eligible to participate in the formal political process on their eighteenth birthday. As one researcher summarized such findings: "I feel as though someone out there waged a war on knowledge, and I've been shellshocked by the 'Ignorants.' Knowledge of Canadian geography is almost nonexistent, political awareness unbelievable, cultural knowledge abysmal."[24] Similar findings were presented in the Report of the Commission on Canadian Studies, which also revealed that little change in such a pattern could be expected for even that small group of students who receive a university education:

The Commission's inquiries among teachers and students alike at all levels of the educational system revealed that most students graduating from high school today lack basic knowledge about Canadian political matters. Moreover, unless they go on to major in political studies at university, their knowledge of the political institutions and public affairs of this country will not likely have expanded appreciably by the time they complete an undergraduate degree. Indeed, in some instances, even if they do major in political studies at university, their knowledge of Canadian political matters may not be much greater because of the comparative neglect of this subject in the curriculum of some political science departments. The problem begins at the school level. But it is reinforced and compounded by policies and attitudes that are often prevalent at the university level of our educational system.[25]

Political affect. Even though levels of political information or political cognition are low, children and adolescents still develop an emotional tie (usually positive) to political leaders and the political

22. Joseph G. Jabbra and Ronald G. Landes, *The Political Orientations of Canadian Adolescents: Political Socialization and Political Culture in Nova Scotia* (Halifax, Nova Scotia: Saint Mary's University, 1976), pp. 22–32.
23. Mel Hurtig, *Never Heard of Them . . . They Must Be Canadian* (Toronto: Canadabooks, 1975).
24. Ibid., p. 10.
25. T. H. B. Symons, *To Know Ourselves: The Report of the Commission on Canadian Studies*, 2 vols. (Ottawa: Association of Universities and Colleges of Canada, 1975), 1:65.

system. The typical pattern is for the child to "personalize" the political system (i.e., to perceive politics initially in terms of leaders) and to
develop supportive attitudes and positive feelings toward the polity
and its leaders and institutions.[26] For example, a comparative study of
English-Canadian and American schoolchildren in grades four through
eight found that the Canadian child's affective response to government's benevolence, dependability, and leadership was greater than
that of his American counterparts.[27] Similarly, Zureik found a "be-
nign outlook" toward politics among children in British Columbia,
while Nova Scotian adolescents manifested a marked predilection to
evaluate political leaders favorably.[28] Although the initial pattern of
political affect is usually supportive or positive, typically the level of
political affect declines during the adolescent years and may even
turn into feelings of alienation and cynicism among a segment of
young people. Such a decline of political affect in the adolescent years
is probably accounted for by a number of factors, including the individual's direct contact with the political system and the influence in
these years of several agents of political socialization (i.e., the mass
media and peer groups) which may present alternative and more critical views of the polity than those presented earlier by the family and
school.[29]

Partisan attachment. One of the earliest emotional ties which a
child develops with the political system is his attachment to a specific
political party. Identifications with political parties begin surprisingly
early among many Canadian children. Several studies of Ontario children discovered that approximately 50 percent claimed a party attachment by the eighth grade.[30] However, the development of party

26. Landes, "The Use of Role Theory," pp. 66–68.
27. Landes, "Political Socialization Among Youth," p. 68.
28. Zureik, "Children and Political Socialization," in Zureik and Pike, eds., *Socialization and Values in Canadian Society*, 1:191; Jabbra and Landes, *The Political Orientation of Canadian Adolescents*, pp. 32–36.
29. Gary B. Ruxh, "The Radicalization of Middle-Class Youth," *International Social Science Journal* 24 (1972):312–25; A. B. Hodgetts, *What Culture? What Heritage?* (Toronto: Ontario Institute for Studies in Education, 1968). In some cases negative views may develop much ear-lier than the adolescent years. See, for example, Anthony P. Cohen, "The Political Context of Childhood: Leaders and Anti-Leaders in a Changing Newfoundland Community," in Zureik and Pike, eds., *Socialization and Values in Canadian Society*, 1:161–84. For possible explanations of this decline in political support during the adolescent years, see Easton and Dennis, *Children in the Political System*, pp. 297–311.
30. Landes, "Political Socialization Among Youth," p. 75; Pammett, "The Development of Political Orientations," p. 139.

orientations among young people shows significant regional variations, with the west having the lowest and Maritimes displaying the
highest rate of partisan orientations.[31] One study of Nova Scotian adolescents found that by the grade seven level, 85 percent were willing
to express a partisan preference.[32] The potential significance of this
early attachment to political parties results from the fact that these
emotive ties precede knowledge and understanding of political issues
and the political structure.[33] Such initial attachments to parties may
provide a basis for the subsequent acquisition of orientations supportive of the wider political system. Moreover, partisan attachments
may themselves be indicative of the individual's support for the political community and regime.

Regional identifications. Numerous studies of Canadian adults have
found strong regional patterns of voting behavior, political attitudes,
and political loyalties. So consistent have these regional patterns
been that the country's overall political culture is usually described as
a composite of a number of regional political cultures or subcultures.
Thus, it is not unexpected that political socialization studies have discovered that these regional identifications begin early in the learning
process and help to produce strong patterns of regional loyalties by
the adolescent years.[34] Differences in patterns of partisanship and political cognition led Gregg and Whittington to conclude that "there
are significant regional differences in the basic orientations to politics
even among very young children."[35] One particularly interesting con-

31. Allan Gregg and Michael S. Whittington, "Regional Variation in Children's Political Attitudes," in *The Provincial Political Systems: Comparative Essays*, ed. David J. Bellamy et al.
(Toronto: Methuen, 1976), p. 78.
32. Ronald G. Landes and Joseph G. Jabbra, "Partisan Identity Among Canadian Youth: A
Case Study of Nova Scotian Adolescents," *The Journal of Commonwealth and Comparative Politics* 17 (1979):62.
33. Ibid., pp. 69–73; Pammett, "The Development of Political Orientations," pp. 137–39.
See also the following studies: Joel Smith, Allan Kornberg, and David Bromley, "Patterns of
Early Political Socialization and Adult Party Affiliation," *Canadian Review of Sociology and Anthropology* 5 (1968):123–55; Allan Kornberg, Joel Smith, and David Bromley, "Some Differences in the Political Socialization Patterns of Canadian and American Party Officials: A Preliminary Report," *Canadian Journal of Political Science* 2 (1969):64–68; Kornberg, Smith, and
Clarke, *Citizen Politicians*, pp. 31–56.
34. Although regional loyalties may develop early, the ability of adults to specify the regional
boundaries of Canada in any consistent manner is low. See, for example, the results of the 1974
national election study presented in Harold D. Clarke et al., *Political Choice in Canada* (Toronto: McGraw-Hill Ryerson, 1979), chap. 2.
35. Gregg and Whittington, "Regional Variation in Children's Political Attitudes," p. 80.

sequence of these regional attachments is the identification by young people in some regions with the provincial rather than the national or local units of government.[36] These strong and early attachments to regions and provinces are a possible factor influencing the low level of national identifications in the Canadian polity.[37] As Johnstone has concluded, "during the adolescent years Canadian young people become aware of the important sectional, regional, and provincial interests in Canadian life," so that the "adolescent years . . . could be characterized as the period of emergent sectionalism."[38]

English-French identifications. Given the fact that historically English-French differences have been the most significant internal political cleavage in Canada, it is not surprising to find that English-Canadian and French-Canadian children and adolescents not only hold different political values, but also view each other with less affection than might be hoped for in a country still trying to forge a common national identity. Numerous studies have shown that English-Canadian and French-Canadian youth are taught different political values in the political socialization process.[39] For example, one study of English- and French-Canadian history textbooks found that almost totally contradictory pictures of historical figures and events were presented.[40] As a result "children overwhelmingly identified with historical figures of their own culture" and "Francophone and Anglophone children identified with different eras of Canadian history."[41] One interesting finding is that francophone students identify with the provincial level of government to a much greater degree than

36. Ibid., pp. 80–83; John C. Johnstone, *Young People's Images of Canadian Society* (Ottawa: Queen's Printer, 1969), pp. 16–22; Ronald G. Landes, "Pre-Adult Orientations to Multiple Systems of Government," *Publius: The Journal of Federalism* 7 (1977):27–39.

37. Jeanne Pierre Richert, "Canadian National Identity: An Empirical Study," *American Review of Canadian Studies* 4 (1974):89–98. For conflicting views on the importance of provincial and national identifications among adults in Canada, see the essays in this book by John Wilson, chap. 7; and by Allan Kornberg and Marianne C. Stewart, chap. 3.

38. Johnstone, *Young People's Images*, p. 22.

39. Paul G. Lamy, "Political Socialization of French and English Canadian Youth: Socialization into Discord," in Zureik and Pike, eds., *Socialization and Values in Canadian Society*, pp. 263–80; H. D. Forbes, "Conflicting National Identities Among Canadian Youth," in *Foundations of Political Culture*, ed. Pammett and Whittington, pp. 288–315.

40. Marcel Trudel and Genevieve Jain, *Canadian History Textbooks* (Ottawa: Queen's Printer, 1970).

41. Jeanne Pierre Richert, "The Impact of Ethnicity on the Perception of Heroes and Historical Symbols," *Canadian Review of Sociology and Anthropology* 11 (1974):156–63.

their anglophone counterparts.[42] Differing views of political authority and levels of political affect have also been discovered, with francophone students more likely to display a personalized view of the political system.[43] In terms of feelings of national identity, "Canada is two nations not just sociologically, but also psychologically."[44] More important perhaps is the finding that differences between francophone and anglophone perceptions increase during the adolescent years, making unlikely the later emergence of any common national identity. Such findings as the above lead to the conclusion that "political socialization in Canada, then, seems to be for young French- and English-Canadians a process of socialization into discord."[45]

Continental political socialization. In both historical and contemporary terms the impact of the United States on Canada has been profound. The American impact on the learning of political values is what is meant by the concept of continental political socialization.[46] Two agents of the political socialization process have been particularly affected: the mass media and the school system.

American domination of the mass media has meant that children are socialized to many American rather than Canadian political values. For example, among grade twelve Nova Scotian adolescents it was found that 70 percent read *Time* magazine, while only 33 percent read *MacLean's* and 5 percent read the *Globe and Mail*.[47] Not surprising then is the finding that Canadian children often know more about the American political system than their own.[48] A similar situation is evident in school textbooks which are overwhelmingly produced by American publishers.[49] As a result students often learn little of the

42. Jeanne Pierre Richert, "Political Socialization in Quebec: Young People's Attitudes Toward Government," *Canadian Journal of Political Science* 6 (1973):303–13.

43. Ibid., p. 313.

44. Forbes, "Conflicting National Identities," p. 302.

45. Lamy, "Political Socialization of French and English Canadian Youth," p. 278. For discussions on the impact of the French-English cleavage on patterns of political support among adults, see in this book the essays by Pammett et al., chap. 12; and Smith and Kornberg, chap. 13.

46. John H. Redekop, "Continentalism: The Key to Canadian Politics," in J. Redekop, ed., *Approaches to Canadian Politics* (Scarborough, Ont.: Prentice-Hall of Canada, 1978), p. 44. For a discussion of the impact of the United States on support attitudes in Canada, see Lawrence LeDuc and J. Alex Murray, chap. 10 in this book.

47. Jabbra and Landes, *The Political Orientations of Canadian Adolescents*, p. 11.

48. Hurtig, *Never Heard of Them*, passim.

49. Redekop, "Continentalism," p. 49; Paul Robinson, *Where Our Survival Lies: Students and Textbooks in Atlantic Canada* (Halifax: Atlantic Institute of Education, 1979).

Canadian political tradition but much about American history and
politics. As one participant in the Canadian Student Awareness Survey concluded, when asked to identify a series of cultural and political leaders, "Never heard of them, so they must be Canadian."[50]

An important possible consequence of the American influence on
the political socialization of Canadian youth is a low level of national
identity among Canadians and the perception of similarities across,
rather than within, national boundaries. Several studies found a
greater perception of similarities between English Canadians and
Americans than between English Canadians and French Canadians.[51]
Combined with the early development of regional loyalties and
English-French differences in political outlooks, the American penetration of the political learning process certainly inhibits the development of support for the Canadian political community and regime.

Implications for Political Support
and Future Research

The above findings on the content of the political socialization process would seem to have some important implications for the nature
and development of political support in Canada. First, the low level
of political cognition among Canadian young people is not only disturbing with respect to traditional theories of the requisites for a successful liberal democracy, but also problematic regarding the acquisition
of supportive attitudes for the political community and regime. For
example, although diffuse support is characterized by its emotional
linkage to political objects, an emotive tie which precedes cognition,
at some point in the development of the individual's political self this
emotive tie will be confronted by political reality. If the initially
learned patterns of diffuse support, which are usually positive to begin with, are not matched by the individual's experience with the political structure in the adolescent and adult years, then a decline in
diffuse support and the development of feelings of alienation, cynicism, and apathy may result. Thus, we are suggesting that diffuse

50. Hurtig, *Never Heard of Them*, p. 13.
51. Forbes, "Conflicting National Identities," pp. 302–3; Johnstone, *Young People's Images*,
pp. 22–36; Landes, "Political Socialization Among Youth," pp. 77–78.

support will be strengthened when it is based on at least a minimal understanding of the structure and operation of the political system. Diffuse support based on an emotive tie founded on ignorance is detrimental to the persistence of the political community and regime, especially when that community and regime are confronted with problems of political change. Moreover, not only is political cognition low, but much of the "knowledge" acquired is simply incorrect, a problem neglected in most assessments of the political learning process. Inaccurate information is probably more devastating for the adaptability of the political community and regime than are the low rates of political cognition.[52]

Low levels of political cognition are especially salient when analyzing the phenomenon of specific support. Hypotheses concerning the determinants of specific support assume that individuals are able to make connections between the outputs of the political system and their satisfaction with that system.[53] Low rates of information raise some serious doubts about the ability of the individual to make such linkages. The impact on the level of political support of low cognition could possibly work in two ways: first, low information could result in overestimating the beneficial impact of the political system, in which case low cognition would enhance political support; or second, low information could result in an underestimation of the outputs of the political system, thus reducing levels of political support. There is some evidence from a recent study of Canadian adults that high rates of information are indicative of higher levels of political support for the political community.

The multiple and reinforcing identities outlined here are strongest among those people who are most knowledgeable about Canada. Most Canadians know a great deal about the United States and feel quite warmly towards Americans, yet they prefer Canada. Similarly, the more extensive their familiarity with several parts of Canada and the more sensitive Canadians are to regionalism, the more they favor the federal government over their pro-

52. The low level of political cognition found among both students and adults is perhaps one reason why the public is manipulated in the process of constitutional reform; see, for example, the argument by Alan C. Cairns in this book, chap. 14.

53. Adults in the 1974 Canadian national election study were able to make a connection between cost-benefit assessments of the federal system and perceptions of political support for the political structure: see Kornberg, Clarke, and Stewart, "Federalism and Fragmentation," pp. 895–98.

vincial governments and the higher they score on the measure of national identity, regardless of provincial, linguistic or social backgrounds.[54]

Such a pattern at least suggests the possibility that support for the political system has some important linkages with the extent of political cognition among the mass public.

Finally, with respect to political cognition, the low levels of political information typically discovered among young people do not mean that specific support is not socialized early. For example, Easton and Dennis have suggested that diffuse support is socialized in childhood, with specific support developing after the child is able to make the connection between outputs and satisfaction with the political system.[55] However, there seems to be considerable evidence that both diffuse and specific support are socialized in childhood, and that both are "mediated" by the various agents of the political socialization process. Such a view is necessary to account for the early acquisition of group identifications, which perhaps can be usefully seen as summary perceptions of the cost-benefit evaluations of the Canadian system by the various subcultures. Children acquire group identifications—and their corresponding evaluations of the polity—early, before they could reasonably be expected to have sufficient knowledge to render such judgments on the basis of their own personal experiences and perceptions. In other words, patterns of specific support, which are often expressed as group identities, are learned early by the child, in contrast to the view of Easton and Dennis. Moreover, such a perspective also suggests that the child's initial contact with the political community and regime is often indirect rather than direct. As a result, the nature of the major socialization agencies, such as the schools and the mass media, may have a profound impact on the origin, development, and intensity of both the specific and diffuse orientations of political support acquired in childhood.

Levels of political affect have been a second major focus of existing studies. The general pattern among Canadian youth of relatively high

54. David J. Elkins, "The Sense of Place," in *Small Worlds: Provinces and Parties in Canadian Political Life*, ed. David J. Elkins and Richard Simeon (Toronto: Methuen, 1980), p. 25. A similar view was expressed by Grace D. Skogstad, "Adolescent Political Alienation," in Zureik and Pike, eds., *Socialization and Values in Canadian Society*, 1:195: "Political awareness and knowledge mitigate political alienation feelings."

55. Easton and Dennis, *Children in the Political System*, pp. 67–68.

affect in childhood and declining levels of support in adolescence requires some explanation. Current research has rarely made the distinction between specific and diffuse support, although affect ratings have been used implicitly as indicators of diffuse support. The variability of the affect ratings, along with their usual decline in the adolescent years, suggests the possibility that what is being measured is specific support for political authorities, especially role occupants, rather than diffuse support for the political community and regime.[56] Another, although not mutually exclusive, possibility is that declining levels of affect in later years represent the result of the individual's direct contact with and experience in the political system. Studies have not investigated the impact of the child's emerging political involvement on political support: the initial interactions between the individual and the political system may be crucial for the development of supportive attitudes such as feelings of political efficacy. If we remember that the concept of political support has both an attitudinal and a behavioral dimension, then direct experiences with the polity should be investigated as an agency of socialization with important implications for the development of political support.[57]

In addition to problems relating to the specific-diffuse distinction and to the impact of direct contact with the polity on levels of political affect, a third problem concerns the intensity of the orientations acquired in childhood. The intensity of the early acquired affective orientations has not been investigated. One would assume that the greater the intensity of the orientations acquired in childhood, the greater their relevance would be in considerations of political support for the political community and regime. What is most significant for the concept of political support is not that children are willing to rate political leaders and institutions on a series of affective or evaluative dimensions, but the strength with which those convictions are held. A study of the intensity problem would also be one way of establishing the linkage between childhood and adult patterns of beliefs and behavior.

Finally, with respect to political affect, it is apparent that the de-

56. Landes, "The Use of Role Theory," p. 68.
57. For examples of the impact of public policy on attitudes of political support, see the chapters in this book on environmental policy by Nord and Weller, chap. 9, and on health policy by Falcone and Van Loon, chap. 8.

clining levels of affect in the adolescent years stand in apparent contradiction with one of the long-held and popular themes of the Canadian political culture; namely, the notion of Canada as a deferential polity.[58] We would suggest that deference is not an appropriate measure of political affect in particular or of diffuse support in general. Deference as an indicator of political support is similar to the concept of compliance—it need not reflect diffuse support.[59] A polity may be deferential in style, while at the same time political support is low or negative for the political community and regime.

While existing research has established the early acquisition of partisan orientations among schoolchildren, several important considerations warrant further study, in addition to the above noted problem of intensity. First, are children's partisan attachments a way of linking them to the wider political community and regime, or do such partisan orientations constitute a divisive force inhibiting the generation of support for the political system? For example, studies of adults have found partisan identifications, especially attachments to the long-dominant federal Liberal party, play an important mediating role between the individual and the political structure.[60] A study of Nova Scotian adolescents discovered a similar pattern: partisan attachments, in particular, influenced the evaluations of political leaders and the child's sense of political efficacy and trust. As with the adult data, Liberal party attachments were associated with positive perceptions of the polity.[61] A second problem with using partisan attachments as an indicator of political support concerns their stability. Existing studies of the political socialization of Canadian youth have utilized cross-sectional sample designs, and thus cannot address themselves adequately to this problem. However, Canadian voting studies have found considerable over-time instability in partisan orientations among adults.[62] We need to know more about the patterns

58. Edgar Z. Friedenberg, *Deference to Authority: The Case of Canada* (White Plains, N.Y.: M. E. Sharpe, 1980); Robert V. Presthus, *Elite Accommodation in Canadian Politics* (Toronto: Macmillan of Canada, 1973), pp. 28–37.

59. Easton, "A Re-Assessment," p. 454.

60. Kornberg et al., "Some Correlates of Regime Support," pp. 201–5; Kornberg et al., "Public Support for Community and Regime," p. 80.

61. Jabbra and Landes, *The Political Orientations of Canadian Adolescents*, pp. 142–46.

62. Clarke et al., *Political Choice in Canada*, pp. 95–110. For additional data on the propensity of people to shift their party identifications, see Smith, Kornberg, and Bromley, "Patterns

of partisan stability and change among the young.[63] If initial partisan attachments are found to be highly variable, then they may be poor indicators of community and/or regime support. Alternatively, one might argue that the variability of partisan attachment itself is a reflection of the more basic factors which tend to produce low levels of support for the political community and regime. Future research needs to investigate such possibilities, and can only do so adequately with longitudinal, rather than cross-sectional, samples.

Numerous studies have dealt with the impact of various group identifications (regional, English-French, continental) on the development of political orientations among Canadian young people. However, these inquiries have rarely clearly delineated their findings with respect to either the two basic types of support or the three objects of support distinguished by Easton. What is needed are studies which incorporate at the design stage indicators for various types and objects of support. One would expect that such research would discover that group loyalties have important effects on both the types and objects of political support.[64]

Also needed are studies which focus on linkages between types and objects of support. How do patterns of specific and diffuse support develop and how do they interact—what is their reciprocal influence on each other? How does support for one political object transfer or condition support for other types of political objects? Is there a "spread of affect" between objects or do they have relatively independent bases of support? On logical and intuitive grounds, we would expect to find a pattern of reciprocal and interactive effects. Relatedly, is there a "progression of loyalties" or a typical pattern of support development from one type of support to the other or from one type of political object to the others? Existing socialization research has implicitly assumed, for example, that regional identities and support for the national level of government are mutually exclusive. By contrast,

of Early Political Socialization"; and Kornberg, Smith, and Bromley, "Some Differences in the Political Socialization Patterns."

63. Research by Kornberg, Smith, and Bromley in Vancouver and Winnipeg indicates substantial instability in partisanship among adolescents and young adults. See their "Patterns of Early Political Socialization" and "Some Differences in the Political Socialization Patterns."

64. On the importance of group identities for political support, see the chapter in this book by Schwartz, chap. 2.

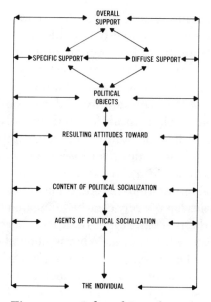

Figure 4.1. *Political Socialization and the Development of Political Support*

recent studies have suggested the overlapping nature of the multiple loyalties for many Canadian adults.[65] As a result, future research needs to investigate how multiple loyalties develop and the interaction between political support levels for the federal and provincial communities, regimes, and authorities. Are there any overarching political values which are not bifurcated by basic sociopolitical cleavages and which would provide a basis for enhancing political support levels for the Canadian political system? One recent study has suggested that support for democratic values "may be one such mechanism of solidarity in the Canadian polity."[66]

Lastly, it can be suggested that new indicators of political support

65. Kornberg et al., "Public Support for Community and Regime," pp. 83–86; Elkins, "The Sense of Place," pp. 1–30; Ronald G. Landes, "The Federal Political Culture in Canada," paper presented at the annual meeting of the Canadian Political Science Association, Saskatoon, Saskatchewan, June 1979.

66. Ronald G. Landes and Joseph G. Jabbra, "The Impact of Socio-Political Cleavages on Support for Democratic Orientations Among Canadians Adolescents in Nova Scotia," *Indian Political Science Review*, forthcoming.

may be necessary to comprehend the nature of supportive orientations acquired in childhood. For example, to measure children's sense of political efficacy probably requires different questions than those used in studies of efficacy among adults. To agree with a statement that "people like me don't have any say about what the government does" may reflect an accurate view of the child's role in the political system, rather than indicating a low sense of political efficacy. Since the child lacks direct involvement in the political system, it might be more appropriate to use measures of social efficacy (i.e., the child's feeling that he is capable of influencing his family and friends) rather than indicators of political efficacy per se. In turn such measures of social efficacy could serve as predictors for the later development of political efficacy and political support during adulthood.

In sum, a review of current knowledge about the origin, nature, and development of political support in Canada suggests that the creation of support is an exceedingly complex phenomenon, a result of the reciprocal and interactive influences of many factors (see figure 4.1). While the existing political socialization literature has produced an emerging body of findings on the content and agents of the political learning process, much work remains to be done before we will understand how political support is generated, developed, and sustained in the Canadian polity.

Conclusion: A Note on the
Engineering of Political Support

If supportive orientations are a result of a learning process and if the level of political support thus developed is lower than desired, then an immediate consideration which arises is whether or not levels of political support could be enhanced by a manipulation of or by a change in the structure and content of the political socialization process.[67] Even if we leave aside a number of important ethical questions raised by such a possibility, it would appear that such an attempt in

---

67. For an important discussion of the problems and prospects of developing a greater level of political participation in Canada, see William Mishler, *Political Participation in Canada* (Toronto: Macmillan, 1979), pp. 153–163. Mishler (p. 160) argues that by "providing more equitable representation of all political interests and fostering more democratic personalities,

the Canadian context would not only be politically unfeasible, but also likely to fail were it to be attempted.

The complexity of the political learning process, combined with our inadequate understanding of it, would seem to limit the opportunity for the successful engineering of supportive beliefs. While changes might be produced in a specific area such as levels of political cognition, other areas such as the affective dimensions of support would seem to be more resistant to change. If one remembers that the present political learning pattern is most often indirect and implicit, then any attempt at political engineering would likely necessitate and result in a major intrusion by the state into the political socialization process. Most people would find such a prospect neither socially nor politically attractive. For example, since the provinces are given exclusive control of the educational process in Section 93 of the British North America Act (except in relation to the protection of minority rights), this major agency of the political socialization process has often been used in Canada as a means of developing provincial rather than national loyalties.[68] Only if education became a federal rather than a provincial responsibility (a most unlikely development) could we even begin to control the content of the political learning process presented by this one agent of political socialization. As the education example illustrates, an effort to change the content of what is learned would necessitate major changes in the structure and control of the agencies of political socialization in Canada.

Attempts at the political engineering of political support, therefore, seem unlikely to succeed. However, levels of political support can still be changed, and probably more effectively, by what government does, and what impact this has on the ordinary citizen. In a democratic political culture, political support is heavily dependent on

increases in participation seem likely to enhance the legitimacy of existing institutions thereby strengthening political order and stability." If Mishler's argument is correct, then increased levels of political participation should result in increased levels of political support for the political community and regime.

68. Trudel and Jain, *Canadian History Textbooks*. See also Rick Ogmundson, "The Sociology of Power and Politics," in *Introduction to Canadian Society: A Sociological Analysis*, ed. G. N. Ramu and Stuart D. Johnson (Toronto: Macmillan of Canada, 1976), pp. 157–211. Ogmundson (p. 181) argues that in Canada, "political socialization via the schools is fragmented because of the ten different provincial systems. This system contrasts sharply to the centralized school systems of other countries which typically give their students systematic exposure to a set of nationalist political ideals about their country."

how citizens evaluate the actions of the government and political system.[69] Thus, the enhancement of political support for the political community and regime in Canada can perhaps be best achieved by government itself becoming more responsive to the needs and concerns of the Canadian public.

69. For a similar argument with respect to the introduction of television into the Canadian House of Commons, see Richard Price and Harold D. Clarke, "Television and the House of Commons," in *Parliament, Policy and Representation*, ed. Harold D. Clarke et al. (Toronto: Methuen, 1980), chap. 4.

Political Support and the Mass Media: The Publicly Financed Communications Agencies

Ronald S. Dick

Can such media as radio, film, and television contribute to the social-ization of political community- and regime-supporting values among the mass publics they serve? The question has particular relevance in the context of Canadian media experience which has been charac-terized by massive and sustained funding of a public sector and by the assignment to that sector of ambitious objectives with politically sup-portive implications. The following examination of the question has four major parts—the first two constitute a chronicle, the latter two, a critique. The chronicle is a necessarily selective review of the objec-tives and the performance record of the federally financed commu-nications agencies in Canada, with specific reference to political support. The critique tries to assess, in the light of what seems rea-sonably evident about the character and the effects of the media, the validity, perhaps even the relevance of certain criticisms of the Cana-dian Broadcasting Corporation, especially the blanket charge that it has "failed in its basic objectives." Are such charges fair?

In any consideration of the media in Canada, two facts must always be kept in mind. They go, so to speak, with the territory. Canadian national sentiment must constantly reckon with: (1) the external pres-sure of American influence which, if not counterbalanced, could be-come total. Canada in a sense is the most culturally exposed country in the world; other nations have large neighbors, but only Canada has 230,000,000 energetic and culturally dynamic people next door who speak the same language as the majority of Canadians; (2) the internal pressure generated by the centrifugal tendencies of the various regions which, if not checked, could lead to the disintegration of the country. Communications transactions among Canadians are intensely affected by these pressures. Moreover, the two main language groups in Canada are for the most part physically separated; they have, not inaccurately, been described as "two solitudes." Consequently, communicating among Canadians is apt to mean to a great extent English Canadians talking to English Canadians, French Canadians talking to French Canadians, and Americans talking to everybody. These are the realities with which Canadian "communicators," past and present, have had to deal.

The Publicly Financed Media: Origins and Development

The nineteenth-century press was Canada's first important means of political persuasion. Early Canadian political authorities had no doubts about the role of the press—it was to be supportive of authority with no qualifications. When John Graves Simcoe, the new lieutenant governor of Upper Canada, remarked in 1791 that "a printer is indispensably necessary," the reason was clear—to help convert his domain into a fortress of Tory and British power. The hope was frustrated. A counterpress arose, equally one-sided, but with libertarian slogans on its banner, and authority as its target. As these newspapers concentrated on political reporting, readers came to know how government operated and it lost its mystery. Press reports of parliamentary speeches brought the assembly closer to the electorate, enhancing the latter's influence. "Political news," notes Paul Rutherford, "better yet 'party reporting,' had undermined executive power and emphasized popular sovereignty."[1] From the point of view of established authority, the press was clearly a disintegrative force.

After this libertarian triumph, as throughout the rest of the nineteenth century, the Canadian press became in the main a party press, extremely partisan in character. The editor of the period was, when in "political heat," a brazen partisan who knew nothing of any "fairness doctrine," and who saw heaven in the victory of his party and hell in the triumph of its opponents. Nonetheless, this disputatious, frag-

1. Paul Rutherford, *The Making of the Canadian Media* (Toronto: McGraw-Hill Ryerson, 1978), p. 20.

mented way of presenting political information was an effective means of socialization to politics. The outstanding effect of the press was, as Rutherford notes, "the exaltation of politics."[2] Its dramatization of political excitements in a country where so much of life tended to come from the outside involved Canadians intensely in that part of their life which truly was their own. Its approvals and disapprovals, its playing up of heroes and villains, reinforced affiliations rather than blurring or confusing them and helped discipline the voting patterns of the electorate. Moreover, the press was much more than a mere instrument of faction. Newspapers in a multitude of ways socialized their readers to a generalized, self-assured, moralistic, and individualistic ethos, reinforcing the values and supporting the institutions of Victorian Canada. They became channels for the communication of a characteristic perspective on the nation, its goals, and its future, providing Canadians not so much with an ideology as a diffuse aggregate of hopes and ideals. Thus the press, which had shown a disintegrative potential in the face of arbitrary authority, was in other respects a powerful integrative force. The nineteenth- and early twentieth-century press may in fact have been unsurpassed in Canada as a successful agent of political and cultural socialization.

It was not until the rise of radio that Canadians were made aware of both the threat and the potential of a true mass medium. An influential group of Canadians was alarmed by the former and fascinated by the latter, a mixture which led to the founding of the most important of the Canadian public media agencies, the Canadian Broadcasting Corporation. The story of the CBC has been told in different contexts and with varying emphases.[3] It is a complicated and at times confusing story, in which theory and practice, objectives and realities, are so frequently at odds that they seem to justify Anthony Smith's comment that "many of the unresolved neuroses from which nations suffer can be found reflected in the ways they choose to organize radio and television."[4] However, two constants underlie the variables and

2. Ibid., p. 34.

3. See, for example, Margaret Prang, "The Origins of Public Broadcasting in Canada," *Canadian Historical Review* 46 (1965):2–31; E. S. Weir, *The Struggle for National Broadcasting in Canada* (Toronto: McClelland and Stewart, 1965); Frank Peers, *The Politics of Canadian Broadcasting, 1920–1951* (Toronto: University of Toronto Press, 1969); and David Ellis, *Evolution of the Canadian Broadcasting System: Objectives and Realities* (Canada: Department of Communications, 1979).

4. Anthony Smith, *The Shadow in the Cave: The Broadcaster, His Audience, and the State* (Urbana: University of Illinois Press, 1973), pp. 14–15.

are relevant to our theme. These are: (1) the particular goals with which this agency was charged, goals which differ somewhat from those of other major national broadcasting systems; and (2) the way in which these goals have been promoted or frustrated by both government generally and by the CBC itself.

It was noted that those whose interest and energy created the CBC were inspired by both the potential and the threat of radio. The potential was symbolized by the biggest politically supportive event in the Confederation's history, the celebration of its Diamond Jubilee in 1927, which was carried on the first national radio hookup and was received enthusiastically. The threat was the rumor that certain private Canadian broadcasting stations were seeking affiliation with the rapidly expanding American networks. So, two concerns—to support and strengthen the national polity and to protect and develop Canadian national consciousness and identity—have remained constants in a long line of statements about the role of the CBC. The Canadian Radio League, a devoted band of post–World War I idealists, interested in seeing that Canada had higher quality broadcasting than the commercial stations of the time seemed likely to offer, quickly found that their arguments for a publicly owned system were more persuasive if they stressed the nation-building potential of the new medium. Without national control, Prime Minister Bennett argued, "radio broadcasting can never become a great agency of communication of matters of national concern and for the diffusion of national thought and ideals; and . . . it can never be the agency by which national consciousness may be fostered and sustained and national unity still further strengthened."[5] Another proponent criticized a potential head of the new organization for not understanding that "it will be used for the purpose of strengthening national unity and healing the rapidly widening gap between the races and sections of Canada."[6] Officials of the fledgling organization spoke of their objectives as being national unity and the bringing about of a better understanding between language groups and regions. So it has gone for almost fifty years. National objectives almost disappeared, except for a stipulation that the broadcasting service should be "basically Canadian in content and character," in the 1958 Broadcasting Act brought in by the Diefen-

5. House of Commons, *Debates*, May 18, 1933, p. 3033.
6. Frank Peers, "Broadcasting and National Unity," in Benjamin D. Singer, ed., *Communications in Canadian Society*, 2nd ed. (Toronto: Copp Clark, 1975), p. 217.

baker government. But they surfaced again in the 1968 Act where Section 3g-iv notes that the national broadcasting service "should contribute to the development of national unity and provide for a continuing expression of Canadian identity." The numerous parliamentary debates involving the CBC during the "crisis years" since 1968 have presumed these objectives in passing judgment on its performance, as did the 1977 Canadian Radio-Television and Telecommunications Commission's *Report of the Committee of Inquiry into the National Broadcasting Service*. The same commission's decision on the renewal of the CBC's licenses (April 1979) leaves no doubt about the matter, declaring bluntly, "Whatever interpretation is given, it is evident that the identity-unity mandate is the raison d'être of the national broadcasting service. Accordingly, one can only measure the success or failure of this service in relation to the fulfillment of this double objective."[7]

It should be noted that in thus officially instructing the national broadcasting service to help both in holding the national polity together, and in finding the national psyche, the Canadian statute of 1968 is unique. The American equivalent is satisfied to talk of "public interest, convenience and necessity"; and successive British statutes rest content with requesting "information, education and entertainment."[8] Only the Canadian statute makes overt reference to national objectives. Clearly, the desire to exploit the "power of the media" as a source of political and cultural support is strongly felt in Canada.

The Record

In pursuing its lofty objectives the CBC has never been permitted to have it all its own way. Early recommendations that it have an outright monopoly came to nothing. Limitations on its funding forced the CBC to give private stations a far greater share in the broadcasting system than its partisans had envisaged. By the mid-1960s, the situation "was not merely that the private sector had grown to a size

7. Canadian Radio-Television and Telecommunications Commission, *Decision: Renewal of the Canadian Broadcasting Corporation's Television and Radio Network Licenses* (Ottawa: 1979), p. 13.

8. Harry Boyle, "The Media Control Institution in Society: Canada and the U.S. Compared," in Singer, ed., *Communications*, p. 196.

never contemplated by Parliament before 1958; it was also that the CBC was now completely outstripped by the private sector, which had gradually assumed the dominant position in budget assets, audience and program 'commercialism.'"[9] Formally, the Broadcasting Act stipulates that the private and public elements of the broadcasting system constitute a single system of which the CBC forms the cornerstone. Parliament eventually decided that "private stations also were to reflect the Canadian identity but only the CBC would be under the obligation to contribute to the development of national unity."[10] In practice, thanks to the maximum utilization of American programs, the private sector has been heavily entertainment-oriented and highly successful with audiences.

The inevitable temptation for the CBC to be drawn into competition for audiences was enhanced by the controversial policy of insisting that it reduce its costs by maximizing commercial sponsorship revenues. Many observers have judged that the policy has confused and divided the CBC's energies, distracting it from its proper goals. In practice, a competitive position has been sustained by a considerable infusion of popular American entertainment which to some seemed to compromise CBC purposes. But, even though great effort was devoted to widening the appeal of programs, public affairs (including subjects related to politics) remained rooted from the start in the public service tradition where standards have rarely been compromised. Discussion with senior CBC management officials has revealed that there was no officially proclaimed priority for political subjects. It never seemed necessary: a strong tradition in this area was firmly established early in the CBC's history and has never been abandoned.

Examination of the programming record would seem to justify this claim. CBC news, both on radio and television, has few peers and is, on the whole, less prone than American networks to feature violence and sensation while also being mature and thorough in its coverage of political affairs.[11] Weekly news reviews and surveys are of high quality. CBC radio's *Sunday Morning* is outstanding. The popular ra-

9. David Ellis, *Evolution of the Canadian Broadcasting System: Objectives and Realities, 1928–1968* (Canada: Department of Communications, 1979), p. 53.

10. Canadian Radio-Television and Telecommunications Commission, *Decision*, p. 12.

11. Benjamin D. Singer, "Violence, Protest, and War in Television News: The U.S. and Canada Compared," in Singer, *Communications*, pp. 312–19.

dio program *As It Happens* combines public affairs and entertainment in brash and energetic fashion. Extensive coverage is given to special events: Royal Tours, openings of Parliament, the peregrinations of the governor general. Recently, partial coverage of the proceedings of the House of Commons, live and on a regular basis, has been added to these activities. The CBC has no formal policies in the political area except in relation to elections and political free time. It used to "grant" free time at its discretion. However, there is now a special law which requires the CBC, along with the other networks, to sell a certain amount of advertising time to all parties at election time. But at other times there is a standing CBC rule against accepting paid political advertisements, which includes any advertising concealing a message on a controversial topic. *The Nation's Business* is a free time political telecast by the four federal political parties, with time divided according to a formula devised by the parties and the Corporation.

On CBC FM radio, *Ideas*, an internationally respected series of talks, discussions, and debates, ranks in quality and in depth of treatment with the best of the BBC Third Programme. Outstanding programs, many of them repeated, have included a comprehensive series, spread over several weeks, entitled *The Concept of Power*. Programs in this series dealt with power politics, the distribution of power, the power of the press, television and its power to shape the image of the politician, the intellectual, and the state, and the diffuse and concealed power of bureaucracy. The 1979 series *Man and the State* explored the sense of powerlessness in modern societies which helps develop distaste for politics and political indifference. First class was the series *Politics and the Imagination*, an extensive look at the relationship between the creative personality and politics, especially the artist's often uneasy relationship with his political environment. Special sections dealt with art and politics, Machiavelli, the political artist, and the intellectual process of radicalization. Conservatism as a philosophy was explored in depth with William Buckley, John Diefenbaker, Ronald Reagan, and Edgar Friedenberg. The 1980–81 series included two four-part studies, one on the history of utopian theory and the other dealing with the ideas of Leon Trotsky. Despite the hazards, satire has not been neglected. On radio, programs like *The Max Ferguson Show*, *Inside from the Outside*, and

The Royal Canadian Air Farce accustomed Canadians to hearing political figures treated with irreverence. CBC TV did a program dealing with political satire featuring Malcolm Muggeridge, and recently it has shown *Paperland: The Bureaucrat Observed*, a tongue-in-cheek study of bureaucracy.

As is revealed by a long line of effective programs (among others, *Close-Up, The Public Eye, This Hour Has Seven Days, The Watson Report, The Way It Is, The Fifth Estate*), CBC TV has never ceased searching for formats and approaches which might arouse the viewer's interest in, and understanding of, the political process. Television has the advantage over radio of not only being able to show politics in action, but also the politician talking about his two favorite subjects—politics and himself. Items of this type have included political insiders like Dalton Camp talking about the types of people attracted to politics; extensive interviews with former politicians of note (e.g., Howard Green, M. J. Coldwell, James Sinclair) on their reasons for choosing a political career; interviews with political figures who review their careers critically and explain their decisions; a defeated politician analyzing his loss; character studies and profiles of party leaders and members of parliament; and politicians talking about politics and the electorate (e.g., Robert Stanfield on cynicism and apathy among the electorate). This general approach has been extended to the past, as in a four-part series dealing with prominent political personalities of the 1930s such as William Aberhart and Maurice Duplessis.

Another considerable group of productions has been concerned with the difficult task of trying to illuminate the structure and operation of the political system. It included programs like *Corridors of Power* (with Norman Ward) which looked critically at the operation of the federal parliament; a cross-country hookup interviewing young people on the subject of republicanism versus monarchy (they preferred the former); and discussions with politicians and political scientists on the importance and dangers of the party system and party politics in a democracy. *What Makes the Country Run* included treatment of the way policy is made, the life and ambitions of the backbench MP, a critique of the Press Gallery and its tendency to play up political flamboyance rather than the substance of government; the role of the cabinet minister and how skillful prime ministers manage their cabinets; the relationship of a minister to the civil service; and the role of the civil servant. In *Some Honourable Members*, the role of the backbencher was given special attention. An interesting experiment was the fictional series *Quentin Durgens* which dramatized the life and activities of a reform-minded Member of Parliament. Making much use of the mechanics of Parliament, it painted a picture of the average politician and of the image-makers and power-brokers of politics that was not entirely flattering.

Yet another group of programs has been concerned with problems of communication in politics. Among these were an examination of how public opinion reaches and influences executives at political party conventions in Canada; a critique of media coverage at political conventions; a program on the debits and credits likely to result from televising parliamentary proceedings; several programs on the theme of "telepolitics"; the invasion of politics by television, especially the fascination it holds for politicians; the question of television's actual influence; and a study of political rhetoric, using excerpts from speeches of Canadian and American politicians to analyze forms of fallacious appeal, distortion, and misinterpretation.

There has been rather a surprising number of efforts to grapple with aspects of political ideas and ideology. Among these were talks like *Conservatism, Liberalism, Socialism: What Do They Mean in Canada?* (with Frank Underhill); Pierre Trudeau describing the influence of Lord Acton and Alexis de Tocqueville on his political thought; Dalton Camp discussing the public's attitude to politicians ("it thinks they are people without navels"); Trudeau talking on the role of intellectuals in politics; leading clergymen discussing the problem of reconciling political and Christian ethics; an analysis of the philosophies of progressivism and conservatism in Canada; several analyses of party ideologies and of party loyalties; and discussion of distortions in government information. *What's Left?* presented an extensive ideological analysis of the fragmentation of the Canadian Left. *The Bible Belt: The Politics of the Second Coming*, undertook an ideological history of the fundamentalist movement of the Canadian prairies, while still other programs focused on subjects such as the pattern of Quebec politics.

This by no means unimpressive record of many-sided attention to political affairs in both their national and provincial contexts on the part of the English-language radio and television network is not matched by Radio-Canada, the French-language network. Here, a much tighter focus on provincial political and cultural affairs and their problematic relationship to the central government tended to predominate. Nor was this tendency balanced to any significant degree by the acquisition or adaptation of available English-language materials. In contrast, it cannot be said that on the English-language networks the contentious issue of Quebec separatism has been neglected. As early as 1963 (before Lévesque was a declared separatist), the topic was the subject of a two-hour special entitled *Quebec Nationalism and Separatism*. After he had officially embraced separatism, a one-hour program was quickly devoted to Lévesque. He and his cause have not lacked attention since. For example, *The Champions*, a CBC-NFB coproduction, was a two-hour special contrasting the backgrounds, political philosophies, and personalities of Lévesque and Trudeau.

The National Film Board, the other major publicly supported media agency in Canada, also owed its inception in 1938 to the desire for a unified and identifiable nation. Its mandate, however, contented itself with assigning to filmmakers the task of "interpreting Canada to Canadians." What won the Board sufferance from the government was its proven capacity (during World War II) to use pan-Canadian contexts in a dramatic way which seemed likely to enhance national feeling. This the Board continued to do, becoming very good at shooting and splicing together scenes from all parts of Canada to suggest a pan-Canadian reality, relating people and activities to the larger whole.

One thing it did not do, however, was concern itself to any degree with the political system. An analysis I undertook for the Board in 1975 revealed that of a total production over the years of some thousands of items, only a dozen or so could be considered seriously concerned with the operation of the political process. As a result of this and further research, production of films in this area was made a priority for a number of years. The resulting films attempted to follow the suggestion of the McGill University political scientist, Dale Thomson, that they "should look at aspects of the democratic process with two questions constantly in mind—what is it supposed to do? Does it work?"[12] The films sought, therefore, to combine information and critique, in that order. *Flora—Scenes From a Leadership Convention*

12. Private communication, July 1976. Dr. Thomson acted as technical advisor to the National Film Board for films dealing with the political process.

looks behind the scenes at the pressures, deals, and disappointments of a leadership race. *I Hate To Lose* follows three candidates through the Quebec provincial election campaign which culminated in the Parti Québécois victory. *The Art of the Possible* is a candid study of Premier Davis of Ontario in action which explores in considerable detail the decision-making apparatus centered around a provincial premier. *Welcome to Smith's Falls* looks at a small town and its politics through the affectionate eyes of its mayor. *The New Mayor* looks at conflicts between establishment groups and political reformers in Winnipeg. *History on the Run* examines the media at work on the campaign trail during the 1979 federal election. Not formally part of the series, but designed to stimulate an interest in politics, is *The Hecklers*, a history of two hundred years of Canadian political cartoons and caricatures. *Solzhenitsyn's Children* looks at the critique of Marxism developed by the New Philosophers in Paris who say that Solzhenitsyn's writings have opened their eyes.

In his advisory capacity, Dale Thomson had suggested that the Board's film program on the political process had a great opportunity "to confront the traditional model of Canadian democracy with representatives of today's public and test the gap of understanding."[13] This is precisely what the NFB's innovative social animation program, *Challenge for Change*, had in fact been attempting. This program was seen by some critics as "antiestablishment," partly because it wanted to arouse people, as one producer put it, "so that they would take up their hammers and build their own world." Hammers aside, the program, in fact, genuinely tried to help people change the system by using the system, and to help the inarticulate and uninfluential win a place in the political process. It was thus fundamentally integrative. The best of these films gave a picture of the problems ordinary people face in dealing with the political system which is remarkable for its realism, accuracy, and candor. Political scientists would not be wasting their time looking at such items as *Halifax Encounter*, *Little Burgundy*, *The Prince Edward Island Development Plan*, *Activator One*, *Organizing for Power*, and *VTR St-Jacques*.

Political socialization through the media is, of course, not restricted to strictly political subjects. The enhancement of "national unity,"

13. Private communication, July 1976.

"national identity," and "national consciousness" has been supported by a tireless and many-sided effort. Both the CBC and the NFB have shown themselves relentlessly ingenious in exploiting any and every device for the literal exploration and dramatization of the pan-Canadian context—from helicopters (*Helicopter Canada*) to Buster Keaton on a railway track speeder (*The Railroader*)! History has been similarly handled in such major efforts as the National Film Board's seventeen-part *The History Makers*, its nine-hour *Struggle for a Border*, and the CBC's *The National Dream, Images of Canada*, and *The Tenth Decade*. That the "search for identity" need not always be a solemn enterprise is shown by the NFB's entertaining *Who Are We?* and *What the Hell's Going on Up There?* On the other hand, *Dreamland*, a history of early Canadian movie making, and *Has Anybody Here Seen Canada?* (CBC-NFB), which deals with the Americanization of the Canadian feature film screen, are clearly distressed by external pressure on Canadian cultural development.

Criticisms

"All right," said a friend who works in the American media, "you have all those media factories up there beating it out for the National Dream. But how come the country is falling apart?" My initial reactions to this facetious question (i.e., the country is not falling apart and the imputation of media insufficiency is grossly unfair) were followed by uncomfortable recollections of what a Member of Parliament, during a debate on the Broadcasting Act of 1968, had called "high-flown language about unity and cultural identity."[14] After so many brave words, somehow a "Canada in Crisis" hardly seemed an appropriate outcome, especially since it could be argued, as this paper has done, that media support for the present Canadian political system has not been neglected.

One explanation of their seeming insufficiency may be that the cumulative effect of much of the media's efforts has been considered unquantifiable. Another may be—despite commendations such as those of the Massey Commission or the Government White Paper of

14. House of Commons, *Debates*, October 17, 1968, p. 3179.

1966—that CBC management's appraisals of their activities in these regards have been overly modest.[15] Certainly, the way in which Canada's national objectives were being realized has not satisfied many Canadian nationalists. External pressure from the giant neighbor seemed to them, if anything, to have increased, intensified by the devastating impact of cable television. And if external pressures had worsened, internal ones had become explosive. To nationalists it came as a shock to realize that support for the pan-Canadian polity was not absolute, being in some cases qualified, in others rejected. The rise to power of an avowedly separatist provincial party threatened that ultimate disaster of the nation-state—physical dismemberment. And in the wake of this, other serious regional discontents, long latent, were awakening. For thoroughgoing nationalists, American penetration, separatism, and regional discontents added up to a national crisis.

This sense of crisis, which was by no means confined to a vocal minority of nationalists, could not fail to influence judgments concerning the performance of the media. In a period which saw the publication of books with titles like *Must Canada Fail?*,[16] most Canadians, while firmly rejecting defeatism, could hardly avoid a sense of disappointment and frustration. Frustration seeks an outlet and does not always find appropriate targets. Moreover, there is always the impulse to blame the messenger who transmits bad news. Much criticism of the CBC over the years had dealt with waste, extravagance, incompetence, and disorganization. But from the late 1960s to the present, more serious criticisms have been made concerning policy and programming. Let us consider the four principal ones.

Americanization. The traditionally large American presence on the Canadian television screen, and especially that on the CBC, became and remained an issue for nationalists, who kept up a steady drumfire emphasizing the danger of "being inarticulate consumers of American

15. For example, Brian Stewart writes: "Presumably these changes would be smaller, and in a different direction, were Canadians entirely dependent on American channels with their preponderance of entertainment programs. If that is not a very spectacular conclusion, it provides some objective justification for a belief in the importance of a Canadian Broadcasting system." W. Brian Stewart, "The Canadian Social System and the Canadian Broadcasting Audience," in Singer, ed., *Communications*, p. 64.

16. Richard Simeon, ed., *Must Canada Fail?* (Montreal and London: McGill-Queen's University Press, 1977).

waste products."[17] In media terms, the arrival of cable television, quickly acquired by a majority of Canadians, had led to greatly increased penetration by American programs,[18] already richly represented on Canadian commercial television and (a more disconcerting fact to many nationalists) on the CBC itself. Regarding the latter, June 1980 figures indicate that aggregate viewing of non-Canadian programs currently runs to about 45–55 percent of all CBC viewing. *M*A*S*H*, *Mork and Mindy*, *Dallas*, *WKRP in Cincinnati*, and *World of Disney* all have two or three times as many devotees on the CBC as the most popular Canadian shows. Despite all efforts by the Canadian regulatory agency, the Canadian Radio-Television and Telecommunications Commission (CRTC), to help Canadian programming through actions such as Canadian-content quotas and prime-time priorities, Canadians still spend more time listening to Americans than they do listening to other Canadians.

The negative or disintegrative effects of the media. As in many other countries, the bewildering pace of social change has raised understandable concern about the apparent decline of traditional Canadian values and institutions. For many people of conservative temper (and these are numerous in Canada) such change has not been good news and, not surprisingly, the messenger has tended to be blamed. The House of Commons has heard angry words about "the morbid preoccupations" of CBC producers. My own research for the NFB's *People and Power* films revealed absolute unanimity among politicians that only negative things were said in the media about the political system and about politicians, and that those who worked in the media regarded the established system at best with indifference, at worst with unconcealed hostility.[19] The CBC's brief fling into "hot seat" confrontation journalism, particularly the program *This Hour*

17. Patricia Hindley, Gail M. Martin, and Jean McNulty, *The Tangled Net: Basic Issues in Canadian Communication* (Vancouver: J. J. Douglas, 1977), p. 8.

18. The figures might well arouse nationalist concern. Whereas in London, Ontario, for example, Canadians without cable had watched American stations only 2.3 percent of the time and Canadian stations 97 percent of the time, those now with cable watched American stations 52 percent of the time. In the same way, post-cable, out of a total of 257 available programs, only 16 percent were Canadian as against 84 percent American. For a typical winter season (1972–73), CBX Audience Research Studies showed that of twenty popular shows with over two million viewers, only two were Canadian, both of them sports events.

19. I found among this influential group almost total unawareness of the wide variety of political programs which had been produced.

Has Seven Days, was much criticized and the House of Commons heard denunciations of the "cynical, deprecating, mud-strewn views of so many at the CBC."[20]

Separatist infiltration of Radio-Canada. More serious accusations of cynicism or indifference (since they imply disloyalty among federal civil servants and misuse of federal funds) have been charges that Radio-Canada is "riddled with separatists" who are suspected of suppressing anything which lends suport to the federal system or a pan-Canadian context, and of replacing it with material favorable to separatism. The result of repeated charges has been an ongoing, indecisive, and slightly maddening debate (in and out of parliament) which has extended, like a television serial, through the crisis years. Among its highlights were, on the government side, Prime Minister Trudeau's suggestion that "judging by the results," the charges were probably true,[21] and his comment that "almost everyone, including the high officials of the CBC, would be prepared to concede that the overwhelming majority of employees of the CBC (Radio-Canada) are of separatist leaning."[22] Despite Secretary of State Pelletier's repeated assurances that such broad charges were unfounded, there were other, rather extravagant extra-parliamentary statements by ministers to the effect that there was a veritable army of separatists in the federal civil service. Holding separatist views, it was suggested, was not a crime, but using a federal function to advance them was. Yet despite some talk of "codes and subterranean communication" during the 1970 FLQ crisis, there was no enthusiasm for Prime Minister Trudeau's hint of controls for the CBC. It is clear that fear of censorship has run deeper than fear of Radio-Canada infiltration. At the same time the CBC's duty to national unity has been frequently proclaimed, as have accusations such as that it "totally ignores the positive side of our democracy, our institutions and our public men."[23] These contradictions seemingly were "resolved" when Mr. Trudeau (in March 1977) invited the Canadian Radio-Television and Telecommunications

20. House of Commons, *Debates*, October 17, 1968, pp. 3957–58.
21. House of Commons, *Debates*, October 24, 1969, p. 32 (quoted by Robert Stanfield).
22. House of Commons, *Debates*, February 25, 1977, p. 3425 (speech by P. E. Trudeau).
23. House of Commons, *Debates*, September 26, 1970, p. 1531 (speech by Andre Fortin).

Commission to investigate doubts about the CBC's fulfillment of its mandate.

Overcentralization. Finally, from opposite ends of the country have come complaints that the CBC is overcentralized, that it represents the "imperial outlook" of Central Canada, and that it gives little thought to helping the regions of Canada speak to one another. In particular it has been charged that the CBC has failed to reflect Canada's fundamental cultural duality, that the English and French networks have had little contact with each other, and that the Corporation has helped to perpetuate, rather than to reduce, the "two solitudes."

The *Report* of the CRTC's Committee of Inquiry says remarkably little about "separatist infiltration" in the CBC but resoundingly confirms all the other criticisms. It then bluntly concludes that the Corporation has failed to "provide for a continuing expression of Canadian identity" and has failed "to contribute to the development of national unity."[24] As these were the objectives described by the CRTC as the "raison d'être" of the CBC, this was tantamount to saying that the CBC was a flat failure.

People who are too long abused often come to see themselves as others see them. This may explain why those who speak publicly for the CBC should finally have come, apparently, to see its sins as its critics see them. Thus, not long ago, the current President of the Corporation excoriated himself and his predecessors for having permitted the "rape" of Canadian culture by American culture. He also confessed to the CRTC Committee of Inquiry that "when you look at what the Canadian broadcasting system is doing to implement the directions of Parliament, it's a pretty sorry story."[25] More Canadianization was recommended, and a determined assault was to be made on the commanding heights of entertainment now largely held by entrenched Americans. More was to be done to overcome the "two solitudes," presumably to the discomfiture of separatism; and, in the same vein, more was to be done to show the various regions of Canada to one another.

24. Canadian Radio-Television and Telecommunications Commission, *Report: Committee of Inquiry into the National Broadcasting Service* (Ottawa: 1977), p. x.
25. Canadian Radio-Television and Telecommunications Commission, *Decision*, p. 13.

It was suggested earlier that the public media in Canada have in no respect lacked vigor in the pursuit of the objectives they have been given. It is suggested here that the constantly implied discrepancy between public media objectives and performance is to a considerable extent the creation of the controlling vision underlying these objectives and the criteria of judgment this imposes. It is further suggested that the criteria of judgment may need reexamination in the light of current realities. Accordingly, the following, rather personal, observations do no more than simply raise the question whether this may not be so with respect to these four areas of persistent criticism: Americanization, the negative effects of the media on political socialization, separatist influence, and the unexploited potential of regionalism.

Appraisals

Americanization. I sometimes think that the CBC takes its nationalist critics too seriously. The CBC is not somehow "responsible" for the American presence on Canadian television or for the rape of anybody by anybody. That is due to geography, technological availability, and bargain prices, but even more to Canadian taste and government policy. Canadians have always had a taste for American entertainment and get angry if someone tries to interfere with their indulging it. Pay television and direct satellite transmission will clearly complicate the situation and even more than cable television. Indeed, if we simply define a nation as a group which has more communications transaction within the group than with outsiders, then as Brian Stewart points out, "the outlook for a Canadian nation is bleak,"[26] so bleak, indeed, that some pessimists have felt that the only valid direction for the CBC is to become an all-Canadian network purged of American programs, whatever the risk in loss of audience. This view, long held by some nationalists, appeared to receive tacit support in the CRTC *Report*'s admission: "It is unrealistic to suggest, in the face of an increasingly active private sector and the availability of cable television,

26. Stewart, "The Canadian Social System," p. 61.

that the mandate of the CBC can any longer be interpreted as demanding majority audiences on a consistent basis."[27] Since "it is not the number of people watching such programming but the significance of the programs to those watching that matters,"[28] the CBC should worry only about providing a quality alternative.

This is a plausible argument, but one which would seem to involve a de facto abandonment of the mass audience (i.e., the general public). It is a long retreat from the prominent role demanded of the CBC relatively recently, let alone from the dominant role hoped for it by its founders. Is the situation really so bad as to justify such pessimism? It is easy to be misled by a kind of audience-numbers game: by aggregates which, without qualitative distinction, are all but meaningless. Most American programs on Canadian television, whether public, commercial, or cable, are entertainment programs, unsurpassed of their kind, and designed to reach the largest possible mass audience. Public affairs, news, and documentary programs are predominantly Canadian. Excellent as these are, they undoubtedly win larger audiences than they might because they share the schedule with more popular programs. Perverse as it may seem, most Canadians prefer their American programs on Canadian stations; they seem to like a mixture of Canadian and American programming. Television viewers tend to develop channel-watching habits. The inclusion of some favorite American programs helps win Canadian viewers away from habit-viewing of American channels and develops a Canadian channel-watching preference. This suggests that if the CBC eliminated all its American programs, it might drive away a large part of its remaining audience.[29]

Assuming that knowledgeable critics are aware of this phenomenon, why do they complain? The truth, in my judgment, is that some of those concerned about the presence of American entertainment on Canadian television simply don't like popular entertainment. More than just snobbery, however, theirs is a genuine concern about the "diffuse" socializing effects of entertainment, particularly popular

27. Canadian Radio-Television and Telecommunications Commission, *Report*, p. x.
28. Ibid.
29. For many Americans, watching the PBS channel is not a habit. NBC, CBS, and ABC undoubtedly exert an influence on American unity and identity. PBS does not, not because it lacks "quality," but because it lacks audiences.

American television drama programs, with their characteristic blend of violence and irreverence and their large audiences. However, behind much solemn talk about "socialization to values other than our own" lurks a reluctance, often rooted in a personal distaste for "commercialism," to recognize the uncomfortable facts that, sociologically, Canada and the United States are branches on the same tree, and that for a majority of Canadians these values are to some extent their own. Paul Rutherford even sees in this sharing in American values a unifying rather than a disintegrative factor for Canada: "Indeed, this very Americanization fostered a common social ethos which acts as a national bond. More and more people in every generation have shared the slang, the heroes and villains, the myths, the values of an American design sufficient to maintain a sense of community among Canadians."[30] Although the thought may outrage nationalists, it is refreshing to find Professor Rutherford taking a dim view of those who wish to purge or purify the Canadian media of the "American presence."

It is certainly possible to take the matter too seriously. Brian Stewart notes that "though Toronto has been open to American signals for many years, there is no evidence that Torontonians are any the less Canadian for it."[31] The much disputed American presence on the CBC, then, may simply reflect a reality of the society and of its tastes. Any attempt to radically reorder that reality could be both costly and self-defeating. An effort to Canadianize all entertainment programs could be an expensive and hazardous venture. Stewart queries whether all-Canadian entertainment programs would necessarily communicate a "distinctive Canadian consciousness" to their audience. The experience of the Canadian Film Development Corporation would seem to suggest that "Canadian-made" and "Canadian" are not synonymous—witness *Meatball* and *Prom Night*!

Negative or disintegrative effects of the media. In a country with a dangerously delicate internal political equilibrium, have the public media helped unsettle or preserve the balance of political forces? Have they been an integrative or disintegrative force? Perhaps no fully satisfactory answer can be given to this question until students of

30. Rutherford, *The Making of the Canadian Media*, p. 102.
31. Stewart, "The Canadian Social System," p. 61.

communications produce a more consistent and coherent conception of media effects than they have to date. Let it be said only that at the popular level the concept of the "awesome power" of the media—not uninfluenced by the pessimism of popular theorists like Ellul and McLuhan—persists. At a more empirical level, the notion of "powerful media" has been considerably qualified over the years by a good deal of respectable research which seems to suggest that television, when not merely a trivializing toy, is more often than not an agent of reinforcement. Continuing research, however, has shown the need for substantial modification of the reinforcement theory. It can be said that the concept of the "powerful media" is slowly reappearing, though tentatively, and with some implications that the media factor in the long run may be ambivalent. On the one hand, we know that the mass media have a certain potential for political support in terms of news, information, and interpretive material within a generally integrative, if critical, frame of reference. On the other, we also know that what strengthening of pan-Canadian federalist signals was achieved did not overwhelm other voices with different and contradictory messages. After twenty years of television, the Canadian crisis is everywhere out in the open. Thus, the medium seemed to have served integrative and disintegrative forces equally.

Recent and contemporary research does not suggest that the ideas of individuals with strong views and real commitment will be changed by efforts at political persuasion. What it does suggest is that the number of people with such convictions is steadily shrinking, as are persons with strong party loyalties. We may infer from this that television is conveying political materials to an immense and increasingly apolitical audience of a kind which no mass medium has ever before commanded. Moreover, an increasing number of analysts believe that television may be helping to create this audience. Relevant in this context is the striking theory of "Videomalaise" developed by Michael Robinson, who argues that the significant increase in information flow brought about by television has not resulted in political movement to left or right, but to political frustration. The obligation to develop two sides to every question inevitably brings all political legitimacies into question. All this "balance" breeds endless disputation, blurs what affiliations people still have, and tends to produce a feeling in the viewer that politics is a debate without end about which he can do very little. The results are in Robinson's vivid term, "Videomalaise," and an ensuing crisis in legitimacy.[32] Without going all the way with Robinson, I would agree that in its cumulative effect television is a disintegrative force. Over the long haul it stands out more as a critic than a celebrant. Television is skeptical, irreverent. This is a matter of something more than iconoclasm (i.e., the *Seven Days* kind of program, with its confrontation tactics, its "bear pits" and "hot seats," designed to rouse controversy for controversy's sake). Television is a genuine and endless debate which puts everything up for grabs. Nothing is beyond dispute. The new Holy Writ, the "fairness doctrine," with its obligation to develop two sides to every issue, brings all legitimacies into question. Nothing is sacred; the most precious truths, the most sacrosanct doctrines, are so many points in an argument. Over a prolonged period, television wears ideas away, breaks concepts apart, does preconceptions in, knocks fond hopes down, and, in sum, gradually "disassociates" already loose aggregates of beliefs and ideals. And at the receiving end of it all, in Michael Robinson's term, sits the "Inadvertent Audience,"[33] its convictions no longer sheltered by selection, belabored by every point of view, increasingly frustrated, alienated, and disaffected. The signs are all around us in the form of quiet withdrawal from, increasing disapproval of, and declining participation in the "system," that sum of things which, amidst endless explanations, becomes less and less comprehensible. "Videomalaise" indeed!

There is also the matter of attitude. Most employees of the mass media are philosophically liberals, concerned, wherever possible, to extend the limits of the permissible. Television in consequence has been a liberating force. It has supported and strengthened the liberal trend in our culture, and has helped maintain the open society, and to open it still further. This propensity will not change: it is a permanent tilt. Michael Novak suggests that we should be grateful "that the social class responsible for the creative side of TV is not a reactionary and frankly illiberal class."[34] Indeed, we should. But those who quite properly decry control or censorship while complaining of media

32. Michael J. Robinson, "American Political Legitimacy in an Era of Electronic Journalism: Reflections on the Evening News," in Douglass Cater, ed., *Television as a Social Force: New Approaches to TV Criticism* (New York: Praeger, 1975), pp. 97–139.

33. Ibid., p. 105.

34. Michael Novak, "Television Shapes the Soul," in Cater, ed., *Television*, p. 21.

"negativism" or "disaffiliation" should be clear just where the liberating force can lead in terms of political support. In the early days of the BBC, Lord Reith said that his organization's responsibility "was to avoid whatever was or might be hurtful."[35] A later BBC policy paper noted that Olympian detachment did not apply "to the basic moral and constitutional beliefs on which the nation's life is founded."[36] Fairly recently, Sir Geoffrey Cox of Independent Television News argued that it is the first duty of broadcasters to support the democratic regime to the utmost. But in the debate which followed, producers maintained that if impartiality was to be the code, it could admit of no exceptions and clearly felt that the achievement of one social value— liberty—meant sacrificing another: commitment to the regime. The distance traveled from Lord Reith had been considerable.

Separatist influence. For Canadians, the issue of the limits of impartiality was posed most sharply by the charges of separatist influence in Radio-Canada. That Olympian detachment on the part of the public media *was* being applied to "the basic moral and constitutional beliefs of the country,"[37] even to the continued existence of the polity, seemed to be implied in the *Report* of the CRTC's Committee of Inquiry. It has little to say about separatism per se; but what it did say is revealing. After accepting the CBC's claim to be a "catalyst for change," the *Report* notes:

It [The CBC] goes on, however, to insist that it cannot be expected to and should not try to take a stand "as between the wide range of political opinions under active discussion in Canada today." That includes "anti-centralist, anti-federalist policies" such as those advocated by Quebec separatists: "The view which the Corporation takes is that its national unity mandate does not require it to take any particular political position in this vexed area of federal-provincial constitutional relations; nor indeed would it be wise or proper for it to do so." This characterization of the current political situation in Canada as a more or less routine federal-provincial constitutional argument certainly suggests an extraordinary coolness in the CBC's attitude. One cannot help wondering, however, whether the coolness is located in the head or in the feet.[38]

35. Lord J. C. W. Reith, *Into the Wind* (London: Hodder and Stoughton, 1949), p. 101.
36. British Broadcasting Corporation, *B.B.C. Handbook 1975* (London: B.B.C., 1974), pp. 284–85.
37. Ibid.
38. Canadian Radio-Television and Telecommunications Commission, *Report*, p. 27.

I would suggest the coolness is at the heart, in the very nature of the media beast. It is clear, of course, that radio and television played an absolutely vital role in the emergence of Quebec nationalism, and that English Canadians who see this movement as identical with the separatist option will deplore and denounce that role. But a distinction must be made. The leaders of the Parti Québécois have been free to utilize television as much or as little, as well or as badly, as any other political party; and they have been fortunate in having a leader with the sort of charisma television appreciates. But the real effects of television in Quebec came immediately before and during the Quiet Revolution. They were the effects of television-as-mirror, and they were devastating. "We looked in that mirror," a producer at Radio-Canada once said to me, "and we didn't like what we saw."[39] The separatist enthusiasm was one way of trying to give general form to a deeper passion for change. But the relatively small number of programs which might reasonably have been considered proseparatist, and which actually were made and used by the media, seem, in retrospect, insignificant beside the number that played a vital role in the transformation of Quebec by holding up an implacable mirror to its realities. This was no merely negative or disintegrative process. Underlying both the eager and long-delayed modernization and the nationalist surge itself, I would argue, was a profound and authentic regionalism of a kind that might inspire a "new national order" for Canada—one which might eventually reduce all its separatisms to historical episodes.

Regionalization. Some years ago I had the pleasure of watching the spirit of true regionalism at work and of seeing what it could accomplish. When the National Film Board moved its facilities from Ottawa to Montreal in the mid-1950s, the francophone filmmakers, who had felt very much in exile in Ottawa (those were the Duplessis days), were, so to speak, reconnected with their roots; they had come back home again. What happened I have described elsewhere:

[T]hey proceeded to explore "their region" and "their people" with all the enthusiasm of those rediscovering themselves, and all the energy that comes from the feeling of an unnatural and too prolonged separation ended, of

39. Private communication, March 1975.

being reunited with one's origins. . . . The result was an extraordinary flowering of talent and achievement. To some, these films had nationalistic, even separatist overtones. But fundamentally they were *regional*. They did not interpret Canada to Quebec, but Quebec to Quebeckers, and to anyone else who cared to watch. . . . These films had a freshness and vividness, a closeness to people, an intimacy with their actual hopes and fears and assumptions, which was new and exhilarating.[40]

What they had was authenticity. Canada is a land of still largely unexplored regionalisms. I suggest that in their further exploration may lie, all appearances to the contrary, an eventual integrative force in terms of political socialization.

There are some obstacles, however. The modern nation-state and regionalism are uneasy partners. Supposedly living in a condition of "creative tension," they easily became mutually suspicious, seeing in each other, respectively, only "provincialism" or "centralist domination." The unthinking identification of regionalism with nationalism, and its further identification in the case of Quebec with separatism (the ultimate horror for any nation-state), acts as something of a mental block. All too easily, regionalism can be made to seem the enemy of national unity and national identity.

The attempt to press the concept of a national identity into service as a socializing agency for a national polity seems particularly dubious in Canada. Northrop Frye has observed:

When the CBC is instructed by Parliament to do what it can do to promote Canadian identity and unity, it is not always realized that unity and identity are quite different things to be promoting, and that in Canada they are perhaps more different than they are anywhere else. Identity is local and regional, rooted in imagination and in works of culture; unity is national in reference, international in perspective and rooted in a political feeling.[41]

Rather than being harnessed in tandem, these two concepts should exist in a state of tension. If this tension is lost there can be serious consequences:

Once the tension is given up, and the two elements of unity and identity are confused or assimilated to each other, we get the two endemic diseases of Canadian life. Assimilating identity to unity produces the empty gestures of

40. R. S. Dick, "Regionalization of a Federal Cultural Institution: The Experience of the National Film Board of Canada" (unpublished paper, 1980), p. 9.
41. Northrop Frye, *The Bush Garden: Essays on the Canadian Imagination* (Toronto: Anansi, 1971), p. ii.

cultural nationalism; assimilating unity to identity produces the kind of provincial isolation which is called separatism.[42]

It is worth noting also the conclusions of another distinguished scholar, Morton Grodzins, who, in *The Loyal and the Disloyal*, argued that national loyalties flourish best by resting on lesser loyalties, not destroying them; and that in a new country in particular, any true national spirit will have to attach itself to older, more familiar loyalties.[43] Loyalty and unity can be built from the ground upward as well as imposed from the top downward. The Canadian scholar, George Woodcock, has written of the "need to decentralize Canada into a working confederation rather than a nonworking nation-state," and of the "relationship between harmful political centralization and a similar tendency in Canadian communications, exemplified particularly in the condition of the Canadian Broadcasting Corporation."[44] There is certainly some truth in Woodcock's irate comment to the effect that, "in the CBC, again as in the Ottawa government, national unity has been mistaken—as it has been so consistently and tragically throughout our history—for the image that English-speaking central Canadians, the true Wasps, have of themselves."[45] Certainly the CBC sometimes gives one the impression of setting forth, like Joyce's famous hero, to forge the uncreated consciousness of its people in the smithy of its downtown Toronto offices! The *Report* of the Committee of Inquiry of the CRTC is therefore on good ground in recommending a much greater accent on regional production. However, this is not simply a matter of making programs from the center *about* the regions, but of having them made *in* the regions by natives of the region. One cannot, as Marshall McLuhan put it, decentralize centrally. Least of all does the answer lie in the forced cultivation of an artificial, irrelevant, and perhaps even unwanted *entente cordiale* between the French and English.

In this respect, the National Film Board's innovative Regionalization Program may point a direction for the future. As of 1980, some 50

42. Ibid., p. iii.

43. Morton Grodzins, *The Loyal and the Disloyal: Social Boundaries of Patriotism and Treason* (Chicago: University of Chicago Press, 1956).

44. George Woodcock, "Introduction," to Hindley, Martin, and McNulty, *The Tangled Net*, p. viii.

45. Hindley et al., *The Tangled Net*, p. 122.

percent of all the NFB's production will be carried out in Regional Production Studios. Filmmakers originally from the various regions, formerly "interpreting Canada to Canadians" from their offices in Montreal, have been "reconnected to their roots," and new filmmakers can develop and work in their home region. Results so far seem to indicate that the creative upsurge previously noted among Quebec filmmakers may, in other forms and styles, eventually be repeated. The program has not been conceived as merely decentralization of an essentially unchanged outlook, but as an attempt to establish a better equilibrium, even (in Frye's sense) a more natural tension between cultural and political loyalties. In the resulting films, the five regional contexts are not subservient to pan-Canadian ones, and discord is not submerged in the celebration of a mythical harmony. This new note is clearly evident in films like *Empty Harbours, Empty Dreams*, a Maritime view of Confederation, or *Blowhard*, a western view of central Canadian "imperialism."

Concluding Observations

Have the public media in Canada then, particularly the CBC, "failed in their major objectives"? In his brief history of the media in Canada, Paul Rutherford concludes that in Canada "the effects of the multimedia had been decidedly mixed," that they have been "contributors to the national distemper," and that they have been "decidedly ambiguous agents of nation-building."[46] Blunter still is his general judgment that "all in all, the multimedia have encouraged a climate of opinion hostile to the old Dominion and Confederation, without generating any widely accepted alternative opinion that might support some new national order. Therein lies one reason for the present day fragility of the nation-state."[47] That the CRTC's Committee of Inquiry concluded that the CBC had failed in its objectives we know. And Prime Minister Trudeau has repeatedly maintained in the House of Commons his view that "the CBC in particular had not contributed in a sufficient way to their mandate, nor to the unity of

46. Rutherford, *The Making of the Canadian Media*, pp. 121, 123.
47. Ibid., p. 122.

Canada,"[48] indeed that it "had been contributing to the division of
Canada."[49]

Although respectful of such eminent opinion, I would suggest that
Canada in fact has been well served by its public media, and not least
by the CBC. A certain paradox has marked Canadian attitudes to "the
people's network." The impressive durability of support for the public-
sector media in Canada has derived less from any demonstrable theory about media effects than from the uncritical assumption that the
media could do anything you asked them, and would surely do it if
you asked them often enough. But, the more presumptive the hope,
the greater the risk of disappointment. The record reveals a paradoxi-
cal pattern of dogged support alternating with outbursts of exaspera-
tion at what, given the premises, could only seem dereliction of duty.
Inevitably criticism has taken on a sharper edge during the years of
crisis in Canada, when the clear dichotomy between aspiration and
reality in the country made charges that the Canadian Broadcasting
Corporation has let the country down more plausible.

There is a story (one rather hopes it is apocryphal) that at the start
of the 1974 CBC license hearings, the then Chairman of the CRTC
declared, "Look! Either we have a country or we don't. Let's decide!"[50] There is a certain breathtaking arrogance in a comment which
reflects both an absurdly low estimate of the exasperatingly complicated and unruly but thoroughly durable Canadian "fact" and an absurdly high estimate of the "awesome power" of the media. Few
would deny some socializing role to the media, but the role seems an
ambivalent one since, as was suggested earlier, the never-ending
flood of the media produces not only a cumulative deposit but a re-
lentless erosion. There is a quality in these systems which swamps
the most carefully contrived selectivities on the part of its minions
and masters alike. In the long run the media (at least in a democracy)
are unreliable allies of those who think to find in them the fundamental contemporary form of social power—the ability to define, to favor
an official view of reality. If the media are indeed a mirror, it is apt,
like that of Perseus's shield, to let us see Medusa.

48. House of Commons, *Debates*, July 22, 1977, p. 7909.
49. Ibid., p. 7908.
50. Bruce McKay, "The CBC and The Public" (unpublished doctoral dissertation, Institute
for Communication Research, Stanford University, 1976), p. 327.

To measure the success or failure of the CBC in terms of an amorphous "unity-identity mandate" is surely both unrealistic and unfair. The CBC has ceaselessly enriched that curious, disorderly, and not entirely unsophisticated Canadian sensibility (the despair of purists) which, without adopting their nationalities, draws as it pleases on things American, British, and French to mix its own myriad identities. And in intensifying the Canadian duality, even its disintegrative elements, may not Radio-Canada and all the Quebec filmmakers merely have been telling us, well in advance of Jane Jacobs, that "the issue of how to combine duality of French and English Canada with federation of ten provinces remains insoluble because it is inherently insoluble!"[51] Insoluble in the old pan-Canadian context, perhaps, but when it *is* solved, and a new angle of vision attained, much that has seemed disintegrative in the media may well seem otherwise.

Meanwhile, tensions—destructive rather than constructive—accumulate and the most fundamental aspects of the polity become open to challenge and change. During such a period, what is needed from the public media is not so much political support in the literal sense (though that remains broadly important), but a difficult, subtle, and carefully spaced process of resocialization, designed to legitimate new concepts of identity and unity. The interposition in all our lives of closer contexts, regional, community, and personal, may produce a new aggregate of *solidarités* to oppose the growing political anomie and "Videomalaise." Here the public media in Canada have a critical role to play. For whatever the limits on the power of these media, if only by telling us what we should be worrying about, they can prepare the way for constructive change.

51. Jane Jacobs, *The Question of Separatism: Quebec and the Struggle Over Sovereignty* (New York: Random House, 1980), p. 89.

Media Agenda-Setting in the 1979 Federal Election: Some Implications for Political Support

Ronald Wagenberg, Walter Soderlund, Donald Briggs, and Walter Romanow

That the media play a critical role in the mobilization of political support is a fact known to every political activist. It is no accident that coup-makers often seize radio and television outlets before they seize armories. However, one need not make reference to anything as dramatic as revolutions to demonstrate the political importance of news media. As the primary disseminators of information and opinion in a political community, they cannot avoid affecting how people think about their country, its political institutions, and those who are elected and appointed to govern.[1] However often "Don't believe everything you read in the paper" may be repeated, the printed word continues to be powerfully persuasive: at the very least, in determining the subjects about which people think. Television is even more persuasive—both in the latter sense and in the sense of specific content—because what is presented is seemingly verified by the viewers' own eyes and thus can easily be interpreted as irrefutable truth.

Anthony Westell has written that in Canada "journalists must accept a large share of responsibility for the current wave of public distrust of government."[2] Such distrust might affect the ability to govern

This research was supported by a grant from the Social Science and Humanities Research Council of Canada. The authors gratefully acknowledge the Council's assistance.

1. See Lee Becker, "Measurement of Gratifications," *Communication Research* 6 (1979): 54–73.

2. Anthony Westell, "The Press: Adversary or Channel of Communication," in *Parliament,*

even a strongly centralized country. But political life in Canada, as is well known, has a strong regional flavor. Do Canadian media contribute to regionalism or do they instead facilitate national integration? A good case might be made for either. With regard to their integrative potential, for example, the radio and television systems are mandated by their governing legislation to act in the interests of national unity and identity. The existence of state-owned broadcasting facilities, though they do not enjoy a monopoly position, at least increases the likelihood such a mandate can be carried out. Contrariwise, the traditions of free speech and press militate against the blatant use of the media as propaganda conduits. The management of the Canadian Broadcasting Corporation was acting in this tradition when it announced during the 1980 Quebec referendum campaign that its policy would be to give adequate coverage to both sides and to cover the debate in as neutral a manner as possible.

With respect to their potential contribution to regionalism, newspapers serve limited regional rather than national audiences. Indeed, even the *Globe and Mail*, the self-styled national newspaper, does not command a large readership outside of Ontario.[3] However, the acquisition of large numbers of newspapers over the years by the major chains has created at least the possibility of central direction and perhaps a bias in the direction of national integration. Moreover, movement of publishers and lesser personnel around the country within newspaper chains and heavy reliance on the Canadian Press wire and syndicated columnists may provide both a buffer against parochial attitudes and a national perspective to Canadian newspapers. Although the chains rarely own newspapers printed in more than one language, and research on editorials during elections has uncovered no evidence of chain direction of editorial policy,[4] it is at least arguable that in the selection and treatment of issues, newspapers facili-

---

Policy and Representation, ed. Harold D. Clarke et al. (Toronto: Methuen Publications, 1980), p. 29.

3. In an attempt to extend its circulation to a broader level of Canadian readership, the *Globe and Mail*, in October 1980, announced its plans to use satellite transmissions to permit publication of the newspaper in Calgary, Alberta, and in Montreal, Quebec.

4. Ronald H. Wagenberg and Walter C. Soderlund, "The Influence of Chain Ownership on Editorial Comment in Canada," *Journalism Quarterly* 52 (1975):93–98; and "The Effects of Chain Ownership on Editorial Coverage: The Case of the 1974 Canadian Federal Election," *Canadian Journal of Political Science* 9 (1976):682–89.

tate national integration.[5] If so, they may contribute to public support for the political community, if not for the regime, or authorities.[6]

Rather than focusing on print media, this essay instead examines the electronic media, where these questions have received less attention and analysis. The specific question to be addressed is whether, in the selection of news items to be presented to the public via national radio and television during the 1979 Canadian federal election, the networks presented a picture that would contribute to support for the political community, to respect for political institutions, and to the establishment of uniform national criteria for assessing the qualities of those who sought political office.

Issues in the 1979 Election and Specific Support

In a democratic political system, an election campaign constitutes a concerted effort to generate specific support for alternative sets of political authorities. In such a system, elections are the means by which political officials are held accountable for their actions in office and authorized to govern for specified, limited terms. Elections also have great symbolic value. In the context of a democratic political culture, the conduct of periodic, free, and open elections affirms the congruence between regime structures and cultural values, legitimizing both the regime and the political community of which it is a part.

In their efforts to generate support at the polls, parties and their leaders raise issues which they hope will touch a responsive chord in the electorate. The media affect the probability of electoral suc-

5. Walter C. Soderlund, Ronald H. Wagenberg, E. Donald Briggs, and Ralph C. Nelson, "Regional and Linguistic Agenda-Setting in Canada: A Study of Newspaper Coverage of Issues Affecting Political Integration in 1976," *Canadian Journal of Political Science* 13 (1980):347–56; and "Output and Feedback: Canadian Newspapers and Political Integration," *Journalism Quarterly* 57 (1980):316–21.

6. Our use of the terms "political authorities," "regime," and "political community" follows David Easton's usage. See *A Systems Analysis of Political Life* (New York: John Wiley & Sons, 1965), pp. 153–219. Thus, "political authorities," as used here, refer to the major political party and leaders holding office and making policy; "regime" refers to the entire constitutional structure as well as such features of the political system as federalism, parliamentary government, and the electoral system, in addition to goals and values. "Political community" refers to the continued legitimacy of the nation-state, Canada, as the perceived ultimate arbiter of political disputes. We believe that over the past decade it is possible to identify "withdrawal of support" at each of these levels.

cess because the ways in which media represent issues to the public in great part determine the reception that will be given to them: whether, for example, the public will perceive issues positively, negatively, or simply ignore them. In turn, the direction of this affect for the issues raised by a particular party and its candidates for office largely will determine their electoral success in a particular election.

The circumstances which existed as the 1979 election campaign began were significant because they were linked to issues which might have affected the level of political support for political authorities and the regime itself. The Liberal Party and its leader, Mr. Trudeau, were especially important in this regard. It has been argued that in the minds of many Canadians the Liberal Party is *the* "government party," that support for the government of Canada is positively correlated to support for the federal Liberals.[7] It also is argued that Mr. Trudeau's preeminent position in the party reflects "French power," a fact that can evoke either positive or negative reactions from members of the public, depending on their ethnicity and region of residence. For these reasons support for the federal regime and the "government of the day" were intertwined in 1979 and the media's coverage of the Liberal Party and its leader may well have spilled over to evaluations of regime.

As well, in 1979, the Parti Québécois government of Quebec was avowedly dedicated to altering the Canadian political community as then constituted. How the media in that province dealt with the interventions of the Parti Québécois and its leader René Lévesque in the federal election, and how various federal parties proposed to deal with the threat of Quebec separatism were even more directly relevant to regime and community support and may have had an impact on levels of public support for those objects, especially among francophones. Of course, media depictions of the issue of language, both in Quebec and the rest of the country, were separate but related matters which could have had a bearing on support. The energy question and the more general problem of provincial control of resources and how the media would represent these issues also could have dramatically affected the level of support for the federal government

7. Allan Kornberg, Harold D. Clarke, and Lawrence LeDuc, "Some Correlates of Regime Support in Canada," *British Journal of Political Science* 8 (1978): 199–216.

and—given the high salience and symbolic importance of these issues in the Western provinces—the regime as well. The possible revamping of the federal constitution raised even more basic questions about the balance of provincial and federal powers. Debate over this issue, and the media's characterization of that debate, also had the potential to affect support levels, as did the media's representation of the seemingly omnipresent issue of regionalism.

In summary, there is no question that during the 1979 federal election campaign there existed a potential for debate on fundamental issues which could have affected political support at the political authorities, regime, and community levels. The way in which the media reported and commented on these issues could have enhanced, detracted from, or failed to affect the level of public support. The findings that follow attempt to explicate the effects on the electorate the media may have had through their agenda-setting function.

Research Framework and Methods

The particular perspective on which this study is founded concerns a rethinking of the concepts of *gatekeeping* and *agenda-setting*—concepts of basic importance in political communication theory. Our perspective is illustrated in figure 6.1. This figure provides a schematic representation of the processes involved between the occurrence of an "event" somewhere in the world and the eventual response of people to it, say in Sydney, Nova Scotia, or Windsor, Ontario. Depending on the location and characteristics of the event, various mass media channels provide crucial links between it and how it is eventually perceived, if indeed it *is* perceived by the mass public. For purposes of analysis, this process may be broken down into two parts: (1) the process intervening between the occurrence and the media reporting of an event (where the event is the independent and the media output the dependent variable); and (2) the process intervening between the media reporting of an event and audience response to it (where the media output becomes the independent and audience response the dependent variable). The first of these processes is examined under the general rubric of *gatekeeping*, the second under that of *agenda-setting*.

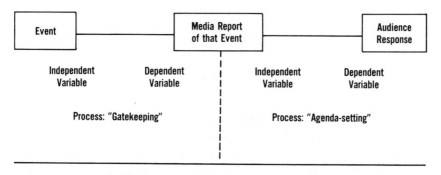

Figure 6.1. *The Media as Gatekeeper and Agenda-Setter*

Mass media research with respect to gatekeeping theory has tended to emphasize particular agents: persons in decision-making positions with regard to news content.[8] There is, however, no reason to suppose that gatekeeping is purely an individual function. Kurt Lewin, in his analysis of gatekeeping, observes that gates are controlled "either by impartial rules or by 'gatekeepers.'"[9] But if "impartial rules" may act as the control agent, then it seems reasonable to assume that there may be still other agents (organizations, for example), and, thus, that it may be useful to define gatekeeping in a broad, macro sense rather than the narrower, micro manner in which it has been interpreted in the journalism literature. Accordingly, gatekeepers may be redefined as any social institutions, contexts, or activities which have, as a consequence of their characteristics or behavior, the effect of modifying media content. It is in this extended definitional sense that we can best understand information movement and gatekeeping forces.

As shown in figure 6.2 all media organizations operate within the context of a culture which constitutes their operational environment. Also, the five activities which are identified in the figure occur within

8. For pertinent examples of the gatekeeping concept, see Wilbur Schramm, "The Gatekeeper: A Memorandum," in *Mass Communications*, ed. Wilbur Schramm (Urbana: University of Illinois Press, 1972), p. 175; Walter Romanow, "The Study of Gatekeepers in Mass Media: A Stance for the Mass Media Critic" (unpublished paper, University of Windsor, 1974); and David Manning White, "The Gatekeeper: A Study in the Selection of News," *Journalism Quarterly* 26 (1950): 394.

9. Kurt Lewin, "Psychological Ecology," in *Field Theory in Social Science*, ed. Dorwin Cartwright (New York: Harper and Bros., 1951), p. 186.

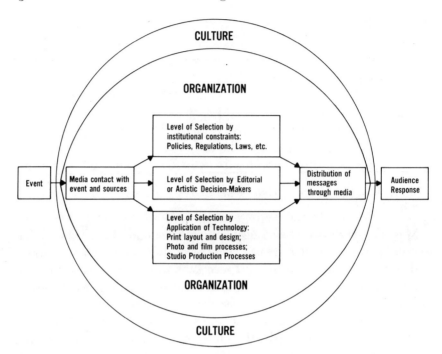

Figure 6.2. *Forces Influencing the Media's Role in the Gatekeeping Process*

a more limited context provided by a particular media organization. Thus, both culture and media organization can be regarded as factors which operate through particular media activities to produce specific outputs. Looked at another way, the cultural environment and organizational context are the macro-gatekeepers, while activities are undertaken within these environments by individuals who constitute the micro-gatekeepers.

Media output is assumed to have an effect and to elicit a response from listeners and viewers. Over the years a number of contending explanations of media effects on audiences have been posited by social scientists.[10] One of these is agenda-setting. According to Donald L. Shaw and Maxwell E. McCombs, "This impact of the mass

10. A summary of these theories is contained in Melvin L. DeFleur, *Theories of Mass Communication* (New York: David McKay, 1968), chap. 7.

media—the ability to effect cognitive change among individuals, to structure their thinking—has been labeled the agenda-setting function of mass communication. Here may lie the most important effect of mass communication, its ability to mentally order and organize our world for us."[11] If we accept the proposition that agenda-setting is a viable interpretation of media impact, then it makes sense to examine radio and television news content, especially where particular themes are selected for prominence in the course of an election.

The preceding discussion has been cast in general terms and encompasses the view that a wide variety of social, technological, and organizational processes, as well as individuals, contribute to the gatekeeping and agenda-setting functions. In the following discussion two macro-gates are examined for their effects on the election information passing through them. The first of these gates is the organizational one, made operational primarily in terms of the television or radio network transmitting the news, and, secondarily, in terms of type (i.e., radio or television). The second gate is culture which, in this discussion, is equated with language, since in Canada linguistic considerations are often equated with cultural survival. In this regard, it is widely hypothesized in media literature that French and English media systems project different agendas to their listening and viewing publics.[12]

The primary research method employed in the study is content analysis. Four major television and two radio networks were studied: CBC-French Television, CBC-English Television, Global Television, and Canadian Television Network (CTV), plus Radio-Canada (the French CBC radio network), and the CBC-English radio network. Beginning March 27, 1979, the day the election was called, and continuing through May 21, the day before the actual election, the major daily newscasts of these several networks were video- and audio-recorded. The recordings then were systematically analyzed for the-

11. Donald L. Shaw and Maxwell E. McCombs, *The Emergence of American Political Issues: The Agenda-Setting Function of the Press* (St. Paul, Minn.: West Publishing Co., 1977), p. 5. (Emphasis is in the original.)

12. See, in this regard, Frederick Elkin, "Communications Media and Identity Formation in Canada," in *Communications in Canadian Society*, ed. Benjamin Singer (Toronto: Copp Clark Publishing Company, 1972), pp. 222–23; Arthur Siegel, "Canadian Newspaper Coverage of the F.L.Q. Crisis: A Study of the Impact of the Press on Politics" (unpublished Ph.D. dissertation, McGill University, 1974); and Arthur Siegel, "French and English Broadcasting in Canada: A Political Evaluation," *Canadian Journal of Communications* 5 (1979): 1–17.

matic content and for evaluative material on political parties and
party leaders. Other variables, such as placement in the broadcasts
and time devoted to each story, also were measured. Stories rarely
were unidimensional, and, therefore, each theme appearing in a particular story was coded.[13] The resulting data set contains 1,758 electoral stories representing the following percentages of total news
items for each network: CBC-French television, 36 percent; CBC-
English television, 27 percent; Global television, 35 percent; CTV,
31 percent; Radio-Canada, 35 percent; and CBC-English radio, 29
percent. Overall, 32 percent of all news stories monitored focused on
the election.

Agenda-setting theory is based on the idea that by selection and
presentation of material the media can "structure our world for us."[14]
Accordingly, the concept of media salience is made operational in two
ways. The first is frequency of mention, the number of times stories
featuring particular issues and political parties were run. The second
is the placement of stories containing these major themes in the sequence of the newscast.[15]

Findings

Data in table 6.1 show the emphasis accorded the ten major campaign issues by the six separate media organizations.[16] Leaders and
leadership are a natural and inevitable focus of election campaign
commentary. Given the variety of forms in which such commentary
may appear—reportorial analysis, criticism of one leader by repre-

13. Intercoder reliability was established at 83.7 using the formula C.R. $= 2M/(N_1 + N_2)$.
See Ole Holsti, *Content Analysis for the Social Sciences and Humanities* (Reading, Mass.:
Addison-Wesley, 1969), p. 140.

14. Lee Becker, Maxwell E. McCombs, and Jack McLeod, "Development of Political Cogni-
tions," in *Political Communications Issues and Strategies for Research*, ed. Steven Chafee (Beverly Hills: Sage Publications, 1975), p. 38.

15. It must be emphasized that the data presented here do not represent the total campaign
dialogue. Nor do they purport to reveal what particular parties or Canadians in general thought
was important during the campaign. The data represent what these six media organizations selected from an entire day's campaign activity for presentation in capsule form in their major
newscasts. That information which passed through the various gates became the networks' campaign agendas.

16. As a corporate entity, the Canadian Broadcasting Corporation is made operational as four
basic network activities: CBC-English Radio; CBC-French Radio; CBC-English Television;
CBC-French Television.

Table 6.1. *Percentages of Electoral Stories Dealing with Major Campaign Issues by TV and Radio Networks (with rank order)*[a]

	Television network								Radio network			
	CBC/FR (N=322)		CBC/ENG (N=306)		Global (N=345)		CTV (N=259)		Radio-Canada (N=266)		CBC Radio (N=260)	
Campaign issue	%	R/O	%	R/O	%	R/O	%	R/O	%	R/O	%	R/O
National unity	22	(2)	24	(1)	14	(3)	22	(2)	16	(2)	15	(1)
Quebec separatism	19	(3)	13	(5)	10	(5)	10	(6)	15	(3)	10	(6)
Federal-provincial relations	13	(5)	9	(9)	6	(8)	6	(9)	8	(5)	13	(3)
Inflation	7	(8)	19	(3)	16	(2)	17	(3)	9	(4)	10	(6)
Unemployment	11	(6)	14	(4)	9	(7)	12	(4)	8	(7)	12	(4)
Tax reform (including mortgage interest plans)	5	(10)	11	(7)	11	(4)	8	(7)	2	(10)	6	(8)
Domestic gas & oil policy (including Petro Can)	9	(7)	12	(6)	9	(6)	7	(8)	8	(6)	10	(5)
Economic development	15	(4)	10	(8)	4	(10)	6	(9)	6	(8)	4	(10)
Leadership	27	(1)	23	(2)	22	(1)	28	(1)	18	(1)	14	(2)
Television debate	6	(9)	6	(10)	5	(9)	10	(5)	5	(9)	4	(9)

a. For ease of presentation, percentages are rounded to whole numbers. Rank-orders based on percentages are correct to one decimal place.

sentatives of other parties, exposition of the virtues of one's own leader—it is not surprising to find the issue among the most prominent. National unity, however, is another matter. The fact that national unity clearly outranked a host of competitive economic issues (though some of these also were among the ten most salient) underscores its special significance in this campaign. The point is further emphasized by the fact that a number of issues which, by virtue of their continuing importance in Canadian society, could reasonably have been expected to receive considerable attention, in fact, were not prominent on the agendas of the electronic media. Among such concerns were agricultural and transportation policy as well as Canadian-American relations. In contrast, the television debate among the leaders of the major parties received substantial coverage. (On the CTV agenda, for example, it was accorded fifth place overall.) The debate, proposed by the television networks, was a media-generated event, relevant to the leadership issue more than to anything else.

Data in table 6.2 show the percentage of electoral stories dealing with the major parties involved in the campaign. The most striking

Table 6.2. *Percentages of Electoral Stories Dealing with Major Parties by TV and Radio Networks*

Party	Television network				Radio network	
	CBC/FR (N=322)	CBC/ENG (N=306)	Global (N=345)	CTV (N=259)	Radio-Canada (N=266)	CBC Radio (N=260)
Liberal	52	51	56	56	43	42
PC	42	43	47	46	33	32
NDP	27	33	31	29	23	29
SC/RC	24	7	4	6	20	6
PQ[a]	12	6	4	4	5	6

a. The provincial governing party of Quebec whose views and attitudes on national unity and Quebec separatism may have influenced the campaign.

feature of this table is the remarkable consistency in the level of attention paid the respective parties by the several media organizations. From each of these organizations the governing Liberal party received the greatest attention, followed by the Progressive Conservatives, with the percentage difference between them being about 10 percent in each case. The New Democratic party, the third largest party in Parliament, always followed the PCs in the rank orders, being mentioned about 10–15 percent less frequently by all of the networks except CBC radio.

An interesting organizational variation is the amount of attention paid the Parti Québécois by the CBC-French television network as opposed to all other media organizations, especially Radio-Canada. This finding juxtaposes the two major media gates. Here is a variation which is clearly related to organization, where, given the governing status of the Parti Québécois in Quebec, a consistency based on language might have been hypothesized.

Table 6.3 provides the basis for investigating the impact which language, culture, and organization have on agenda-setting. The table presents Spearman rank-order correlations among all the organizational agendas found in table 6.1. All the correlations are positive, the two highest (0.84 and 0.82) being those between CBC-French television and Radio-Canada and between CBC-English television and Global TV. The lowest (0.25) is between CBC-French television and Global TV. If the data are grouped by media type, thus producing composite television and radio agendas, the rank-order correlations

Table 6.3. *Spearman Rank-Order Correlations between TV and Radio Network Agendas*

	CBC ENG	Global	CTV	Radio-Canada	CBC/ENG Radio
CBC/FR	0.53	0.25	0.36	0.84	0.59
CBC/ENG	—	0.82	0.80	0.52	0.68
GLOBAL	—	—	0.74	0.62	0.56
CTV	—	—	—	0.59	0.55
Radio-Canada	—	—	—	—	0.79

between these agendas is 0.72. If, on the other hand, the data are grouped according to language of transmission, the correlation between the English and French agendas is only 0.49. We may infer from this analysis that both organizational and cultural gates were kept open to a broadly similar range of issues and that issues passing through one gate were not subjected to significant blockage by the other. Thus, it can be argued that there was an "electronic media agenda" in the 1979 Canadian election,[17] whose significance for political support will be explored shortly.

The existence of an electronic media agenda does not preclude linguistic-cultural and/or media type variations. With regard to the former, a number of instances of marked dissimilarity were evident. Quebec separatism, as might be expected, was an issue which received greater attention in French-language media. Other issues seemingly affected by language-culture were tax reform, inflation, federal-provincial relations, and economic development. However, on coverage of the Parti Québécois, (where one might have expected linguistic-cultural similarity) Radio-Canada's coverage of the PQ was closer to the English-language media than it was to CBC-French television. The linguistic-cultural gate seemed to be most active in filtering out material on the NDP, while paying relatively frequent attention to the Ralliement de Créditistes, a party which was an electoral contender only in Quebec.

A comparison of radio and television coverage of the campaign reveals that the overall rank-order correlation between the composite

17. Differences between the electronic media and print media in election coverage are examined elsewhere by the authors as a separate study which includes campaign coverage data for twenty-three newspapers, representing every province and both major language groups.

agendas is quite high. With respect to issues, radio paid more attention to federal-provincial relations and less to tax reform than did television. What is most clear from the data, however, is that in the aggregate the percentages of stories dealing with nearly all of the major
parties and issues in the campaign were noticeably smaller on radio
than on television. For example, television ran approximately 10 percent more stories featuring the two major political parties than did
radio. Similarly, television news also featured more stories than did
radio on leading issues such as national unity, leadership, and inflation.

In addition to the frequency of mention of particular issues during
the course of the campaign, the place accorded them in program sequence is an additional variable which sheds some light on the concept of agenda-setting. To examine the sequencing of issues in programs we will focus on the numbers and percentages of news stories
dealing with a particular theme which appear in the lead position,
and positions 2 through 4 in the news broadcasts. Looking at the
number and percentages of lead stories which deal with major parties, there is clearly less unanimity than was evident in the analysis of
the total number of stories on each party (table 6.2). Specifically,
while CTV had fewer news items dealing with the PCs than with the
Liberals, a slightly higher percentage of the PC items was accorded
lead story status (data not shown in tabular form). Similarly, even
though the magnitude of difference is small, both the CBC-English
television and radio networks slotted a larger percentage of NDP than
PC stories into the lead position. Some interesting modifications in
the rank-order data can be observed if we examine specific issues. For
example, while it was pointed out that the French-language agenda
gave greater prominence to the issues of Quebec separatism, federal-
provincial relations, and economic development, there is no evidence
of an attempt to highlight these issues by placing them first in the
news program.

The difference between measuring the media salience by rank-
ordering the frequency of mention as opposed to the placement of
stories in newscasts is best illustrated by examining CTV's treatment
of the leadership and domestic gas and oil policy issues. Using the
rank-order measure, leadership had first place on CTV's agenda, with
seventy-five total stories. However, only seven of these (10 percent)
were lead stories. In contrast, domestic gas and oil policy merited

only eighteen total stories but five of them (28 percent) led off the newscasts. A similar pattern is evident in Global's treatment of the leadership and federal-provincial relations issues.

While this study focuses on agenda-setting, it is apparent that in setting their agendas networks are either unable or unwilling to avoid portraying leaders and parties favorably or unfavorably. By so doing they may have a direct bearing on the degree of support the public ascribes to parties, their leaders, perhaps even the regime itself. In terms of coding criteria, stories were judged as either positive or negative only when they were *obviously* favorable or unfavorable to a party, its policies, or its representatives.

Table 6.4, which shows the percentage of stories that included comments on major party leaders, reveals that the commentary pertaining to Mr. Trudeau and Mr. Clark tended to be negative rather than positive. This tendency is less pronounced in radio than television coverage. It must be remembered that the percentages cited here refer to total stories (e.g., CBC-French, $N = 322$). If one refers to table 6.1, it will be seen that stories including leadership themes account for between 14 and 28 percent of all stories. Thus, the percentages shown in Table 6.4 represent a significant proportion of stories with leadership themes. For Mr. Trudeau, the percentage of negatively oriented stories ranged from a low of 3 percent on Radio-Canada to a high of 11 percent on the CBC-French television network. For Mr. Clark, the range was from 4 percent (Radio-Canada) to

Table 6.4. *Percentages of Electoral Stories Reflecting Positively or Negatively on Major Party Leaders by TV and Radio Networks*

	Television network								Radio network			
	CBC/FR (N=322)		CBC/ENG (N=306)		Global (N=345)		CTV (N=259)		Radio-Canada (N=266)		CBC/ENG Radio (N=260)	
	Pos	Neg	Pos	Neg	Pos	Neg	Pos	Neg	Pos	Neg	Pos	Neg
Trudeau (LIB)	3	11	3	10	4	7	4	9	2	3	2	5
Clark (PC)	2	7	3	8	1	6	2	13	2	4	2	4
Broadbent (NDP)	1	2	1	2	2	a	4	2	2	a	2	a
Roy (SC/RC)	1	1	1	1	0	1	a	a	a	0	0	0
Lévesque (PQ)	0	1	0	1	a	a	0	a	0	0	0	0

a. $\geq$ 0 but < 0.5%.

13 percent (CTV). In contrast, the percentage of positively oriented stories on Mr. Trudeau varied from a low of 3 percent on both radio networks to a high of 4 percent on CTV. Mr. Clark enjoyed his most favorable treatment (3 percent) at the hands of CBC-English television; the least favorable (1 percent) was Global's coverage. Mr. Broadbent, although receiving less coverage overall (and therefore less salient in terms of agenda-setting theory), was the object of more positive than negative commentary on the CBC television networks. Similarly, CTV accorded him both the most positive and the most negative treatment (4 percent and 2 percent, respectively). Fabien Roy and René Lévesque were the subjects of very little evaluative commentary. In summary, it is evident that the leaders of the two major parties were, on balance, unfavorably represented by all six media organizations. Only NDP leader Edward Broadbent received more positive than negative comments, but, overall, there were fewer references to him than to Trudeau and Clark. The two French-language networks provided the most and least favorable coverage of Mr. Trudeau, indicating there was no common linguistic position on the Liberal leader.

In the material they broadcast on the major parties, the six media organizations cast them both—government and electoral alternative alike—in a negative light (see table 6.5). Interestingly, only the NDP was cast in a positive light more often than in a negative one by all six organizations. Considering the treatment of various parties by particular media, the CBC-English television network was most negative toward the Liberals with 17 percent of its total stories being negative in tone. Radio-Canada was second with 16 percent negative. The Liberals fared best on CTV; 9 percent of the stories were positive in nature. Even on this network, however, 12 percent of the stories dealing with the Liberals were negative. The Conservatives were treated unfavorably in 12 percent of CTV stories, while its most positive treatment came from Global (8 percent). However, the latter network also represented the PCs unfavorably in 10 percent of its stories. CBC-English television accorded the NDP both its most positive and negative treatments, 7 and 4 percent, respectively. Finally, it should be noted that there do not appear to be language-culture differences in the amount of positive and negative coverage devoted to the several parties.

Table 6.5. *Percentages of Electoral Stories Reflecting Positively or Negatively on Major Parties, Their Policies, or Personnel by TV and Radio Networks*

	Television network								Radio network			
	CBC/FR (N=322)		CBC/ENG (N=306)		Global (N=345)		CTV (N=259)		Radio-Canada (N=266)		CBC/ENG Radio (N=260)	
	Pos	Neg	Pos	Neg	Pos	Neg	Pos	Neg	Pos	Neg	Pos	Neg
Liberal	5	14	6	17	6	15	9	12	2	16	5	14
PC	2	9	8	11	8	10	7	12	5	9	5	5
NDP	2	1	7	4	4	3	7	3	5	2	5	2
SC/RC	1	1	1	2	0	3	a	1	1	1	0	0
PQ	a	1	0	1	0	3	a	2	a	1	0	2

a. ≥ 0 but < 0.5%.

Media Coverage of Elections and Political Support: Conclusions

An election is a manifestation of the support process in a democratic political system. The manner in which an election campaign is reported by the electronic media must therefore be accorded some significance in this process. It is notable, therefore, that—notwithstanding some obvious differences between the French-language and English-language agendas—the data presented above support the view that there exists a national electronic media agenda, with what might be called a French variation thereon. Perhaps particularly significant in this regard was the finding that when evaluating the major parties and their leaders, all the networks shared a common, critical orientation. It can be argued that the existence of such a national political agenda tends to promote a common conception of the problems facing the community—thus serving as an agent of national integration. This is true even across linguistic barriers, although to a lesser extent. If Canadians in different parts of the country are being presented with a basically consistent agenda of the problems faced by their national community, they at least have a common view of what should concern them, even if they have widely different regional or linguistic attitudes about viable solutions to these problems. It is at least plausible that this is preferable, in terms of heightening community support, to the continuance of two or more "media solitudes" which de facto inhibit intergroup communications processes.

Donald Smiley has observed that prior to 1960 a variety of factors including "institutional self-segregation" and "mediation at the summit" combined to provide for a stable French-English relationship.[18] In these circumstances a common national media agenda was neither likely, necessary, nor perhaps even conducive to the maintenance of the Canadian polity. After 1960, however, the oft-repeated question "What does Quebec want?" bore testimony to the degree to which persons outside of Quebec were ignorant of the aspirations of Québécois. By the time of the 1979 election, the electronic media at least were providing a picture of the disagreements and possible solutions to problems as they were perceived by politicians and citizens in different parts of the country. In the present context, where traditional elite accommodation and mass segregation patterns of consociational democracy appear to have broken down, it seems preferable—in terms of long-term support for the existence of a political community called Canada—that we have a relatively common agenda, even if that agenda itself generates controversy.

Although the media may have facilitated support for the national political community, the negative balance in the coverage of the major parties and their leaders suggests they may have eroded public support for political authorities. No attempt is made here to establish a direct link between media coverage and audience attitudes, but it does seem reasonable to assume that if the public is at all influenced by media evaluations, it could scarcely have avoided formulating negative opinions about both the Liberals and Conservatives, the two parties with a realistic chance of forming a government. The relationship between support for political authorities, particularly the Liberals and Trudeau, and support for the regime is suggested by the bitter reaction in the west to the reelection of the Liberals in 1980. Not only were many upset by the results per se, there also was widespread anger with an electoral system that enabled the east to foist an unwanted government on the west, one in which westerners felt almost totally unrepresented.

It can be inferred from the performance of the electronic media in the 1979 election that individual Canadians receiving their news from

18. Donald Smiley, *Canada in Question*, 2nd ed. (Toronto: McGraw-Hill Ryerson, 1976), pp. 163–68.

different media organizations (from radio or television, in French or in English), were presented with basically similar pictures of the campaign. The reasons for this homogeneity are not readily apparent, nor is there a universally accepted answer to the question of whether, aside from the contribution to national integration, it should be a cause for satisfaction or concern. Regarding similarities in media coverage, three potential explanations may be adduced: (1) collusion between the various networks (the authors rule this out); (2) a manifestation of the kind of "pack journalism" described by Timothy Crouse in his book on the 1972 American presidential campaign,[19] and detected by Clive Cocking in his treatment of the 1979 Canadian campaign;[20] and (3) the major party campaign strategies of stressing various issues and leaders were more or less successful, in that the national electronic press faithfully reported what the politicians were saying rather than highlighting rival "press agendas" for the election.

Whatever the explanation, the fact that the electronic media presented voters with basically similar agendas has both advantages and disadvantages. Certainly, it is not surprising that politicians and political parties highlight issues they believe will win for them and studiously avoid those seen as problematic. Insofar as the media's role is concerned, it can be argued, on the one hand, that during an election they have the responsibility of providing coverage of those issues and problems the contending parties regard as most salient. It is not their business to structure an alternative agenda. In a properly functioning democracy it is the political parties which have the responsibility of governing (rather than the media) and they should be the arbiters of which issues need to be articulated. On the other hand, it also can be argued that the function of a free press (print and electronic) in a democracy is to educate citizens during an election campaign by putting hard questions to politicians and by reporting what is *not* as well as what *is* said. In this regard our research suggests that in their coverage of the 1979 election, with the exception of the negative portrayals of the Liberal and PC leaders, the electronic media in Canada were holding a fiddle for the parties, their leaders, and candidates to play, rather than attempting to call the tune for them.

19. Timothy Crouse, *The Boys on the Bus* (New York: Ballantine Books, 1974), pp. 7–15.
20. Clive Cocking, *Following the Leaders: A Media Watcher's Diary of Campaign '79* (Toronto: Doubleday, 1980), p. 106.

Of course, this type of election coverage can have advantages in a political community historically beset by ethno-linguistic and regional cleavages. There is no evidence any of the media made a deliberate effort to comply with the mandate of the Canadian Broadcast Act to promote the "national interest," or that the CBC networks overtly pursued their mandate of fostering national unity.[21] But the mere fact that the media tended to report the same set of basic issues and to evaluate the campaign in a relatively similar fashion meant that Canadians were presented with a unified picture of the political problems facing the country and of the policies and programs the several parties and politicians offered as possible solutions to them. As argued above, a significant secondary impact of this rather undifferentiated passage of information through media gates to the Canadian public could well be the enhancement of support for the national political community in all parts of the country.

As a more general conclusion, it bears reiterating that this study has argued that the gatekeeping process, and the news agenda which it produces, is not simply the result of conscious individual decisions of news gatherers and disseminators. Rather it is the end result of a very broad and inclusive system in which culture and institutional organization combine to provide a diffuse but nevertheless real framework in which some decisions are more likely than others. The behavior of electronic media in the 1979 election campaign does not provide a basis for discerning clear relationships between these macro-gates and the selection and portrayal of particular issues by the micro media gatekeepers. Nevertheless, it is clear that decisions by the latter heavily influence the quantity and quality of political information available to the Canadian electorate. Thus, the proposition that both voting behavior and elections as well as broader patterns of political support for the political regime and community are affected by the operation of the media gatekeepers remains an important hypothesis deserving closer scrutiny.

21. The Canadian broadcasting system is mandated in this manner: ". . . the Canadian broadcasting system should be effectively owned and controlled by Canadians so as to safeguard, enrich, and strengthen the cultural, political, social and economic fabric of Canada"; and, in the case of the Canadian Broadcasting Corporation, to "contribute to the development of national unity and provide for a continuing expression of Canadian identity." See Canada, *Broadcasting Act 1968* (Ottawa: Queen's Printer, 1978), Part I, 2(b) and (g).

On the Dangers of Bickering in a Federal State: Some Reflections on the Failure of the National Party System

John Wilson

"Our whole political machinery," Lord Balfour wrote in 1927, "pre-supposes a people so fundamentally at one that they can safely afford to bicker."[1] The parliamentary system may well thrive on the contest between government and opposition, but when the struggle becomes bound up with differences which go to the very root of a political community's existence the resolution of the conflict will likely require a degree of compromise which undermines the customary role of political parties in a properly functioning democratic system. And if the conflict turns on the competing claims of different parts of the country—as in the nature of the case it frequently will in a federal state—the resulting party struggle may destroy the effectiveness of parliamentary government altogether. In short, parliamentary government and federalism do not necessarily work well together.

It is not surprising, therefore, that several generations of observers have claimed a special role for the national party system in Canada. Beyond merely performing the primary functions of aggregating and articulating competing interests, our political parties, in John Meisel's words, "have a special role to play as agencies for the creation of national symbols, experiences, memories, heroes, and villains. . . . An absolutely critical latent function of the party system in Canada is . . . the role it plays in the development and fostering of a national politi-

---

1. Introduction to the World's Classics edition of Walter Bagehot's *The English Constitution* (London: 1928), p. xxiv.

cal culture."[2] In a political community such as Canada, where virtually no other institution generates the necessary support for the integrity of the system itself, only the party system can bring about the
degree of national reconciliation and integration which the continued
existence of the country requires. Nor is this view of the character
and purpose of the Canadian party system simply a product of the
post–World War II evolution of the federation. It can be found in
even the earliest accounts of the practice of Canadian politics. In 1906
André Siegfried recognized that the absence of ideological conflict in
the Canadian party system was due to the need to keep the country
together.[3] Lord Bryce advanced much the same argument a decade
later,[4] and the view that Canadian political parties have no alternative
but to suppress the pursuit of political principle in deference to the
higher goal of maintaining national unity has remained the central argument of virtually every account of the character of our system since
that time. The particular focus of each observer may be different, but
the ultimate conclusion is the same.

What these different commentaries represent, of course, is the
declaration for Canada of the necessity of the practice of brokerage in
our party politics. The case was most bluntly stated, perhaps, by
Frank Underhill in his famous 1950 essay in the *Canadian Forum* following the death of Mackenzie King:

Mr. King's leadership in domestic matters was based upon two fundamen-
tals. . . . One was that Canada cannot be governed without the consent and
cooperation of the French Canadians; and the other was that in a loosely knit
continental community like ours, with all its diverse interest-groups, a political party that aspires to the responsibility of government must not be a
class party but must be a loosely knit representative collection of voters from
all groups. . . . In other words, the federalism which is the essence of both
North American countries must be reflected in their political parties.[5]

To be sure, the idea that the practice of brokerage politics is absolutely necessary for the preservation of the Canadian union has not

2. John Meisel, "Recent Changes in Canadian Parties," in Hugh G. Thorburn, ed., *Party Politics in Canada*, 2nd ed. (Scarborough: Prentice-Hall, 1967), p. 34.
3. See the often-quoted passage in his *The Race Question in Canada*, ed. F. H. Underhill (Toronto: McClelland and Stewart, 1966), pp. 113–14.
4. James Bryce, *Modern Democracies* (London: Macmillan, 1921), pp. 524–28.
5. "Concerning Mr. King," reprinted in F. H. Underhill, *In Search of Canadian Liberalism* (Toronto: University of Toronto Press, 1960), p. 136.

been without its critics, but Canadian political parties—including, in more recent years, even the New Democratic party—have nonetheless assiduously sought to avoid any kind of conflict which might divide the nation in an ideological way and have instead developed appeals designed to please every sector and every interest. The difficulty is, of course, that this strategy has not worked.

Viewed from the perspective of the beginning of the 1980s, the Canadian party system is more badly divided on a regional basis than at almost any time since Confederation. It is not simply that the Liberals have no elected members of Parliament west of Winnipeg, or that the Conservatives have been reduced to one elected member in Quebec, or that the NDP has no representation at all east of Oshawa. Rather it is the case that each of the parties gets very little voter support in each of these regions. The Conservatives—with just under 13 percent of the vote in Quebec in 1980—are at their lowest level of support in that province since Confederation (with the single exception of the election of 1945 when they won fractionally over 8 percent of the vote there). The Liberals are only marginally better off in the Western provinces than they were in 1979, and in either case have less support than at any time since the 1921 election (leaving aside the Diefenbaker sweep of 1958). The NDP has substantially improved its position in the west but, even with the help of a revised Elections Act that provides for a massive infusion of public funds into its campaign, the party remains unable to make significant inroads in Ontario. Except for its traditional support base in Cape Breton Island, it remains very much on the fringe in Atlantic Canada. Today, no party can fairly claim to speak for the country as a whole.

To make matters worse, it does not appear that anything can be done to rectify the situation. The cry for electoral reform which followed hard on the heels of the 1980 election made much of the fact that despite the parliamentary results there *were* Liberal voters in the west, Conservative voters in Quebec, and NDP voters in Atlantic Canada, suggesting that a carefully designed system of proportional representation would resolve the problem and contribute to the maintenance of national unity and the traditional role of the parties as brokers between the competing interests of the regions. What was not noticed, however, was that virtually every scheme which was proposed—including even the very peculiar plan recommended by the

Task Force on Canadian Unity[6]—would have done little more than
enable Mr. Trudeau to create a cabinet drawn entirely from the House
of Commons with representatives from every province. It remains
the case that in the west the Liberals are very much a third party
while in Quebec only the Liberals have an even remotely respectable
level of voter support. In short, if the role of the national party system
is to promote national integration and minimize the impact of regional variation in Canada it is difficult to avoid the conclusion that
the system has failed.

Such a judgment holds out very little hope for the future well-being
of Canada. For if it is true that no other institutions are able to generate the necessary support for the national system, and if the party system can no longer do the job, there can be little prospect at any time
in the foreseeable future of an amicable resolution of the regional conflict which now wracks the country. There are, however, a number of
very good reasons for supposing that such a judgment is not only premature but founded on an analysis of the nature of party competition
and voter support in Canada which is at the very least misguided, if
not wildly wrong.

The Conventional Wisdom

Apart from setting out the traditional prescription for the behavior
of our national parties (sometimes the commitment to the necessity of
brokerage politics is only implicit but it is invariably there) most modern analyses of the character of Canada's national party system have
been preoccupied with explaining the apparent peculiarity that we
have had more than two electorally successful parties at the national
level for a quite considerable period of time. The reasons given vary
all the way from Leon Epstein's attempt to demonstrate the unsuit-
ability of parliamentary government—with its rigid party divisions in
the legislature—in a federation where regional demands require special attention,[7] to accounts of the several different kinds of cleavages

6. Task Force on Canadian Unity, *A Future Together: Observations and Recommendations*
(Ottawa: Minister of Supply and Services, 1979), pp. 105–6. The scheme is fully explained in
William P. Irvine, *Does Canada Need a New Electoral System?* (Kingston: Queen's University,
Institute of Intergovernmental Relations, 1979), pp. 64–67.

7. Leon D. Epstein, "A Comparative Study of Canadian Parties," *American Political Science
Review* 48 (1964): 46–59.

in the electorate which are said to cause a national pattern of party support only intermittently able to provide an overall parliamentary majority for any one party.[8] Specific sectors of the country—not particular provinces at all, but rather only certain parts of some provinces such as Northern Ontario or Cape Breton Island or the lower mainland of British Columbia—have been willing to support parties other than the Liberals or the Conservatives, apparently for reasons which are associated with the character of these places.

There is, of course, disagreement about which cleavage is the most important in determining these varying results. As a general rule, the class cleavage has not been considered very significant, although it is usually conceded that it may have some role to play in certain parts of the country. Equally, the geographic cleavage—whether cast in terms of central Canada against the periphery or rich provinces against the poor—has not found much support even though it is generally regarded as more important than the class cleavage.[9] But by far the most common explanation of the character of the Canadian system depends upon what might loosely be called the cultural cleavage— French against English, Catholic against Protestant, or specific partisan support due to other ethnic and religious divisions in the population—and here it is usually argued that the varying patterns of party support across the country can be attributed primarily to varying concentrations of these different groups in the electorate.

For some observers the cultural cleavage is all that matters, but others have combined it with the effect of other cleavages in trying to account for our behavior. Some years ago, for example, after a detailed statistical analysis of both aggregate and survey data Jean Laponce concluded that "the Conservatives are rich and Protestant, the Liberals are Catholic and French, the NDP is working class and Protestant. Canada is thus no exception among western industrial nations. Its party system is organized around the usual regional, religious, and social class oppositions to which is added a specific linguistic cleavage."[10] The difficulty is that such a conclusion is simply not true. If

8. For a general discussion see John Meisel, *Cleavages, Parties and Values in Canada* (Beverly Hills: Sage Professional Papers in Contemporary Political Sociology, 1974).

9. See Douglas McCready and Conrad Winn, "Geographic Cleavage: Core vs. Periphery," in C. Winn and J. McMenemy, eds., *Political Parties in Canada* (Toronto: McGraw-Hill Ryerson, 1976), pp. 71–88.

10. Jean Laponce, "Post-dicting Electoral Cleavages in Canadian Federal Elections, 1949–1968: Material for a Footnote," *Canadian Journal of Political Science* 5 (1972): 284.

this description of the characteristics of Canadian party support may be taken as accurate (and in a general sense it likely is accurate) then Canada is *not at all* like other western industrial nations. In Great Britain, for example, there is general agreement that, of the many different factors which might affect the outcome of elections, social class has for many years had the most influential role.[11] The precise measurements may vary from election to election, but as a general rule roughly two-thirds of the working class votes Labour and four-fifths of the middle class votes Conservative, with the two parties frequently being of almost equal strength in total support. Even when the Liberal vote is as strong as it has been in recent years it comes more from the middle class than the working class and draws more heavily from the Conservatives than from Labour. Much the same kind of description of the social composition of party support, stressing the importance of social class, has usually been given for most other western industrial nations. The relationship may not always be as intense as it apparently is in Great Britain, but in both Australia and New Zealand, and generally throughout western and northern Europe, there seems to be little doubt about the dominant role which social class plays.[12] Even in the United States, where there is no national party which even remotely resembles the British Labour party (or the various continental and Commonwealth parties of like mind) in its commitment to the ideals of social democracy, most studies have shown that a very substantial majority of the working class ordinarily votes for the Democratic party.[13] In presidential elections, of course, the relationship may be from time to time undercut by other factors, but it has generally been sufficient to ensure a Democratic majority in the House of Representatives.

The Canadian case, in other words, remains unique. Viewed from the national level there is no single social cleavage which explains the character of the party system.[14] Instead, there is a mixed bag of dif-

11. See, for example, David Butler and Donald Stokes, *Political Change in Canada*, 2nd college edition (New York: St. Martin's, 1976), chap. 4.

12. This is true even in countries where regionalism has an important role in the national system. See, for example, the collection of essays in Seymour M. Lipset and Stein Rokkan, eds., *Party Systems and Voter Alignments: Cross National Perspectives* (New York: The Free Press, 1967).

13. Marian D. Irish and James W. Prothro, *The Politics of American Democracy*, 3rd ed. (Englewood Cliffs: Prentice-Hall, 1965), pp. 177–78.

14. For further documentation of this observation based on a detailed analysis of data from the 1974 national election survey see Harold D. Clarke et al., *Political Choice in Canada* (Toronto: McGraw-Hill Ryerson, 1979), chap. 4.

ferent kinds of cleavages which appear to vary in strength from one part of the country to another to such an extent that for most observers the national parties have no other alternative but to play the broker's role of seeking to mediate between the many conflicting interests of the country. That is what may be called the conventional wisdom with respect to the character of the Canadian party system. There is no room for class politics in Canada simply because the addition of one more cleavage of that kind to a system already badly divided would almost certainly destroy the polity.

In fact, however, there are really *two* versions of the conventional wisdom. While they may appear to differ fundamentally in their respective analyses of the character and purpose of the Canadian party system, what they have in common is more revealing of the shortcomings of most contemporary accounts of what is happening to the Canadian political system as a whole.

If adherents of what I will call the "old" conventional wisdom regarding the Canadian party system—the traditional view that our national political parties must always be merely brokers between the conflicting interests of the country—now have to face the fact that brokerage politics does not appear to have prevented the development of severe regional divisions in the party system, their critics have no difficulty in isolating the cause of the problem. So far from being a mechanism for keeping the country together, the practice of brokerage politics, it is said, is itself responsible for the deep divisions which now confront us. Simply by pursuing the role of mediator between the competing cultural and regional sentiments each of the national parties has, by its example, encouraged Canadians to regard the things which divide them as more important than the things which unite them. Because the parties have continually sought to be all things to all people, so the argument runs, they have never seriously tried to create a better understanding throughout the country of the varying needs of its parts. They have, in short, put political expediency—winning the next election—ahead of national unity.

The critics of the brokerage theory, adherents of what I will call the "new" conventional wisdom, have made what is regarded in some quarters as a devastating case against the "old" conventional wisdom. The focus of the criticism varies, of course. For some the emphasis on personalities in politics to which the practice of brokerage inevitably leads—thereby undermining the practice of national parliamentary

government—is what is most objectionable.[15] For others it is the
failure to develop a more "creative politics." This is directly attributable to the fact that brokerage politics seeks to obscure social divisions which ought to be constructively harnessed to the operation of
the political system.[16] For still others what is most offensive is that the
brokerage theory masquerades as a nonideological set of prescriptions
for the behavior of Canadian political parties but is itself a doctrine
which almost exclusively serves the interests of the middle class.[17]
These variations aside, however, virtually all of the adherents of the
"new" conventional wisdom argue that greater ideological conflict between parties—stemming from party competition becoming more
openly based on social class divisions across the whole electorate—
would be more likely to unite the country than the continuing stress
which the brokerage theory places on other differences based on region, race, or religion. As Gad Horowitz has put it, "the promotion of
dissensus on class issues is a way of mitigating dissensus on many nonclass issues."[18] The two conventional wisdoms thus appear to be poles
apart in their perceptions of the capabilities of the party system as
well as in their prescriptions of the most appropriate kind of party
behavior for the promotion of national integration.

    But that is not the most important point of comparison between
them. Because *both* views approach the question from a *national*
perspective they miss the significance of a number of key facts about
the character of party competition in Canada, and as a consequence
we do not have the kind of understanding of how the system works
which might enable us to find a genuine solution to the problem of
national unity.

    We learn nothing, for example, about the forces at work in Cana-
dian politics from an analysis which attributes the multiplicity of parties to the combination of parliamentary government and federalism
(especially when Australia does not appear to have analogous difficulties) when most of the comparative evidence suggests that multi-
partyism *only* arises in parliamentary systems if there are social and

    15. John Wilson, "The Myth of Candidate Partisanship: The Case of Waterloo South," *Jour-*
nal of Canadian Studies 3 (1968): 21–23.
    16. John Porter, *The Vertical Mosaic* (Toronto: University of Toronto Press, 1965), p. 374.
    17. Gad Horowitz, "Toward the Democratic Class Struggle," *Journal of Canadian Studies* 1
(1966): 8–9.
    18. Ibid., p. 10.

economic forces, *not* institutions, loose in the country that are sufficiently strong to promote it. It simply is not good enough to conclude
that Canada has a "two-plus" party system,[19] and leave it at that without further exploration, when the fact is that such a party system is a
rarity in the democratic world. As a general rule one finds either
"pure" two-party systems (where the two leading parties share between themselves roughly 90 percent of the votes cast) or else clear
three-party systems (where no party contesting every possible seat
wins less than 20 to 25 percent of the vote). It is almost impossible to
find a system of the kind which has existed in Canada since 1921; and
where one can be found it invariably has only a comparatively brief
period of existence before disappearing.

We learn nothing from an analysis which says that for the foreseeable future Canada will have two fairly strong major parties and one
middling major party, along with the occasional minor party, and that
this kind of party competition is now to be regarded as "normal." We
need to know *why* this happens in Canada and nowhere else. It is not
enough to point to the existence of different regions, or to the many
conflicting interests in the country—French and English, Catholic
and Protestant, east and west, urban and rural, and so on—and to
conclude from these facts that brokerage politics is necessary at the
national level. These observations tell us nothing about the character
of the party system which would not be obvious to anyone who follows the national news on a regular basis.

Nor are we any more enlightened by what I have called the "new"
conventional wisdom—the very trenchant criticism of the brokerage
theory and its consequences which has appeared in recent years. No
doubt it is true that the practices of brokerage politics undermine
the quality of Canadian parliamentary democracy. It is equally true
that the conflicts which fragment the country are reinforced by the
traditional behavior of the parties, and it seems entirely probable that
in practice the brokerage theory has an insidious ideological character
of its own which precludes the development of a more "creative politics" based on confrontation between left and right. But the solution
which the adherents of the "new" conventional wisdom suggest, that
is, the development of class-bred party competition in the national

19. The phrase is Leon Epstein's.

system, assumes that large numbers of Canadian voters are ready and waiting to respond to that kind of political appeal.

In short, both conventional wisdoms assume that there is a kind of *uniformity* to the national party system; that leaving aside certain regional idiosyncracies people behave politically in much the same way wherever they are found in the country, and that all that is needed is a little more imaginative leadership from Ottawa and our problems will go away. And because they view the system from this national perspective, when the two conventional wisdoms are confronted with the hard facts of the contemporary degree of regional partisanship they have no alternative but to conclude that the party system has failed. For the "old" conventional wisdom it has become a "stalled omnibus"[20] no longer able to eliminate regional conflict by persuading all sectors that they are getting exactly what they want. The Liberals, we are told, do not understand western Canada, and the Conservatives do not understand the special circumstances of Quebec. For the "new" conventional wisdom, on the other hand, the party system has failed because it has approached the problem in the wrong way. In either case the prospects for Canada seem bleak.

But if it is recognized that neither of the conventional wisdoms has taken into account every aspect of what has been known for years about the Canadian political experience, and that both of them make the same questionable assumption about the character of party competition in Canada, it may be possible to demonstrate that the fault lies less with the national party system than with the conventional wisdoms' analyses of its purpose. It may be, in other words, that the national party system has been expected to do something which in the nature of the case cannot be done.

The Failure of the Conventional Wisdoms

If Canada may be regarded as a nation in any of the customary senses of that term, it would be reasonable to expect the national party system to perform in either of the ways prescribed by the con-

20. The phrase was coined by John Meisel from G. V. Ferguson's description of the differences between the Liberal and Conservative parties. See his "The Stalled Omnibus: Canadian Parties in the 1960's," *Social Research* 30 (1963): 367–90.

ventional wisdoms. If, for example, our people habitually regard themselves as Canadians, rather than Ontarians, or Nova Scotians, or Albertans, or whatever, or if there is an underlying kind of uniformity to our political behavior such that regional variations in party support can indeed be seen as nothing more than expressions of the idiosyncratic differences one expects to find in a pluralistic society, then the dispute between the two schools of thought would represent little more than the usual argument between left and right based on differing ideological perceptions of the purpose of political society. But if that is not the case, if Canada is not a nation in any of the customary senses of that term, then the conventional wisdoms' insistence on viewing the performance of the party system exclusively from a national perspective may be the real source of our inability to see a way out of the contemporary dilemma. For if there are regional loyalties which transcend commitment to the nation as a whole, or, even if that is not the case, if there are differences between the regions more fundamental than the "old" conventional wisdom would have us believe, it may be necessary to reverse our conception of what the national parties can contribute to the quest for national unity, if not also our conception of the character of the Canadian federation in the second half of the twentieth century.

It is no longer necessary, as it might have been ten years ago, to parade the evidence attesting to the strength of regional political differences.[21] But while few people would now claim that these differences are not worth recognizing, the conviction remains that they are not so very great that determined national leadership will not be able to overcome them and thereby develop a greater sense of national identity. In short, the conventional wisdom prevails, nicely illustrated, it may be observed, by Ottawa's proposal in the fall of 1980 to patriate the British North America Act, complete with an entrenched charter of rights binding on all of the provinces and an amending formula which would permit the federal government to appeal to the people over the heads of the provincial legislatures through the use of a national referendum.[22] These are not issues, however, which could

21. The literature of recent years has become far too extensive to summarize in a footnote, but a good recent discussion of the question can be found in the essays in David Elkins and Richard Simeon, eds., *Small Worlds: Provinces and Parties in Canadian Political Life* (Toronto: Methuen, 1980).

22. Gallup Polls taken during the summer of 1980, showing very substantial majorities across

be expected to reveal profound differences from region to region because they do not turn on varying perceptions of the most appropriate
solutions to pressing social and economic problems. But differences
in partisan support usually do depend on such varying perceptions, or
at least on differing assessments of the most important problems facing political society, derived from the varying significance attached to
specific social and economic interests. There is some reason to believe that the now very obvious regional political differences in Canada are linked to precisely these kinds of varying perceptions and that
the gulf between the different regions of the country goes beyond the
capacity of a single national party system to bridge it.

The point can be very easily demonstrated by a closer examination
of the assumptions made by the "new" conventional wisdom. On the
face of things it is probably true that class-based party competition
could contribute to the growth of greater national unity where emphasis on the things which divide us—such as race, religion, and region—cannot. There are social classes everywhere in the country and
it does not seem unreasonable to assume that they can be mobilized
to create an ideological contest between the parties which cuts across
regional divisions and therefore makes those divisions irrelevant. But
the assumption that class politics is capable of eliminating the significance of differences which have a regional focus depends for its validity on the prior assumption that *all* of Canada is ready for class politics. That may very well not be the case.

Some evidence now exists, based on analysis of the 1965, 1968, and
1974 national survey data, that Canada has several different political
cultures based in different regions.[23] Some years ago I sought to ex-

the country for many of Ottawa's proposed changes—for example, 91 percent in favor of guaranteeing "basic human rights to all Canadian citizens"—were frequently quoted in the debate as
proof of the wide support which existed for the federal government's initiative and the extent to
which the opposition of most provincial premiers was unrepresentative of popular opinion. Less
often quoted were Gallup Polls from the same period showing that 36 percent of the Canadian
people believed the provinces should have more power (compared to 20 percent favoring
greater power for Ottawa), or that 73 percent thought constitutional change should come about
by agreement of at least a majority of the eleven governments involved (within this group 26
percent wanted unanimous agreement) while only 8 percent approved of the federal government deciding such matters on its own.

23. See Richard Simeon and David Elkins, "Provincial Political Cultures in Canada," in their
Small Worlds, pp. 31–76. This is a revised and updated version of their "Regional Political Cultures in Canada," *Canadian Journal of Political Sciences* 7 (1974): 397–437.

plain that phenomenon by arguing that some parts of the country are more developed in their leading political values, and some less developed, precisely because these areas were also more (or less) developed in economic terms.[24] I do not want to go over that ground again, but since the original argument has been variously rejected as too ideological[25] or too lacking in acceptable empirical support[26] to merit serious consideration it may be useful to restate those points which bear directly on the question at hand—differences between the provincial party systems and what these can tell us about regional differences in general in Canada.[27]

One of the things which I tried to establish with that argument was the extent to which different parts of the country could be said to behave differently politically (leaving aside the question of attitudes and beliefs) because they were more (or less) advanced in terms of their economic development. No doubt it is difficult to accept the suggestion that Saskatchewan, for example, can be characterized as an industrially developed province, or that there is no significant difference in this respect between, let us say, the Atlantic provinces and Ontario, but even if it is said that too much can be made of these kinds of variations it is quite clear that there are different kinds of party systems operating in these provinces. These different party systems, however, are the outward evidence of qualitatively. different kinds of societies, that is, societies at different stages of economic development.

The relationship between these phenomena is illustrated in figure 7.1.[28] Put in its simplest possible terms, I have argued that the

24. "The Canadian Political Cultures: Towards a Redefinition of the Nature of the Canadian Political System," *Canadian Journal of Political Science* 7 (1974): 438–83.

25. Donald V. Smiley, *Canada in Question: Federalism in the Seventies*, 2nd ed. (Toronto: McGraw-Hill Ryerson, 1976), p. 226.

26. David Bell and Lorne Tepperman, *The Roots of Disunity: A Look at Canadian Political Culture* (Toronto: McClelland and Stewart, 1979), pp. 188–90.

27. I take it for granted that when we speak of regional variations of party support in Canada we are really speaking of provincially based variations. It is important to recognize for the argument which follows that I view each province as an independent society, for the reasons advanced in "The Canadian Political Cultures," pp. 439–44.

28. Figure 7.1 may be instructively compared with the diagram attempting to illustrate the same set of relationships in Bell and Tepperman, *The Roots of Disunity*, p. 191. The causal arrows are not in the same place because I regard *both* political culture and political behavior as caused by something else, and *neither* as causally related to the other. Moreover, the development will presumably continue into postindustrial society and beyond.

Table 7.1. *The Federal and Provincial Elections of 1945 in Ontario*

	Registered electorate	Nonvoters	Liberals	Conservatives	CCF	Others
Provincial election of June 4	2,469,960	704,167	526,433	781,345	395,708	62,307
Federal election of June 11	2,457,937	642,970	734,402	756,762	260,502	63,301
Change	−12,023	−61,197	+207,969	−24,583	−135,206	+994
Percentage share of registered electorate						
Provincial		28%	21	32	16	3
Federal		26	30	31	11	3
Change		−2	+9	−1	−5	0

particular character of any party system is dependent upon the underlying characteristics of the society's economy or, more specifically, the economic relationships among people which are supported and encouraged by those characteristics. Of course, those characteristics change over time, and as they do the party system itself will undergo changes. The pattern will be recognized by anyone familiar with the evolution of the party systems of western Europe over the past 150 years.

At the beginning of the nineteenth century there was no sign of anything remotely resembling a labor party anywhere in western Europe. The condition which generally gave rise there to the appearance and later political success of social democratic parties was the development of industrial society, and particularly those circumstances of such a society which promote the success of worker-oriented parties. Those circumstances are easily described. As the consequences of the growth of industrial society begin to spread across the whole face of the social system, people become more and more economically dependent on each other. Very few people in modern times have jobs where they are free to make their own decisions without reference to others. In fact, for by far the largest part of the population, economic well-being, or security in the search for economic well-being, depends upon decisions made by others. The leading characteristic of industrial society is that individuals do not control their own economic destiny in the way their ancestors did up to roughly the end of the eighteenth century. What these circumstances generally lead to is a very substantial increase in the willingness of many people to support a political party which aims to redress the balance between management and worker. Not everyone who is economically dependent will support such a party, of course, partly because many such people hope themselves one day to be on the other side and partly because many others regard the present balance of forces in the economic system as proper—even if they are often on the short end of it. In other words, with the rise of industrial society we generally also find the beginning of class politics. This is a perfectly normal reaction to the circumstances of a society where the things which are most important to people are not equally distributed among them.

The key point in understanding the contemporary Canadian situation, however, is the reverse of these observations. Working-class parties, that is, labor parties or social democratic parties, are not going to appear unless there are circumstances in existence to cause their appearance. Unless, in other words, there has been some development toward industrial society—and, specifically, the development of perceptions within that society which say that the degree of economic inequality usually associated with the rise of industrial society is wrong—there is not going to be in that society any support for class-based party competition. If this is the case, and if the Atlantic provinces, for example, are not as economically developed as the rest of Canada then it follows that there will not be any significant degree of support there for class-based party competition. Without the kind of development that characterizes the growth of industrial society and the different political values associated with that growth, there will be no need for class politics. And if provinces such as Quebec, Ontario, Manitoba, and British Columbia are only partly developed—not so much in economic terms as in the extent to which their people have developed political responses to these economic changes—then in these cases there will be only marginal support for the idea of class-based party competition. In other words, the solution which the critics of the brokerage theory, the adherents of the "new" conventional wisdom, have advanced as a mechanism for integrating the Canadian people and promoting greater national unity is not the least bit likely to work. There cannot be a *national* party system based on class politics if only *some* parts of the nation are interested in social class as a vehicle for political expression while the rest are not.

But if accepting the consequences of this analysis creates problems—perhaps because the argument linking changes in the character of party systems to different stages of economic development is difficult to accept on some more general philosophical ground— exactly the same conclusion may be reached simply by turning the reasoning around. It is quite clear that there is no significant support for the NDP in Atlantic Canada (apart, of course, from the isolated case of Cape Breton Island). Presumably that is because people there generally see no point in voting for the NDP. But the NDP is, explicitly, a class party. That is, it formulates its attitudes toward what should be done by governments in terms of an analysis of Canadian society which reflects concern with the weaknesses of industrial capitalism. We must therefore assume that the people of the Atlantic provinces generally see no point in voting NDP because they do not think that the party's approach is relevant to their circumstances. In other words, the people of Atlantic Canada are generally not interested in class politics.

However the argument is presented it seems quite clear that an insufficient number of people believe in class politics to make the idea that it could be a solution to the problem of national unity really rather misguided. The critics of the brokerage theory, even though they have found some very serious weaknesses in the reasoning of the "old" conventional wisdom, have therefore missed the essential characteristics of party competition in Canada simply because they have approached the question exclusively from a national perspective and have made no allowance for the seriousness of regional differences.

Moreover, if their advice were followed the political parties would very quickly demonstrate by their behavior that the "new" conventional wisdom will not only fail to solve the problem of national unity but will also perpetuate the practice of the older view. Because what would happen if the national parties did begin to compete with each other in class terms is that they would almost immediately run into the apparent lack of interest in class politics in Atlantic Canada, and into the relatively minor interest in it in Ontario and some other parts of the country. Because the parties are interested in maximizing the number of votes they can win in order to capture office they would simply not practice class politics in Atlantic Canada or in certain other parts of the country. Instead, they would appeal to people in these regions on other grounds, while still using the class appeal elsewhere. And if they did that, they would of course be doing exactly what the critics of the brokerage theory say is so shameful about its practice— they would be dividing the country by not dealing with it as a single nation but rather as a collection of regions with very different interests. They would, in short, be practicing brokerage politics. The "new" conventional wisdom, then, merely reinforces the "old" conventional wisdom.

That is not to say, however, that the older view provides a more satisfactory account of the character of party competition in Canada. The brokerage theorists themselves have also missed the point— because they also make the assumption that there is a national party system which has an underlying kind of uniformity in their terms. They assume that there are varying interests, only some of which are regionally based, that require the political struggle to be carried on in this way. No proponent of the brokerage theory has ever justified it on the ground that there is economic inequality in Canada—not inequality between regions, but inequality between people. Adherents of the "old" conventional wisdom have in fact always said that the things which divide us are religious differences, ethnic differences, and differences between the regions due to their natural circumstances. Ontario is rich, it is said, because she has access to tremendous hydroelectric resources and is close to the markets of the northeastern United States. Alberta has her oil and British Columbia her natural gas and her forest products. The brokerage theory has always claimed either that class differences do not exist in Canada or that if they do they should have nothing to do with politics.

But significant class differences *do* exist in the various parts of the Canadian party system. There is no doubt at all that there are parts of the country where class politics is practiced[29] with quite remarkable degrees of success (that is to say, without destroying the capacity of

29. Analysis of aggregate election results at the provincial level together with census data indicates that in parts of Ontario and Quebec, and more or less throughout British Columbia, Saskatchewan, and Manitoba, social class is an important determinant of the vote, while it appears to have very little effect in Alberta and Atlantic Canada. The number of cases outside Ontario and Quebec is usually too small in national surveys to test the relationship properly, but where they exist provincial surveys tend to confirm this view. See, for example, John Wilson

the society to carry on as a political community). If we fail to come to terms with that fact by failing to develop a view of the nature of party competition in the country which accounts for it, we cannot claim to have understood party politics in Canada at all. What is wrong, indeed, with the conventional views of the character of the Canadian party system can be stated very simply: the critics of the brokerage theory assume that there is a basis for class politics *everywhere*, while the brokerage theorists assume that class politics cannot be practiced *anywhere*. Thus, neither the "new" nor the "old" conventional wisdom provides an adequate explanation of the contemporary Canadian dilemma and we must look elsewhere for an answer.

The Significance of Regional Party Systems

The obvious alternative to the assumption that there is a single national party system in Canada in which everyone participates (either in the same way or in ways which vary only for purely local reasons) is the possibility that there are independent party systems operating in each of the provinces which have very little connection with each other. I have already developed the argument which supports this view elsewhere, drawing attention to the very different kinds of party systems which appeared to exist in the provinces in 1974.[30]

Although a number of changes have occurred in recent years, none of them has in any significant way altered the essential character of each system. The four Atlantic provinces continue as examples of rather less developed two-party systems with NDP strength in Nova Scotia still largely confined, as it has been since the 1930s, to Cape Breton Island.[31] In Quebec, the extraordinary success of the Parti Québécois (the first left nationalist party there which has not effec-

and Jo Surich, *Report to the Manitoba New Democratic Party on the Results of a Survey of Political Opinion in the Province* (Waterloo, 1973, mimeo), pp. 13–19.

30. "The Canadian Political Cultures," pp. 457–74. For an argument from a different perspective but which reaches similar conclusions see David Elkins, "The Structure of Provincial Party Systems," in Elkins and Simeon, eds., *Small Worlds*, pp. 211–41.

31. Even the sudden upsurge of NDP strength in Newfoundland in the 1979 federal election—resulting in the retention of the seat in Corner Brook won in a 1978 by-election—very quickly dissipated in 1980, suggesting that nothing of consequence had changed in that province.

tively disappeared at the next election after its first entry into provincial politics), together with the recovery of the Union Nationale
in 1976, suggests that a transitional phase in the party system is
well under way.[32] In Ontario, even though the clear three-party
system which has persisted there since the end of the Second World
War shows no sign of disappearing, there is some possibility that the
1975 and 1977 elections—both of which resulted in minority governments—may represent a new stage in the transitional phase.[33] And
although there has been a marked further decline in the strength of
the Liberal party in both Manitoba and British Columbia to the point
where both provinces effectively have two-party systems, it would be
premature without a good deal more evidence to claim that the transition has been completed in these cases. In short, the characterization of the provincial systems which seemed appropriate in the middle of the 1970s appears to be equally appropriate for the early 1980s.[34]
Even in the cases of Saskatchewan and Alberta, where developed
two-party systems (although of different kinds) were said to be operating, no change of consequence has occurred. All that has happened
in Saskatchewan is that the Conservative party has replaced the Liberal party as the principal opponent of the NDP, and in Alberta there
is still no sign that the system might in fact be merely entering the
transitional phase rather than having already completed it.[35]

Nor has the similarity within each province between federal and
provincial election results, in terms of the character of the party system itself rather than the leading competitors, changed at all. After a
careful analysis of federal and provincial results in this century up to
and including 1974 Richard Johnston concluded that

with the major exceptions of Quebec and British Columbia, the system has
done a better job of holding levels together within provinces than of holding

32. Given the collapse of the Union Nationale in the 1981 Quebec election it is possible that a
fundamental realignment is now taking place in that province of the kind one expects following
the transitional phase.

33. For a discussion of the factors which may force the transitional phase toward a conclusion—such as a prolonged diet of minority government—see John Wilson and David Hoffman,
"Ontario: A Three-Party System in Transition," in Martin Robin, ed., *Canadian Provincial Politics: The Party Systems of the Ten Provinces*, 1st ed. (Scarborough: Prentice-Hall, 1972),
pp. 236–37.

34. See table IV in "The Canadian Political Cultures," p. 474.

35. The likely validity of this alternative interpretation of the situation in Alberta is examined
briefly in footnote 48 in "The Canadian Political Cultures," p. 471.

provinces together within levels. In the old English-speaking provinces, dissimilarity between levels seems no more than should be expected of elections whose dates do not coincide. No dynamic seems to push levels apart for more than an election or two. Even the Prairie provinces seem to indicate the system's ability to integrate levels. While the interlevel differences beginning in 1958 persisted for some years, they now seem on a path to disappearance.[36]

But rather than being a commentary on the behavior of the national party system these remarks suggest that, in fact, there is no national party system at all. What we have instead is a collection of ten provincially based systems which by chance are called upon occasionally at the same time to render an electoral judgment.

That is, of course, precisely the conclusion to which an analysis based on developmental differences between the regions leads. The peculiarities which the conventional wisdom cannot explain—the existence of a "two-plus" party system at the national level, and widely varying results from region to region in virtually every federal election—are exactly what one would expect to find if all that happens every four or five years is that a number of undeveloped two-party systems, several transitional three-party systems, and at least one advanced two-party system which follows the British model are simply added together to produce a national result. If it is true that what we usually regard as exclusively provincial circumstances do, in fact, govern behavior in federal elections it should hardly be surprising that the result is inconclusive or regionally imbalanced. In other words, once it is understood that we can only make sense of it by looking through regional rather than national eyes, there is nothing at all peculiar about the character of the Canadian party system in comparison with other democratic systems.

That is not to suggest that Canada is not a nation at all, but rather that it is not a nation in the conventional sense of the term—where the attention of the people is focused on the national capital, where national rather than regional symbols dominate political experience, where people habitually attach greater importance to the things they

36. "Federal and Provincial Voting: Contemporary Patterns and Historical Evolution," in Elkins and Simeon, *Small Worlds*, p. 159. It is, of course, questionable whether Quebec (at least before 1970) and British Columbia are really exceptions, particularly if allowance is made for the very similar *functions* performed by parties with different names at each level. On this see "The Canadian Political Cultures," pp. 464–71.

have in common than to the things which divide them, and where there is a widely shared sense of having accomplished great things together in the past and an intention to do so together in the future. The forces which work to fragment the Canadian nation exist in almost every corner of our experience, and we should therefore expect that fragmentation to be reproduced in the party system.

Nor am I saying that we quite literally do not have a national party system. Very clearly we do. There are national leaders, candidates for office in the national parliament, regular national elections, and all the other characteristics ordinarily associated with political competition in a healthy democratic state. What I am saying, however, is that Canadians do not perceive themselves as operating at two different levels of political activity. They may distinguish between federal and provincial elections, but their behavior in each case can be seen more as a continuous process of political participation in an ongoing single system based in their province rather than as a deliberate rendering of a judgment which varies according to the context. Of necessity, therefore, overall federal election results are often inconclusive, because the motivations governing political behavior vary quite sharply from one part of the country to another. Canadian political behavior, in short, arises from conditions which exist in each province individually and not from conditions which exist in the country as a whole.

But if this is the case, the fact that Canada remains badly fragmented politically as we move through the last quarter of the twentieth century can hardly be said to be due to the failure of the national party system. That system cannot be expected to promote national integration if political behavior is governed to the extent I have suggested by exclusively provincial circumstances—and, indeed, circumstances which in many cases have very little connection from one province to another. On the other hand, if there is any reason to believe that residents of Ontario, or Alberta, or Newfoundland, or of any province, can set these sentiments aside at the time of a national election and make their voting decision within the context of a set of issues or, perhaps, party loyalties which transcend provincial boundaries, then there is at least a possibility not only that a national party system exists in Canada in a more fundamental sense but that it ought to be able to perform the integrative function.

On the face of things, of course, this is exactly what happens. It does appear to be the case that at least some of our people—estimates vary from province to province but for the country as a whole the figure may be as high as 30 percent of the electorate, depending on who is counted[37]—behave very differently in federal and provincial elections in their own area, leading to strikingly different rates of success for the parties in certain instances at different levels. In other words, it appears that many people do recognize the simultaneous existence of both a national and a provincial system where they live. The character of the party system at each level may be much the same, that is, underdeveloped two-party, transitional three-party, or developed two-party, but if many people switch their vote from one level to the other it must surely be the case either that they perceive themselves as having different interests depending on the context of the election, or that their interests cannot be served by the same party at both levels. In either case it seems likely that these people see themselves as actors in two different kinds of party systems—one which bears only on the circumstances of their province and one which goes beyond that to encompass the whole country.

Moreover, the mere fact that such people exist opens up the possibility that many others may think the same way even though they always vote for the same party in every election irrespective of the level. If that is the case there would be little ground for doubting the capacity of the national party system to promote a greater degree of national integration—if only because such perceptions on the part of voters would seriously undermine the importance which might otherwise be attached to political differences among the provinces. No doubt a proper resolution of the question would require a detailed examination of the contextual perceptions of all voters whether they change from one level to the other or not. At the same time, the fact that some people change their votes highlights the character of the problem in such a dramatic way that for the limited (and very conjectural) purpose at hand it may be sufficient to examine these cases alone. Without at least a better understanding of what causes partisan

37. Analysis of the interlevel changes reported in the 1965, 1968, and 1974 national surveys indicates that 32, 30, and 32 percent, respectively, of the national electorate voted differently in the provincial election immediately preceding the federal election being studied, although these figures include, again respectively, 14, 9, and 13 percent who said that they had not voted at one of the two levels. These data do not reflect cases where the respondent could not remember (or refused to say) how he or she had voted at one of the two levels.

shifts between federal and provincial elections, any attempt to sketch a broader canvas—to say nothing of speculation about the future of the country based on the idea that the provinces are at different stages of political development—would be premature.

Theories of Federal-Provincial Voting Change

Varying types of party success in federal and provincial elections are not a new thing in Canadian politics. For example, in the last century it was almost invariably the case that the Conservatives scored substantial victories in Ontario at the federal level, despite the fact that the Liberals remained in office at Queen's Park continuously from 1871 to 1905. Such changes were, apparently, regarded as perfectly natural responses to the leading issues of the day. One political commentator of the time, accounting for the results of the 1878 federal and 1879 provincial elections in the province, asserted that: "It was Reform votes that gave Ontario to Sir John A. Macdonald, last September, by a majority of 66 against 22. Protection being secured, Ontario Reformers came back to their party allegiance and sustained Mr. Mowat by 58 to 30."[38] It was taken for granted that regional sentiments existed which would lead, from time to time, to sharply different electoral results at different levels in each province, and these were evidently seen as nothing more than confirmation of the wisdom of the Fathers of Confederation in insisting that the new nation would have a federal structure rather than the legislative union Sir John A. Macdonald had originally wanted. In other words, it was assumed that a national party system existed for the whole country along with party systems for provincial purposes in each of the provinces and that voters understood that they had different political roles to play depending on the level at which an election was being fought.

It is hardly surprising, therefore, that from the beginning attempts

38. "The Ontario Elections," *Canadian Monthly and National Review* (September 1879): 228. It is worth noting, however, that while the number of seats won by each party frequently varied enormously from one level to the other their percentage shares of the vote hardly changed at all during this period and were often very close to each other. Clearly, the different results in terms of seats owed a great deal to Mowat's ability to "redistribute constitutencies with Christian humility and partisan ingenuity," as Sir John Willison put it, and there is ample evidence that Macdonald did the same thing.

to explain the phenomenon of varying rates of party success between federal and provincial elections have always taken for granted the existence of both a national party system and regional systems based in each province. In fact, the most prominent theories which have been advanced in the years since World War II not only make this assumption but also try to account for the differences which occur between the two levels by some variation of a general argument that there is a fundamental hostility between Ottawa and the provinces which can only be accommodated by the opportunity the federal structure provides for people to express themselves differently at different levels. Indeed, all of them attribute to the electorate, or at least to major sections of it, a capacity for what we call "strategic" voting which goes well beyond the claims for voter rationality made by most modern studies of political behavior. But quite apart from this weakness it is easily shown that each of these theories seriously misrepresents the character of the changes from one level to another which actually take place and therefore fail to provide an adequate explanation of why people shift their vote between federal and provincial elections.

The earliest general account of the phenomenon was provided by MacGregor Dawson, in what I will call the "cyclic" theory, although it is now usually regarded as so obviously fallacious that reference is rarely made to it.[39] The argument, however, was quite straightforward. Success for one party at the federal level generates in due course success for the other party at the provincial level, and after a time, when the other party has won control of most of the provincial governments, that springboard enables it to vault back into power at Ottawa and the whole cycle begins anew. In other words, Dawson was saying, once people have put one party in power in Ottawa they begin to turn away from it by voting for the other party at the provincial level in increasingly larger numbers, and then—presumably in some temporary fit of absentmindedness—vote for the same party briefly at both levels in order to start the constant process of change again.[40]

39. *The Government of Canada*, 1st ed. (Toronto: University of Toronto Press, 1947), pp. 581–83. The account occupied some seven paragraphs in the early editions of Dawson's textbook, all of which have been removed by Norman Ward in the current edition, although his rewriting of the last paragraph on p. 486 of that edition—where the only reference to the phenomenon now occurs—implies a qualified approval of Dawson's original view.

40. It is some testimony, perhaps, to the persistence of older ideas about the character of

The cyclic theory was meant to apply to the whole country, that is, to explain the behavior of all Canadians, but of course, as it deals only with conflict between the Liberals and the Conservatives (since no other party has ever held power at Ottawa), it cannot be used to account for what happens in the four Western provinces without a number of further assumptions which Dawson does not appear to have made.[41] There is a far more serious objection to it, however, which may well explain its suppression in the most recent editions of the textbook. A careful reading of Dawson's own description of the process at work indicates that he *did* make the assumption that when a party has won power nationally it has also won in each province in that election. Indeed, if that assumption is not made the cyclic theory is simple nonsense as an explanation of varying federal and provincial voting behavior—because unless people vote one way federally and turn around and do something different provincially right across the country there may in fact be no conflict between the levels at all in some places. But it is rarely the case that a party's national victory is founded on victory in all of the provinces, and we may therefore dismiss the cyclic theory as an explanation of anything.

If Dawson's theory cannot tell us why parties other than the Liberals and the Conservatives have had considerable success at the provincial level, the theory advanced by Seymour Lipset in his famous review of C. B. Macpherson's book on Social Credit in Alberta sets out an entirely plausible explanation for the phenomenon which continues to have some currency.[42] What is perhaps best described as the "protest" theory of differential federal and provincial voting argues that in western Canada, particularly in Alberta and Saskatchewan, people realized that they could not stimulate the federal government to protect their specific regional interests because the members of parliament they elected were bound to be outnumbered in either the Liberal or the Conservative caucus by the much larger group of MPs elected from eastern Canada, and in any case their freedom to ex-

Canadian party competition that a number of journalists, to say nothing of Mr. Clark himself, saw the Conservative federal victory of 1979 as simply the natural consequence of the fact that by that time the Liberals were not in office in any of the provinces. It is more difficult, however, to use the cyclic theory to explain the 1980 election.

41. For example, that a Social Credit provincial vote is the same as voting Conservative, or that voting CCF provincially is analogous to voting Liberal federally.

42. "Democracy in Alberta: Part I," *Canadian Forum* 33 (November, 1954): 176.

press a regional point of view would have to take second place to the
unified party position required by the circumstances of the parliamentary battle. What the people of the prairies did, therefore, was
elect their own parties to power at the provincial level, enabling them
to bargain with Ottawa for a better deal for the west within the federal
system.

On the face of things, the protest theory offers a quite reasonable
account of the often sharply different rates of party success in federal
and provincial politics in western Canada, but it cannot be applied to
the country as a whole because its validity depends—in the first instance at least—on the conflict between the two levels being between
one of the older parties and one of the newer parties. In Ontario,
where the Liberals have won most of the federal elections which have
occurred since the end of the Second World War, it makes no sense at
all to explain the uninterrupted success of the Conservatives at the
provincial level in this way. If the people of Ontario were trying to
serve their special regional interests by putting the Conservatives in
office at Queen's Park one would think they could accomplish a great
deal more by sending them to Ottawa as well. But in Alberta and
Saskatchewan, according to the protest theory, there was no hope of
their parties coming to power nationally and so people had no alternative but to follow the provincial route.

In fact, however, the electorate in both provinces *did* try to follow
the federal route as well, by voting in national elections in almost exactly the same way they were voting provincially. When the Social
Credit party first appeared in Alberta, 54 percent of the electorate
supported it in the 1935 provincial election. In the federal election a
few months later, 47 percent did so. Evidently, the major part of the
support that had gone in previous federal elections to the United
Farmers of Alberta was now simply transferred to Social Credit, just
as it had been at the provincial level in order to put the Social Credit
party into office. The similarity of federal and provincial electoral behavior in Alberta, at least as far as Social Credit is concerned, continued right up until the late 1950s when the Conservative party's
success nationally destroyed the party at the federal level. After that,
and until the party fell upon hard times at the provincial level as well
following their defeat in 1971, provincial Social Credit voters generally switched to the Conservatives in federal elections. In more re-

cent years there has been a much less marked difference between federal and provincial elections in the province in levels of support for all parties.

This record does not altogether dismiss the phenomenon of vote-switching between the two levels in Alberta; but it is arguable that shifts between the Conservatives and Social Credit are in reality simply exchanges between two parties that both serve a middle-class-representation function.[43] Yet, it is not what we would expect to see if the protest theory were a satisfactory explanation of why that happens. Rather than Social Credit having come to power in Edmonton in order to give Albertans a more effective voice in the federal system, it seems much more likely that the party served a particular need which Alberta society had at the time.[44] In any case, the fact that so many people were willing to support the party at *both* levels, and for such a long time, is simply inconsistent with the pattern of behavior which the protest theory predicts.

Much the same kind of record exists in Saskatchewan where again, if the protest theory were an adequate explanation of the phenomenon of partisan shifts between federal and provincial elections, we should expect to find much less support for the CCF in federal elections than occurred at the provincial level. In 1944, when the CCF first came to power, it won 53 percent of the vote in the province, and at the federal election of the following year 44 percent. In other words, at almost the same time as the people of Saskatchewan decided to put the CCF in office in Regina, they apparently sought to do the same thing for the nation as a whole. Of course there was vote-switching between federal and provincial elections in the province, although of a much smaller magnitude as far as the CCF was concerned than occurred with Social Credit in Alberta up to the end of the 1950s, and it is equally true that in the period since that time the inroads which the Conservative party under John Diefenbaker's leadership made into CCF and NDP federal support in the former province have only very slowly dissipated.[45] Nonetheless, there is no more

43. See "The Canadian Political Cultures," pp. 468–70.
44. A very persuasive argument that something of precisely this nature is the real explanation for the rise of Social Credit in Alberta can be found in David E. Smith, "A Comparison of Prairie Political Developments in Saskatchewan and Alberta," *Journal of Canadian Studies* 3 (1969): 17–26.
45. The fact that the Conservatives have replaced the Liberals as the principal opposition

evidence in the case of Saskatchewan than there is in Alberta's that the protest theory will do as an explanation of why these changes occur.

Among the remaining provinces, until very recently only British Columbia and Manitoba could have been candidates for the application of the protest theory—since in every other case the federal-provincial contest was primarily between the Liberals and the Conservatives[46]—and in neither of these can its requirements be met. When the Social Credit party first came to power in British Columbia it apparently carried a very substantial proportion of its provincial support over into the next federal election,[47] but since that time there has been a progressive decline in its popularity at the federal level to the point where in the 1980 election candidates could be found for only five of the province's twenty-eight seats. At the same time, the virtual disappearance of the Conservative party in provincial elections there after the collapse of the Liberal-Conservative coalition on the eve of the 1952 contest, coupled with the fact that the provincial Liberal party never regained its former strength, meant that almost from the beginning the Social Credit party in British Columbia was in reality nothing more than an alternative way of carrying on the struggle against the CCF (and later the NDP).[48] In these circumstances it seems quite unrealistic to attribute the party's success to the kinds of voter motivations which the protest theory would suggest, just as it

party at the provincial level in Saskatchewan has very much reduced the contrast between federal and provincial election results there. In the federal election of 1979, for example, the NDP won 36 percent of the vote against 41 percent for the Conservatives, which can be compared to 48 percent and 38 percent, respectively, in the provincial election of 1978.

46. In Quebec, regarding the Union Nationale as the inheritor of the Conservative tradition generally reduced the problems involved in the comparison to insignificance, but the rise of the Parti Québécois is another matter altogether. On the basis of the available evidence there ought to be some transference between the PQ and the NDP at the federal level but the extent to which that occurs is clearly very small. For the moment, in fact, Quebec may be the only case where the protest theory makes some sense, although observers of the 1976 election there would be unlikely to attribute the PQ's success to a fear of the province's inability to affect the way in which decisions are made in Ottawa.

47. Comparisons are complicated by the alternative voting system in use in the province in those years, but in 1952 and 1953 the party's first count strength was 27 percent and 38 percent, respectively, against the 26 percent it won in the federal election of 1953.

48. Some support for this view may be drawn from the fact that the current British Columbia cabinet has more former Liberals and Conservatives in it than people who have built their political careers inside the Social Credit party, as well as from the fact that even the elder Bennett avoided as much as possible references to original Social Credit doctrine in his descriptions of the party's purpose.

seems unrealistic to regard voting shifts by its provincial supporters
to the Liberals and Conservatives in federal elections as anything
more than an expression of an opinion they consistently hold at all
levels—namely, that the NDP must be avoided at all costs.

In the years following the end of the Second World War, Manitoba
would not have been regarded as a case where the protest theory
could be applied any more than Ontario is today, but the greatly increased strength of the NDP there in recent years might suggest that
it should now be examined in that light. In fact, of course, support for
the CCF (and later the NDP) in the province has nearly always reproduced in subsequent federal elections, and today the difference is
barely worth talking about.[49] In short, the protest theory leaves a
good deal to be desired as an explanation of why the changes which
take place between federal and provincial elections in any province
actually occur. In most cases these changes simply are not very great.

Indeed, if we set the case of contemporary Quebec aside it appears
that Ontario is the only place where a change of any consequence occurs. But as I have already suggested, the protest theory does not apply to Ontario at all. To find an explanation of the peculiar fact that
the Liberals have been unable to make any significant headway in the
province for nearly forty years while they often have fared very well
in federal elections we are obliged to turn to the oldest of all theories
of federal-provincial change.

The "balance" theory, as it is now commonly called, has been a part
of the arsenal of journalistic comment on Canadian politics ever since
the days of Mowat's confrontations with Macdonald in the last century, but its classic modern statement was given by the late Frank Underhill in his famous Dunning Lecture, delivered at Queen's University in 1955:

By some instinctive subconscious mental process the Canadian people have
apparently decided that, since freedom depends upon a balance of power,
they will balance the monopolistic power of the Liberal government at Ottawa by setting up the effective countervailing power not in Ottawa but in
the provincial capitals. Her Majesty's loyal Canadian opposition now really
consists of the Social Credit governments in Alberta and British Columbia,
the C.C.F. government in Saskatchewan, the Conservative governments in

49. In the 1980 federal election the party won an all-time high of 34 percent of the province's
vote, only four points less than its strength in the provincial election of 1977.

Ontario and New Brunswick, and the Union Nationale government in Quebec. These are all governments who get elected in their own Provinces in order to save their people from the malign influence of Ottawa.[50]

The theory was obviously intended to apply to the whole country, but it has come to be associated primarily with Ontario, if for no other reason than that Professor Underhill's own writing had so frequently drawn attention to the peculiarity of the Ontario case. In a 1946 essay in the *Canadian Forum*, for example, he had suggested that the behavior of the Ontario electorate had changed very little between the Macdonald and King eras:

In the 1870's and 1880's and early 1890's many a good Ontario citizen would vote Grit in provincial politics, and then, appalled at the thought of Grit domination of the whole of Canada, he would turn around and help re-elect Macdonald in federal politics. Just so today. Thousands of Ontario voters last summer, after putting Mr. Drew into office, turned round within a week and helped the rest of Canada to make sure that Ontario tories should not dominate the Dominion.[51]

In fact, however, a careful examination of what actually happened in the two 1945 elections in the province, the only time in our modern history when a federal and provincial campaign overlapped (until the British Columbia election of 1979 clashed with the federal election of that year), shows that Professor Underhill's characterization of the results was very substantially wide of the mark. Thousands of Ontario Conservatives did indeed change their vote for the federal election, but as table 7.1 shows, that was far from being the main source of the new federal Liberal strength. Even allowing for the slightly smaller number of eligible voters, there can hardly be any doubt that it was a massive shift of provincial CCF supporters (roughly a third of the party's provincial vote), together with people who had not voted at all in the earlier election, which accounted for the change. This is demonstrated by the figures in the lower part of table 7.1 which show each party's vote (and the number who abstained) as a percentage of the total registered electorate.

This pattern of change is not the least bit consistent with the balance theory. No doubt the aggregate results presented in table 7.1

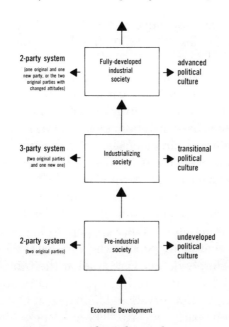

Figure 7.1. *The Relationships among Economic Development, Party Systems, and the Development of Political Culture*

conceal a wide variety of interlevel exchanges between the parties; but to assume that a large number of CCF voters switched to the Conservatives federally, as must be assumed in order to claim, as the balance theory would have us believe, that a significant number of provincial Conservatives voted for the Liberals in the 1945 federal election, is to ignore the circumstances of Ontario politics in those years. The 1945 provincial campaign was marked by an extraordinary degree of bitterness between the CCF and the Conservatives,[52] and it hardly seems likely that it could have dissipated to this extent in so short a time. The balance theory, therefore, does not appear to square at all with the probable behavior of Ontario voters at the end of the Second World War.

Nor is there much evidence that it explains the pattern of federal-

52. See Gerald L. Caplan, "The Ontario 'Gestapo' Affair, 1943–1945," *Canadian Journal of Economics and Political Science* 30 (1964): 343–59.

provincial change that has continued in the province since that time. In fact, it was more or less taken for granted for a number of years that increased Liberal strength in federal elections in Ontario was primarily due to CCF (and later NDP) voters at the provincial level shifting their allegiance, either because there was some kind of ideological affinity between the two parties, or because CCF supporters recognized that their party had little chance of winning a federal election given the political circumstances of the country as a whole.[53] More recently, however, it has been suggested that what is merely hinted at in the data for 1945 presented in table 7.1—that people who abstain at the provincial level may have something to do with the federal result—has a good deal more to do with federal Liberal success in Ontario than anything else.[54] What appears to happen, according to this argument, is that many people who vote for the Liberal party in federal elections simply do not vote at all at the provincial level, either because they have no interest in provincial politics or because, after so many years of Conservative dominance at Queen's Park, they do not believe their party can win. There is some evidence as well that this pattern varies considerably from one part of the province to another, and that there may be both an ethnic component and a social-class component affecting the frequency with which it occurs.[55] Although data from surveys taken in Ontario during the last fifteen years generally do not confirm the relationships suggested by analysis of the aggregate data, and particularly do not indicate any major role being played by abstention in provincial elections,[56] it is impossible not to be struck by the picture which emerges for the province when federal and provincial results are presented in the fashion used in figure 7.2, where each party's vote at each level is shown as a percentage of the registered electorate to allow for the effect of abstention.

53. See, for example, Howard A. Scarrow, "Federal-Provincial Voting Patterns in Canada," *Canadian Journal of Economics and Political Science* 26 (1960): 295.

54. John Wilson and David Hoffman, "The Liberal Party in Contemporary Ontario Politics," *Canadian Journal of Political Science* 3 (1970): 179–204.

55. "The Liberal Party in Contemporary Ontario Politics," pp. 184–90.

56. Some surveys of Ontario long have suggested that people who vote Liberal federally and Conservative provincially are much more likely to be middle class than the population as a whole but Richard Johnston's analysis of the 1965, 1968, and 1974 national surveys sees only a comparatively minor role for either social class or religion in the changes which take place, and in Ontario virtually no role at all for abstention. See "Federal and Provincial Voting," in Elkins and Simeon, *Small Worlds*, pp. 160–72.

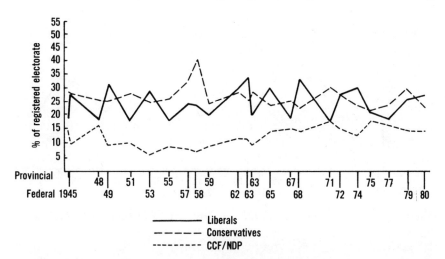

Figure 7.2. *Party Vote as a Percentage of the Registered Electorate, Ontario Party System, Federal and Provincial Elections since 1945*

There is a remarkable uniformity in the movement of the Conservative and CCF/NDP vote. Indeed, it is almost as if they were competing in a single party system which responds from time to time to the changing circumstances of the society. In contrast, the Liberal vote varies in a way which makes it clear that something must be interfering at regular intervals with the party's capacity to appeal to the electorate.[57] If we now add the number of people abstaining at each election (set out on the same scale in figure 7.3) it seems obvious that the increased rate of abstention at the provincial level is closely linked with the Liberal party's difficulty. No doubt all parties are affected to some degree by the phenomenon; but the aggregate data at least suggest that the Liberals are more seriously affected than others.[58] If that is the case, however, the extent of real shifts between the parties between provincial and federal elections is no more dramatic in Ontario

57. The points along the horizontal axis of the graphs in figures 7.2 and 7.3 are spaced as far as possible so as to exactly represent the elapsed time in months between each election.

58. Although virtually all available survey data discount the role which is played by abstention at the provincial level in the Ontario case it may be worth noting that sample surveys are likely not at all reliable with this aspect of voting behavior. Not only are there the standard problems of recall or "bandwagoning" when past behavior is being probed, but people are noticeably less willing to report that they did not vote at all. Even the most representative samples invariably understate the actual level of nonvoting in any given election.

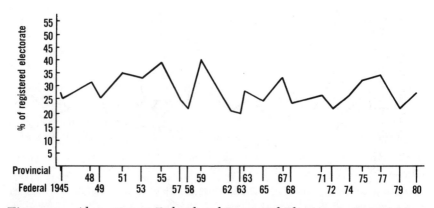

Figure 7.3. *Abstention in Federal and Provincial Elections in Ontario since 1945*

than it is anywhere else in Canada, and we are left with the original dilemma. Like both the cyclic theory and the protest theory, the balance theory fails to explain the changes which actually occur simply because it vastly overstates the magnitude of those changes by ignoring the overall *similarity* which exists between federal and provincial voting behavior within each province.[59]

And yet the misconception persists. A number of years ago Steven Muller developed what is sometimes regarded as a fourth theory to account for the peculiarities of party competition in Canada.[60] In reality, however, his argument (I will call it the "safety-valve" theory) is little more than an ingenious combination of the three theories just discussed, and as such is easily shown to be just as mistaken. The core of his view lies in the notion of an imagined "second layer" of the national party system where competition between the parties is specifically directed to the federal-provincial conflict, thus providing an outlet for the expression of sectional interests without damaging the

59. The 1974 national survey contained a question designed to probe the extent of agreement with the balance theory, finding that opinion was much the same in each province. Approximately 25 percent of all respondents agreed that "the same political party should not control both the federal government in Ottawa and the provincial government here in [province] at the same time"; roughly 10 percent said that they felt very strongly about this view, 12 percent fairly strongly, and three percent not very strongly, while 65 percent said it made no difference.

60. "Federalism and the Party System in Canada," a paper presented to the 1961 annual meeting of the American Political Science Association and later published in Aaron Wildavsky, ed., *American Federalism in Perspective* (Boston: Little, Brown, 1967), pp. 144–62.

stability of the nation as a whole. In the "first layer" of the national party system there is the conventional contest from coast to coast dominated by the Liberals and Conservatives, with only a minor role being played by other parties which may nonetheless be significant actors within their own provincial party systems. What prevents this otherwise potentially divisive pattern of party competition from breaking the country up is the fact that office at the provincial level enables the leaders of regional parties to expend their energies in bargaining with Ottawa to obtain a better deal for their people. In this way national politicians are left free to pursue ends which may not always please certain regions but which may gain them votes in other parts of the country, while regional politicians have the opportunity to appear to be doing something for their own province.

This bargaining process between different political groups is the principal activity of the "second layer" and is, in Muller's conception, separated both from the "first layer" of the national party system and from party competition at the provincial level. Moreover, he argues, the electorate itself recognizes the wisdom of this arrangement, confident that their special sectional needs are being dealt with away from the direct light of open party conflict at the national level:

The most virulently divergent pressures away from national consensus exist among French Canadians and in the West. It is then perhaps no accident, that until 1960 Quebec voters for years chose to support the Union Nationale in the province while usually voting Liberal in Dominion elections. Also, the Western provinces, with the very recent exception of Manitoba, are each in the control of a party not affiliated with either of the main contenders for Dominion power. . . . These circumstances are scarcely understandable except in terms of Canadian federalism and a second layer of the national party system. The so-called ideology of Social Credit seems scarcely relevant to the conduct of provincial government by the party, and of almost equal irrelevance to its voters. The Union Nationale, given the leadership of the late M. Duplessis and French Canadian nationalism, was and is not encumbered with an ideology that could be so labelled. There is, of course, a socialist-progressive point of view that distinguishes the C.C.F. ideologically, but there is little evidence of its relevance to provincial voting in Saskatchewan. It seems most likely that voters in general support these provincial parties with a pragmatic perception of the federal circumstances under discussion, i.e., with recognition of the two layers comprising the national party system.[61]

61. Ibid., p. 156.

In other words, the success of different parties at the provincial level is due to the people themselves understanding that there is a need both to protest against the policies of the federal government and to balance Ottawa's power by providing an alternative administration in the provincial capitals. Resolution of federal-provincial conflict in this way, says Muller, has been a continuing feature of Canadian federalism, for "the logic of the second layer lays down its own classic cyclical pattern." This is nicely illustrated by the fact that when the federal Liberals came to power in 1935 they were already in office in all but one of the provinces, and when they were defeated by the Conservatives in 1957 they held power in only three provinces, two of which fell to the Conservatives immediately afterward.[62]

We may legitimately ask, however, why it should be suggested that there is a national party system in Canada with these characteristics when support for parties such as the CCF (and later the NDP) and Social Credit in these years tended to run at much the same level in both federal and provincial elections, not just in the west, but in Ontario as well. The fact is that although the Liberals and the Conservatives may be the largest parties across the country as a whole, they were not then, and are not today, "the main contenders for power" at either level in most of these provinces. But if that is so it is surely perverse to insist upon a distinction between the two layers of the national party system when that system, in effect, is not in operation at all in at least these cases.

Indeed, it is difficult to avoid the conclusion that the assumption that there actually is a national party system operating across the country as a whole is what lies at the root of the problem all of these theories have in explaining the phenomenon of voting shifts between federal and provincial elections. Our interest in the phenomenon, however, is in discovering to what extent the fact that it occurs can be used to establish the existence of a national party system as well as provincial party systems—in order to make a judgment concerning the capacity of the national system to perform the integrative function which traditional interpretation has assigned to it—and for this purpose none of the standard theories will do. These theories' accounts

62. Ibid., p. 150. The illustration is not one which Dawson could have used, given the dates involved, but there can be no doubt about the source of the idea in Muller's mind.

of why people change their vote from one level to the other do not square with the available data regarding electoral behavior, and they depend, in the end, on a kind of circular reasoning with respect to the real character of party competition in Canada. Unless it is assumed that our people see themselves as participating in two different systems depending on the level of the election, it makes no sense to claim that their provincial vote is used generally to oppose the power of the federal government—whether merely to express growing disapproval of Ottawa's policy, or to protest their exclusion from the national debate, or to create a balance between the two levels of government. But the fact that some people do vote differently at the two levels is not *by itself* proof that they see themselves as having a role to play in two different party systems. In the absence of any compelling independent evidence that a national party system exists, it would be just as reasonable to suggest that the process begins with these people casting a provincial vote, not in response to national pressures, but in order to serve the interests and goals they have in the context of that provincial society. When they are called on to vote in a federal election they continue to express those interests. That is to say, it is entirely possible that federal and provincial elections are all of a piece for our people. In fact, since most Canadians vote the same way in federal and provincial elections it seems much more likely that something of this kind is the case. If we set aside the undemonstrated assumption that a national party system exists apart from the provincial systems, it is easy to see the variations which occur from one province to another in federal elections as simply expressions of different views about the conduct and purpose of politics rooted, perhaps, in more fundamental differences which may exist between the provinces. Nonetheless, there are people who change their vote from one level to the other, and unless we can get some measure of why that happens we cannot assume that their behavior is necessarily provincially rather than nationally directed.

An Alternative Explanation

If the conventional theories which have been developed to explain voting shifts between federal and provincial elections are unsatisfactory because they all make assumptions which are unwarranted, it would make sense to take advantage of modern techniques of public opinion measurement and simply ask those people who make this kind of change why they do it. Unfortunately, however, that question is rarely asked in voting surveys despite the fact that it is now customary to obtain a quite complete account of respondents' federal and provincial voting histories.[63] Moreover, where the question has been asked it has usually been in connection with the respondent's *past* behavior in a federal or provincial election. This introduces problems of accurate recall of the vote in the more distant case (to say nothing of the reasons why it was different from what had been done more recently), and of the effect which rationalization born of the respondents' current behavior has on their explanation of past behavior.[64]

It may well be that this latter problem can never be entirely eliminated, but it may nonetheless be useful to examine data from a survey where the question was put following questions concerning the *current* provincial and federal voting *intention* of respondents. This has the advantage of isolating people who at the same time expect to vote differently at the two levels.[65] Table 7.2, which summarizes responses to the two voting intention questions asked in the Manitoba study in 1973, provides an indication of the maximum number of people who could be said to make a deliberate shift between the two levels.[66] If we

63. This has meant that virtually all of the more recent attempts to explain the phenomenon of federal-provincial voting shifts have been forced to guess about the possible causes of this kind of behavior by exploring its relationshp with other respondent traits such as interest in politics, degree of political involvement, or appropriate social and economic characteristics. See, for example, the very careful examination of these possibilities in Richard Johnston, "Federal and Provincial Voting," in Elkins and Simeon, *Small Worlds*, pp. 160–72.

64. I know of only three studies where a question of *why* people voted differently in federal and provincial elections was asked: in two 1967 constituency surveys reported in George Perlin and Patti Peppin, "Variations in Party Support in Federal and Provincial Elections: Some Hypotheses," *Canadian Journal of Political Science* 4 (1971):280–86; in a 1973 survey of Manitoba conducted by John Wilson and Jo Surich; and in the 1974 national election survey. Only the Manitoba study dealt with the voting intention of respondents at both levels.

65. The survey of Manitoba from which the data reported here are taken was done in late February and March of 1973, on the eve of the provincial general election of that year. It was based on an area probability sample, stratified by 1969 provincial vote, of 858 residents of the province eligible to vote in the 1973 provincial election. The sample was weighted to 1,109 cases, to compensate for Winnipeg having been undersampled in relation to the rest of the province. Interviews were conducted in every constituency except those of the far north, covering a universe representing nearly 94 percent of the 1973 registered electorate. The data deck and codebook for the study are held in the Centre for Election Studies in the Department of Political Science at the University of Waterloo.

66. It is worth remembering that when we are examining aggregate change between two elec-

Table 7.2. Federal and Provincial Voting Intention in Manitoba in March 1973[b]

| | Provincial voting intention | | | | | |
	Liberal	Conser-vative	NDP	Other	Don't know[c]	Total
Federal voting intention						
Liberal	13	2	7	1	3	26
Conservative	1	27	6	a	3	37
NDP	a	—	18	a	1	19
Other	a	a	a	1	a	1
Don't know[c]	1	1	3	a	12	17
Total	15	30	34	2	19	(1,109)

a. Less than half of one percent.
b. Each cell, including the marginal totals, is shown as a percentage of the total number of cases = 1,109.
c. Includes respondents who refused to answer and a small number who said they would not vote.

consider only direct exchanges between the parties (leaving aside the 261 cases who were undecided at either or both of the levels) there were 199 respondents who anticipated changing their vote. These constituted 18 percent of the whole sample and 23 percent of the 848 respondents who had made up their mind.[67] By far the greatest proportion were persons who intended to vote for the NDP in the next Manitoba election and for one of the other parties at the federal level.

How the direction of these changes is characterized, of course, may make some difference in any judgment about the existence of different party systems at the two levels. On the basis of the data in table 7.2, for example, we could say either that NDP voters are very loyal

---

tions at different levels that are separated by some length of time there are a number of factors that have nothing at all to do with individual voter shifts that may contribute to the overall apparent pattern, such as new entrants to the electorate or different rules regarding voter eligibility at the two levels. For a thoughtful discussion of these possibilities see Johnston, "Federal and Provincial Voting," in Elkins and Simeon, *Small Worlds*, pp. 160–61. The effect of new entrants to the electorate on the changes which take place between federal elections is discussed in some detail in the abridged edition of Harold D. Clarke et al., *Political Choice in Canada* (Toronto: McGraw-Hill Ryerson, 1980), chaps. 12 and 13.

67. For the purposes of this analysis, respondents who were undecided about how they would vote in either election but who expressed a preference for one of the parties after probing (in each case roughly half of all those who were initially undecided) have been added to each party's number of decided supporters for the relevant election.

to their party because nearly all the federal NDP vote is retained in provincial elections, or that NDP voters are particularly fickle since a very large number of them change to another party in federal elections. We could describe Liberal and Conservative voters in much the same way, although in this case the stability would be said to exist from provincial to federal elections since the losses appear to run in the other direction. But in either case we would be making assumptions about the primary location of political activity that might lead to very different explanations of the phenomenon of party exchanges between the two levels, and hence to quite different judgments about the character of the national party system. Great care must be taken, therefore, to ensure that the question asked to determine why people change their vote between federal and provincial elections does not imply a particular direction in which the change is assumed to occur, thereby encouraging responses which may conceal the real motivation of respondents.

Given these considerations, it may well be significant that, although the question which was asked in the Manitoba study had, if anything, a slight bias favoring the assumption that the change occurs moving from federal to provincial elections (simply because federal elections were mentioned first),[68] the number of responses which can be clearly identified as reflecting a change moving from provincial to federal elections is actually the larger of the two possibilities. Table 7.3 groups all respondents who said that they intended to vote for different parties at the two levels by various combinations excluding only those pairs where the number of cases is too small for analysis. The table distinguishes between the different directions of the intended change on the basis of the reasons given by each respondent. Although more respondents appear to begin at the provincial rather than the federal level, which suggests that they see themselves primarily as actors in the provincial system since they appear to think that their answer to the question should justify the federal voting deviation, the more interesting fact emerging from table 7.3 is that more than half of all people who change do not make a directional

68. The question was: "Many people vote differently in national and provincial elections. I notice that you intend to do something different in the next national election than you intend to do in the next Manitoba election. Is there any one special reason for changing between the two elections?" It may be, of course, that respondents automatically put the provincial election first, either because of the clear provincial focus of earlier questions in the interview or simply because it was well known at the time that a provincial election would likely occur that spring.

Table 7.3. *Reasons for Intending to Vote Differently in Provincial and Federal Elections in Manitoba, 1973*

Provincial voting intention Federal voting intention	New Democrat		Conservative	Liberal	Total intending to change[a]
	Liberal	Conservative	Liberal	Conservative	
Change appears to occur from provincial to federal elections	%	%	%	%	%
It depends on the federal candidate	3	5	—	21	4
I like/don't like Trudeau	5	—	—	7	} 6
I don't like Stanfield	—	—	12	—	
I don't like Lewis	3	2	—	—	
I like federal Liberal policies	5	—	4	—	} 7
I don't like federal NDP policies	1	8	—	—	
NDP can't win a federal election	12	15	—	—	9
Change appears to occur from federal to provincial elections					
It depends on the provincial candidate	3	3	—	—	1
I like Schreyer	9	3	—	—	5
I like provincial NDP policies	8	13	—	—	7
Liberals can't beat NDP provincially	—	—	44	—	6
Direction of change unclear					
It depends on the candidate	16	23	12	7	21
Leaders (unspecified)	7	2	8	21	6
Policies (unspecified)	5	7	4	—	4
Don't want same party at both levels	4	8	12	14	7
No particular reason, don't know	19	11	4	29	17
Number of cases	(75)	(61)	(25)	(14)	(199)

a. Includes twenty-four cases involving seven different combinations not shown separately.

distinction at all between the two levels. That is, of course, exactly the pattern to be expected if voters view political participation as occurring within a single party system.

What is most intriguing, however, is that, whether the direction of the change is obvious or not, there is hardly any hint of partisanship in the reasons given for changing by most of the people who intend to do so. In fact, nearly half of them—the 26 percent who say that their vote at either or both levels is determined by the characteristics of the local candidate and the 17 percent who are unable to give any reason for changing—appear to be completely nonpartisan in their political activity. This may also be true of those who are motivated by their feeling toward specific party leaders or toward leaders in general. Indeed, even those people who say that they like or dislike the policies of a particular party may not all be expressing more clearly partisan feelings than others—among the respondents classified in table 7.3 as giving an unspecified policy-oriented response there are a number who say that their vote depends on the particular issues at the time.[69]

Interpretation of the meaning of what may be called the strategic reasons for a different federal and provincial voting intention is less easy. It seems likely that all of them reflect a decidedly nonpartisan attitude. Persons whose votes are determined by wanting to be on the winning side or by the principle which is said to underpin the balance theory are surely not going to be very strongly attached to any party.[70] Support for the idea that different parties should be in power in Ottawa and the provincial capitals represents a much clearer recognition of the existence of different party systems at the two levels than either of the other two "strategic" responses shown in table 7.3. It is interesting that nearly equal proportions of those who intend to vote NDP provincially and for either the Liberals or the Conservatives federally say that they will do that because the NDP is not strong enough to win a federal election across Canada as a whole. That suggests a kind of random choice of alternatives which in turn implies that the two groups are more alike than they are different. This may mean that

69. Five of the nine respondents classified in this way mentioned issues rather than party policies. The policy category generally in table 7.3—whether linked to a specific party or not—may be too loose a classification for the purpose of this analysis since it includes both people who simply said that they liked or disliked a particular party and those who singled out particular policies, as well as the more clearly issue-oriented responses, along with one individual whose answer "I hate the Liberals" was intended as an explanation for a federal Conservative and provincial NDP vote.

70. Responses endorsing the balance theory were almost equally divided between explicit assertions of the principle that the same party should not be in power federally and provincially at the same time and the more general, but similar, "what's good for Manitoba is not necessarily good for Canada."

their provincial vote is the more significant one.[71] But the more important point is that these people really are saying, "If I thought the
NDP could win a national election I would vote for it," a view which
is just as consistent with the idea that a federal election is an occasion
for collecting the results from several different party systems as it is
with the idea that a national party system exists apart from Manitoba's
where the character of party competition is quite different. It is not at
all clear, therefore, that a different federal and provincial vote by
these people can be taken as recognition that distinct systems exist at
both levels. Equally, the federal Liberals who intend to vote for the
Conservatives provincially in order to be sure of defeating the NDP
can be characterized as saying, "If I thought the Liberals could beat
the NDP in Manitoba I would vote for them," a view which suggests
that keeping the NDP out of office is more important as far as these
people are concerned than any difference that might exist between
the two older parties. But that suggests that these people attach little importance to a differential federal-provincial vote of this kind. If
that is the case there is at least some doubt whether it represents any
kind of recognition of the existence of different party systems at the
two levels.[72]

Even if we assume, however, that most of the cases of strategic voting changes between federal and provincial elections, along with the
major part of those shown in table 7.3 as changing for policy reasons,
do represent instances of changed partisanship between levels, it remains the case that well more than half of all the respondents in the
Manitoba study who intended to vote differently in the two elections
do not look at all like voters with strong party loyalties at different
levels.[73] Instead, they appear to be people who could change their
vote at any time. But if that is the case, that is, if most of those who
change their vote between federal and provincial elections are pri-

71. The very rough similarity generally in the responses of provincial New Democrats
who intended to vote Liberal or Conservative federally, as shown in table 7.3, may suggest the
same thing for at least all of the provincial New Democrats who were contemplating changing
their vote.

72. Much the same reasoning probably applies to interlevel exchanges between the Liberals
and Conservatives federally and Social Credit provincially in British Columbia, which is why
that province may not be the striking case of federal-provincial variation it is often held out
to be.

73. This conclusion is consistent with an analysis of interlevel variation in party identification
based on data from the 1974 national survey which found that those identifying with different

marily motivated by the characteristics of either the local candidates or the party leaders, or else don't know why they change,[74] then they are likely to change their vote whatever kind of election comes along, and no greater significance should be attached to the fact that they make the change between different levels than would be attached to similar changes at the same level. They are, in short, behaving as if they were acting within a single party system.

That conclusion necessarily leads to the rejection of the conventional wisdom regarding the nature of party competition in Canada. It is possible, of course—since what appears to happen in Manitoba may not happen everywhere else in Canada—that in some provinces there may be a greater recognition of two distinct contexts for political participation divided between federal and provincial elections. Establishing the extent to which that is the case would require a detailed examination of the motivations of those who switch their vote between the two levels in every province. But, even if it could be shown that what appears to happen in Manitoba also occurs in only a few of the other provinces, it would still be necessary to reject the conventional wisdom. Unless there is a capacity for the national party system to operate *everywhere* in Canada it cannot be expected to play the integrative role that has been traditionally assigned to it.[75] In any case, it seems improbable that there will be many instances where a widespread recognition of the alleged difference between the two levels of political participation exists. For the fact is that quite a large

parties at each level tended to have a weaker attachment to their party in both cases than those who were consistent identifiers across levels. See Clarke et al., *Political Choice in Canada*, unabridged ed., p. 145. It may also be the reason why Richard Johnston could not find any strong evidence of socioeconomic characteristics which distinguished people who change their vote between federal and provincial elections from the rest of the population. There is no reason to believe that nonpartisanship is a particular trait of any social class or religious faith. See "Federal and Provincial Voting," in Elkins and Simeon, *Small Worlds*, pp. 166–72.

74. These groups represent 60 percent of all those intending to vote differently at the two levels shown in table 7.3. If half of those intending to change for "policy" reasons are included, on the ground that they are responding to specific issues rather than to the platform of a particular party, along with those "strategic" changers whose behavior is not motivated by belief in the balance theory, then another 9 percent and 15 percent, respectively, can be added to the total, leaving only 16 percent of all changers who could be said to be people who recognize the existence of distinct party systems at the two levels. This represents 32 cases in the Manitoba study, or 3 percent of the whole provincial sample.

75. The implications of "multiple loyalties" are explored in David Elkins, "The Sense of Place," in Elkins and Simeon, *Small Worlds*, pp. 1–30. But preliminary analysis of the responses to the question in the 1974 national survey probing for respondents' explanations of a different past federal and provincial vote indicates that in all provinces except Quebec a substantial majority of those who switched between the two levels gave reasons analogous to those

number of persons identify with the same party federally and provincially;[76] and while there may be particular occasions when they will vote for another party, as a general rule they don't like to leave their "own" party without a compelling reason for doing so. It is unlikely, therefore, that very many of them customarily shift back and forth between federal and provincial elections. But if it is true that the people who do make these changes are largely those with only a very weak party identification at either level, or people with no identification at all who could change their vote at any time, then there is very little reason to believe that such differential rates of party success as clearly do occur between the two levels in various provinces should be taken as evidence of the existence of a national party system alongside each of the provincial systems. It seems more likely, in fact, that most voters see themselves as involved in a continuous process of political participation in a single system which has its roots in their province.

So far, therefore, from Canadian political behavior representing the expression of a *national* electorate with merely idiosyncratic regional variations, it may be the case that the circumstances of *provincial* politics direct the fate of the country as a whole; and if it is true that these vary from one region to another in terms of different stages of political development, then no amount of compromise or conciliation through the medium of a national party system could be expected to foster the growth of greater Canadian unity. In other words, our contemporary dilemma can hardly be blamed on the failure of the national party system. The problem is much deeper than that.

The Future of the Federal System

The consequences of such a view are of course enormous. For if the national party system cannot, in the nature of the case, perform the

which in the Manitoba data I have characterized as nonpartisan—that is to say, behavior consistent with a voting change at any time at either level—which suggests that it may indeed be the case in most of the country that people perceive themselves as acting in a single system which has its origins at the provincial level.

76. Analysis of data from the 1974 national survey indicates that 67 percent of those who report any kind of party identification (more than 90 percent of the whole sample) identify with the same party at both levels, although about a third of these do not show the same strength of identification in each case. See table 5.2 in Clarke et al., *Political Choice in Canada*, unabridged ed., p. 141.

task assigned to it by the conventional wisdom, and if no other existing institutions can be expected to focus attention on the well-being
of the country suppressing regional divisions and disagreements, we
may have to rethink completely our understanding of the character of
the Canadian federation. That is more easily said than done because,
as Alan Cairns observed in his 1977 presidential address to the Canadian Political Science Association, the tradition of Canadian political
inquiry has put far more emphasis on the role of the national government than was warranted by careful consideration of political developments since the end of World War II.[77]

No doubt there are many reasons for this institutional version of
the assumption which the conventional wisdom has visited on analysis of the nature of party competition in Canada, but among them
must be the fact that for years the only comprehensive treatment of
the peculiar characteristics of Canadian government and politics was
to be found in MacGregor Dawson's textbook. Whole generations of
political scientists were raised on Dawson's view of things which, because it paid virtually no attention at all to the importance of the provinces, simply reinforced the conviction that all of our troubles could
be traced to the decisions of a pair of eccentric British law lords, or to
the misplaced convictions of a few narrow-minded provincial politicians who had been misinformed about the terms of the 1867 bargain.
As short a time as twenty years ago there were no courses in our universities on provincial politics in general, let alone on the history and
politics of individual provinces, and the literature of the discipline
was mute testimony to the fact that the federal government was
widely regarded as the only government worth talking about.[78]

There is also a partisan reason for this attitude on the part of even
many modern political scientists. The Liberals (of whom Dawson was
one) were much more interested in the national situation because
that was where all the Liberal action was: the party had been in
power in Ottawa for the better part of this century. The Conservatives and socialists, on the other hand, had a natural preference

77. Alan C. Cairns, "The Governments and Societies of Canadian Federalism," *Canadian
Journal of Political Science* 10 (1977): 697–98.
78. The sheer volume of the current literature on almost every aspect of Canadian regionalism shows, of course, that the older view is no longer as popular as it once was. But the intellectual residue remains in the fact that most Canadian political scientists still appear to regard the
federal government as the most important government in Canada.

for national solutions to our problems: the Conservatives because their ideological position inclined them to regard the nation as more important than its parts, and CCF and NDP supporters because they believed in equalizing circumstances all across the country and viewed the federal government as the only instrument that could accomplish this goal. The parties themselves, of course, did not necessarily share these views. But Canadian political scientists in general did. And, when they were confronted with the hard facts of variation in party support from one region to another, or with the extraordinary growth in political power on the part of provincial governments, they began to devise explanations of these phenomena to fit their conviction that it was the job of the party system, and of the federal government, to knit the country together.

But time is rapidly running out on that view. As each year passes without any noticeable change in the balance of power which has evolved between the two levels of government since 1945, Canadian society becomes more and more populated by people who have never known anything except the dominance of the provincial governments. This dominance, indeed, regenerates itself simply by the fact that the provinces are in near-sovereign control of a major part of the legislative authority which governs the social and economic life chances of our people.[79] As a consequence, before very long there may not be many left in Canada who will be prepared to support the federal government in an outright confrontation with the provinces. There is intriguing confirmation of this possibility in the answers regarding the level of government which was most important to them given by respondents under the age of thirty-five in the 1974 national survey, as compared to those provided by older citizens. Data showed that across the country as a whole the younger group was more likely to favor their provincial government. The older group either favored the federal government or saw the two levels as equally important.

This is not, of course, very surprising, for if people are socialized into a federal system during a period of increasing decentralization one would expect them to have these kinds of opinions and to regard

79. The role which governments can play in shaping the character of a society is too often ignored. On this point generally see Cairns, "The Governments and Societies of Canadian Federalism," pp. 695–725. For analogous observations cast in a slightly different light see my "The Canadian Political Cultures," pp. 440–43.

them as perfectly normal, just as a much older generation of Canadians which remembers the sudden shock of the arrival of the depression in the 1930s has never quite been able to convince itself that we now know how to avoid that kind of disaster and that total economic collapse is not necessarily always lurking just around the corner. On questions as fundamental as these, people tend to adopt the political ideas of the era in which they grew up. Once adopted, such ideas are not very easily changed. Nor is there any reason to believe that the condition of the Canadian federation which these circumstances herald for the future is likely to change. Younger people do not take this view merely because they are young; much the same distribution of opinions regarding the relative importance of the two levels of government exists in the group under thirty, as in the group under twenty-five. In other words, aging by itself does not bring with it a greater respect for federal government. Rather, it appears to be the case that persons under thirty-five have acquired these views quite literally because they are accustomed to a substantial degree of governmental decentralization in Canada and see nothing wrong with it. But that means that in due course a large majority of the Canadian people will have a similar set of attitudes toward the conflict between the two levels of government. Thus, except in circumstances which none of us wishes to contemplate, the task of replacing regional loyalties with a higher sense of national identity may become impossible.

We need not conclude, however, that there is now no chance of a proper sense of national unity developing on the northern half of the North American continent. The preoccupation with the nation as a whole which has consumed most of the commentary on our present discontents has disguised the fact that there are alternative ways of managing a federation and that a quite satisfactory sense of national togetherness can be based on greater understanding of, and more toleration for, the fundamental regional differences in Canada without insisting that people must be treated in the same way wherever they happen to live.

The most serious consequence of the conventional wisdom's certainty that there must be *national* solutions to our problems, whether imposed by the heavy hand of the federal government or by some form of "cooperative" federalism which nonetheless treats all of the provinces in the same way, is that it causes us to lose sight of the original purpose of political society. When we talk about the problems of the Canadian federation all that is ever discussed is what the relative balance of powers ought to be between the two levels of government without any consideration ever being given to the kind of society—in terms of human social relationships, or the attitude people have toward each other—that relative balance will create. We ignore, in other words, the impact which the behavior of governments can have in affecting the value system of their societies, and in doing so we suppress assumptions about the character of human behavior which need a good deal more exposure.

The conventional wisdom rejects the idea of greater decentralization of authority within the Canadian federation out of hand, apparently because it is taken for granted that an increase in the strength of the provincial governments (whether the federal government grows weaker or not) cannot, by definition, lead to a qualitatively better society. If people are increasingly socialized politically into regional societies where all, or nearly all, the good things come from their provincial governments, then they will ultimately conclude that their provincial governments are much more important than Ottawa. They will, we are told, turn in upon themselves, and when they are asked to make sacrifices for those poorer, disadvantaged Canadians who live in less prosperous parts of the country they will not willingly do so, and may even punish at the polls governments who propose that they should. The alternative, therefore, is either greater power for the federal government or a system which masquerades as decentralization but is in fact a carefully contrived arrangement where Ottawa enables the provincial governments to do certain things on condition that their programs meet some kind of national standard.

For roughly the past thirty years we have followed this second option—under the very misleading title of "cooperative" federalism—having given up on the first not long after the Reconstruction Conference of 1945. It is widely believed that the increasing willingness of the federal government during this period to hand over nominal federal powers to the provinces has been the cause of the decline in national feeling since the end of World War II. But that is not the real problem. The fact is that both options are cut from the same ideological cloth, and either one was likely to lead to the same conclusion.

What is most objectionable about our modern practice of federalism is not that it has encouraged the growth of regional and provincial strength, but rather that as a system for managing the Canadian federation it does nothing to inhibit the growth of a narrow provincial self-satisfaction, and nothing to force us to cast our vision on a wider scale. Requiring the provinces to bargain with the federal government for this or that tax point, or for a greater or lesser degree of federal participation in specific provincial programs, merely promotes competition and greed on the part of each government. This set of attitudes is in turn transmitted into the political value system of their people. Each province is treated, as it were, as simply another individual with insatiable demands in the society of Canadian federalism, and each is left to itself to do what it can to promote its own ends.

Indeed, cooperative federalism looks very much like the nineteenth-century liberal view of government itself. In that view, political society is seen as a collection of self-seeking individuals who have abandoned an intolerable presocial state of nature for the limited purposes of community living. For these purposes it is necessary for each individual to succumb to the collective will of the whole, but only so far as is necessary to ensure that each individual's freedom to do as he or she pleases is not more restricted than that of any other member of the society. Each individual is expected to guard his or her own rights jealously, and each individual in this liberal view of political society typically, and quite properly, makes claims only for himself and ignores the rest. It is taken for granted that everyone is behaving in the same way and that out of this collective self-seeking the general good of the society as a whole will result. If this view of political life is applied to modern Canadian federalism—by thinking of the provinces as ten individual members of our federal society—what results is what we have come to call cooperative federalism. It is, in a word, laissez-faire for the federal government—*the* government in this federal society. It is taken for granted that each province is out only for itself and that if suitable arrangements are made to enable them equally to promote themselves somehow the general national good will result.

But of course laissez-faire no more works with the Canadian federal system than it did with nineteenth-century government. All that happens is that the rich get richer and the poor get poorer. In due course a revised version of the liberal view of political society takes over. That view makes the same set of assumptions about the fundamental character of human motivation but says that it has become clear that individuals require a very substantial degree of government intervention to ensure socially responsible behavior. In modern liberal society, therefore, we have a welfare state; and in modern Canadian federalism we have an increasing demand that the federal government assume more power.

Neither of these views represents a satisfactory solution to our current dilemma. Both will encourage the continued growth of individual self-seeking on the part of the provinces largely because both are founded on a view of the fundamental motivations of the provincial governments which takes their selfishness for granted. There are, however, other ways to approach the problem. All that is necessary to see how we might resolve the dilemma is to adopt a different set of assumptions about the character of political society and those who participate in it.

Political society is undeniably composed of individuals, but whether they behave in a competitive or cooperative manner is another matter. There are at least three schools of thought on the question. Some say that people are naturally greedy if left to themselves; others say they are naturally willing to share; and still others say they are neither, that people learn to behave one way or the other through their experience. For those who adhere to the first school of thought there are generally two options. Either people will be allowed to do as they like with only very limited interference by the state, or there will be very considerable state regulation in order to curb the excesses of individual greed and to provide an equal opportunity for variously gifted individuals to compete in the marketplace. For our purposes the other two schools of thought can be lumped together. In either case the role of government is to so arrange things as to encourage the sharing, whether it is naturally motivated or only learned through experience.

Just as I am inclined to think there is some doubt about whether or not human beings are naturally greedy, I also can see no reason why it should be assumed that the Canadian provinces are necessarily greedy. It is true, of course, that they often make quite extraordinary demands on Ottawa even to the point of being willing to keep their natural resources in the ground in order to force a better bargain when times are difficult. On the other hand, however, there is no evidence that any of them is opposed, for example, to the practice of equalization between all of the provinces. In fact, just as it may be argued that the apparent selfishness of individuals is less due to any natural human motivation than it is to a society which encourages that attitude, so we may say that the behavior of the provinces is as much due to the manner in which the federal system has been managed over the last thirty years as it is to any regional particularisms which are inherent in their circumstances. If we were to assume, therefore, that these ten individuals of Canadian federal society are either willing to share or can learn to do so, then the role of the central government is to enable them to do that, not by imposing rules and regulations, but by creating an environment in which each of them will be able to grow up in its own way.

Given Canada's circumstances, that is likely to mean much greater decentralization of authority than we have ever contemplated before, accompanied, of course, by mechanisms which will allow those who are well off to share their wealth with those less fortunate than themselves. In the end, the pattern of federal-provincial relations which has evolved in the years since the end of the Second World War may not be the disaster that the conventional wisdom would have us believe it is, and the apparent impossibility of our being able to develop a national party system to bridge regional differences may therefore be literally irrelevant. Instead, we have an opportunity to forge a new kind of union—from the ashes of the old, as the saying goes—and that, in its way, has much grander implications for the future of the country than Sir John A. Macdonald ever dreamed.

· III ·

Policies

Public Attitudes and Intergovernmental Shifts in Responsibility for Health Programs: Paying the Piper without Calling the Tune?

David Falcone and Richard J. Van Loon

This paper examines the impact of Canadian health policy on public support for the federal government which is conceived of as a set of institutions and processes rather than as the party in power: the object Canadians commonly label "Ottawa." Health is an appropriate area to examine if one wishes to better comprehend the role public policy plays in generating or eroding public support for a national government in a federal system in which the subunits are major political actors. Since good health is a matter of concern to virtually everyone, governmental policies that bear on it are extremely salient. One would assume that if these policies generate programs that provide adequate coverage and effective services at reasonable cost to the public they will significantly enhance support for the federal government. Our analysis of the origins and development of health policy in Canada suggests this may be too easy an assumption—that divided jurisdiction and baroque funding arrangements have confused the public, heightened federal-provincial conflict, and may even have eroded rather than enhanced public support for the national government.

As our overview will indicate, Canadian health policy has both federal and provincial government origins. The federal government was the first to make a formal proposal but Saskatchewan was first to enact a program. Despite major changes in funding arrangements in 1975 and 1977, health insurance programs remain a divided responsibility. After describing the programs and speculating about their likely consequences for differential public support for the federal and provincial systems, survey data will be examined which provided limited, indirect, and somewhat conflicting evidence on this issue and the more general question of what, if anything, can a federal government do to enhance support for itself.

National Health Insurance: The Federal Right to Tax and the Provincial Duty to Spend[1]

The cornerstones of Canada's hospital insurance program and medical insurance program (the Hospital Insurance and Diagnostic Services Act of 1957 and the Medical Care Act of 1968, respectively) were laid as a result of a disjointed series of proposals and enactments, some provincial and some federal. Many seem to have been based upon purely pragmatic and straightforward political grounds before and after the federal-provincial conditional grant insurance program. Seven of these are highlighted by Malcolm Taylor as critical events in the creation of the Canadian health insurance system: the six-and-one-half year gestation of the 1945 federal health insurance proposals which, though not implemented, set the stage for later federal-provincial negotiations in this area; the Saskatchewan Hospital Services Legislation of 1946 which provided the first universal hospital insurance program in North America; the 1957 Ontario Hospital Insurance Plan that, after the earlier enactment of such programs by Saskatchewan, British Columbia (1948), and Alberta (1950), triggered the federal government's conditional grant hospital insurance program; the evolution of that program from the 1945 proposals; the highly controversial Saskatchewan Medical Care Insurance Program of 1961, again the first of its kind in North America; the conditional grant National Medicare Program, following the enactment of different forms of governmental medical insurance in Alberta, Ontario, and British Columbia; and the federally induced Quebec Medicare Program of 1979 and subsequent strike by specialists in that province.[2]

1. This section relies heavily on David Falcone and Richard J. Van Loon, "Centralization and Devolution of Health Policy," paper delivered at the Carleton-Duke Conference on Centralization and Devolution, July 1979; and Richard J. Van Loon, "From Shared Cost to Block Funding and Beyond: The Politics of Health Insurance in Canada," *Journal of Health Politics Policy and Law* 2 (1979): 453–78.
2. Malcolm Taylor, *Health Insurance and Canadian Public Policy: The Seven Decisions that*

The 1945 proposals follow a familiar pattern. An Interdepartmental Advisory Committee on Health Insurance submitted a comprehensive report on health services to Health Minister Ian Mackenzie recommending a comprehensive universal national health insurance program using the grant-in-aid mechanism to avert constitutional problems. (Earlier the Rowell-Sirois Commission had suggested the desirability of a national health insurance plan financed through taxes rented to the federal government but, of course, not using the conditional-grant device.) The recommendation was generally endorsed by major interest groups and provincial ministers of health.

At that time this would have been a boldly interventionist federal program. However, because of shifts in cabinet priorities, national health insurance was not given independent status. Instead, it was included in the general social reconstruction program to be discussed at an upcoming Dominion-Provincial Conference of First Ministers. In order that it not threaten the entire program, the health component abandoned the uniform legislation requirement and made other concessions that diminished its interventionist character. Despite these concessions, the conference did not endorse the proposals. The chief stumbling blocks were the rental fields requested by the federal government. Basing their attack on the "contract" theory of confederation, Premiers Duplessis of Quebec and Drew of Ontario were able to abort the conference, despite the fact that other provinces appeared to favor the federal offer.

According to Taylor, despite the demise of the conference, the proposals had a significant impact:

The majority of provincial governments, previously relatively unconcerned with the economic and health problems of their citizens, had now to face both an aroused public opinion and, for the first time, the prospects of the compelling pressures of federal grants inducing them to action in an area clearly of provincial constitutional jurisdiction, and despite the fact that for some of them there was neither ideological commitment nor political party rivalry justifying the political, administrative, and financial hazards.[3]

The provinces responded to these pressures in varying ways. In the early stages of the conference, Saskatchewan had already begun to consider a hospital insurance plan. With federal participation uncer-

---

Created the Canadian Health Insurance System (Montreal: McGill-Queen's University Press, 1978).

3. Ibid., p. 68.

tain, the Cooperative Commonwealth Federation (CCF) government nonetheless passed legislation providing for a universal, compulsory hospital care insurance system in 1946. Taylor dubs the Saskatchewan Plan "the policy decision to go it alone," and, the later Ontario Hospital Insurance Plan, "the decision not to go it alone." Given Ontario's proportion of the population and economic resources of Canada, it is not surprising that they did not *have* to face going it alone. Moreover, it had been Ontario's opposition that deadlocked the Dominion-Provincial Conference. But in the more than ten years that elapsed between the Conference and the Ontario Hospital Insurance Plan, George Drew had become leader of the national Progressive Conservative Party and Leslie Frost had become Premier. Taylor gives Frost's advocacy of national hospital insurance much of the credit for its adoption, an attribution which should somewhat undermine the confidence of determinists or others cynical about the relevance to policy of the attitudes and ideologies of politicians. All of the alternative national insurance programs under consideration would have resulted in a reallocation of resources at the expense of the citizens of "have provinces." Although the taxation requirements on the governments of those provinces might have been made easier, had Ontario opposed in 1956, its opposition might very well have had the same effect on national hospital insurance as it had had earlier. At the very least, Ontario could have postponed a program, given Louis St. Laurent's lack of enthusiasm for early enactment.

With the exception of Saskatchewan's, the provincial plans were object lessons in how not to formulate a government-financed hospital insurance program. Blue Cross's administrative capabilities in British Columbia were overtaxed, which did not augur well for the use of private intermediaries elsewhere. Alberta's indirect inducement to municipalities to participate in a shared cost scheme was heavy-handed and so unsuccessful that only 38.6 percent of hospital income (compared to 85.7 percent in Saskatchewan and 73 percent in British Columbia) came from government.[4] When Newfoundland entered confederation in 1949, it brought with it a cottage hospital scheme covering 47 percent of the population in which the government directly provided services. Such a "state" plan clearly was not politi-

4. Ibid., p. 168.

cally feasible outside that province. As another testament to the adage about politics and bedfellows, Saskatchewan's CCF-initiated program provided a model hospital insurance program and a Progressive Conservative government in Ontario provided the clout to see that a version of it was effected nationally.

The impetus to act that was spurred by Ontario coincided with a gradualist stance on the part of the federal government so that, like the programs in Saskatchewan and Ontario, national health insurance began with coverage of hospital services. This occurred despite the fact that the federal government, like the provincial governments where hospital insurance was first introduced, was made well aware of the inflationary substitution of hospital for outpatient services that this program encouraged. On the one hand, the program covered the most costly health services and avoided the most politically threatening opposition. On the other, by accelerating the aggregate cost of health services—even if the total cost to governments was less than would have been the case with a comprehensive health insurance program—it foreshadowed the eventual dominance of cost control as a concern in health policy.

Another inflationary aspect of the program was the use of a virtually open-ended (i.e., limited only by the extent of a province's ability to spend) conditional grant method of cost-sharing. Again, policy makers had been advised of the consequences of "combining the federal right to tax with the provincial duty to spend" (as former Finance Minister John Turner once put it) as early as the Rowell-Sirois Report. According to the formula, if a provincial hospital insurance plan met federal conditions, the federal government "matched" expenditures on covered services. "Matched" was qualified, because the federal contribution consisted of 24 percent of the average Canadian per capita cost for hospital services, and 25 percent of the average per capita cost in the province times the number of insured persons in the province. Thus, low-cost (therefore low income, although per capita income and cost are imperfectly correlated) provinces were intended to receive slightly more than 50 percent of the cost of the program, high-cost/income provinces, slightly less.

For a province to receive funds, its program had to be: universal (operationally, this meant it had to cover 95 percent of the population and no financial deterrent to utilization could be imposed); portable, with travel or a change in residence; comprehensive (covering almost the entire range of inpatient services, accommodation, and meals at the standard ward level and, at the option of the provinces, a wide range of outpatient services); and not-for-profit (in effect, provincially administered). In setting these conditions the federal government had largely accommodated the provinces (e.g., Ontario's insistence that universal did not mean compulsory). Nevertheless, in many ways the *responsibility* for the administration of the program was centralized. As Taylor notes:

> The degree of control was extraordinary. Every essential requirement for the operation of the program was prescribed by the federal government. The provincial government would have to establish a hospital planning division; it must license, inspect, and supervise hospitals and maintain adequate staff standards; it must approve hospital budgets; it must approve the purchase of furniture and equipment by hospitals; it must collect the prescribed statistics and submit the required reports; and the province must make insured services available to all on uniform terms and conditions.[5]

All provinces had accepted the federal "offer" by 1961.

The evolution of the National Medical Care Insurance followed a pattern similar to that of hospital insurance. One could use the 1945 proposals as a basis for viewing the federal government as the initiator of the policy. However, it was Saskatchewan which first implemented a plan and bore the consequences, a physicians' strike. Saskatchewan's experience may have averted a similar reaction to the federal government's later and substantially similar plan.

Partly to provide a trophy for the recently formed New Democratic Party, Saskatchewan intended its health insurance plan to serve as a national model. In its brief to the Hall Commission (Royal Commission on Health Services) in 1962, the provincial government called upon Ottawa to enact a medical services plan along the same lines as the Hospital Insurance and Diagnostic Services Act. The provincial plan was nearly sabotaged by Diefenbaker's victory in 1962. The Conservative victory was interpreted as a defeat for the medicare concept advocated by the Liberals. Further, an early staunch advocate of Saskatchewan's plan, Tommy Douglas, lost his federal seat. Nevertheless, the plan was implemented despite the political cost (some hold

5. Ibid., p. 230.

the mismanagement of the physicians' strike partly responsible for the Liberals' electoral victory in Saskatchewan in 1964) and was successful, at least in the view of the Hall Commission.

Other provincial plans in force at the time used private intermediaries to subsidize the cost of participation of persons who were unable to afford the premiums. It was this sort of plan that a Canadian Association–Canadian Health Insurance Association coalition had expected the Hall Commission to recommend when it urged the Commission's appointment. The Commission considered such a plan in a typically pragmatic Canadian fashion. Using consumer survey data, it found that the average Canadian allocated about 4 percent of his income to health services. In the interest of improved national health, it judged that policy makers probably would want to set the lower limit at 5 percent. In this event, given the Canadian income distribution, almost three-fourths of income earners would have required subsidization (i.e., would have to have been means-tested in some way). Therefore, it is not surprising that on administrative grounds alone the Commission found the universal Saskatchewan plan more attractive than that of Alberta, British Columbia, or Ontario.

The Hall Commission's Report[6] helped generate both support for and opposition to medical care insurance. The Diefenbaker government had appointed the Commission and, when the Progressive Conservatives became the opposition, the fact that the Report's recommendations were not yet implemented gave them something to exploit. Naturally, the NDP supported federal legislative embodiment of its provincial showpiece. The primary threat to a national plan was provincial opposition, which was formidable. By the mid-1960s negotiations between the federal and provincial governments were analogous to international relations among near equals who were not necessarily allies. Shared cost programs were under attack; Quebec had opted out of the Canadian University Foundation grants programs and had set up a pension plan similar to, but distinct from, the Canadian Pension Plan. Taylor sums up the centripetal-centrifugal balance at the time as follows:

. . . coinciding with the emergence of the new autonomy-seeking Quebec Premier Lesage, the Liberal government in Ottawa found itself also con-

6. Hall Commission, *Report* 1 (1964); 2 (1965).

fronting other provincial governments with strong, determined leaders no longer content to accept Ottawa's largesse if it meant accepting Ottawa's dictates. Clearly the centralization-decentralization pendulum had reached its apogee and was commencing its back-swing to the provinces.[7]

Pearson's government, then, was in the unenviable position of having to act in a way that was certain to alienate the provinces. A fixed per capita grant was economically unacceptable to the provinces but a conditional grant program was overly interventionist. As a result, the federal government marketed the conditional grant program as one in which the federal and provincial governments set the conditions at the outset: "The proposal does not require detailed agreements governing the Medicare plan. It calls only for a general Federal-Provincial *understanding* as to the nature of the health programs which will make a Federal government believe that there are four criteria on which such an understanding should be based."[8]

The conditions (i.e., portability, comprehensiveness, universality, not-for-profit administration) remained. However, they were stated generally and required neither ongoing detailed federal government audits nor specific federal-provincial agreements. The matching formula was simplified (the federal contribution was based on the national average per capita cost, which had a more reallocative effect) and a more redistributive effect was achieved than with the hospital insurance program. In effect, ten provincial programs were created.

By 1971, each province provided medical care insurance that covered virtually all residents. This did away with almost all out-of-pocket expenses. The exceptions, ones which were later to be consequential in judging the availability and accessibility of services provided, were the provisions for "opting out" or "extra-billing" on the part of physicians.[9] The former issue precipitated the strike in Quebec; labor was adamant that opting out not be permitted whereas

7. Taylor, *Health Insurance*, p. 354.

8. Remarks by former Prime Minister Lester Pearson, cited in Taylor, *Health Insurance*, p. 354.

9. Under a province's plan the physician may either bill the patient who then seeks reimbursement from the insurer, or he can simply submit a bill to the plan on behalf of the patient for services rendered. In effect, when a physician bills a patient directly, he is charging more than the given percentage of the negotiated (Provincial Medical Association–Provincial Plan) fee schedule. The patient is reimbursed by the plan for the percentage of the fee covered (e.g., 90 percent) and the difference between this and the amount he or she pays is an out-of-pocket expense.

the organization representing medical specialists was equally committed to the provision. The result was a government compromise that specified a limit on the percentage of specialists who could opt out, a compromise which satisfied no one.

The consensus view of the Canadian health insurance system is that by and large it accomplished what it set out to do: make a comprehensive range of high-quality health services available and accessible to all at little direct cost.[10] Geographic maldistribution of personnel and facilities remained, but some discrepancies were noticeably reduced and there was increased utilization, particularly of hospital services, by lower-income persons.[11] Some services, such as home care, were not covered by all provinces, although they were not only needed but may have proved to be cost effective. The health manpower supply grew to the point where it was regarded as an embarrassment of riches.[12] Even some improvement in outcome measures has been attributed to national health insurance: chiefly, the infant mortality rate, which declined from 20 percent over the United States level in 1958 to a figure below that of England and Wales by 1973.[13] Further, survey data show that health insurance is the most popular "government" program.[14] Still, from the very outset, there was dissatisfaction with the program on the part of governments. Some provinces, notably Ontario and Quebec, complained that their priorities were distorted by the program, that they had to make expenditures on covered services irrespective of how appropriate these were. The federal government's concern centered primarily on the fiscal arrangements, namely, that they were inflationary and, since they were open-ended, unpredictable.

It should be noted that although costs are now a pressing concern, no dramatic increase can be traced to either the hospital or the medical care programs. As one would expect, particularly since Canada

10. Spyros Andreopoulous, ed., *National Health Insurance: Can We Learn From Canada?* (New York: Wiley, 1975).

11. Peter Enterline et al., "The Distribution of Medical Services Before and After 'Free' Medical Care—The Quebec Experience," *New England Journal of Medicine* 289 (1973): 2274–378.

12. Robert A. Armstrong, Director of Health Insurance, Health and Welfare Canada, personal interview, May 1976. See also, James Bennett and Jacques Krasny, *Health-Care in Canada*, reprint from the series appearing in *The Financial Post*, March 26–May 7, 1977.

13. Ibid.

14. Van Loon, "From Shared Cost," pp. 454–78.

had an excess hospital bed supply, hospital utilization increased after the Hospital Insurance and Diagnostic Services Act. Accordingly, this component of health expenditures also increased. Further, although utilization did not rise, expenditures went up after Medicare, if only because bad debts were eliminated.[15] However, overall health care expenditures did not increase at a much different rate from those of the United States which had no such program. Also, from 1971 to 1976 (the period of greatest expressed concern about aggregate health costs) the ratio of health expenditures to Gross National Product actually fell from 7.3 to 7.1.[16] Essentially, it seems that in each country relative price inflation has been due to the same interrelated forces: an aging population; third-party reimbursement; and, probably more than anything else, the technological imperative in health care.

In any event, what is important is that in the mid-1970s Ottawa perceived that costs were rising too rapidly and that divided responsibility was a large part of the cause. The federal government, therefore, began to propose alternative cost-sharing mechanisms in the early 1970s which were rejected by the provinces. The denouement of centralization occurred in 1975 when the federal government imposed a ceiling upon its contributions to costs over the next three years that was tied to the rise in GNP. In the budget speech announcing this ceiling on federal contributions to the Health Insurance Program, the federal minister of finance also gave notice of federal intention to terminate the Hospital Insurance agreements and to renegotiate. A formal proposal to combine the new negotiations with those for general federal-provincial fiscal arrangements followed in June 1976. For the purposes of this discussion, the fine print of the final settlement matters less than the overall impact and the nature of the negotiations. Those with a love for complex formulae are referred to the legislation itself,[17] but, in essence, there are four parts to the arrangement. First, there is a per capita block grant amounting to about one-half of the former federal contribution which is based on 1975 payments and will escalate annually according to population and GNP increases. This block grant is payable only if provinces continue

15. Robert G. Evans, "Beyond the Medical Marketplace: Expenditures, Utilization and Pricing of Insured Health in Canada," in Spyros Andreopoulous, ed., *National Health Insurance*, p. 46.
16. Van Loon, "From Shared Cost," pp. 454–78.
17. *The Federal-Provincial Fiscal Arrangements and Established Programs Financing Act* (1977).

to meet the appropriate, if ill-defined, program conditions. Since the amount of the grant is about one-quarter of the cost of popular programs, it was felt that the provinces would comply. Second, the federal government agreed to vacate 13.5 percentage points of personal and 1 percentage point of corporate income tax and to equalize the yield from these sources in the same way as other income tax points. Third, a $20-per-capita unconditional annual payment was to be provided; it will be escalated annually in the same way as the block payments, but payable "in respect of extended health care services" such as home nursing, ambulatory services, and long-term institutional care. Most of these presumably lower cost alternatives were not covered by earlier cost-sharing legislation. Finally, there is a transitional adjustment payment to ensure that the provinces do not suffer financially as a result of the changes.

With respect to the negotiations themselves, there was very little to distinguish health from other policy areas; indeed, postsecondary education was included in the same formulae but was treated in an even less conditional manner. The four basic medical conditions (comprehensiveness, universality, portability, and public administration) and the key hospital insurance condition (access unencumbered by financial barriers) were to be ensured by tying the block grant to them. A separate block grant was provided specifically for extended care, but that is about the extent to which specifically health-related concerns entered the final discussion. No meetings of federal and provincial health ministers were held to consider the final formulae (although several meetings between 1971 and 1975 did discuss earlier drafts) and final negotiations took place almost exclusively among federal and provincial Finance Treasury, and Prime Minister's Office or Premiers' Office, officials.

The current funding arrangement can be described as part of a devolution of program responsibility; but, in effect, it amounts to a concentration of interest in resource allocation since a dollar spent by a provincial government is now just that and health spending must be viewed in the context of a consolidated budget. Not surprisingly, then, provinces have experienced a heightened cost-consciousness and have placed caps on health expenditure levels. They also have responded to the incentive built into the funding formula to test both the public's and the federal government's tolerance for the limits of the conditions, for by minimizing compliance they can make the

Table 8.1. Total Health Expenditures by Provincial Governments (a) and Related Federal Contributions (b), by Province, 1975–76 to 1979–80

Province	Provincial expenditures					Federal contribution[a]					Percent federal contribution[b]				
	1975–76	1976–77	1977–78	1978–79	1979–80	1975–76	1976–77	1977–78	1978–79	1979–80	1975–76	1976–77	1977–78	1978–79	1979–80
	$ millions					$ millions					Percent				
Newfoundland	209.6	225.7	239.6	266.0	297.8	85.6	100.5	113.1	132.7	152.1	40.8	44.3	47.2	49.9	31.1
Prince Edward Island	42.0	44.9	56.1	59.3	62.9	19.0	21.7	22.7	28.6	32.8	45.2	48.3	40.5	48.2	52.2
Nova Scotia	288.6	322.5	330.1	389.4	437.5	118.7	140.4	166.2	191.5	221.6	41.1	47.5	47.5	49.2	30.7
New Brunswick	221.8	254.0	279.9	307.8	363.6	97.0	116.5	134.2	159.8	183.4	43.7	46.8	47.9	51.9	50.4
Quebec	2,614.2	3,062.2	3,271.1	3,626.4	3,992.2	1,017.1	1,182.0	1,362.5	1,517.2	1,692.8	38.9	39.1	41.7	41.8	42.4
Ontario	3,181.0	3,638.3	3,991.0	4,354.7	4,705.6	1,286.3	1,479.5	1,736.3	1,960.4	2,211.2	40.4	40.7	41.5	45.0	47.0
Manitoba	413.0	467.7	508.4	531.7	577.2	166.2	193.2	206.7	241.3	269.5	40.2	41.3	40.7	45.4	40.7
Saskatchewan	327.7	397.7	449.5	483.3	558.9	142.2	169.2	191.6	215.3	248.8	43.4	42.5	42.6	44.6	44.5
Alberta	748.9	852.4	921.8	1,088.3	1,284.7	280.9	329.6	395.4	459.8	523.6	37.5	38.7	42.9	42.1	40.8
British Columbia	991.8	1,091.8	1,220.7	1,417.6	1,616.8	378.3	433.2	507.1	593.1	680.3	38.1	39.7	41.5	41.8	42.1
N.W.T.[c]															
Yukon															
Canada	9,039.4	10,321.2	11,288.2	12,524.5	13,897.2	3,591.3	4,168.4	4,385.8	5,499.9	6,216.1	39.7	40.4	42.8	41.9	44.7

a. Includes all relevant federal contributions under H.I.D.S., Medical Care, E.P.F., Canada Assistance Plan, Health Resources Fund and Professional Training Grant. Note particularly that federal contribution allocated to hospital insurance and medical care programs under E.P.F. excludes one income tax point and its cash equivalent.

b. Federal contribution as a percentage of total health expenditure by provincial government.

c. Data for the Yukon and Northwest Territories were not available.

Source: The Hon. Emmett M. Hall, CC, Q.C., Canada's National-Provincial Health Program for the 1980's (Ottawa: Government of Canada, 1980).

block transfer basically unconditional, thereby putting the funds to other uses. Since the federal government was stuck with an unrealistic "all or nothing" sanction (funds could not be partially withheld), it was, in effect, powerless except for moral suasion. However, provincial publics and opposition parties have not proved to be overly tolerant of breaches of conditions. Consequently, some severe abuses which arose in 1978 and 1979 have been corrected by provincial governments themselves. Nonetheless, as an overall result, the federal portion of health program financing actually has increased at the same time as it sometimes seems to be bearing the blame for the need for provincial fiscal restraint (see table 8.1). There are several ways that this situation could be portrayed as an anomaly, but it is not. It is a natural consequence of blurred and bifurcated responsibility for a heretofore popular policy which has significant consequences for the distribution of political support.

These consequences are discussed in the ensuing section. The foregoing account of the development of federal-provincial relations in the health policy arena should make the survey findings that will be presented less than surprising; in health policy (as well as education and welfare) the federal approach has been motivated by an ideological preference for equity and income redistribution. These concerns have been coupled with an aversion to overt constitutional squabbling and have unintentionally provided a recipe for public disaffection with Ottawa. As will be seen, we are not confident that there is a feasible remedy for this problem, particularly in the fiscally conservative environment of the 1980s. However, the federal government seems to be opting for a strategy of highlighting its activities in the delivery and funding of health and other social programs.

Public Attitudes toward Federal and Provincial Governments

Conrad Winn and Associates have compiled a significant body of opinion survey data on public attitudes toward the federal and provincial governments. The main data sources are: thirteen omnibus surveys conducted between 1976 and 1980 by CROP Inc., a Montreal-based national survey organization; studies commissioned from CROP by the federal government; and one especially pertinent survey conducted by Gallup in 1977. Winn's principal conclusion is that: "The federal government is held in declining esteem, the provincial governments are the beneficiaries of increasing public trust, and the Canadian public is sympathetic to provincial demands for more power."[18] There are important qualifications to this statement. Some are due to basic ambiguities in the survey results which will be noted in passing. However, one has most telling implications for federal government policy. It involves Milton Rokeach's distinction between attitudes toward *objects* and *situations*.[19] Since the former, which are exclusively tapped by CROP surveys, by and large indicate a comparative bias toward the provinces, they tempt us to accept the hypothesis that the structure of program responsibility—health in this case—has eroded federal support. On the other hand, the scant data on public attitudes regarding which level of government should have responsibility for specific programs are inconsistent with this conclusion. They serve as another reminder of the hazards involved in asserting researchers' impressions of consistency in interpretations of public attitude patterns. Let us elaborate.

The CROP survey findings first indicate declining support for the federal government. Consonant with this are the opinions, next examined, that the federal government is less efficient than the provinces and, less conclusively, that Ottawa is chiefly to blame for federal-provincial conflict. Following this is a discussion of attitudes toward the provincial (not just Quebec) independence issue and toward the appropriate balance of power between federal and provincial governments. Finally, data on public opinion about federal provincial responsibility for social policy are assessed. In light of Rokeach's distinction and, combined with other data, they form the basis for our caution in offering easy generalizations about "support." They also temper inferences about what should be the federal government's optimal strategy for securing more support.

Declining satisfaction with the federal government. Figure 8.1 depicts the public's increasing satisfaction with provincial as opposed to the federal government; the broken line measures overall satisfaction

18. Conrad Winn and Associates, *Report* (August 1980 study commissioned by Health and Welfare Canada), passim.

19. Milton Rokeach, "The Role of Values in Public Opinion Research," *Public Opinion Quarterly* 32 (Winter 1968–1969):547–59.

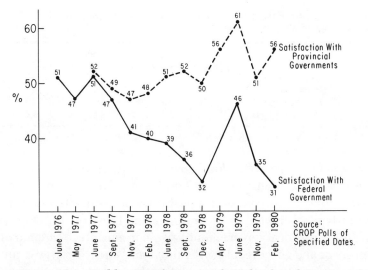

Figure 8.1. *Public Satisfaction with Federal and Provincial Governments (in percent)*

with provincial government (i.e., the percentage of respondents saying that they are "very satisfied" or "satisfied"). The unbroken line measures overall satisfaction with the federal government. The gap between the two seems to have begun in September 1977, with the largest gap occurring in February 1980. Supporting this finding is the fact that responses to other questions reported below show that the federal government is not highly esteemed. There also is a general tendency for all regions and social groups to be dissatisfied with the central government; hence a summary score measuring Canada-wide dissatisfaction does reflect the general attitudes of Canadians and is not the result of skewing by the extreme views of one social group. There is one departure from the downward trend in satisfaction with the federal government (June 1979). However, it is easily explained by the public's "honeymoon" with the newly elected Clark government.

Perceived inefficiency of the federal government. Table 8.2 presents CROP data gathered in September 1978 which reveal that respondents felt the federal government was less "efficient" than

Table 8.2. *Public Perceptions of the Relative Efficiency of Three Levels of Government*

	Local	Provincial	Federal
Very efficient	14%	10%	5%
Somewhat efficient	54	54	43
Not efficient	20	25	40
Don't know / N.A.	12	11	12

Source: CROP Survey, September 1978.

provincial and, especially, local governments. Fourteen percent of respondents rated their local government as "very efficient" as compared to the 10 percent and 5 percent who, respectively, evaluated their provincial and federal governments in these terms. Only 20 percent felt their local government was "not efficient," as compared to 25 percent and 40 percent for the provincial and federal governments, respectively. These data suggest that the relative smallness of the unit of government being evaluated may be a critical variable in determining favorable public perceptions, a possibility we will consider shortly.

Blame for federal-provincial conflict. In June 1979, CROP explored the extent to which the Canadian public was aware of federal-provincial disagreements, as well as the way in which blame for such disagreements was allocated. Respondents were asked: "Generally speaking, do you feel that the provincial and federal levels of government have usually, sometimes, rarely, or never, been able to work together effectively?" Nationwide, only 15 percent expressed the view that cooperation "usually" took place. For those not feeling this way, a supplementary question was asked: "Do you put the blame for this mainly on the provinces, mainly on the federal government, or both equally?" As table 8.3 indicates, twice as many respondents (16 percent vs. 8 percent) blamed the federal rather than provincial government. Moreover, the federal government was blamed more frequently in every region. The federal government was especially unpopular in the west, where it was three times more likely to be blamed than provincial governments. Winn and Associates' arithmetic cannot be disputed on this point. However, what may be most significant about the responses to this question is that 64 percent placed

Table 8.3. *Public's Allocation of Blame for Federal-Provincial Conflict by Region*

	Canada	Atlantic	Quebec	Ontario	West
Mainly federal government	16%	13%	21%	9%	20%
Mainly provincial government	8	6	12	5	6
Both equally	64⎱	81	67	86	74
Don't know / N.A.	12⎰				

equal blame on both levels of government, suggesting a general dissatisfaction with the conduct of intergovernmental affairs that may be working in favor of a strong federal position. We will take up this issue in the section on policy implications.

Provincial independence. In December 1978 and in January 1979, CROP asked respondents for their views about Canada's constitutional future. The question was "As you know, there has been a lot of discussion about Canada's future. Here are some proposed options. If a referendum were held today, which one option would you vote for?" Table 8.4A, below, shows the distribution of the responses. As might be expected, "revised federalism" and the "status quo" were the preferred alternatives. But it is striking that "provincial independence" was more than twice as popular as the option signifying more power for the federal government. The fact that more than one of every seven Canadians appeared to favor provincial independence might be disturbing information for federalists. Among the young (aged eighteen to twenty-nine), almost one-fifth (18 percent) favor provincial independence. The provincialism of the young may be temporary (e.g., Maurice Pinard has observed a tendency for Quebec francophones to become less *indépendantiste* as they age). But one cannot rule out the possibility that support for provincial independence will increase as the generation aged eighteen to twenty-nine (when interviewed in December 1978–January 1979) becomes older and inculcates its views among succeeding generations.

Table 8.4 displays the regional distribution of responses favoring provincial independence. In Quebec, fully 26 percent favored provincial independence as compared to 17 percent in British Columbia and 10 percent in Ontario. Among the regions and subregions for which CROP provides breakdowns, the lowest support for indepen-

Table 8.4. *Public Attitudes toward Various Constitutional Options*

A. *Preferred constitutional options of Canadian public*

Political independence for your province with an economic association with the rest of Canada	15%
Revised federalism negotiated between the provinces and the federal government	37
Status quo, that is, keeping things as they are	26
Give the central government in Ottawa more power over the provinces than it now has	7
None of the above or don't know	14

B. *Regional support for provincial independence (in percent)*

Major regions		CROP subregions	
Atlantic	12	Montreal	22
Quebec	26	Toronto	3
Ontario	10	Alberta	10
West	13	B.C.	17

Source: CROP survey during December 1978 and January 1979.

dence (3 percent) occurred in Toronto. Toronto also expressed the greatest support (12 percent) for more centralization of power in Ottawa. At least at the time of these surveys, support for independence was not higher in Alberta (10 percent) than in Ontario (10 percent). From this datum, it may be inferred that Albertans are less likely than, say, British Columbians to support a separatist movement. But, it should certainly not be inferred that Albertans are more satisfied with the conduct of the federal government or system in light of other attitudinal data.

Balance of powers. In recent years, Gallup and CROP have elicited the views of Canadians with respect to the desirable distribution of power between the two levels of government. CROP asked the same question on two different occasions. A Gallup survey sought public attitudes toward the federal-provincial balance of power in the fields of taxation and social policy. In all three surveys, the public expressed support for a further decentralization of power. Table 8.5 displays the regional breakdown of responses to the Gallup survey taken in July 1977. The question was worded as follows: "As you know, provincial

Table 8.5. Public Support for Greater Provincial Power in the Fields of Taxation and Social Policy

	Canada	Atlantic	Quebec	Ontario	Manitoba	Saskatchewan	Alberta	B.C.
Approve	53%	46%	59%	46%	69%	55%	63%	57%
Disapprove	25	32	24	25	25	27	16	28
Undecided / N.A.	21	22	17	28	6	18	21	15

Source: Gallup survey, July 1977.

governments are asking for more responsibilities in such areas as taxation and social security measures like welfare, pensions, and so on.
Would you approve or disapprove if the provincial governments had
more power in these fields and federal government had less?" Across
the country as a whole, an absolute majority (53 percent) favored
more provincial power, as did majorities in Quebec (59 percent) and
in each of the Western provinces (60 percent). Only one-fourth of respondents opposed provincial demands. Albertans were least likely to
oppose the devolution of power (16 percent).

In December 1978, and again in September 1979, CROP asked the
following questions: "Assuming that a referendum were held today
regarding *federalism*, which *one* of the following options would you
vote for?" The three substantive options consisted of more power for
the provinces, more power for Ottawa, and a rearrangement of responsibilities without a change in the balance of power. In both years,
those favoring more provincial power substantially outnumbered
those favoring more federal power. For the two years, the average in
favor of more provincial power was 21 percent as opposed to the
10 percent who favored more federal power. In the September 1979
CROP poll, every generation, social group, region, and subregion
(except Ontario and Toronto) favored more provincial power. As might
be expected, the groups most supportive of decentralization were
Quebec francophones, Albertans, and the young. Among the generation aged eighteen to twenty-nine, 25 percent preferred more provincial power while only 9 percent preferred more power for Ottawa.
Among educational strata, the one least inclined to the provincial
viewpoint consisted of those with grade-school educations or less.

Social policy. In the light of the foregoing catalogue of primarily
negative attitudes toward the federal government, the survey results
regarding the appropriate distribution of responsibility are curious.
They highlight the necessity of interpreting public opinion data with
Rokeach's "object-situation" distinction in mind and with a respect for
Canadians' abilities to tolerate what seemingly are inconsistencies in
their political attitudes.

In June 1979, CROP elicited views on the desirable distribution of
responsibility for public sector activities. Many opinion surveys elicit-
ing the attitudes of Quebecers on this subject have indicated that

large pluralities of Quebec francophones—often absolute majorities
—favored the devolution of large sectors of federal government activities to the provinces. CROP's June 1979 survey is the first one Winn
and Associates were able to find that presented the opinions of all
Canadians on this matter. Table 8.6 contains the distribution of
responses to questions about whether education, communication,
culture, and social security policy should be "only" or "primarily"
federal or provincial or should be shared equally between the two levels of government. Column 6, a summary measure reflecting the proportion who thought the federal presence in a given field should be
equal or greater than that of the provinces, shows that respondents
were most willing to concede a significant role for the federal government in social security (74 percent) and least willing to do so in education (41 percent). Since the BNA Act defined education as an exclusively provincial matter, the willingness of 14 percent of respondents
to consider "only" a federal role and another 16 percent to consider
"primarily" a federal role is somewhat unexpected. Even in the (normally thought to be) sensitive field of culture the federal government
appears to have a publicly sanctioned role; almost half the respondents wanted it to have at least equal responsibility.

Thus, there seems to be an inconsistency between the public's generalized, broad-brushed sympathy for provincial governments and its
support for a moderately strong federal presence in specific sectors of
social policy. It could be that the seeming inconsistency is real, that
Canadians *demand* public programs but object to *supplying* them,
and that the resultant excess demand breeds alienation from the
"taxing government." This inconsistency has been noted in the case of
the United Kingdom by James Buchanan.[20] He regards it as a natural
consequence of government's collective provision of a good which can
be consumed in divisible quantities.

On the other hand, while it is difficult to question the reliability of
the many surveys showing declining public esteem for the federal
government, it is possible that the single CROP survey of attitudes
toward federal and provincial roles in specific sectors is invalid. Another possibility is that the CROP survey of attitudes toward specific

20. James Buchanan, "The Inconsistencies in the NDS," in James Buchanan and Richard Toli-
son, eds., *Theory of Public Choice* (Ann Arbor: University of Michigan Press, 1972), pp. 27–45.

Table 8.6. Public Attitudes toward Federal and Provincial Responsibilities in Four Sectors within or adjoining Social Policy

	Only federal	Primarily federal	Primarily provincial	Only provincial	Equal	Don't know or N.A.	"Only federal" plus "Primarily federal" plus "equal"
Education	14%	16	27	26	11	6	41
Communications	30%	27	14	8	14	7	71
Culture	16%	16	23	21	17	7	49
Social security	40%	21	10	12	13	4	74

Source: CROP survey, June–July 1979.

public sector activities represents a more realistic *situation* to respondents. There is another explanation (not at all inconsistent with the first two) for the public's generally negative view of the federal government and its apparent support for a federal presence in specific sectors of activity; the public's disaffection with the federal government is partly due to an exaggerated view of the extent of its role in society and the economy. This explanation has some empirical support[21] and has a bearing on the kind of strategy the federal government might adopt to exploit popular programs in order to enhance its public image. The more general question is how can specific support for individual policy decisions of a government be used to generate and sustain an acceptable level of diffuse support? The latter, in our judgment, is simply an amalgam of people's reactions to individual government policies which cannot readily be articulated in the cost-benefit terms upon which they are based. This is a question often raised by policy makers, although not necessarily in these terms.

Programs and Attitudes

Obviously neither the federal nor provincial governments *intended* that the several health programs that were separated should undermine federal support (if, in fact, they have done so). Indeed, the timeworn adage that is twisted in the title of this paper suggests that federal officials expected the opposite (i.e., that they would receive increased public support). They appear to have assumed that the cost-sharing arrangements could be structured in ways that would *require* the provinces to give them due credit. They were wrong. Moreover, although at the inception of the programs most provincial politicians probably underestimated their potential for generating support, it did not take long for them to realize how popular they were. Not surprisingly, the more popular they became the more tenaciously they guarded their turf. In fact, in some cases there is no overt indication that the federal government is involved in the programs. For example, Ontario calls its plan—more than 92 percent financed by fed-

21. Ronald Morris et al., *Attitudes Toward Federal Information: A Summary Report for the Task Force on Government Information* (Toronto: York University, 1970).

eral transfer and direct premiums—The *Ontario* Hospital Insurance
Program (OHIP). This raises the question of whether the federal government should try to enhance its visibility as a joint (indeed, in some
cases, primary) sponsor. Unfortunately, there is no definitive answer.

On the one hand there is no reason to think that Canadians are immune either to the fear of "big government" currently afflicting citizens of the United States, or to the sentiments in favor of reprivatiza-
tion that seem to have been growing in the United Kingdom, the
Federal Republic of Germany, Australia, and elsewhere in recent
years. If some of the Canadian dissatisfaction with Ottawa can be attributed to this malaise, then advertising the fact that the federal government is even bigger than Canadians had previously suspected
would clearly be inadvisable. On the other hand the premise of the
foregoing statement may not be valid. That is, Canadians may *not* be
afraid of big government[22] and they may not want to reprivatize
health. Moreover, although recent cost-containment imperatives may
be eroding favorable opinion somewhat in some provinces, available
surveys indicate that health programs continue to be popular.

Complicating any attempt to answer the question of whether the
federal government should make the public more aware of its role in
providing and funding health care programs is the seeming public ignorance of which government has jurisdiction over health and other
public policy areas. Illustrative of this apparent lack of knowledge are
the dramatically different findings of two surveys, one carried out in
1968, the other in 1974. Using data derived from the 1968 Government Information Survey, Robert Presthus[23] estimated that 43 percent of respondents thought the medicare program was federal, 26
percent considered it the responsibility of both levels of government,
and only 16 percent viewed it as a provincial concern. This misper-
ception was not confined to medicare. It extended to eleven of four-

22. When a 1977 national sample of the public was asked to specify how much effort the government should put into different policy areas and cautioned to remember that putting more
effort in one of these would require a tradeoff—less effort in another, or higher taxes—more
than half of the interviewees want "more" or "much more" government effort in twelve of
twenty-one areas. Conversely in only three areas did as much as a quarter of those questioned
want "less" or "much less" effort. For a discussion of demands on government, see Allan Kornberg, William Mishler, and Harold Clarke, *Representative Democracy in the Canadian Provinces* (Toronto: Prentice-Hall, 1982), pp. 75–78.

23. Robert Presthus, *Elite Accommodation in Canadian Politics* (Toronto: Macmillan, 1975),
p. 48.

teen other policy areas. The responses in the case of medicare could be expected since Parliament had passed the act only a year earlier. Public estimates of federal responsibility in other areas, however, suggest that the federal presence has been seen as more dominant than it actually has been.

If the results of the Government Information Survey are valid, then it appears there was a remarkable shift in misperceptions between 1968 and the 1974 Federal Election Study. Although this survey asked about hospital insurance—as opposed to medicare—the public *probably* did not perceive a difference in these programs for purposes of assigning responsibility for health policy. (Supporting this assumption is the fact that the shift in perceptions about health policy coincided with a similar shift in views about educational programs.) Clarke et al. report that only 27 percent of respondents thought the insurance program was federal, 62 percent thought it was provincial, and only around 11 percent attributed responsibility to both levels of government.[24] These contradictory findings lend force to the argument that the structure of Canadian federalism has become so complex and its intergovernmental fiscal arrangements so baroque that ordinary citizens cannot possibily sort out the complexities of Established Program Financing and its relationship to health (and other) programs.

Despite or perhaps *because* of this confusion, federal officials seem to have decided on a program of public enlightenment. Concomitant with increased assertiveness and encouraged by popular support for its stance on constitutional revision and energy policy, the federal government is taking an aggressive stance with respect to its visibility in health and other policy areas. It is even being suggested that the arena of federal-provincial conflict should be institutionalized at the federal level via a "German solution" (i.e., the establishment of a legislatively effective upper house to represent provincial interests, thus obviating the sometimes cumbersome exigencies of "executive federalism").

One other feature of Established Program Financing should be considered because it is a datum that has relevance for the attribution of

24. Harold Clarke et al., *Political Choice in Canada* (Toronto: McGraw-Hill Ryerson, 1979), p. 78.

federal as opposed to provincial support. A systematic campaign to make the public more aware of the existing assignment of responsibility for programs and revenues may most alienate the upper income classes constituting the "attentive public" in what may be an unusually inattentive political culture. As matters stand, the provinces visibly administer programs such as health and postsecondary education that are attractive to the middle class; the federal government handles income transfers, such as those that would be in effect under a now contemplated guaranteed annual income program. A campaign of enlightenment may make the attentive public more aware of the federal role in health and education. However, it also will bring home to them the fact that Ottawa "takes" as much or more than it "gives." In short, the expected "benefit" in public support that may derive from spotlighting its role in health and education may not offset the liabilities Ottawa incurs in making manifest its position as the "taxing" government. The perceptual assumptions underlying this argument and their consequences for the generation and maintenance of specific support need to be explored much more carefully in future surveys because, however removed from a person's *explicit* decisional calculus and attitudinal posture, the outputs of government largely determine an individual's support for the system, or so we would argue.

Summary

The development of federal hospital insurance and comprehensive health programs illustrates the fact that, like other areas of social policy, health policy is a product of complex federal and provincial stimuli. The funding of health programs and those in related areas also illustrates the ambiguities and complexities of fiscal federalism and that federal officials, through a series of decisions of their own making, have placed themselves in the unintended and unanticipated position of being collectors of taxes. In contrast, provincial officials are able to represent themselves as the providers of highly valued public goods. Not surprisingly, therefore, numerous surveys have indicated that provincial governments generally are more highly regarded than their federal counterparts. Despite this high regard, other survey data indicate that Canadians are willing to see the federal government have major or partial responsibility in a number of *specific* policy areas. One reason for these seemingly contradictory findings may be that most average citizens are ignorant of the level of government having jurisdiction over and responsibility for funding programs in the several areas of social policy. Given the complexities of fiscal federalism, this is hardly surprising. Nor is it especially surprising that federal officials have read these opinion surveys and concluded that they can improve their "image" if they clarify and advertise the extent of their "provider" role. Whether this beating of their own drum is an optimal strategy to pursue is problematic. However, it seems clear—even if they do not think of it in Eastonian terms—that these officials have decided that publicizing their involvement and responsibility will enhance both the level of specific and diffuse support Canadians ascribe to their federal government.

Environmental Policy and Political Support

Douglas C. Nord and Geoffrey R. Weller

Political Support and the Environmental Connection

In recent years a number of distinguished political observers in North America and Europe have warned that the modern liberal-democratic nations of the West are confronted with a major challenge to their continued political viability. Some suggest that this common danger comes in the form of a dramatic decline in the degree of public support which is accorded government policies and institutions within Western democracies. A number of scholars have pointed to a developing "crisis of confidence" in the political structures and processes of these states.[1] It is argued that this "crisis" is a consequence of the increasing demands made on the political systems of Europe and North America. Policy arenas have become overburdened with new and frequently conflicting demands generated by diverse interest groups and lobbies. Key political actors and institutions have been unable to address or respond effectively to the major policy concerns of these groups in that they appear incapable of developing satisfactory remedies to important societal ills. As a result, the citizens of the Western democracies have become more "alienated" from their established political systems—their levels of political participation, trust in government, and own sense of political efficacy all having been significantly reduced during the decade of the 1970s.[2]

1. Harold and Margaret Sprout, *The Context of Environmental Politics* (Lexington, Ky.: University of Kentucky Press, 1978), pp. 92–96.
2. William Mishler, *Political Participation in Canada* (Toronto: Macmillan, 1979); Sidney Verba and N. H. Nie, *Participation in America* (New York: Harper and Row, 1972); Guiseppe

Though a number of political analysts have made note of this rapid decline of political support in Western democracies, few have attempted to closely study its constituent elements or its likely long-term consequences for existing political regimes. Instead, there has been a marked preference to treat the problem of political support as merely a subsidiary concern of the broader public policy-making process. Scholars have tended to focus their primary attention on the manner in which new policy demands are introduced into the political arena and subsequently transformed into policy decisions by the activities of major political actors and institutions. Relatively little concern has been paid to the "feedback loop" of the policy-making process by which policy outcomes are evaluated by the members of the political society. In particular, a minimum of interest has been accorded the degree to which policy outcomes have both direct or mediated influences on the extent of public support for governmental activities within an individual community.[3]

Of the limited number of scholars who have wrestled with the complicated question of political support, perhaps the research of Gerhard Loewenberg, John Wahlke, Edward Muller, and David Easton has been the most effective in pointing out the importance of popular support both for regime stability and as a measure of political change.[4] Easton's studies, in particular, have helped clarify the extent to which political support is a vital ingredient in the smooth functioning of an overburdened political system. In his various writings, he has drawn attention to the fact that long-time, well-established popular support for existing political institutions and processes can prove to be an effective counterweight to negative reactions that may develop to temporary malfunctions of the public policy process. Noting the vital im-

Di Palma, *Apathy and Participation* (New York: Free Press, 1970); Allan Kornberg, Harold D. Clarke, and Lawrence LeDuc, "Some Correlates of Regime Support in Canada," *British Journal of Political Science* 8 (1978): 199–216.

3. David Easton, "A Re-Assessment of the Concept of Political Support," *British Journal of Political Science* 5 (1975): 435–37.

4. John C. Wahlke, "Policy Demands and System Support: The Role of the Represented," *British Journal of Political Science* 1 (1971): 271–90; Edward N. Muller, "Representation of Citizens by Political Authorities: Consequences for Regime Support," *American Political Science Review* 65 (1970): 1149–77; G. R. Boynton and Gerhard Loewenberg, "The Development of Public Support for Parliament in Germany 1951–1959," *British Journal of Political Science* 3 (1973): 169–80; David Easton, "Theoretical Approaches to Political Support," *Candian Journal of Political Science* 9 (1976): 431–48.

portance of such a storehouse of positive commitment, Easton has suggested that "diffuse" political support within a society may be conceived as "a reservoir of favorable public attitudes or good will that helps members to accept or tolerate outputs to which they are opposed or the effects of which they see as damaging to their wants."[5]

Nonetheless, Easton and other students of political support have been quick to point out that this "reservoir of favorable attitudes" toward the political system cannot compensate indefinitely for perceived public policy failures. More than one scholar has noted that a single disastrous policy outcome can generate significant opposition to the established political leadership of a nation.[6] Further, it has been observed that successive policy shortcomings can threaten a government's electoral mandate and lead to its eventual defeat. In such cases, "specific" political support for a current government may be withdrawn and vested in new political leaders. In similar fashion, it has been suggested that the repeated inability of a government—regardless of party label—to develop effective public policy can lead to major popular disaffection from the established political system. Faced with a government that appears unwilling or unable to fashion acceptable policy decisions, individual citizens may find themselves rejecting not only its political leaders and programs, but also ongoing political structures and processes. It should be noted, however, that the erosion of support for an existing regime is usually a consequence of a *series* of policy disappointments rather than a public's negative reaction to a single policy outcome.[7]

In the support-maintaining process, political leaders and institutions attuned to a particular series of societal demands may find themselves at a considerable disadvantage when new policy concerns like "environmental protection" are added to the established policy agenda. At one and the same time they are confronted with the challenge of developing policies to accommodate such new demands while trying to maintain the support of established groups who may oppose them. Unfortunately, attempts at accommodation are often unacceptable to many of the most committed political actors, new and old. As a result, public officials may face the necessity of sacrificing

5. David Easton, *A Systems Analysis of Political Life* (New York: Wiley, 1965), p. 273.
6. Ibid., p. 219.
7. Easton, "A Re-Assessment of the Concept of Political Support," pp. 448–49.

the specific and diffuse support of *particular* interest groups if they are to fashion policies agreeable to a *broad* spectrum of the political community.[8] This paper explores some of the problems political leaders encounter in their attempts to maintain political support in an era of changing policy concerns. More specifically, we first will examine the manner in which the environmental issue was introduced into the Canadian policy arena. We then will assess its impact on political institutions and processes, especially the extent to which the environmental issue has affected both specific and diffuse political support for them.

Environmental Policy and Political Support: The Canadian Model

Although demands upon government in Canada for better protection of the environment always must be seen in the context of competing demands for further development, there has not been such a clear polarization between environmental and developmental forces as there has been in the United States. Moreover, the Canadian policy-making process is designed to produce diffuse and specific support from both groups. Diffuse support is encouraged by incorporating as many policy actors representing environmental and developmental concerns as possible into the policy-making process in an effort to achieve compromises. Attempts also are made to generate specific support by balancing regulatory and distributive policy outputs so that no major set of groups in either camp is thoroughly displeased. Before examining these actions in detail let us consider some of the major forces in the environmental arena.

The business and industrial sector in Canada might better be described as "prodevelopment" than as "antienvironmental." The emphasis is on convincing governments and the public of the need for economic development and growth. As Woodrow[9] has indicated, the peak associations at the federal and provincial levels try to foster a set of public and governmental attitudes conducive to development. In-

8. Charles F. Andrain, *Politics and Economic Policy in Western Democracies* (Belmont, Calif.: Duxbury Press, 1980), pp. 31–38.

9. R. Brian Woodrow, "Resources and Environmental Policy-Making at the National Level: The Search for a Focus," in O. P. Dwivedi, ed., *Resources and the Environment: Policy Perspectives for Canada* (Toronto: McClelland and Stewart, 1980), pp. 23–48.

dustry and trade associations at the national and provincial levels such
as the Canadian Pulp and Paper Association and the Ontario Forest
Products Industry are concerned not only with generating attitudes
favorable to their specific industry but also obtaining advantageous
public policies. Their general posture is that economic development
and growth are dependent upon continued exploitation of natural resources and that attempts to do so either should not be overly restricted by environmental regulations or, if regulated, industries
should be given public funds with which to meet at least some of the
costs involved.[10] The prodevelopment groups have substantial political resources with which to influence the policy-making process.
They generate considerable wealth for the nation, help the balance
of payments situation, employ large numbers of people, have close
links with influential groups such as municipal governments and
chambers of commerce, and also have financial resources enabling
them to promote their positions more vigorously than groups opposing development.

Groups whose demands relate either to the need to protect the environment or restrict further development, or to both, constitute a
loose amalgam of environmental organizations, professional groups,
and native peoples' organizations. The formation of environmental
pressure groups, nongovernmental organizations (or NGOs as they
are now frequently called), was the most immediately apparent consequence of the increase in environmental awareness in the late
1960s and early 1970s. Thousands of groups developed in those years
but relatively few survived. Most that did are restricted either by
region, ideology, or specific area of interest, despite bearing such
grandiose titles as the "National Survival Institute." Greater unity is
developing among these groups but the pace has been rather slow.

Concomitant with the rise of new environmental interest groups
has come a renewal of interest in the environment on the part of organizations and professions (especially forestry) associated with older
conservation movements. Heightened awareness of environmental
issues also led groups previously not directly involved in environmental issues per se (e.g., native peoples and labor unions) to adopt them
as legitimate ones for their members, or to use them to advance tradi-

10. Royal Commission on the Northern Environment, *North of 50°*, No. 2, (Dec. 21, 1977),
p. 5.

tional group objectives such as land claims or occupational health and safety. In general, the viewpoint of these groups is that economic development and growth should not be the overriding concern of society; if further exploitation and development are to take place it should be strictly controlled so that damage to the environment will be minimal. Moreover, most of the groups hold the view that the polluter, not the public, should pay any costs incurred. However, only a few would argue that some areas should be preserved against exploitation in perpetuity.[11] Conservationist groups generally demand regulatory policies from governments, but they are not unequivocally hostile to the generation of "distributive" or "incentive" policies if these promise to achieve their goals. The political resources of conservationist, environmental, and related groups are not negligible, but because many are still organizationally fragmented and financially weak, they are not able to promote their views as effectively as are prodevelopment forces.

The rise of environmental groups and the general concern of the public for environmental matters has meant that governments in Canada increasingly have been cross-pressured and found it difficult to develop responses that ensure continued support from both proenvironment and prodevelopment forces. Unlike their American counterparts, however, they have not stood aside while the opposing forces battled and then ministered to the victorious side. Instead, they have attempted to promote diffuse support by incorporating as many of the policy actors as possible into the search for policies that are intended to be compromises. Both mechanisms (incorporation and compromise policies) have been referred to by Easton as ways of creating diffuse support or of reducing stress in a political system. These mechanisms, by creating or preserving that "reservoir of favorable attitudes or good will," are said to express themselves in two forms, namely "trust as against cynicism" and "in belief in the legitimacy of political objects."[12] Attempts also have been made to generate specific support, which, in Easton's terminology, is "directed to the perceived decisions, policies, actions, utterances, or the general style"[13] of authorities. They have tried to accomplish this by walking a

11. Royal Commission on the Northern Environment, *North of 50°*, No. 1 (Oct. 15, 1977), p. 15.
12. Easton, "A Re-Assessment of the Concept of Political Support," p. 447.
13. Ibid., p. 439.

tightrope, balancing regulatory with distributive policies, so that no major set of groups is thoroughly displeased. Let us consider some of the ways in which they have gone about these efforts to generate support.

A typical response of governments to a new public concern is to create a bureaucratic unit (an agency, in time, even a ministry) to indicate that they share the public's concern. Specialized agencies were created in the 1950s and 1960s; in the 1970s most Canadian governments integrated them in ministries of the environment. The creation of these ministries symbolized the new status environmental issues occupied on the policy agendas of the several governments. They also helped ensure that environmental concerns could compete on favorable terms (with other ministries articulating the concerns of other societal groups) in the "competition for scarce resources" that is one of the principal stages in the Canadian policy-making process.[14] Ministries of the environment also are useful vehicles for incorporating nongovernmental organizations of all kinds into the policy-making process, thereby enhancing their sense of political efficacy, as well as their trust in and support for political authorities and the regimes of which they are a part. Indeed, many interest groups have been given permanent advisory roles in ministries. For example, the Ontario ministry has numerous advisory committees and boards on everything from pesticides to waste management.[15] The ostensible purpose of this kind of incorporation is to offer advice to the ministry and although advice is offered, the advisory function also may be used to coopt, placate, and influence important groups as well as to enable the government and bureaucracy to try to effect compromises among different interests in a policy arena.

Another method of generating diffuse support has been to encourage public participation in environmental policy making. Indeed, lengthy and detailed public hearings have become "normal" on any

14. A. Paul Pross, "The Coastal Management Debate: Putting an Issue on the Public Agenda," in Dwivedi, ed., *Resources and the Environment: Policy Perspectives for Canada*, pp. 107–32. With regard to the importance of bureaucratic units themselves in the competition for scarce resources and the attention of cabinets, Pross notes that the issue of coastal zone management was put on the policy agenda by the environmental agencies themselves rather than by environmental pressure groups.

15. Ontario Ministry of the Environment, *Annual Report, 1978–1979* (Toronto: Queen's Printer, 1979).

controversial environmental matter. The federal Department of the Environment, for example, recognized that both prodevelopment and proenvironment nongovernmental organizations might feel left out of the process of making environmental regulations because matters of administrative law are not discussed at the parliamentary level. Consequently, the department has developed a draft policy on public consultation and information availability[16] calling for regular consultation and the provision of full information. Provisions for dealing with toxic wastes illustrate the manner in which consultation occurs. The process begins when the department sends a list of substances they are considering regulating (together with their justifications for the proposed action) to concerned organizations. The list and the rationalizations are intended to focus discussion. After preliminary discussions a tentative regulation is announced and a "Rationale for Regulation Report," together with a "Control Measures Report," is circulated to as comprehensive a list of groups as possible. After sixty days one or more public meetings is held. Following this, a "Proposed Regulation Report," which synthesizes the results of the consultations and which offers specific recommendations, is distributed to the groups involved. The department waits for further approaches and then publishes the proposed regulation in the *Canada Gazette*. This is followed by another sixty-day waiting period. If a formal objection is received, a board consisting of nongovernmental members assesses the evidence and recommends to the minister whether he should proceed with the regulation.

Royal commissions, such as the Ontario Royal Commission on the Northern Environment, and other public inquiry vehicles also are intended to facilitate public participation. Typically, they have funding programs to enable individuals and a wide range of groups to prepare oral and written briefs. They also hold public meetings, workshops, and surveys which result in reports and recommendations to a commission. The entire process is intended to convey a sense of governmental concern and a willingness to listen, thereby generating a sense of political efficacy and trust among a wide variety of groups. Still another channel of public participation is provided by the environmental impact assessment process. Public participation usually

16. Environment Canada, *Draft Policy for Public Consultation and Information Availability* (Ottawa: Environment Canada, June 19, 1980).

occurs at the hearing stage after proponents of a development have prepared a report. Although these hearings take place when the process is well along, they provide another publicly visible forum for the accommodation of various political forces involved, as well as an opportunity for a kind of public catharsis of their grievances.

The federal and provincial governments also have sought to generate diffuse support by various symbolic actions. Perhaps the most significant was the creation by act of Parliament of Environment Week in 1971. To our knowledge Canada is the only country in the world to have such legislation. On the more practical side Canadian governments, largely through their ministries of the environment, have encouraged and supported the entrenchment of environmental concerns in schools, universities, community groups, service clubs, businesses, industry, and government itself. This is done by sponsoring or subsidizing meetings, tours, displays, programs, and other activities. The objective is to create a general awareness of environmental issues among all sectors of the population.

Governments have tried to create *specific* support through the generation of a judicious mix of regulatory and distributive policies, in combination with a strongly stated commitment to "responsible" economic development. In view of the tightrope governments must walk between the competing demands of proenvironment and pro-development groups, their policies have been basically piecemeal, and there has been little in the way of comprehensive planning. Since group pressures are not equal, policy outputs have tended to favor development interests, but not to such a degree that the environmental forces have become alienated.

As was noted above, the late 1960s and early 1970s witnessed the emergence of a great many environmental groups and the peaking of public concern for the environment. This coincided with the promulgation of new environmental regulations and governmental adoption of a polluter-must-pay principle. In Ontario, for example, the Ontario Water Resources Act was revised in 1970, the Environmental Protection Act was passed in 1971, the Pesticides Act in 1973, and the Environmental Assessment Act in 1975. Ontario standards are determined in consultation with Ottawa. The provincial government negotiates individual compliance schedules with each major polluter. The compliance schedules vary, therefore, from polluter to polluter within the same industry and from industry to industry. Regulations under these acts are largely enforced by fines.

Regulatory policy of this type is, of course, pleasing to proenvironment groups. If pursued with reasonable effort, it is likely to create support among them for the minister of the environment, his ministry, and, indeed, for the entire complex of institutions and processes people normally call "government." However, this type of policy output is not, by and large, pleasing to prodevelopment groups. Many of the proenvironment groups recognize that "their" minister is up against powerful economic forces in society and, indeed, in the cabinet. Thus, less than satisfactory policies (from their perspective) do not necessarily result in withdrawal of support. Further, many environmental groups take comfort in the fact that the stick of regulation is not the only way to achieve a desired objective; it can be supplemented by the carrot of incentives. As the 1970s progressed, this was increasingly the case: not only because of a backlash effect, but also because it became increasingly evident that regulation can have unanticipated costs. As a consequence, Canadian governments have emphasized incentives while simultaneously conducting sophisticated cost-benefit analyses intended to bring benefits—such as those derived from levying effluent charges—to light. By way of illustration, both levels of government have given tax writeoffs to various industries and provided grants for the installation of equipment to reduce air and water pollution. Incentives are provided not only to established industries but also are frequently attached (almost as riders) to economic expansion grants. Both levels of government also have helped municipalities upgrade their sewer and water facilities since they facilitate both economic *and* environmental goals.

Public Perceptions and Support for Environmental Policies and Programs

Although public interest in environmental problems has remained high in the United States, in Canada a debate has taken place over the extent of public interest and whether interest can be maintained in the 1980s. The orthodox position seems to be that there has been a gradual decline in public interest. This is the view of Woodrow,

Winham, Munton, and many others.[17] This position is, however, challenged by people such as Donald Chant and Ross Howard[18] who hold
that the concerns of the general public have stabilized at a relatively
high level. Public opinion polls are cited in support of both points of
view. Those espousing the orthodox view note that polls indicate little interest in environmental matters prior to 1969, a rise in interest
in 1970 (the year which saw the founding of most of the major proenvironment groups), and a drop-off after 1971.[19] The unorthodox
view is that although environmental issues may no longer be number
one on the public's list of concerns, many polls conducted after 1971
have indicated that public interest has been consistently high.[20] Moreover, they indicate that other prominent issues like energy are environmentally related.

A related orthodox view is that the environmental issue is becoming too complex for the public, not only technically, but also in terms
of the time and expense required to be informed or active. Politically,
the issue has become enmeshed in fragmented governmental jurisdictions which, in turn, has led to localism or parochial self-interest.
The unorthodox reply is that the general public has become more sophisticated, both about the technical aspects of the environmental
issue and the governmental processes affecting it. The orthodox

17. Gilbert Winham, "Attitudes on Pollution and Growth in Hamilton, or 'There's An Awful
Lot of Talk These Days About Ecology,'" *Canadian Journal of Political Science* 3 (1972):384–
401; Don Munton, "Great Lakes Water Quality: A Study in Environmental Politics and Diplo-
macy," in Dwivedi, ed., *Resources and the Environment*, pp. 153–78.
18. Donald Chant, "A Decade of Environmental Concern: Retrospect and Prospect," keynote
address to the Environmental Challenge for the 80's Conference, Toronto, October 1980; Ross
Howard, "Public Opinion and Environmental Concern," paper presented at the Environmental
Challenges for the 80's Conference.
19. The *Gallup Report* (Mar. 25, 1970) indicated in a nationwide survey that 91 percent of
respondents were aware of pollution problems and 69 percent felt them to be "very serious."
The *Gallup Report* (Dec. 2, 1970) indicated in another nationwide survey that pollution was the
issue seen as requiring the most attention from government. *Gallup Report* surveys of Feb. 26
and Aug. 19, 1975, suggested that few respondents regarded pollution as a major political issue.
20. Many surveys have indicated that although pollution may not be the first-ranking issue
with the public it remains very important. A 1977 nationwide probability sample of 3,288 Canadians aged eighteen or older revealed that 47.2 percent of respondents desired more government effort to protect the environment and 30.5 percent desired "much more" activity. For details see Tom Atkinson and others, *Quality of Life Project* (Toronto: Institute for Behavioral
Research, York University, 1977). Similarly, a survey analysis of the most important issues facing
the country in the period 1978–80 revealed that "environment and pollution" consistently
ranked as the third most important issue concern reported—only after "inflation" and "unemployment." See Lawrence LeDuc and J. Alex Murray, "A Resurgence of Canadian Nationalism:
Attitudes and Policy in the 1980s," chap. 10 in this volume.

view further argues that the general public, and the proenvironment groups, are on the losing end of the jobs-versus-environment argument which has become especially salient in a period of recession. The unorthodox response is that there has been growing public understanding that the environmental issue is not just a simpleminded equation between environmental protection and jobs, but is closely related to a wider range of issues such as the energy future, the protection of wildlife, land use, and recreation. This is reflected in the rise of a large number of new groups interested in these issues which supplement rather than rival existing environmental groups. Another unorthodox view is that public support will continue because the environmental issue has become entrenched in the political arena, in the bureaucracy, and in the universities and public schools. Those espousing the orthodox position are less sure about the depth of the entrenchment. For one thing environmental issues have never been a major area of partisan conflict. For another, Canadian legislators are hampered by their lack of specialized knowledge about matters pertinent to these issues.

Since these and other differences cannot be resolved in this paper, let us consider whether the major actors in the Canadian environmental policy process feel politically efficacious and trusting, since these feelings can affect the levels of both the specific and diffuse support. Our view is that the major proenvironment groups, those incorporated into the advisory process and having close links to the bureaucracy, *are* likely to feel politically efficacious—as are those prodevelopment groups which either have not suffered extensively from regulation or have benefited significantly from the incentive policies of governments. These groups are likely to find regulatory and distributive outputs acceptable because they probably have played a part in their creation. For similar reasons, they also are likely to trust and support both governments' political leaders. Donald Chant's view,[21] that while much remains to be done, much was accomplished in the 1970s, is probably typical of most of the major environment and development groups. From their perspective, regulations have been put into effect that have had salutary effects and more are planned. Moreover, governments are beginning to set environmental

21. Chant, "A Decade of Environmental Concern."

priorities. Although some prodevelopment groups may not be entirely enamored with the number of regulations Canadian governments have enacted, they have received substantial financial assistance to help meet the costs imposed by some of these regulations. The forest industry, for example, can take credit for the fact that a number of recent development grants to the industry include funds for installing pollution-control devices. (The industry had argued that its competitiveness would be damaged and jobs within it endangered if firms were required to pay the full costs of such equipment.) Although the magnitude of these grants may not always have been regarded as sufficient, the fact that Canadian governments made them available and did not rely exclusively on regulations suggests that the positions of prodevelopment groups have received a sympathetic reception.

Minor proenvironment groups which have not been significantly incorporated into the advisory process and do not have close links to the bureaucracy also are not likely to feel politically efficacious. Nor are prodevelopment groups which have not been incorporated into the policy process or have not received various governmental incentives. Good examples of proenvironment groups which have not been incorporated into the policy process, which probably lack political efficacy, and which also do not trust governments much are native peoples' groups. Illustrative of a lack of trust is the observation of Chief Andrew Rickards that for Indians to trust the government was like "asking Colonel Sanders to babysit our chickens."[22]

More generally, a number of proenvironment and prodevelopment groups are skeptical of the motives and actions of governments. Proenvironment groups point, for example, to denials by some governments that environmental problems exist, to their relaxation of regulations, their levying of minimal fines, or their exemption of certain projects from environmental impact assessments. There also is suspicion that Royal Commissions, while they promote public participation, in practice rely on internal reports as a basis for their recommendations. Environmental impact assessments are further criticized because the proponents of development projects prepare these as-

22. Royal Commission on the Northern Environment, *North of 50°*, No. 2, (Dec. 21, 1977), p. 5.

sessments and public participation begins only after assessments and reviews are completed.[23]

On the other hand, prodevelopment groups find many regulations too restrictive and the incentives governments offer too small. Although there has been some pressure for deregulation by prodevelopment forces, more typical is a concern that governments may carry regulation too far in the future. As a spokesman for Griffith Mines put it, "there is a danger of overcontrol on the part of the government, and mine management is fearful that controls will become so unreasonably rigid that industrial growth will be drastically cut and the economy will become stagnant."[24] Accordingly, no matter how often an agency such as the Ontario Ministry of the Environment may contend that "the argument that environmental standards are driving away investments in Ontario is largely unsubstantiated,"[25] at least some prodevelopment groups probably will continue to adhere to this belief.

The Canadian approach to environmental and related issues may be best illustrated by a case study of the problems of northwestern Ontario. The 3 percent (250,000) of the population of Ontario living in the region constituting 40 percent of the land mass of the province is markedly affected, either directly or indirectly, by the process of resource exploitation. The economy of the region is dominated by the forest and mining industries. In the more remote areas some families subsist on fishing, hunting and trapping. Although there is some secondary processing and manufacturing, opportunities for the expansion of this sector of the economy are distinctly limited by remoteness from mass markets, the consequent high operating and transportation costs, as well as by the lack of a large skilled labor pool.[26] In the late 1960s and early 1970s there was considerable conflict over environmental matters in the region. Local proenvironment groups were formed to protest what they perceived as a large number of environmental problems. Environmental groups based in southern Ontario

23. John Eichmanis, *Freedom of Information and the Policy Making Process in Ontario* (Toronto: Ontario Commission on Freedom of Information and Privacy, February 1980), p. 97.

24. The Northern Development Research Group, *A Selected Overview of Ontario's Public Decisional Framework of Northern Primary Resource Development* (Toronto: Northern Development Research Group, March 1980), pp. 63–70.

25. Royal Commission on the Northern Environment, *North of 50°*, No. 1 (Nov. 29, 1977), p. 20.

26. Ibid.

also became involved in the region. Among the issues raised were: overharvesting of timber; effects of the proposed construction of major hydroelectric projects on rivers on the Hudson's Bay watershed; possible construction of the Polar Gas pipeline; the Reed Company's mercury pollution of the English-Wabigoon river system; and that same company's desire to greatly expand its timber limits. The region's largest city, Thunder Bay, faced problems from grain dust emissions from the local elevators and from asbestos fibers (which came from Silver Bay, Minnesota) in its drinking water. The conflict on many of these issues was intense. For example, the Reed mercury/ expansion issues achieved national notoriety and led to the publication of several books.[27]

As the decade progressed, the environmental problems of the region were tackled by both levels of government, employing a mixture of regulatory and incentive policies and attempting either to incorporate major policy actors or to encourage them to participate in the policy process. A series of regulatory policies on air and water pollution were passed which—although they affected the province in general—affected the pulp and paper industry in particular. The industry had been widely identified by government (especially the Federal Minister and his department) as the most serious industrial polluter. The response of the industry to these regulations was to largely ignore them. By the mid-1970s only three of thirty-one pulp and paper companies had complied with biochemical and oxygen standards set in 1969; the Kapuskasing Spruce Falls plant, for example, was producing twenty-four times the allowable limit.[28] Clearly, government (federal and provincial) had not extracted a great deal of specific support from industry. It then lost the support of proenvironment groups as well by allowing the situation to go on and by continually either relaxing standards or extending time limits for compliance. Contributing to the erosion of specific support was government's seeming denial of the existence of asbestos in Thunder Bay's drinking water. It

27. For general background see Ontario Ministry of Natural Resources, *Strategic Land Use Plan, Northwestern Ontario: Background Information and Approach to Policy* (Toronto: Ontario Ministry of Natural Resources, 1974); and Geoffrey R. Weller, "Resource Development in Northern Ontario: A Case Study in Hinterland Politics," in Dwivedi, ed., *Resources and the Environment*, pp. 243–68.
28. See, for example, Warner Troyer, *No Safe Place* (Toronto: Clarke Irwin, 1977); and G. Hutchison and Dick Wallace, *Grassy Narrows* (Toronto: Van Nostrand and Reinhold, 1977).

also seemed incapable of tackling mercury pollution near Dryden and it excused the Marmion Lake Generating Station from conducting a "mandatory" environmental impact assessment.

The situation began to improve from about 1977. In that year stricter pollution abatement regulations were passed. At the same time the federal and Ontario governments began to cooperate to provide incentives to industry to modernize and install pollution abatement equipment. The sums involved were enormous, amounting to several hundreds of millions of dollars.[29] For example, grain elevator companies were helped to install abatement equipment; the city of Thunder Bay was provided with assistance in building a filtration system; and the Ontario government guaranteed Great Lakes Pulp and Paper that it would pay any legal settlements above $15 million resulting from the company's takeover of Reed Paper.

Two major institutions concerned with regional matters also were created in 1977. One was the Federal Ministry of Northern Affairs. It was intended to consolidate all northern programs, create a political focus for the north, and promote economic development in the region. The other was the Royal Commission on the Northern Environment, originally intended only to inquire into the granting of new timber limits to the Reed company, but which became, more or less, all-encompassing. The commission has provided funding to a wide range of prodevelopment and proenvironment groups. It has helped individuals prepare oral and written briefs, has held public meetings and workshops, and sponsored surveys leading to a large number of submissions and presentations. These activities are intended not only to symbolize the commission's concern with environmental issues but also to provide institutionalized opportunities for interested individuals and groups to vent any grievances.

As a consequence of these steps, public discontent over the handling of environmental problems largely has been defused. By way of illustration, grain dust emissions in Thunder Bay have ceased to be a serious problem, mercury waste is no longer being dumped in the English-Wabigoon, air and water emission standards are beginning to have an effect, and sundry other advances have been made. At the same time, there is evidence that both levels of government are com-

29. Douglas H. Pimlott, "The Water Equation," *Alternatives* 7 (1978):26–29.

mitted to economic development. We may infer, therefore, that governmental policies have succeeded in preserving or reestablishing a sense of political efficacy, trust, and, therefore, support among most environmental and development groups in the region.[30]

Conclusion

The approach of Canadian governments to the solution of environmental and related problems has been to involve components of their own bureaucracies as active participants in the search for acceptable and effective policies and programs. By actively involving themselves in the task of seeking accommodations between or among various groups interested in environmental policies, bureaucratic officials have been able to represent themselves as part of the "solution" to perceived environmental problems rather than as mere observers of the environmental condition. The long-term implications of such a "participant role" are open to question. From the perspective of maximizing public participation, for example, the growth of environmentally related governmental agencies, each following an accommodative policy strategy, may eventually reduce the degree of open discussion of ecological concerns, because it may remove the latter from the public forum and place their consideration and resolution in the several federal and provincial bureaucracies. If so, there may well be an accompanying decline in the general public's sense of efficacy, trust, and support of government—not because it has failed to address environmental issues, but because it seems to be monopolizing the entire process. The line between policy accommodation and policy dictation can be a narrow one.

These long-term possibilities notwithstanding, environmental policy making by both the federal and provincial governments currently is receiving careful public scrutiny. Large numbers of Canadians have become increasingly aware of the dangers posed to their society by unchecked environmental pollution. A smaller number are equally conscious of the need to reconcile their demands for effective

30. By 1980, most of the environmental groups based in southern Ontario had become more or less inactive in the north, whereas most of the northern groups either had gone out of existence or—like Environment North and the Non-Nuclear Coalition—become inactive.

environmental policies and programs with the need for continued economic growth. The ability of Canadian governments to continue to formulate policies that accommodate both—to "square the circle," in a sense—may become a major test of their ability to maintain what Easton has termed "adequate" levels of diffuse and specific support for themselves, their policies, and, perhaps, for the regime itself.

A Resurgence of Canadian Nationalism: Attitudes and Policy in the 1980s

Lawrence LeDuc and J. Alex Murray

In spite of widely recognized measurement problems, the distinction between diffuse and specific support as advanced by Easton has proven useful in developing and extending our theoretical and empirical understanding of important political processes.[1] In Canada, several recent attempts have been made to operationalize these concepts for purposes of measuring support for federal and provincial political authorities, regimes, and communities.[2] As in the Canadian research, the support concepts generally have been applied within a single nation state (or political entity, as in the case of the Canadian provinces). However, there are circumstances where underlying levels of affect for foreign nations, or attitudes toward specific policies vis-à-vis those

1. See especially David Easton, "A Re-Assessment of the Concept of Political Support," *British Journal of Political Science* 5 (1975):435–57; and Easton, "Theoretical Approaches to Political Support," *Canadian Journal of Political Science* 9 (1976):431–48. See also Edward Muller and Thomas Jukam, "On the Meaning of Political Support," *American Political Science Review* 71 (1977):1561–95; Muller, "Behavioral Correlates of Political Support," *American Political Science Review*: 455–68; and P. Abramson and R. Inglehart, "The Development of Systemic Support in Western Democracies," *Comparative Political Studies* 2 (1970):419–42. On problems of measurement, see G. Loewenberg, "The Influence of Parliamentary Behavior on Regime Stability," *Comparative Politics* 3 (1971):177–200; Muller and Jukam, "On the Meaning of Political Support," pp. 1561–65; Allan Kornberg, Harold Clarke, and Lawrence LeDuc, "Some Correlates of Regime Support in Canada," *British Journal of Political Science* 3 (1978):199–216; and Michael Atkinson, William Coleman, and Thomas Lewis, "Studying Political Support in Canada: An Evaluation of Indicators," paper presented to the annual meeting of the Canadian Political Science Association, Montreal, 1980. See also the exchange between Kornberg et al. and Atkinson et al. in the *British Journal of Political Science* 10 (1980):402–16.

2. In addition to the works by Kornberg et al. and Atkinson et al. cited above, see Allan Kornberg, Harold Clarke, and Marianne Stewart, "Federalism and Fragmentation: Political Support in Canada," *Journal of Politics* 41 (1979):889–904; and Kornberg, Clarke, and Stewart, "Public Support for Community and Regime in the Regions of Contemporary Canada," *American Review of Canadian Studies* 10 (1980):75–93.

nations, may be of relevance for understanding policy processes and their impact on political support in a particular polity. Such an instance may be found in the Canada–United States relationship, as treated from the Canadian domestic political perspective. This is so because of the high salience of the United States as a distinct political object, and because policies toward the United States in such areas as trade, investment, and defense are of considerable importance to federal and provincial political authorities and, indeed, to a large part of the Canadian citizenry.

The application of the idea of specific support with respect to relationships between Canada and the United States is fairly obvious, in that a particular decision or action affecting foreign policy or foreign trade may inspire praise or blame in the same sense that any public policy may increase or decrease support for Canadian authorities or for the institutions with which they are associated. The concept of diffuse support may also be useful for understanding developments in the Canada–United States relationship. The United States as a familiar political object engenders positive or negative feelings that transcend particular policies or individuals. Strongly pro- or anti-American attitudes have been commonplace throughout Canadian history, and today the United States inspires feelings of love or hatred among individual Canadians without reference to any specific policy, personality, or action. As in Easton's exposition of diffuse support for a regime, it might be expected that such attitudes will be the product of socialization, or of long experience, and that they will be relatively resistant to change.[3] Such fundamental affective orientations, comparable in some respects to feelings of patriotism or strong ideological commitment, may well determine the receptivity of Canadians to proposals such as a North American common market, new trade arrangements, or increases in American investment, to a greater extent than will evaluations of these policies on their own merits.

This is not to say that evaluations of the impact of these policies are unimportant. Indeed, how political elites and the general public perceive such impacts can be expected to influence levels of support for Canadian political authorities, and indirectly, other aspects of the Canadian political system. Also, such perceptions may influence levels

3. Easton, "A Re-Assessment of the Concept of the Political Support," pp. 445–47.

of specific and diffuse support for external political entities, i.e., the
United States. In sum, following Easton, we view feelings of specific
and diffuse support for political objects internal and external to a political system as standing at "either end" of the policy process. Reactions to the outputs of this process by political elites and the general
public constitute important aspects of feedback loops, the operation
of which can alter levels of specific and, ultimately, diffuse support for
these objects.

The skeins of causality implied by this perspective are complex and
thereby difficult to disentangle empirically. Moreover, as many have
recognized, distinguishing empirically between diffuse and specific
support is often difficult. We shall not be concerned in this paper with
the development of new measures of support for Canada, the United
States, or for a North American political regime or trading bloc. We
will, however, be interested in the extent to which a variety of indicators suggest the existence of attitudes that are more characteristic of
diffuse than of specific support, and in the extent to which one can
thereby generalize about the nature of the Canadian-American relationship independently of specific policies or initiatives. Further, we
shall be interested in exploring the interaction between feelings of
diffuse and specific support as variables in the Canadian policy process, for explaining, for example, the growth of Canadian nationalism
and the extent to which generalized nationalistic feelings, particularly
vis-à-vis the United States, constrain or promote particular policy options in present-day Canada.

Attitudes toward the United States and Public Policy

There is considerable evidence that, independent of particular policies or authorities, many Canadians hold positive or negative attitudes toward the United States. Information on these attitudes is contained in national surveys conducted in 1974 through 1980. In these
surveys, a 100-point "thermometer" scale—commonly employed as a
general indicator of support[4]—was used to measure feelings of Cana-

4. Kornberg et al., "Some Correlates of Regime Support." See also Kornberg et al., "Federalism and Fragmentation," pp. 892–94. For an application of the 1974 thermometer scores as
measures of "continentalist" or "devolutionary" attitudes, see Joel Smith and David Jackson,
"Canadian Provincial Socioeconomic Systems, the United States, and Potential Opinion Climates for Future Devolutionary Proposals," Duke University (mimeo).

Table 10.1. *Mean Thermometer Scale Ratings of the United States, Canada, and Other Nations, 1974 and 1979–80 Canadian National Samples*

	United States	Canada	Britain	France	(N)
1974	48	84	51	43	(2362)
1979	56	80	a	a	(2743)
1980	62	83	a	a	(1758)

a. Not asked in 1979–80 surveys.
Source: Harold Clarke, Jane Jenson, Lawrence LeDuc, and Jon Pammett, 1974 and 1979–80 Canadian National Election Studies.

dians toward the United States and other countries. These measures show that affect for the United States increased significantly over the six-year period between the two surveys.[5] This pattern is quite different from those for Canada and the other countries included in the survey (table 10.1). Similarly, a 1976 survey conducted by the United States Information Agency[6] found that Canadians' opinions about the United States were more positive and more strongly held than were attitudes expressed toward other nations (table 10.2). When pondering the meaning of these data, it is noteworthy that in all of these surveys the questions asked were independent of any reference to specific events, personalities, or policies, and were intended to indicate generalized feelings of positive or negative affect.

A relationship has long been observed in Canada between generalized feelings about the United States such as those described above and domestic policy in areas such as trade and investment.[7] Although

5. This finding should be treated with caution because of the possibility that Watergate and related events may have depressed the 1974 figure. There is, however, a statistically significant increase between the 1979 and 1980 surveys as well.
6. This survey was conducted under the sponsorship of the United States Information Agency (now ICA). A national sample of 1,350 Canadians was interviewed in October 1976 on the subject of trade, investment, images of the United States, and related issues. A report of this survey may be found in Office of Research, International Communication Agency, *Canadian Attitudes Toward the U.S. Economic and Cultural Presence in Canada*, ICA Research Report No. R-35-78, 1978.
7. Terrence A. Keenleyside, Lawrence LeDuc, and J. Alex Murray, "Public Opinion and Canada-United States Economic Relations," *Behind the Headlines* 35 (1976). Among other reports based on these surveys, see J. Alex Murray and Lawrence LeDuc, "Public Opinion and Foreign Policy Options in Canada," *Public Opinion Quarterly* 40 (1976):38–40; Lawrence LeDuc and J. Alex Murray, "Canadian Nationalism: Pause or Decline?" paper presented to the

Table 10.2. *Attitudes of a 1976 Canadian National Sample toward the United States and Other Countries*

	United States	Britain	France	Japan
Percent indicating a "good" or "very good" opinion of the country	70	62	49	47
Percent indicating "strong" or "moderately strong" feelings (positive and negative)	68	58	34	30
(*N* = 1350)				

Source: 1976 USIA Survey.

care must be taken in attributing causality in such relationships, it is clear that the first initiatives to restrict foreign (primarily American) investment and to reduce trade dependence on the United States coincided with a steady and sustained shift of public opinion in a direction increasingly critical of the Canada–United States relationship which occurred in the 1960s and early 1970s. Evidence of this shift may be found in public opinion data. For example, while in 1956 only 27 percent of the Canadian population agreed with a C.I.P.O. question which hypothesized "too much U.S. influence in the Canadian way of life," the percentage agreeing with that statement had risen to 53 percent in 1966 and peaked at 57 percent in 1974 (figure 10.1).[8] This shift in public opinion was only one of several elements that might lead one to characterize the late 1960s and early 1970s as a period of rising Canadian nationalism. A growing volume of literature critical of the traditional Canada–United States relationship began to appear. George Grant, Donald Creighton, Walter Gordon, Kari Levitt, Mel Watkins, Abraham Rotstein, and Gary Lax were among those who wrote books critical of the United States' economic influence in Canada during this period.[9] At the end of the 1960s, the Waffle

Conference of the World Association for Public Opinion Research, Oslo, Norway, (August 1977); and J. Alex Murray and Lawrence LeDuc, "Attitudes of Canadians Toward Current Foreign Policy and Trade Issues," paper presented to the Canada Today Conference, Heidelberg College, 1979.

8. The USIA survey shows this figure declining to 43 percent in 1976. The question wording, however, is not exactly comparable. See ICA, *Canadian Attitudes Toward the U.S. Economic and Cultural Presence in Canada*, pp. 34–36.

9. Mitchell Sharp, "Canada-U.S. Relations: Options for the Future," p. 17. See also Denis Smith, "Nationalism and The Third Option," paper presented to the Conference on Canada/U.S. Relations, Department of External Affairs, 1975, *Statements and Speeches*, no. 75–1.

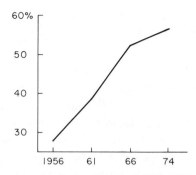

Figure 10.1. *Percent Indicating that There is "Too Much U.S. Influence in the Canadian Way of Life," CIPO National Samples, 1956–74*

Group, a radical wing of the New Democratic Party, argued that the nationalization of foreign firms was the only way for Canada to regain control over its economy. In 1970, the Committee for an Independent Canada was organized as a broadly based group to press for increased Canadian control over the Canadian economy.

Another characteristic of the period was the release of several government reports dealing with Canadian-American economic relations that served to generate additional public discussion of this area of foreign policy. In 1968, a special task force created by the Liberal government issued a report (the Watkins Report) which noted that foreign investment in Canada had been largely beneficial to the Canadian economy, but was encroaching upon the country's sovereignty and influencing its foreign policy. It made a number of positive recommendations to enhance economic independence, including the creation of an agency to coordinate policies regarding multinational enterprises, a government export trade agency to prevent the extraterritorial application of alien laws from interfering with the exports of subsidiaries when those exports conformed to Canadian law and foreign policy, and the creation of the Canada Development Corporation to act as a large holding company with entrepreneurial and management functions and to assume a leadership role in Canada's business community. In 1970, the House of Commons Standing Committee on External Affairs and National Defense issued a report (the Wahn Report) recommending that major subsidiaries be required to sell 51 percent of their stock to Canadians. Finally, in May 1972, the Trudeau government tabled a long-awaited report on foreign direct investment in Canada (the Gray Report) which put forward three strategies for dealing with foreign investment, with particular emphasis on the need to establish a foreign investment screening agency.[10]

In 1973, such an agency, the Foreign Investment Review Agency (FIRA), was established under terms of the Foreign Investment Review Act. The intention was to make all new foreign direct investment subject to review, except those by companies already established in Canada and made within their existing line of business. FIRA was seen as a significant new initiative for dealing in a comprehensive fashion with the problem of foreign investment. Once in operation, however, the agency was subject to considerable criticism for operating in a weak and indecisive manner.[11]

Between the introduction of the first draft bill and the passage of the Foreign Investment Review Act, the government also released a paper under the signature of then Secretary of State for External Affairs Mitchell Sharp, entitled "Canada-U.S. Relations: Options for the Future." The paper put forward three options for the direction of Canadian-American relations: (1) maintenance of the existing relationship with the United States with a minimum of policy adjustments; (2) deliberate movement toward closer integration with the United States; or (3) the pursuit of a comprehensive, long-term strategy to develop and strengthen the Canadian economy and other aspects of our national life and in the process to reduce Canadian vulnerability. A proposal to adopt the "third" option, implicit in the paper, was made explicit in a 1975 speech by then Secretary for External Affairs Allan MacEachen. Thus, Canada officially adopted the policy of pursuing enhanced economic independence via a comprehensive strategy, one aspect of which was the Foreign Investment Review Act. However, Sharp's paper clearly indicated that the strategy

10. Canada, Privy Council Office, *Foreign Ownership and the Structure of Canadian Industry* (Ottawa, 1968); Canada, House of Commons, Standing Committee on External Affairs and National Defence, *Proceedings*, 28th Parl., 2nd sess, No. 33, July 27, 1970; *Foreign Direct Investment in Canada* (Ottawa, 1972). For a complete review of the topic, see John Fayerweather, *Foreign Investment in Canada: Prospects for National Policy* (White Plains, New York: International Arts and Science Press, 1973), pp. 169–95.

11. See, for example, Charles J. McMillan, "After the Gray Report: The Tortuous Evolution of Foreign Investment Policy," *McGill Law Journal* 20 (1974):213–60.

was keyed to exports and that its basic focus would be the diversifica-
tion of the country's economic relations: "The object is essentially to
create a sounder, less vulnerable economic base for competing in the
domestic and world markets and deliberately to broaden the spectrum of markets in which Canadians can and will compete."[12]

It is impossible to ascertain precisely the extent to which public
opinion influenced the various initiatives in the areas of Canadian-
American relations outlined above. That the measures taken were accompanied by a gradually escalating public concern with respect to
Canadian economic independence is, however, clear from survey
data collected over this period.[13] The percentage of successive national samples willing to categorize United States investment as basically a "good thing" for the Canadian economy declined steadily
throughout this period, reaching its lowest point of 45 percent in the
1974 survey, one year after the passage of the Foreign Investment Review Act (figure 10.2). This proved, however, to be the end of the
period that might loosely be categorized as one of rising Canadian nationalism and decreasing support for closer trade and investment relations with the United States. Slowly, throughout the middle and
late 1970s, public opinion began to shift, so that from 1977 to the end
of the decade a majority of respondents judged that United States in-

12. Sharp, "Canada-U.S. Relations," p. 17. There has been a substantial amount of commentary, both supportive and critical of the Sharp paper. See, among others, Dale C. Thomp-
son, "Option Three: What Price Tag?," Louis Balthazar, "Achieving a Stronger Identity,"
Harry C. Johnson, "The Advantages of Integration," Abraham Rotstein, "Shedding Innocence
and Dogma," and Jeremy Kinsman, "Pursuing the Realistic Goal of Closer Canada-EEC Links,"
all in *International Perspectives* (1973):3–13, and 22–27. Some reactions to the proposals and
additional commentary also may be found in "Canada-U.S. Relations: Options for the Future,"
No. 1 "American Reaction," and No. 2 "Canadian Reaction," *Behind the Headlines* 32 (1973).
Commentaries involving the "third option" may be found in Alex Inglis, "A New Approach to
the Discussion of Canadian-American Relations," and Christopher Young, "End of an Era or a
Constant in Political Vocabulary?" both in *International Perspectives* (1975):3–15; and Denis
Smith, "Nationalism and the Third Option," paper presented to the Conference on Canada-
U.S. Relations, Department of External Affairs, February, 1975.
13. The data reported here were derived from surveys conducted annually by Elliott Research Corporation (Toronto, Ont.) and the International Business Studies Research Unit at the
University of Windsor (Windsor, Ont.). The surveys are based on national quota samples of
approximately 3,000 respondents, controlled for province, rural-urban location, age, and gender. Some reports which have utilized data from past surveys in this series are J. Alex Murray
and Mary C. Gerace, "Canadian Attitudes Toward the U.S. Presence," *Public Opinion Quarterly* 36 (1972):388–97; J. Alex Murray and Lawrence LeDuc, *Canadian Public Attitudes Toward U.S. Equity Investment in Canada*, (Ontario Economic Council Working Papers series,
1975); Lawrence LeDuc and J. Alex Murray, "Public Attitudes Toward Foreign Policy Issues";
J. Alex Murray and Lawrence LeDuc, "Public Opinion and Foreign Policy Options in Canada."

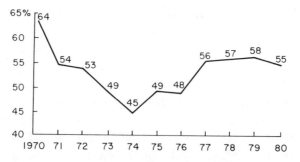

Figure 10.2. *Percent of a National Sample Who Believe that U.S. Investment in Canada Is "a Good Thing," 1970–80 (excluding "no opinion" and "qualified" answers)*

vestment was good for the economy. At the same time, the new policies which had been pursued by the federal government under the Foreign Investment Review Act were quietly set aside, and critics charged that FIRA was "falling apart in the face of corporate obstinacy and government indifference."[14] Herb Gray, the author of the Gray Report and father of FIRA was dropped from the cabinet, and ministers such as Jean Cretien, who were less sympathetic to the goals of the Foreign Investment Act, became responsible for its implementation and enforcement.

Similarly, the "third option" fell into decline as a goal of Canadian foreign policy almost as soon as it was given official sanction in 1975. A much heralded "contractual link" between Canada and the European Common Market, one of the few tangible elements of the third option policy, failed to have any real impact on trade relationships or on other areas of government policy.[15] In spite of statements made in support of the various government reports on the subject, the government did not intend a major reorientation of Canadian foreign or trade policy.

Survey data for this period suggest that this cautious approach to the issue of Canada's foreign policy orientation was consistent with trends in public opinion. At the time that the third option policy was announced as the official position of the government, public support

14. Ian Urquart, "FIRA: Watchdog or Lapdog?" *MacLean's* (July 11, 1977): 18–20.
15. David Humphreys, "Canada's Link with Europe Still Not Widely Understood," *International Perspectives* (1976): 33.

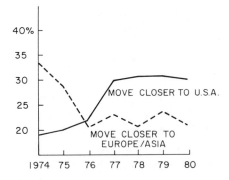

Figure 10.3. *Percent of National Sample Favoring a Change in Canadian Foreign Policy, 1974–80*

for this approach was already in decline. In 1974 (the first year for which survey data on this issue were collected), 34 percent of a national sample indicated a preference for closer relations with Europe and only 19 percent favored closer relations with the United States. By 1977 these positions had been reversed, with 30 percent favoring closer United States ties and only 21 percent receptive to forging stronger ties with Europe (figure 10.3). The third option policy never recovered from this sharp decline in public support, levels of which stabilized until the end of the decade. Throughout the 1977–80 period about a third of the population continued to favor closer ties with the United States.

Attitudes toward Trade and Investment: Some Recent Trends

It is evident that the late 1970s represented a period of declining economic nationalism. As noted, government policy with respect to trade and investment during these years was consistent with these prevailing trends in public opinion. In retrospect, policies intended to increase the country's control over its domestic economy and to lessen trade dependency on the United States had been initiated just at a time when public acceptance of Canada–United States economic interdependence was beginning to decline; and these same policies were later curtailed as public attitudes toward the Canadian-American relationship grew increasingly favorable. Now, in the early 1980s, there

are signs that a revival of the nationalism of the early 1970s may be
beginning. The evidence to this effect in the survey data reported
thus far is slight, but, nevertheless, unmistakable. Following five con-
secutive years of increasingly favorable public attitudes toward the
role of American investment in the Canadian economy, there has
been a small but statistically significant decline in the proportion of
persons who regard United States investment as a "good thing" (figure 10.2). Also, by 1980, the proportion who regard foreign investment as a "serious problem" had risen to 38 percent, only one percentage point below that recorded in 1976. In short, there is evidence
that the level of foreign investment may once again become a viable
political issue, inviting new government initiatives of the type begun
in the early 1970s.

Regarding these trends, although there is surprisingly little variation in the overall pattern, it might be noted that the modest resurgence of nationalism evident in the most recent survey data is not
completely uniform throughout the country. Currently, the percentage favoring American investment varies from a low of 45 percent in
British Columbia to a high of 51 percent in the Prairie provinces. The
largest year-to-date decline in the proportion of respondents who feel
this way has taken place in Ontario and the Atlantic provinces. However, opinion shifts are evident in other regions as well. Not all of
these are in the same direction. For example, between 1979 and
1980, the percentage favoring United States investment dropped
nine percentage points in the Atlantic region, while increasing by one
point in British Columbia.

It is also noteworthy that the distribution of reasons given by respondents to justify their position on the foreign investment issue has
not changed appreciably over the period during which this question
has been included in our annual surveys. Respondents who feel that
United States investment in the Canadian economy is basically a bad
thing have tended to give general nationalistic responses ("Canada
should control its own affairs," "should be more independent," etc.),
or to cite the pervasiveness of United States influence in Canada.
Those, on the other hand, who feel that foreign investment is basically a good thing for the country consistently have cited economic
growth and development benefits (table 10.3). Nearly half of the respondents in this latter group have given answers specifically relating

Table 10.3. *Reasons for Believing that U.S. Ownership of Canadian Companies Is a Good or Bad Thing for the Canadian Economy, 1980*

Reasons for a good thing	Total Canada	Reasons for a bad thing	Total Canada
Creates more employment	49%	U.S. taking over Canadian economy; Canada / Canadians should control their own business / economy	37%
Need outside investment for expansion / development of industry / resources	18		
Brings more into Canada; more money is circulated	16	Profits / money leave the country; does not benefit Canada; U.S. profits from Canada's resources	35
Raises / expands the economy (better standard of living; helps Canada / Canadians)	15	Canadians can do it themselves; should be more independent (not depend on United States)	12
Canadians are not willing to invest (too cautious—need a push); if United States did not do it, some other country would	12	Take jobs / business away from Canadians	9
		Canadians take risk / initiative / invest in their own country; keep Canadian investment in Canada	9
Creates a friendly relationship / cooperation; stabilizes; keeps Canada par with United States; help each other	6	No employment security; they can move out any time it suits them especially when going gets rough	4
Most of what we have now is because of U.S. investing; Canadian economy is based on U.S., could not operate without United States	5	Tend to "Americanize" / change Canada / Canadian methods; will lose Canadian identity	3
Better / more products; world market, more to export / trade	3	Discrimination; unequal trade; do not get a square deal; Canadians pay more; manpower drain, etc.	2
Miscellaneous reasons	4		
(*N* = 1145)		Miscellaneous reasons	5
		(*N* = 886)	

Percentages total more than 100 because multiple responses to the survey question were permitted.

to employment, and many more have mentioned such considerations as resource development or the improvement of living standards.

Regarding responses to a question measuring the extent to which foreign investment is seen as a "problem," an increase in the proportion of respondents who regard foreign investment as a serious problem may be observed in each region of the country except Quebec and in virtually every sociodemographic group.[16] Although there are variations between the regions, the largest year-to-year increases in the percentage of respondents defining foreign investment as a serious problem may be found in Ontario and the Atlantic provinces, a pattern similar to that observed for the foreign investment issue more generally. British Columbia, however, continues, as it has in previous surveys, to contain the largest proportion of persons who perceive foreign investment as a problem which must be faced.

Widespread recognition that foreign investment is either a present-day or future problem generally has not been accompanied by broad public sentiment in favor of direct government action to control foreign investment. In previous surveys, only a minority of those identifying foreign investment as a problem were found to advocate direct government regulation through agencies such as FIRA, although some did opt for selective controls in certain industries. More have favored incentives for Canadian business or alternate investment schemes such as the Canada Development Corporation. In the most recent survey, the proportion of respondents calling for government regulation increased slightly from its low point in 1979 (table 10.4); but still this approach is advocated by no more than 26 percent of those who believe foreign investment is a problem. However, this increase, following several years of successive declines in the percentage of the population favoring government controls, is indicative of the modest resurgence of nationalism found generally in the 1980 survey data. As noted earlier, this slight shift in opinion has been accompanied by policy and personnel changes which suggest a strengthening of FIRA and a new resolve on the part of the federal government to limit the extent of new United States investment.

These same general observations may be made regarding the current orientation of Canadian foreign policy. Following a sharp rise in 1977, the proportion of respondents who advocate closer ties with the United States has leveled off in recent surveys (figure 10.3). There are, however, modest variations in this pattern by region. The per-

16. The sociodemographic correlates are generally similar to those noted for the foreign investment benefits question. Men and older respondents are slightly more likely to feel that foreign investment is *not* a problem. New Democrats (49 percent) are much more likely than Liberals or Conservatives (each 35 percent) to define foreign investment as an *immediate* problem. Relationships with socioeconomic status variables are not significant.

Table 10.4. *Proposed Solutions to the Foreign Investment Problem, Selected Surveys (only respondents who viewed foreign investment as a problem)*

	1980	1979	1976
More support for Canadian business	32%	35%	34%
Government regulation	26	24	31
Canada Development Corporation	20	18	17
Selected industry controls	13	13	14
Investment from many countries	7	9	7
All other	1	2	2
No opinion	4	2	2
	(*N* = 1874)	(*N* = 2354)	(*N* = 2300)

Percentages total more than 100 because multiple responses to the survey question were permitted.

centage of respondents favoring closer relations with the United States has declined nine percentage points in the Atlantic provinces, but has shifted only slightly elsewhere. In all parts of the country except Quebec and the Prairies, the percentage of the sample desiring to maintain the status quo in foreign policy has risen significantly. The leveling off of the proportion calling for closer ties with the United States thus has not been accompanied by a resurgence of pro-European sentiment and does not therefore in itself suggest a revival of the third option policy. Rather, it suggests an increasing caution in Canadian foreign policy and skepticism regarding the desirability of closer economic ties with either the United States or other countries. Current levels of support for the status quo in foreign policy therefore may reflect dissatisfaction with the two major alternatives that have been propounded in recent years rather than satisfaction with existing policy.

Consonant with these shifts in public opinion, recent trends in the posture of the federal government toward trade and investment issues have been cautiously more nationalistic. After the Liberal party's defeat in the 1979 federal election, pressures developed within the party for policies that would more clearly reflect a concern for the level of foreign investment in the economy and the degree of trade dependence on the United States. Following the Liberal return to power in 1980, these policies gained wider acceptance within the cabinet. Relatedly, the renewed prominence of ministers such as

Herb Gray and Allan MacEachen also may be considered indicators of a "tilt" in the direction of more nationalistic trade and investment policies, in line with the new trends in public opinion.

Canadian Nationalism: Stability and Change

Canadians always have demonstrated a considerable degree of pragmatism in their political and economic beliefs.[17] This is certainly true with respect to attitudes toward the United States. Although we may speak of Canadians as becoming more or less favorable to American investment and more or less supportive of closer relations with the United States, it would be misleading to conceptualize such attitudes as parts of a highly constrained political ideology. For example, negative attitudes toward the high level of American investment are not necessarily accompanied by support for greater intervention by agencies such as FIRA. This pattern is shown by a cross-tabulation of attitudes toward the foreign investment issue and the characterization of foreign investment as a "problem" to be dealt with by government (table 10.5). Only slightly more than half (57 percent) of those who see United States investment in Canada as a "bad thing" for the country also feel that it is a serious problem. Treated as a proportion of the total sample, only 21 percent feel that United States investment is a bad thing *and* it is also a problem that must be solved. Significant proportions of the sample (6 percent and 7 percent, respectively) feel that although United States investment is a bad thing, it is at most only a potential problem for the country. The converse is likewise true. Respondents who characterize United States investment as a "good thing" have varying opinions about whether or not such investment is a problem. Thus, fully one-quarter of this group (12 percent of the total sample) believe that foreign investment is a good thing, but that it is also a serious problem. Such persons may well be positively disposed toward new American investment in Canada but also desirous of stronger controls on such investment. Clearly, these issue orientations are not unidimensional. While there is a relation-

17. See, for example, the content of political party images held by Canadians which display very low levels of ideological content. Harold Clarke, Jane Jenson, Lawrence LeDuc, and Jon Pammett, *Political Choice in Canada* (Toronto: McGraw-Hill Ryerson, 1979), pp. 194–202.

Table 10.5. *Relationship between Feeling toward U.S. Investment as a Good or Bad Thing and Identification of Foreign Investment as a Serious Problem, 1980 (diagonal percentages; row percentages shown in parentheses)*

	Foreign investment a problem?				
	Yes, a serious problem	*No, not a problem*	*Maybe a future problem*	*No opinion*	*(N[a])*
U.S. Investment					
Good	12	21	13	3	(1490)
	(25)	(42)	(26)	(7)	
Bad	21	6	7	2	(1116)
	(57)	(17)	(20)	(5)	
Qualified	3	3	3	—	(244)
	(40)	(30)	(26)	(4)	
No opinion	1	1	1	2	(187)
	(20)	(18)	(23)	(40)	
					(3037)

$V = 0.26$
$(p \leq 0.001)$
a. Weighted.

ship between these two questions ($V = 0.26$), the degree of independence is far greater than would be expected if a single underlying attitude such as nationalism or pro- or anti-Americanism were determining responses to both questions. It is likely, then, that levels of specific support for particular trade policies or alternatives, rather than more general and diffuse supportive sentiments for the United States as a political or economic entity, best characterize how public opinion influences policies and policy making.

The same general point may be made with respect to the relationship between attitudes toward foreign investment and trade policy options. These reveal an even greater degree of independence (table 10.6) than do the two foreign investment questions. Knowing someone's attitude toward United States investment in Canada is at best a weak predictor of his or her attitudes toward trade options. As is seen in table 10.6, of those respondents who feel that United States investment is a good thing, only a minority (39 percent) also opt for closer trade relations with the United States. Nearly as many of this group (36 percent) favor maintaining the status quo in Canadian-American relations, while 18 percent would prefer a third option policy. Simi-

Table 10.6. *Relationship between Attitudes toward Foreign Investment in Canada and Support for Changes in Canadian Foreign Policy, 1980 (diagonal percentages; row percentages shown in parentheses)*

	Status quo	Closer to U.S.A.	Closer to Europe/Asia	No opinion	(N[a])
U.S. Investment					
Good	18	19	9	3	(1490)
	(36)	(39)	(18)	(7)	
Bad	15	8	10	4	(1116)
	(42)	(22)	(27)	(10)	
Qualified	3	2	2	1	(244)
	(32)	(26)	(30)	(13)	
No opinion	3	1	—	2	(187)
	(44)	(21)	(7)	(28)	
					3037

V = 0.15
(p ≤ 0.001)
a. Weighted.

larly, a feeling that United States investment is a bad thing for Canada does not necessarily indicate support for the third option in trade relationships. Twenty-two percent of those with negative attitudes toward United States investment actually advocate closer relations with the United States; only a slightly higher percentage of this group (27 percent) supports the third option. By far the largest proportion (42 percent) favors the status quo in relations with the United States. Viewed differently, the two groups whose attitudes are fully consistent with "pro-American" or "anti-American" positions on both issues (i.e., those who believe that United States investment is good *and* who support closer relations with the United States as opposed to those who feel that United States investment is bad for the country *and* favor the third option), comprise only 19 percent and 10 percent of the total 1980 national sample, respectively.

Generally, the pattern of attitudes on these several issues suggests that for many Canadians feelings about issues like foreign investment or trade agreements are based on practical rather than on emotional considerations. Issues involving elements of nationalism might be expected to be highly emotional in character and related to deeply held feelings about the particular political objects in question: feelings that, like diffuse support, are the product of long experience or of socialization and tend to resist change. Easton notes that feelings of diffuse support, even when derived from experience, will tend over time to "become transformed into generalized attitudes toward authorities or other political objects and . . . to take on a life of their own." In this sense, he argues, they are similar to ideological orientations or commitments.[18]

What we might call Canadian nationalism, however, does not appear to conform to this pattern or to resemble, at least for the bulk of the population, a type of ideological commitment. Undoubtedly, there are Canadians who are true "nationalists." But, there appear to be many more whose attitudes toward matters such as trade and investment are highly pragmatic and keyed to specific issues rather than anchored in more basic ideological commitments. This tendency is illustrated by the substantial numbers of survey respondents who recognize foreign investment as a "problem" but nevertheless also consider it a "good thing" (table 10.5), or by those who welcome American investment, but do *not* favor closer trade ties with the United States (table 10.6). The fact that a number of these combinations exist suggests that nationalistic attitudes in Canada are not unidimensional in character and probably do not for the most part derive from more general feelings of diffuse support for various political entities.

Even at a time when nationalistic attitudes and policies are increasingly evident the tendency toward pragmatism in trade and investment policies in fact may be increasing. This is not necessarily a contradiction. For example, the 10 percent (table 10.6) of the national sample who can be characterized as the strongest nationalists (i.e., those who consider United States investment a "bad thing" for the country *and* who favor a third option trade policy) actually is slightly smaller than a comparable percentage of the 1979 survey.[19] In fact, the former percentage is only slightly higher than the percentage of respondents who feel that United States investment is bad for the country but favor closer relations with the United States (8 percent of the total sample), a seemingly inconsistent position

18. Easton, "A Re-Assessment of the Concept of Political Support," p. 446.

19. In 1979, 11 percent of the national sample were strong nationalists, also indicating a preference for the third option policy. A 1 percent decline, however, even for the total sample, is not statistically significant.

when considered in terms of nationalism as ideology. The segment of the population which might be characterized as most consistently pro-American (i.e., those who consider American investment as a good thing and who favor closer relations with the United States) has also declined slightly (19 percent of the total sample in 1980).[20]

An increasing tendency to reject ideological nationalism also may explain why attitudes on *specific* issues such as foreign investment seemingly have become more nationalistic and why policies in this area have been strengthened although *generalized* attitudes toward the United States appear to have grown more positive. As measured by the thermometer scores in table 10.1 discussed earlier (the measure which perhaps most closely approximates diffuse support for the United States), attitudes toward the United States in general terms have grown consistently more favorable in the past few years. Attitudes toward specific trade and investment issues, however, have not moved in the same direction. Indeed, they have shown an opposite tendency in the most recent of the annual surveys. This finding might be considered unusual only if it is argued that attitudes toward specific issues such as American investment in Canada or trade relations with the United States are tightly tied to generalized attitudes such as diffuse support. The contradictory tendencies shown by these several indicators might be taken as additional evidence that, as we have argued here, they are not.

In recent years, Canadians have been preoccupied with domestic economic issues to a much greater extent than with foreign policy or trade. All of the most recent surveys have shown inflation and unemployment to be the issues of greatest salience (table 10.7), followed by a growing concern with energy and environmental issues. It is likely, therefore, that trade and investment policies are more likely to be evaluated in terms of domestic costs and benefits than by other standards. In an earlier survey,[21] respondents who were asked to indicate whether Canada should have more trade agreements with the United States similar to the Auto Pact divided almost evenly on the question

20. In 1979, 20 percent of the sample considered the United States involvement a "good thing" and also favored closer relations with the United States.

21. In 1975, the following question was asked of a national sample of 5,000 Canadians: "Should Canada have more trade agreements with the United States like the Canada/U.S. Automotive Pact?" The outcome was Yes-27 percent, No-28 percent, Depends on Industry-30 percent, and No Opinion-15 percent.

Table 10.7. *Most Important Issues Facing the Country, 1978–80*

	Most important			Total mentions		
	1980	1979	1978	1980	1979	1978
Inflation	50%	43%	36%	83%	83%	79%
Unemployment	18	30	38	65	78	81
Environment & pollution	11	8	7	33	29	26
Energy	8	2	3	42	19	25
Provincial-federal relations	4	4	4	19	22	18
National unity	3	6	8	19	25	32
Taxation	3	3	3	23	28	25
U.S. investment	3	3	3	14	15	13
(*N* [1980][a] = 3030)						

Totals to more than 100% because multiple mentions were permitted in the survey.
a. Weighted.

(27 percent in favor and 28 percent against). The largest percentage of the sample, however, responded in qualified terms that "it depends" on the industry or the specifics of context and timing. We believe that these same attitudes persist in today's political and economic climate. Policies that are perceived to confer tangible economic benefits will be supported by a majority of the population. But trade agreements or investment policies which are not so perceived—whether they involve the United States or other countries—cannot rely on a reservoir of diffuse support built up in previous years or in other circumstances. Although diffuse support for various political objects remains one element in the complex of inputs which affect policy making in Canada, in the present era its effect would appear to be much less than that of specific support for more narrowly defined policies or actions.

Nationalism and Political Support in the 1980s

The Liberals interpreted the results of the 1980 election as a mandate to enhance Canada's control of its economy, and a number of steps to accomplish this already have been taken, or at least contemplated. First is the strategy (embodied in the National Energy Program) to raise Canadian control of the oil and gas industry from just 36 percent at present (as measured by assets of Canadian-held companies) to at least 50 percent by 1990.[22] The strategy, if it succeeds, will shift into Canadian hands more of the tremendous financial clout that has been accumulated by the oil and gas companies. More generally, increased Canadian control of natural resources has been advocated by strong nationalists such as Energy Minister Marc Lalonde and Industry, Trade and Commerce Minister Herb Gray, who have argued that "the public, as indicated by opinion polls, is very supportive of these kinds of initiatives."[23]

Public support for increased government thrusts into the private domain already has proved worrisome to foreign investors and other overseas analysts,[24] and the United States and other governments have attempted to apply pressure on Canada to relax or eliminate entirely its new foreign investment controls. Moreover, Gray is also interested in expanding the powers of FIRA, which is bound to further dampen the enthusiasm of American and other foreign investors, and cause them greater concern. At the same time, the support that the government has received and expects to continue receiving for its anticipated strategy of Canadianization will be tested by regular opinion surveys designed to monitor the public's mood. Above, it has been argued that the extent to which the public will favor government initiatives such as those dealing with foreign investment will be governed largely by short-term, cost-benefit evaluations rather than longer-term, more general nationalistic sentiments. In Easton's terms, specific rather than diffuse support will be of paramount importance.

The question of a policy reversal which may be engendered because of foreign pressure or changes in public opinion has yet to be faced by the Canadian government. Depending upon trends in such opinion in the years ahead, the 1980s may provide an excellent opportunity to study the significance of public attitudes in the process by which Canada's foreign investment policy is determined. Such an inquiry promises to bolster our understanding of the interplay among factors governing the operation and outputs of the policy process and the impact of the latter on support for various aspects of the Canadian political system and prominent actors in its environment.

22. "Trudeau's Drive to 'Canadianize' Industry," *Business Week* (Oct. 6, 1980): 126–31.
23. Ibid., p. 126.
24. "More West German Firms Want to Invest in Canada," *The Financial Times*, Oct. 18, 1980, pp. S1–S10. See also Arthur Donner, "Canadianization Holds Some Hidden Dangers," *The Globe and Mail*, Oct. 6, 1980, p. B4.

· IV ·

Crises

Nationalism in Quebec: The Transition of Ideology and Political Support

François-Pierre Gingras and Neil Nevitte

Nationalism is the most significant thread running through Quebec politics during the last 150 years. Historically, the particular character of Quebec nationalism, however, has been a function of the nature of Quebec society itself; changes in Quebec society have produced transformations in the style, substance, and form of Quebec nationalism. Today, most observers view the "Quiet Revolution" of the early 1960s as the single most important turning point in Quebec's recent history. For many it marked Quebec's coming of age, the moment when Quebec moved into the modern era. Traditional social, political, and cultural institutions, which in the past had been the pillars of a traditional order, came under attack. Not surprisingly then, for many, contemporary Quebec nationalism of the sort advanced by the Parti Québécois is directly related to the transformations implied by the Quiet Revolution.

This chapter has two goals. The first is to illustrate the continuity of Quebec's nationalism by tracing, in very broad terms, the socio-historical backdrop of contemporary Quebec nationalism. It will be suggested that the decline of the Alliance Laurentienne and the rise of the Rassemblement pour l'Indépendance Nationale (RIN) in the early 1960s represent prima facie evidence of the decisive ideological shift toward modern nationalism in Quebec. The second goal is more theoretical. It will be argued that the changes encompassed by the Quiet Revolution are not as complete as many have suggested and that the tension between the forces of tradition and the forces of modernity constitutes a key focus for understanding contemporary

Quebec politics. Specifically, it will be shown that the push for secularization in Quebec, secularization being the cutting edge of the Quiet Revolution, has not run its course, and as a result religious values remain important in Quebec society. Moreover, the coexistence of traditional religious values and modern secular values in contemporary Quebec carries important consequences for political support and the expression of contemporary nationalism.

Nationalism or, more specifically, the idea of national autonomy has been a prominent theme in Quebec politics for a long time. For example, the *Patriotes* issued a declaration of independence proclaiming Lower Canada a republic as early as 1838. A few years later, after the rebellion was crushed, Lafontaine and a majority of francophone members of Parliament believed that French Canadians had won the struggle for autonomy within the union of the two Canadas.[1] Nevertheless, different groups which have supported the idea of independence have displayed widely divergent ideologies in other respects. In other words, the purposes of independence for these organizations have been very different.

Historically, the Roman Catholic Church exercised the most profound influence on traditional Quebec and consequently on the definition of traditional Quebec nationalism. The church's total penetration of society and its unparalleled organizational capacity made it a critical actor in the politics of the province and as such it was uniquely qualified to articulate national aspirations. These aspirations, summarized in the phrase *la survivance*, presumed that institutions such as the parish, the confessional schools, and the family would remain as the chief pillars of French Canadian society.[2] Substantively, tradi-

1. Following the 1837–38 rebellion, London appointed Lord Durham as high commissioner. In his famous *Report on the Affairs of British North America* he recommended "subjecting the Province (of Lower Canada) to the rigorous rule of an English majority." See Gerald M. Graig, ed., *Lord Durham's Report* (Toronto: McClelland and Stewart, Carleton Library, 1963), p. 159. The Union Act of 1840 brought Lower Canada (Quebec) and Upper Canada (Ontario) into a single political community.

2. While French Canadians developed a kind of institutional completeness in the control of most of their political, social, cultural, and religious institutions, they found themselves excluded from economic institutions. This was as apparent in 1831 as in the 1970s. See A. de Tocqueville, *Journey to America*, ed., J. P. Mayer (New Haven: Yale University Press, 1959), pp. 184–94. See also J. M. Veaudelle, *Les siéges sociaux et l'environment québécois*; and P. E. Laporte, *L'usage des langues dans la vie économique au Québec: situation actuelle et possibilités de changement*. These latter studies were prepared in 1973 and 1974, respectively, for a Quebec government commission on the status of French language and linguistic rights.

tional nationalism called for the safeguarding of religious and cultural rights and institutions, the rejection of liberalism, the protection of a traditional rural life-style, freedom from government intervention, and provincial autonomy. Not surprisingly, increased levels of industrialization and urbanization represented a challenge to these ideals, and progressively traditional Quebec nationalism took on the appearance of the collective reactions of a minority which perceived itself to be under siege.

The Origins of Contemporary Quebec Independentism

The contemporary independence movement in Quebec is usually traced back to 1957.[3] The transition to modern Quebec nationalism, however, was characterized by considerable ideological polarization. On the extreme right, the Alliance Laurentienne which was created in 1957 and which slipped into political oblivion in the mid-1960s stood in stark contrast to the nationalism of the left which, though organizationally disparate, found expression through such publications as *La Revue socialiste*. In fact, in many respects the independentism of the Alliance Laurentienne may be viewed as the last gasp of the reactionary nationalist tradition. It played upon the nostalgic themes popularized during the religiously inspired nationalism of the 1920s and 1930s, advocating protection of the French Catholic and humanistic civilization surrounded by the "otherwise so materialistic and so unreligious English-speaking North America." According to one important exponent, "We are, on this land of old Quebec, the only Catholic nation which may oppose itself to American infiltration as an unassailable bulwark . . . we are the only ones to resist the ascendancy of Matter over the Mind."[4] The Alliance wanted a form of social corporatism where the political role of the citizen would be channeled through a multilevel complex of interest groups and where the role of political parties would be diminished.

At the other end of the ideological spectrum, nationalists claiming

3. François-Pierre Gingras, "L'idéologie indépendantiste au Quebec: de la revendictation au project social," *Cahiers internationaux de sociologie* 59 (1975): 273–84.
4. Abbé Wilfrid Morin, *L'indépendance du Quebec: le Québec aux Québécois* (Montreal: Editions de l'Alliance Laurentienne, 1960), p. 128. This book had been published in 1938 as *Nos droits à l'indépendance politique* (Paris: Guillemat).

to be the "only authentic left in French Canada" also denounced capitalism. They spoke out against the economic ghettoization of French Canadians and denounced English-speaking Canadians as "colonialist ogres."[5] Although the extreme left remained marginal within the independentist movement, it constantly challenged the ideology and tactics of independentists such as Pierre Bourgault, André d'Allemagne, and Marcel Chaput who were significant figures in the gestation of mainstream modern nationalism.

The Rassemblement pour l'Indépendance Nationale, created in 1960, was the first distinct organizational vehicle for modern Quebec nationalism. At the outset it advocated a form of nationalism which favored no specific socioeconomic group or political doctrine. Although the RIN advanced a number of national claims which had been part and parcel of the traditional independentist movements, such as French unilingualism and territorial claims to Labrador, the importance of the RIN was that it represented a significant departure from the essence of traditional nationalism. The RIN's nationalism was not a defensive ideology reacting to unsatisfied demands, but a moderately aggressive nationalism which could not be satisfied by concessions from, or "outputs" of, the federal system.[6]

The RIN was also the first independentist organization to attempt to articulate how an independent Quebec might participate in the international political arena. An important part of the party program discussed Quebec's role in the United Nations, its nonalignment, the kinds of bilateral and multilateral agreements Quebec might sign with Canada, the United States, and the European Community as well as the Third World. Domestically, the RIN wanted to promote a "nonconfessional social democracy" which would feature a mixed economy where private companies, state corporations, and cooperatives could coexist, where public utility monopolies would be nationalized, and where worker participation could be developed. In the words of RIN's program, "The RIN has set its goal to establish the necessary prerequisites for the full development of the Québécois nation. Such a full development will be attainable only if and when the nation becomes responsible for its own destiny, particularly when it will have recuperated its entire initiative in the political realm and

5. *La Revue socialiste*, I (1959); Raoul Roy, quoted by *Le Devoir*, June 15, 1961, pp. 1, 6.
6. See Morin, *L'Indépendance*, p. 5.

oriented the economy to the satisfaction of collective needs."[7] The RIN program called for an interventionist role for the state and the advance of new secular values.[8] In fact, these changes did not occur overnight; they developed gradually between 1960 and 1968, the period generally regarded as the watershed of the Quiet Revolution.[9]

The RIN was formed only a few months after Jean Lesage's Liberals had defeated the Union Nationale, whose leader and founder, Maurice Duplessis, had died. Since the reforms of the Lesage regime are widely regarded as having set in motion the changes identified with the Quiet Revolution, it is necessary to outline the nature of the Quiet Revolution in order to appreciate the context and direction of the RIN's program.

In general terms the Quiet Revolution represented a fundamental, qualitative change in the orientation of Quebec society. This involved an impetus toward greater participation by Québécois in a modern industrial economy, and a reorientation of values particularly with respect to the reaffirmation of the authenticity of Quebec culture. These two basic themes, the socioeconomic development of Quebec and the Québécois, and the value of orientations leading to cultural affirmation, were viewed as complementary. Attitudes toward Quebec culture changed: *survivance*, which expressed the culturally defensive posture of old Quebec, was replaced by *rattrapage*, reflecting a new confidence coupled with the realization that precious time had been lost in the social and economic development of Quebec. In all dimensions, political and economic, cultural and social, the Quiet Revolution was, according to conventional historiography, a transition from an old to a new order.

Over the years, independence became perceived by its advocates

7. Rassemblement pour l'Indépendance Nationale, *Programme politique du R.I.N. 1966–1967* (Montreal: Secrétariat du R.I.N., 1967), p. 3.

8. Many members of the RIN as well as readers and contributors to the Marxist journal *Parti-Pris* also belonged to the anticlerical Mouvement laique de langue française, whose acknowledged objective was to secularize Quebec. Writer André Major is typical of these radical intellectuals. See his "Arms in Hand," in Frank R. Scott and Michael Olivier, eds., *Québec States Her Case* (Toronto: Macmillan, 1964), pp. 73–82. See also Denis Monière, *Le développement de la pensée de gauche au Québec à travers trois revues: Cité Libre, Socialisme et Parti Pris*, M. A. thesis (Political Science), University of Ottawa, 1970, chap. 3.

9. Some may prefer to equate the Quiet Revolution with the six years (1960–66) during which Jean Lesage's Liberals were in office. To the extent that the authors consider the Quiet Revolution to be unfinished business, the dates of 1966 or 1968 make little difference. The year 1966 may have seen the Union Nationale return to office, but 1968 witnessed the founding of the Parti Québécois.

more as an instrument than as a goal per se. Independence represented the key to social and economic planning which was to be
guided *by* the Québécois, *for* the Québécois. As Pierre Bourgault,
the leader of the RIN, commented, "So far, we have never known
where we were heading for, because others were deciding. We now
want to decide ourselves, and be responsible for our successes as well
as for our failures."[10] The RIN postulated that the Québécois should
invent a new, unique socioeconomic system that would take into account their cultural uniqueness as well as the North American context. Some independentists have argued that the party developed a
brand of Québécois socialism. Whatever one's assessment, it is clear
that the leaders of the RIN had accomplished a singular achievement:
no political party had ever before submitted to the Québécois such a
developed program. Some of the concrete proposals had proceeded
from a careful analysis of foreign systems, especially those of the
United States, Israel, France, Yugoslavia, the USSR, and most importantly, Sweden. The program's continual reference to the uniqueness
of some of Quebec's own institutions and traditions resulted in a
syncretism typically associated with ideological constructions in
emerging nations. The party's socioeconomic and political proposals
involved a balance of tradition and innovation, of tributes to the national heritage and character as well as the adoption of solutions
which had proved successful elsewhere. In this sense, the RIN differed from earlier separatist movements that had attributed paramount importance to the past. For the RIN, the future was what
counted and the future had to be planned.

The Central Planning Office was pivotal to the RIN design for an
independent Quebec; it was to be responsible for the formulation of
short-term as well as long-term planning alternatives taking into account regional, sectoral, and national priorities. The objective was to
have the Central Planning Office staffed by experts who would perform technical functions which were to be defined by the entire population and which would be implemented through interest groups
such as trade unions, parent-teacher associations, and the like. In
fact, the uniquely Québécois brand of democracy that was advocated
represented a blend of corporatism (inherited from the nationalist

10. Pierre Bourgault (personal communication).

movements of the 1920s and 1930s and the Alliance Laurentienne)
and of socialism (more or less inspired by the neo-Marxist wing of the
movement).

The Parti Québécois emerged as the principal vehicle for contemporary Quebec nationalism in the wake of the RIN's annual convention in 1968. A severe crisis in the RIN featuring a split between the
revolutionary neo-Marxist faction and Pierre Bourgault's middle-
of-the-road faction culminated in a resolution to terminate the existence of the party. Actually, a considerable portion of the party's
membership had already joined the newly created PQ, probably because the PQ was perceived to have better electoral prospects than
the RIN. The PQ itself was an outgrowth of the Mouvement Sou-
veraineté Association formed in 1967 by René Lévesque, a high-pro-
file and well-respected former cabinet minister in the Lesage government of 1960–66.[11]

Sovereignty-Association: Ideological
Compromise and Electoral Success

There were several reasons why Lévesque thought the Québécois
might one day be in favor of independence. He argued that Quebec
needed more economic and political flexibility than that which the
Canadian federal system had been able to allocate to the provinces.
Furthermore, he wanted French Canadians to be recognized as equal
partners with English Canadians in the Canadian federation. The
long-standing superior/inferior relationship had to be replaced by a
healthier one: "There will be a new Canada, otherwise Quebec will
secede," Lévesque told a Toronto audience in 1963. Furthermore, he
believed that "if the Québécois cannot get Canadians to accept bina-
tionalism, then we will have to think about separating."[12] There were
definite demands in these statements for symbolic outputs from the
political system. But there were also demands for more concrete outputs as well. In the early 1960s, the provincial Liberal government of

11. The MSA had started with the "working hypothesis" of a sovereign Quebec, economically
associated with (the rest of) Canada, in a new mutually agreeable union. It was primarily a constitutional design aimed at solving a constitutional crisis.
12. *Le Devoir*, June 3, 1963, p. 9, and Nov. 4, 1963, p. 1.

Quebec requested additional resources for the province and thereby precipitated a major clash with the federal government. First, Quebec demanded an immediate increase in the share of personal and corporate taxes (that is, a significant, if partial, withdrawal of the federal government from the fields of personal income taxes, corporate income taxes, and succession duties, to the benefit of the provinces); and second, a gradual redistribution of the taxation fields themselves (that is, the complete withdrawal of the federal government from some fields, or the transfer of 100 percent of the revenues from some tax fields from the federal to the provincial governments). "If this were not possible, we would be left with no alternative but to separate," said Lévesque in a famous Quebec government "ultimatum" in 1963.[13]

Later, Lévesque wrote that Quebec demands "obviously exceed the best dispositions manifested in the other majority."[14] Nevertheless, he always remained confident that, if the Canadian political community could not support a plan for equal partnership, Canadians would accept a redefinition of the relationship between Quebec and the rest of the nation without necessarily choosing total rupture. "Necessary arrangements with Ottawa can be worked out while satisfying the aspirations of our nation," Lévesque told the *New York Times* in 1964.[15]

Since the early 1960s, virtually all Canadian politicians have, at one time or another, suggested possible alternatives for new constitutional arrangements. Lévesque himself first supported the "Associate States" formula, by which Quebec and English Canada would each have a semi-independent status in a new Confederation based primarily on monetary and other ties of an economic nature. When the MSA was founded in 1967, the organization, composed of Lévesque and dissident Liberals, felt that "Quebec is altogether moving in the irreversible direction of sovereignty."[16]

The core of the independentist construction has been a belief in a uniquely Québécois collective personality manifested by a deeply rooted attachment to "this only corner of the world where we may be

13. See *Le Devoir*, Oct. 30, 1963, p. 3.
14. René Lévesque, *Option Québec* (Montréal: Editions de l'Homme, 1968), p. 35.
15. *The New York Times*, Feb. 24, 1964, p. 1.
16. Jean Blain, "Preface," *Option Québec*, p. 11.

fully ourselves."[17] This has implied the maintenance of French as the normal language of use despite tremendous North American pressures in the direction of assimilation. More generally, not only do Québécois have the right to safeguard their collective personality (the right of all nations to live), but also they have a moral obligation not to betray the heritage preserved and developed through generations at the cost of uninterrupted efforts and sacrifices. Thus, independentists believe Québécois have two alternatives: on the one hand, there is the "comfortable" solution of losing the collective self through assimilation;[18] on the other, there is the difficult solution which involves struggling for a status congruous with the size, personality, and perceived aspirations of the Québécois nation.

According to independentists, the achievement of the second solution is dependent upon the ability of the Quebec government to autonomously determine and implement its own policies in the fields of citizenship, immigration and manpower, communications, social security and health, justice, the economy, international relations, the internal constitution, and territorial integrity. They do not regard the Canadian political system as sufficiently flexible to allow for such a measure of autonomy. As a result, rupture is regarded as inevitable if Québécois decide to fully assert their collective self. To achieve their goals, René Lévesque and his supporters in the MSA attempted to define a new Quebec political community on the basis of "the two major trends of our times: that of national freedom and that of freely accepted political and economic communities."[19]

For the MSA, as earlier for the RIN, sovereignty appeared as a tool, as a means to recuperate jurisdictions, resources, and decisions —powers which would allow the Québécois, mainly through government intervention, to set their priorities and choose their models for development. The ultimate objective was the creation of a "new society" that would truly reflect the uniquely Québécois personality. However, the MSA did not articulate the substance of this new society—its major concern was the constitutional dimension.

17. Lévesque, *Option Québec*, p. 19.
18. During the 1960s several independentists had little respect for English culture—an attitude further reinforced by English Canadians who argued that "Quebec" is what makes Canada different from the United States.
19. Lévesque, *Option Québec*, pp. 38–39.

In 1968, the MSA merged with other groups to form the Parti
Québécois. The new party emphasized the instrumental nature of independence rather than the possibility of an association with English
Canada. During its first few years of existence, the new party's strategy was to recruit members on the basis of their sympathy for the
idea of sovereignty (or sovereignty-association) and the respectability
brought by Lévesque to the movement; to develop a sophisticated
social democratic program; and to try to persuade the electorate to
"buy" the program (social democracy and independence). The program itself was largely inherited from the MSA and the RIN and was
based on three key themes: planning, efficiency, and decentralization. It had clear technocratic biases, vesting in the government a
major role in the definition and organization of the community.

In the 1970 provincial election the PQ won seven seats (of a possible 108) and 23 percent of the popular vote. These totals represented
significant increases over 1966 when the independentist candidates
attracted the support of 9 percent of the electorate and failed to gain a
single seat in the National Assembly. While the results were encouraging they were still wide of the mark. As with other movement parties, the early days of the PQ were marked by a concern for ideological purity rather than electoral success. By 1972, however, the party
had shifted its strategy in a pragmatic direction by making a more
concerted effort to identify with the problems facing the public at
large.[20] Between 1972 and 1976 Péquistes became actively involved in
a wide range of interest groups, from labor unions to business associations, from citizens' committees to school boards, from charitable organizations to gay groups. The party which had consistently represented those seeking reforms also expressed its understanding for
those "in a hurry" calling for revolution. At the same time, unlike the
RIN, the PQ managed to maintain its respectability by studiously
avoiding any active participation in extraparliamentary demonstra-
tions. The stated objective was to achieve a political synthesis of "all
valid approaches" leading to the full development of the collective
personality so that a majority of Québécois could recognize themselves in the PQ.[21]

20. Manifesto of Nov. 27, 1971.
21. See René Lévesque's "Presentation," in *La Solution, le programme du Parti Québécois*
(Montréal: Editions du Jour, 1970); and André Larocque, *Défis au Parti Québécois* (Montréal:
Editions du Jour, 1971).

The pragmatic drift of the PQ was accelerated after the 1973 election—a contest which saw the party increase its popular vote total to 30 percent but capture only six assembly seats. The party largely abandoned its earlier "educational mission," to display instead an image of being *the* alternative to the status quo. PQ strategists understood that in searching for popular support a new party had to stress three elements, namely, the identification of personal and collective interests reflected in the emphasis placed on the need for control over one's personal/collective destiny, including good government in the short run; the symbolic manifestations of these aspirations, such as slogans like "Quebec to the Québécois" and "for a real government," designed to confirm the loyalties of the supporters and to recruit new sympathizers; and the deep-rooted cultural values of the population, that is, nationalism, the French language, social and economic development.

The agenda that PQ strategists tried to set involved issues such as the need for a "real" government, freedom from the political scandals of the Liberal administration, reformed party financing, and so forth. Also, the party made an effort to recruit new members (and in the 1976 campaign, to gather votes) on semi-ideological and nonideological terms, while trying to "ideologically educate" the members after they had joined (instead of before). The rationale for the strategy was the view that the objective of independence might be accepted and shared only as the result of individual analyses and ideological maturation.

In the 1976 election the strategy was successful; it brought the party 41 percent of the vote and enough seats to form a majority government. In this election the PQ did not ask the Québécois to vote for the elaborate program, but instead to cast a ballot for "good government." According to the logic of the party's leadership, good government implied an eventual constitutional rupture (with anticipated economic association) as only limited improvements might be made within the existing constitutional structure. And the Québécois, through a referendum, would tell the government when to go that far in the development of their collective self.

In 1976, the PQ promised to hold a referendum on sovereignty-association during its first term of office. After considerable procrastination May 20, 1980, was chosen and the Québécois were asked to give the government a mandate to *negotiate* sovereignty-association. All observers agree that the actual "soft" wording of the question was designed to draw more supporters than would have been attracted by a "straight" question calling the Québécois to express their support for sovereignty-association . . . or even independence. Some claimed that it was "an effort to deflect the discussion away from the theme of basic change in the Canadian political community and toward the interpretation that what was being proposed was a series of changes to the regime."[22] The strategy was successful to the extent that, according to data collected by Maurice Pinard and Richard Hamilton, more than 40 percent of those who voted "oui" wanted to set in motion negotiations on a renewed federalism rather than to support sovereignty-association.[23]

However, the presence of a substantial number of "neo-federalists" among "oui" voters was insufficient as 60 percent of all voters cast a "non." A majority of Québécois were unwilling, or unready, to go even as far as giving a mandate to negotiate sovereignty-association. In fact, as will be argued later, this result suggests that a majority of Québécois have not yet accepted all of the new value orientations developed during the Quiet Revolution, including the polarized nationalist values conveyed in the independentist movement.

Prior to the Quiet Revolution, value orientations were largely religious-based as the Roman Catholic Church played a central role in Quebec's social and political life. But since that time, other new and more important forces were presumed to be at work in the province. According to some theorists, the institutional and structural changes in Quebec during the 1960s were merely symptoms of, and secondary to, the essence of the Quiet Revolution. For example, Guy Rocher has argued that it "was characterized by changes of mentality, attitudes and values among French Canadians in Quebec much more than by a change in the institutions and in the social structures as such."[24] Similarly, Kenneth McRoberts and Dale Posgate have main-

22. Jon H. Pammett, Harold D. Clarke, Jane Jenson, and Lawrence LeDuc, "Political Support and Voting Behavior in the Quebec Referendum," in this volume, chap. 12.

23. Their survey was conducted May 4–9, 1980. See also Maurice Pinard and Richard Hamilton, "Les Québécois votent NON: Le sens du vote" (Montréal: Université McGill, 1980, unpublished), p. 6.

24. He goes on to say, "During the '60s the changes that were to take place and that have finally come to be known as the Quiet Revolution centered around two main areas: the role of

tained that traditional beliefs and assumptions were "to a large extent abandoned,"[25] while Fernand Dumont has referred to the Quiet Revolution as a profound transmutation of yesterday's arguments[26]—arguments articulated by the leading upholders of the old order, the Roman Catholic Church. The Quiet Revolution, therefore, to the extent that it constituted a reaction against the past, represented a fundamental challenge to the heretofore untested hegemony of the Roman Catholic Church as the definitive director of the social order. Secular spokesmen articulated a new vision of Quebec; a vision which was aclerical if not anticlerical. Moreover, the elites engineering Quebec's transformation from the old to the new order were not reluctant to implicate the Church as the agent responsible for the social, economic, political, and cultural retardation of the Québécois. Some observers hold, then, that the creation of a new order requires not only the participation of the Québécois in the modern sectors of the economy but also, analogously, participation in *new and modern values*. So it is assumed that the atrophy of the institutions of the Roman Catholic Church, particularly the educational and social service institutions, has been paralleled by atrophy in the pertinence of Roman Catholic values traditionally understood.

The argument of the Quiet Revolution theorists is powerful. By all accounts, at least until 1960, Quebec culture *was* a traditional and essentially religious culture. Thus Québécois nationalism, until 1960, may be interpreted as a religious nationalism. If the dissociation of the religious component of Quebec culture, under such motors as secular postsecondary education, reached fruition in the Quiet Revolution, then a fundamental reorientation of Quebec society, a genuine "cultural revolution," has indeed taken place.[27]

---

the Roman Catholic Church and the educational role . . . the Church [lost] the powerful grip it had upon the mentality of the French-Canadians." Guy Rocher, "The Quiet Revolution and Revolutionary Movements among Quebec French Canadians," paper prepared for the Bicentennial Conference on Revolution and Evolution (Durham, NC: Duke University, 1976), p. 2. A more detailed version of Rocher's argument can be found in *Le Québec en mutation* (Montréal: Hurtubise H.M.H., 1971).

25. Kenneth McRoberts and Dale Posgate, *Quebec: Social Change and Political Crisis*, rev. ed. (Toronto: McClelland and Stewart, 1980), p. 94.

26. Fernand Dumont, "Our Culture: Between Past and Future," in *The Vigil of Quebec* (Toronto: University of Toronto Press, 1974), pp. 50–55; originally published in French in the November 1970 issue of *Maintenant*.

27. See Rocher, "The Quiet Revolution," p. 3; Dumont, "Our Culture," p. 50.

First, there can be little disagreement with Michel Brunet's view that the question of complete redistribution of power between church and state has been settled.[28] Clearly, the institutional power of the Church has declined and the once organic relationship between church and state has been ruptured by the introduction of hospital insurance and medicare, the creation of the Ministries of Cultural Affairs and of Education, and the establishment of an integrated network of state agencies providing basic as well as specialized health and social services. Second, at the grass-roots level, Quiet Revolution theorists point to falling attendance rates at Mass as further evidence of the decline of the Church. Also, the number of priests ordained in the Roman Catholic Church fell 58 percent between 1960 and 1969.[29] And interest in the parish, particularly among the youth, has declined. Third, the Church has become disconnected from significant interest groups in Quebec. With the death of Maurice Duplessis, the Roman Catholic Church lost an important and sympathetic ally. By 1960, the Church had lost its influence even with the Catholic Trade Unions in Quebec.[30] Most professional and student organizations and public interest committees created in the 1960s did not bother to appoint chaplains.

The evidence supporting the Quiet Revolution view of Quebec's social change since 1960 is impressive. But, from the theoretical perspective adopted here, it cannot yet be considered conclusive. The first point to be made relates to the institutional evidence that Quiet Revolution theorists bring to support their interpretation of Quebec's transformation. In our view, the institutional evidence does not easily fit the Quiet Revolution framework. The victory of Quebec's provincial Liberal party in 1960, said to represent grass-roots endorsement of a program of social change, actually involved only a net loss of slightly more than 2 percent of the eligible electorate by the Union Nationale, compared to its vote total in the 1956 election.[31] The so-called consolidation of modernization values in the 1962 election also added only

28. Michel Brunet, "Historical Background of Quebec's Challenge to Canadian Unity," in Dale C. Thomson, ed., *Quebec Society and Politics* (Toronto: McClelland and Stewart, 1973), pp. 39–51.

29. Nive Voisine, *Histoire de L'Eglise catholique au Québec 1608–1970* (Montréal: Fides, 1971), p. 83.

30. Roger Chartier, "Chronologie de l'évolution confessionnelle de la C.T.C.C. (C.S.N.)," *Relations industrielles* 16 (1961): 102–12; A. Fraser Isbester, "A History of National Catholic Unions in Canada; 1901–1965," unpublished Ph.D. thesis, Cornell University, 1968, p. 342.

31. As a percentage of the total registered electorate, Union Nationale support fell from

3 percent of eligible voters to the Liberal party's vote total. Insofar as the Union Nationale represented traditionalism in the 1960s, it cannot be said that the values associated with the old order were "swept aside overnight."[32]

Nor can it even be said Quebec society has embraced religious neutrality: as late as 1975, a study prepared for the Reorganization Committee of the School Council of the Island of Montreal reported that "more than 80 percent of Catholics want religious instruction in school" and, "most parents, especially Catholics, think these classes should be compulsory."[33] Attempts to deconfessionalize the school system have met with staunch opposition from an overwhelming majority of Protestants and Roman Catholics alike. Four years after the election of the Parti Québécois, president Robert Gaulin of the Centrale de l'enseignement du Québec blamed the PQ government for not yet having shown the courage to have the province shed the "strait-jacket of confessional education."[34]

The second reservation specifically relates to the role that Quiet Revolution theorists conventionally assign to the Church in Quebec. Viewing the disengagement of the Roman Catholic Church from the Quebec polity as synonymous with the secular, progressive thrust of the Quiet Revolution implies that the Church (at least in Quebec) is once and for all against change, and that the most significant dimension of religious influence in Quebec is institutionally expressed. Perhaps the capacity of the Church to respond to change has been underestimated to the extent that its homogeneity as a conservative organization has been overestimated. To be sure, there are conservative forces within the Church hierarchy, but there are also liberal, even radical elements which have exercised important influence through such bodies as the Sacerdotal Commission on Social Studies. Church-sponsored institutions such as the School for Social Studies at Laval

---

39.9 percent in 1956 to 37.5 percent in 1960. Because the rate of voter turnout increased from 78.3 percent in 1956 to 81.7 percent in 1960, the minor decline in Union Nationale support is paralleled by somewhat more important gains for the Liberals, who polled 41.3 percent of the registered electorate in 1960, compared to 34.6 percent in 1956. See Vincent Lemieux, Marcel Gilbert, and Andre Blais, *Une élection de réalignement: l'élection générale du 29 avril 1970 au Québec* (Montréal: Editions du Jour, 1970), chap. 1.

32. In fact, popular support for the Union Nationale declined marginally in absolute terms. It was roughly the same in 1966 (948,928 votes) as in 1956 (956,082). Of course one must keep in mind that during this decade the total registered electorate increased by 34.6 percent.

33. Normand Wener, "Montreal Parents on Religion and the School," *Unisson* 4 (1975):3.

34. See *La Presse*, Sept. 13, 1980.

University, in fact, trained many of the leaders of the Quiet Revolution.

Encouragement for the Church to respond to the "revolution" in Quebec's social environment came not only from outside forces but also from within. For example, the Second Vatican Council urged greater responsiveness to the needs of the working class; it urged that the Church reflect and respond to cultural particularism and to symbolically democratize Mass. The Roman Catholic Church in Quebec, as the Dumont Report[35] clearly shows, became self-conscious of the need to reassess its societal role. Roman Catholic laity have taken advantage of their increased role in Church affairs by offering direction and criticism. The motivation of the Church to respond to the demands for change from within and outside is clear; bishops knew that to win the support of the Québécois the Church had to identify with their aspirations. By the fall of 1971 Abbé Norbert Lacoste argued that the Church's infrastructure was ready to meet the needs of the future.[36] He was probably right.

Although the Catholic Committee of the Superior Council of Education disagreed with the pragmatic approach to education outlined in the Dumont Report, it endorsed its critical appraisal of the Church's role in modern Quebec. In its important document *Religion in Today's School*, it argued, "We need only point out how much greater is the range of ways of belonging to the Church or professing the Christian faith since the Vatican II Council. Thus an *internal* pluralism within the Christian community is added to the *external* pluralism of society in general, all of which makes matters still more complex."[37]

Institutional measures of the progress of the Quiet Revolution tend to oversimplify the nature and scope of the transitions that took place within the Church itself.[38] Although the Church bore the brunt of the institutional changes of the Quiet Revolution, it is far from convinced that such changes forecast a secular society. To quote the caretakers of

35. Fernand Dumont chaired the Commission d'étude sur les laics et l'Eglise; the actual title of the "Dumont Report" is *L'Eglise du Québec: un héritage, un projet* (Montréal: Fides, 1971).
36. Norbert Lacoste, "The Catholic Church in Quebec: Adapting to Change," in Thomson, *Quebec Society and Politics*, p. 167.
37. The Catholic Committee of the Superior Council of Education, *Religion in Today's School* (Quebec: Superior Council of Education, 1975), p. 20 (originally published in French in 1974 as *Dimension religieuse et projet scolaire*.)
38. Some American sociologists have cautioned against any oversimplification of the secularization process. See, for instance: Peter Berger, *A Rumor of Angels* (New York: Doubleday, 1969); Andrew Greely, *Concilium* (January 1973):1; Andrew Greely, *Unsecular Man, the Persistance of Religion*, (New York: Schocken, 1972).

Catholic instruction in Quebec, there may have been a "secularization of social institutions and of cultural expression," but this has not necessarily led to the dominance of "secularism, a new ideology of a self-contained world watching the fade-out of religious reality."[39]

Our third reservation about the Quiet Revolution framework concerns the assumed relationship between changes in institutions and changes in societal values. Specifically, while Quiet Revolution theorists argue that it is values, not institutions, that are at the core of social change, the only evidence that is presented in support of the case is institutional and we have already questioned the integrity of these types of data. Thus Leon Dion's assertion that declining attendance at Mass signaled the emergence of a "new man-centered rationality" and a "spirit of self-determination"[40] makes an inference which, in our view, remains open to question. Clearly, structural and/or legal changes such as secularization can lead or lag behind the changes in values taking place within the general population. This may be the case even within the Church.

As early as 1966, former *Le Devoir* editor Claude Ryan, whose close ties with the Church are well known, commented on the secularization movement in the following terms: "I am quite struck by the rather quiet way in which the transition takes place. It can't be said that we are witnessing a revolution of the laity against the clergy. There are many clerics who favour those changes; and there are many lay people who are opposed to those changes. . . . I have the impression that the power of religious values themselves remains quite considerable."[41] The fact of the matter is that the Quiet Revolution was elite-induced social change. Thus, the institutional reforms of the 1960s may be a more accurate reflection of the interests of areligious elites rather than the values of the bulk of the Quebec population. Indeed, some interpreters of the Quiet Revolution agree on this point.[42]

39. Catholic Committee, *Religion in Today's School*, p. 19.

40. "Few societies have experienced such profound changes in so short a space of time as Quebec [during the 1960s]. . . . Today, many . . . churches are abandoned and for sale. . . . Breaking the bonds which tied them so securely to a familiar world, Quebecers find themselves suddenly cut off from old beliefs, now obsolete." Leon Dion, "Toward a Self-Determined Consciousness," in Thomson, *Quebec Society and Politics*, pp. 27, 28.

41. Claude Ryan, "Pouvoir religieux et sécularisation," in Fernand Dumont and Jean-Paul Montminy, *Le pouvoir dans la société canadienne-française*, special issue of *Recherches sociographiques* 7 (1966): 108, 109.

42. "The Quiet Revolution was the ideology of the dominant political group, but it is hard to

In sum, in our view the conventional interpretation of the Quiet Revolution as an explanation of contemporary Quebec politics appears to contain serious weaknesses. The flaws are not fatal but they may be misleading. The above reservations, collectively, are sufficiently significant to cast doubt on the straightforward view that the Quiet Revolution represented a sudden and wholehearted change for most Québécois. To summarize our critique, the conventional view of the Quiet Revolution can only be sustained by ignoring the evident capacity of traditional institutions, such as the Roman Catholic Church, to respond to change; by focusing only on a selectively narrow range of institutional evidence; and by assuming that elite-led institutional changes corresponded to changes in the attitudes of the Quebec population as a whole.

Most intellectuals, academics, and other observers now take for granted the idea that, in the two decades following 1960, new, non-traditional Quiet Revolution values have filtered down and are now almost universally accepted by the Quebec public. They are surprised to see a "religious" Claude Ryan elected leader of the Quebec Liberal party and they are surprised to see the PQ referendum defeated at the hands of a coalition of "traditionalists" and federalists.[43] The unquestioning acceptance of the conventional interpretation of the Quiet Revolution has prematurely foreclosed debate about the coexistence of "traditional" along with "modern" values in Quebec and their impact on politics. The debate must continue precisely because the most important aspect of the Quiet Revolution, changed *value* orientations, has not received sufficient attention.

Traditional and Modern Values in Contemporary Quebec

The idea that the institutional disengagement of the Roman Catholic Church is a measure of the "religious neutrality" of Quebec culture can be questioned partly because the concept *secularization*

---

believe that it was the ideology of the majority of the French-Canadian Quebeckers," Rocher, *The Quiet Revolution*, p. 17. See also Marcel Rioux, "Quebec—From a Minority Complex to Majority Behavior," in Henry J. Tobias and Charles E. Woodhouse, eds., *Minorities and Politics* (Albuquerque: University of New Mexico Press, 1969), pp. 39–52. See also McRoberts and Posgate, *Quebec: Social Change and Political Crisis*, chap. 6.

43. One might argue that the reelection of the PQ in 1981 confirms the long-term secular trend initiated during the Quiet Revolution. The authors would point out, however, that, be-

has much more than an institutional dimension. Even if the Church has been participating less effectively in political life, it cannot be assumed automatically that traditional religious values are now politically or socially irrelevant. To explore directly the "values" dimension, this chapter uses data derived from a mail questionnaire survey of the Quebec general public conducted in November 1976.[44]

To argue that the Quiet Revolution has to do primarily with the secularization of Quebec society raises important theoretical questions about the meaning of the term "secular." This is not the place to retrace a complex sociological debate. Suffice it to say that it is implicit in the definition of secular society that religious values may be privately held. One of the Quiet Revolution's challenges to Quebec's traditional social order was to restrict religious values to the private sphere; the purpose was to disarticulate the political impact of the Church, not to banish all aspects of religion in toto. The critical issue in the analysis of secularization in Quebec, then, concerns the extent to which religious values continue to impinge on society. Two aspects are of particular interest: first, to what extent do religious values play an important role in the definition of the Québécois collective identity? and second, to what extent do religious values structure the political domain? Attention must be directed not only to the privately held beliefs of the Québécois (personal religiosity) but also to the public aspects of religious beliefs (hereinafter designated cultural religiosity).

There are empirical as well as theoretical reasons for preferring indicators of cultural religiosity over personal religiosity. The marginals in table 11.1 indicate the scope of the subjective, private importance

---

tween 1976 and 1980, popular vote for the Liberals rose from 34 percent to 46 percent, compared to the PQ's 40 percent and 49 percent.

44. A 106-item questionnaire was mailed to 2,980 households in Quebec. The research design used a random sample drawn from telephone directories of the province. The sample was regionally stratified between Montreal, Quebec City, and the rest of the province. Eight hundred and fifty usable questionnaires were returned, a response rate of about 30 percent which is quite acceptable under the circumstances. Two systematic biases can be reported but neither is considered significant given the way we use the data. First, it was expected that a sizable proportion of Québécois whose mother tongue was other than French would not respond. Less than 1 percent of the sample indicated a mother tongue other than French. When we refer to "Québécois" we generalize only about francophones in Québec. Second, there is a slight overrepresentation of respondents under thirty-five years of age. To the extent that age is used as an independent or control variable the bias is not problematic. When age is not controlled for, conservative value orientations are underestimated in our data. Further details about the sample can be acquired by written request from either author.

Table 11.1. *Opinions of Québécois of the Personal and Cultural Importance of Religion*

Importance of religion to French-Canadian culture	Personal importance of religion				
	Very important	Important	Of little importance	Not important	Total
Very important	57%	17%	9%	1%	24%
Important	24	38	26	6	23
Of little importance	10	30	42	17	24
Not important	9	16	24	76	29
(N =)	(255)	(155)	(213)	(174)	(797)
Gamma = 0.70					

Percentages may not add to 100 because of rounding error.

of religion (personal religiosity), in Quebec as well as the importance attributed to religion in the definition of French-Canadian culture (cultural religiosity). Table 11.1 further shows that even though there is a strong association between both measures of religious orientations (gamma = 0.70), close to one-fifth of those for whom religion was personally "very important" attached little or no significance to religion for French-Canadian culture. This also was the case for 46 percent for whom religion was personally "important."

A more important general finding also is apparent in the marginal distributions shown in table 11.1: only 29 percent of the Québécois sampled thought that religion was not important to French-Canadian culture, while nearly half of the respondents (47 percent) regarded religion as important or very important to French-Canadian culture. On that basis, it is difficult to make the argument that Quebec in 1976 had a truly secular culture. Furthermore, while it may be contended that Quebec is moving closer to possessing such a culture, on the grounds that younger generations tend to be both personally (table 11.2) and culturally (table 11.3) less religious than older generations (gammas = 0.55 and 0.47, respectively), it could be suggested that cultural religiosity has declined less than personal religiosity, since absolute percentage differences between extreme age cohorts are smaller for the former measure than for the latter (37 percent compared to 51 percent in the "very important" category).[45]

Our data show that a majority of the Québécois still considered re-

45. It is, of course, difficult to assess the possible effects of maturation on cultural religiosity without longitudinal data.

Table 11.2. *Personal Importance of Religion by Age (horizontal percentages)*

| Age | Personal importance of religion | | | | |
	Very important	Important	Of little importance	Not important	(N =)
18–34 years	13%	17	35	35	(335)
35–55 years	37%	27	23	13	(227)
56 years +	64%	14	13	9	(132)
Gamma = 0.55					

Percentages may not add to 100 because of rounding error.

Table 11.3. *Cultural Importance of Religion by Age (horizontal percentages)*

| Age | Importance of religion to French-Canadian culture | | | | |
	Very important	Important	Of little importance	Not important	(N =)
18–34 years	10%	21	27	42	(330)
35–55 years	28%	28	24	21	(224)
56 years +	47%	26	15	13	(131)
Gamma = 0.47					

Percentages may not add to 100 because of rounding error.

ligion a component of French-Canadian culture. But the fact that only 29 percent of the Québécois are not culturally religious does not discredit the position of Quiet Revolution theorists; it only discredits the oversimplification that the Quiet Revolution heralded a communal reorientation away from religious values for all Québécois. The reorientation has taken place among the young, and data not presented here confirm that the educational reforms of the 1960s were instrumental in the reorientation. Not surprisingly, the Church has reacted, proposing in 1974 "a complete reversal of attitude towards questions concerning religious education in the school," arguing that religious education "should be an integral element of any open and liberal school" because "the religious dimension is included in the concept of the complete man" as well as "rooted in our whole cultural heritage."[46] In sum, our data suggest that the conventional inter-

46. Catholic Committee, *Religion in Today's School,* pp. 9, 31, 34.

pretation of the Quiet Revolution does apply, but only to a relatively restricted segment of the Québécois—those under thirty-five years of age. For the other Québécois, religion continues to play an important role in the definition of French-Canadian culture. In our view, the fact that most Québécois do *not* carry a secular view of French-Canadian culture is crucial because it argues against the indiscriminate use of the conventional interpretation of the Quiet Revolution, and it gives further support to the idea that the process of secularization is far from complete.

At the outset it was argued that the style of nationalism in Quebec was related to the nature of Quebec society itself. The argument can be extended in a more formal way. Since nationalism depends upon the consciousness of belonging to the nation and since "the nation" can be viewed as a political analogue of culture, the extent to which religious values impinge upon the definition of culture has potential consequences for nationalism. A strong case can be made to support the view that, historically, the Roman Catholic Church systematically nurtured the religious component of French-Canadian culture thereby effecting a fusion between the religious and national identity of French Canadians. As a result, religious rights became a partial substitute for national rights because the culture (nation) had an entirely religious definition. Using our survey data, we are in a position to explore the relationship between cultural religiosity and national identity in contemporary Quebec.

Table 11.4 shows that the least culturally religious Québécois are more likely to see themselves as Québécois only or Québécois first (32 percent and 30 percent), while the most culturally religious are more likely to attribute equal or more importance to their Canadian identity (51 percent and 21 percent). However, it cannot be said that the culturally religious identify primarily with Canada. Since slightly more than half (51 percent) the culturally religious see themselves equally as Québécois and Canadians, cultural religiosity actually encourages identification with the Québécois nation; this is characteristic of traditional nationalism, from Louis-Hyppolite Lafontaine to Henri Bourassa to Claude Ryan. It is also noteworthy that the "Québécois only" are much more likely to view religion as culturally unimportant (55 percent) than are the "Canadians only" or the hybrid Canadian/Québécois (22 percent and 21 percent, respectively). The

Table 11.4. *State-Nation Identification by Cultural Religiosity*[a]

| State-nation identification | Importance of religion to French-Canadian culture | | | | |
	Very important	Important	Of little importance	Not important	Total
Québécois only	7%	8%	17%	32%	17%
Québécois first	22	37	36	30	31
Equally Québécois and Canadian	51	37	31	25	36
Canadian first[b]	21	17	16	13	17
(N =)	(190)	(187)	(190)	(229)	(797)
Gamma = −0.30					

a. *State-nation identification* was measured with the following question: "Vous considérez-vous comme étant: Québécois seulement; Québécois d'abord, Canadien ensuite; Egalement Québécois et Canadien; Canadien d'abord, Québécois ensuite; Canadien seulement?"
b. Also includes Canadian only.
Percentages may not add to 100 because of rounding error.

Table 11.5. *Attitudes toward Independence by Cultural Religiosity*

| Attitude toward independence | Importance of religion to French-Canadian culture | | | | |
	Very important	Important	Of little importance	Not important	Total
Favorable	21%	32%	38%	50%	36%
Undecided	9	8	15	17	12
Opposed	70	61	47	33	52
(N =)	(192)	(186)	(190)	(229)	(797)
Gamma = −0.36					

Percentages may not add to 100 because of rounding error.

corollary also holds true: the "Québécois only" are much less likely to view religion as very important to the culture than the "Canadians only" or the hybrid Canadian/Québécois (data not shown in tabular form).

Given the tendency of culturally religious Québécois to identify with the Canadian state as well as the Québécois nation, it is unlikely that religious national identifiers would express national claims in the form of independentism. This expectation finds support in table 11.5 which shows that half of those who have an entirely secular view of French-Canadian culture are independentists. In contrast, only 21 percent of the culturally religious are independentist. While culturally secular Québécois dominate the ranks of the independentists, detailed analysis of the data indicates that only 16 percent of Quebec national identifiers opposed to separation are culturally secular. Cultural religiosity thus decreases the likelihood of nationalists favoring independence.

Political Support and Traditional/Modern Values

So far our analysis has focused on the general question of the changing character of Quebec society and the consequential shifts in the nature of Quebec nationalism. Having shown that many Québécois still hold a traditional view of Quebec society, it remains to be demonstrated that the existence of both traditional and nontraditional orientations have significant consequences for political support in Quebec. The survey on which the following analysis is based coincided with the historic November 1976 victory of the Parti Québécois. Insofar as the PQ is seen as the vehicle of contemporary Quebec nationalism, it is appropriate to examine some theoretically relevant characteristics of its supporters, comparing them with Liberal and Union Nationale partisans. We will address the following specific questions in order: To what extent were PQ supporters really favorable to independence? Did they hold a traditional religious or a secular view of the national culture? To what extent were they recruited from the Quiet Revolution cohort? What were their issue priorities during the 1976 campaign?

Regarding the relationship between attitudes toward independence and party support, table 11.6 shows that even though the issue of independence had been appropriated by the Parti Québécois, 28 percent of PQ supporters in 1976 were not in favor of independence. As for supporters of other parties, Lemieux and his associates have suggested that the 1970 election marked the beginning of a long-term realignment of partisan orientations around two major competitors, the Liberals and the Parti Québécois.[47] A large section of the Union Nationale clientele, therefore, constituted a potential reservoir of support for the two major parties. Our data for 1976 indicate that Union Nationale supporters were even more likely to oppose in-

47. Lemieux, Gilbert, Blais, *Une élection de réalignement.*

Table 11.6. *Attitudes toward Independence by Provincial Party Support,*
November 1976

Attitude toward independence	Provincial party support					Total
	Parti Québécois	Liberal	Union Nationale	Other parties[a]	No party	
Favorable	72%	7%	3%	0%	31%	37%
Undecided	15	8	10	22	11	12
Opposed	13	84	88	78	58	52
(N =)	(342)	(313)	(40)	(37)	(55)	(787)

a. Other parties include Créditistes (*n* = 36) and Parti National Populaire (*n* = 1).
Percentages may not add to 100 because of rounding error.

dependence (88 percent) than Liberals (84 percent) or supporters of "other" parties.

Regarding religious values, in spite of the fact that the Liberal party institutionally initiated the Quiet Revolution, the benefactors of the Quiet Revolution attitudes, insofar as they may also be equated with areligiosity, should, according to our hypothesis, be the Parti Québécois. And indeed, the difference between supporters of the PQ and other parties proves to be substantial in this respect. The findings presented in table 11.7 illustrate the point clearly. More than three-fifths of those with an entirely secular view of French-Canadian culture supported the PQ, and about three-quarters of those who regard religion as very important to French-Canadian culture did not support the party. According to the data, a higher proportion of the Union Nationale partisans (nearly 80 percent) had a religious orientation than any other party, followed by the Créditistes and the Liberals in descending order. A close inspection of table 11.7 shows that even the most secular of these three parties, the Liberals, displayed a relationship between cultural religiosity and party support which was markedly different from that of the PQ.

We have already commented on the strong relationships between orientations toward religious values and age. In this regard, it is worth noting that the significance of age to Parti Québécois support is amply documented in contemporary literature on recent electoral behavior in Quebec. Hamilton and Pinard, Rioux, and others have shown that the young overwhelmingly support the party.[48] Similarly,

48. Hamilton and Pinard, "The Bases of Parti Québécois Support;" M. Rioux, *Jeunesse et Société Contemporaine* (Montréal: Presses de l'Université de Montréal, 1964); Harold D.

Table 11.7. *Provincial Party Support, November 1976, by Cultural Religiosity*

Provincial party support	Importance of religion to French-Canadian culture				
	Very important	Important	Of little importance	Not important	Total
Parti Créditiste	9%	3%	4%	2%	5%
Parti Libéral	50	48	37	26	40
Parti Québécois	25	38	48	61	44
Union Nationale	10	6	2	2	5
No party	5	5	9	9	7
(N =)	(185)	(184)	(186)	(223)	(778)

Percentages may not add to 100 because of rounding error.

in our 1976 survey the relationship between age and party support was both significant and strong; the old tended to support the Liberals and the Union Nationale and the young, i.e., those under thirty-five years of age, supported the PQ.

In addition to the structural and value-oriented questions, the survey inquired about salient issues.[49] Parti Québécois supporters were distinguishable on several counts. They were more concerned with the federal government's attempts to take power away from the provinces, corruption in government, and foreign control of the economy than were Liberal or Union Nationale supporters. While Péquistes tended to be concerned about nonfrancophone immigration to Quebec, they were distinctly less concerned with traditional issues such as "law and order" and the loss of importance of religion than were adherents of the other provincial parties. In short the issue-related data further substantiate the view that PQ partisans have a secular nationalist profile which is characteristically linked with the Quiet Revolution. Union Nationale supporters shared many of the same concerns of the Péquistes. They gave the federal-provincial power equilibrium high priority, which is congruent with the view that the Union Nationale is a nationalist party too. Also like the PQ, Union Nationale

Clarke, "Partisanship and the Parti Québécois: The Impact of the Independence Issue," *American Review of Canadian Studies* 8 (Autumn 1978):28–47.

49. Specifically, the questionnaire asked respondents to assign a score which indicated the importance they attached to each issue. Nine issues were presented: Non-francophone immigration into Quebec; corruption in government, federal "intrusions" into provincial life, inflation/unemployment, loss of religion in society, law and order, the impact of Anglo-American culture in Quebec, urbanization, and foreign control of the economy.

supporters ranked corruption in government as a serious problem. But, quite unlike the Péquistes, Union Nationale partisans were very concerned about "law and order" and they were much less likely to attach low salience to the loss of religion in Quebec society. Evidently, it is those ingredients in the party platform which appealed to a very different profile of party supporters, i.e., the traditional nationalists. Relative to Union Nationale and PQ supporters, the Liberals tended to be more concerned about "pragmatic" questions. Typically, they were least likely to identify the incursion of Anglo-American culture, foreign control of the economy, government corruption, and the increased power of the federal government as salient issues. Rather, unemployment and inflation and law and order were their characteristic concerns.

To summarize, the above analysis suggests that significant political consequences flow from the incomplete secularization of Quebec society. First, a secular orientation to Quebec national culture is linked to an exclusivist orientation to the Quebec nation whereas a religious conception of the national culture encourages a dual set of loyalties; adherents are attracted simultaneously to the Quebec nation and to the Canadian state. These two conceptions, in turn, produce two varieties of nationalist ideologies which exist side by side. On the one hand, the secular nationalists are attracted to an independentist solution; on the other hand, the traditional nationalists, who also seek to promote and defend Quebec's national interest, tend to believe that Quebec's aspirations can be achieved within a Canadian federal state. The incomplete secularization of Quebec also has consequences for the distribution of political support. In our 1976 survey, the secular elements in Quebec, the Quiet Revolution cohort, tended to support the Parti Québécois. The nonsecular were divided between the traditional nationalists who supported the Union Nationale, and those who were less nationalist in orientation and were attracted to the Liberal party. Finally, the different orientations of each group of supporters are reflected in the different priorities assigned a cluster of issues in 1976.

Conclusion

This chapter started from the position that Quebec nationalism—
the making of claims by Québécois to defend and enhance the national
collectivity—has been a coherent and protracted theme throughout
Quebec's political history. At the same time, the kind of nationalism
expressed in Quebec has changed markedly. At the outset, we identified the broad characteristics of different stages in the evolution of
Quebec nationalism. In the early period of nationalism, the traditional stage which lasted until the late 1950s, the Roman Catholic
Church played a dominant role. Historically, the Church pressed for
national claims while accepting the legitimacy of existing constitutional structures. Early nationalist political parties tended to reflect
the profound influence of the Church in the sense that they sought to
defend the values of a religiously defined national culture.

The second stage of Quebec nationalism refers to the Quiet Revolution period when the religious domination of Quebec society was
called into question. The Quiet Revolution challenged not only the
preeminence of clericalism but also, by extension, the traditional conception of the Quebec national culture. The onset of modernization
encouraged a kind of pluralism which in turn produced a number of
different nationalist groupings. While all factions agreed that the national interests of Quebec had to be defended, their visions of what
the Quebec nation should be and how the national interest should be
advanced differed widely. On the right the Alliance Laurentienne
still promoted a traditional Catholic view of Quebec; on the left,
Marxist fragment groups proposed a completely different solution.
The RIN emerged from this second stage as the first independentist
political party to attract substantial popular support and articulate an
integrated plan for nationalism in a modern Quebec. The third stage
represents, broadly, the consolidation of modern nationalist forces
culminating in the electoral victory of the Parti Québécois.

The second part of this chapter focused on the theoretical status of
the Quiet Revolution. Our understanding of the Quiet Revolution,
widely regarded as the watershed of modern Quebec, is of considerable practical significance because such social transformations lead to
changes in the character of nationalism and the structure of political

support in general. As such, the Quiet Revolution paradigm deserves careful evaluation.

The argument advanced here is that conventional interpretations of the Quiet Revolution can be misleading. There is no question that the Quiet Revolution did unleash secular forces in Quebec, enormously significant forces which, for example, were probably responsible for the victory of the PQ in 1976. What is problematic, however, according to our evidence, is that an uncritical acceptance of the Quiet Revolution paradigm tends to overdramatize the scope and nature of Quebec's sociopolitical change with the result that the continued significance of the tension between modernity and tradition has been diminished. Certainly, a fundamental realignment in Quebec politics has taken place, but the evidence clearly shows that the process of transformation from a traditional religious to a secular society is far from complete. Indeed, the coexistence of religious and secular orientations represents a very significant cleavage in Quebec—one which makes the outcomes of political events such as the referendum uncertain. Therefore, to presume that the values associated with the Quiet Revolution changed "overnight" or that they have percolated through all of Quebec society at the mass level produces an oversimplified image of contemporary Quebec politics.

To suggest that the transformation of Quebec politics is incomplete encourages the inference that the movement to a secular society in Quebec will be completed. Although the analysis of attitudes of Québécois does not use longitudinal data, it could be argued that, since the Quiet Revolution involved seemingly irreversible reforms in areas such as education, the attitudes of the Quiet Revolution cohort will eventually be extended to the whole population. This is a tempting and perhaps powerful argument. At the same time, this argument too may be something of an oversimplification, one which ignores other factors. A survey of patterns of political support in advanced industrialized societies, societies which in fact left clericalism behind a long time ago, clearly shows that religious values are remarkably resilient and that the "religious factor" remains a powerful though often indirect force informing political preferences. The implication is that, even with the advancing Quiet Revolution cohort, future support for independentist goals such as sovereignty-association is far from a foregone conclusion in Quebec. Not only is it difficult to predict what patterns of political support will emerge from a maturing Quiet Revolution cohort—conventional wisdom holds that such cohorts tend to become progressively less "revolutionary"—but it is also plain that many Québécois continue to subscribe to traditional values. The unfortunate consequence of conventional Quiet Revolution interpretations is that attention is deflected away from this evidently significant traditional element in Quebec. The result, in our view, is that debate about the importance of such factors as religion has been prematurely foreclosed, or at least preempted.

Political Support and Voting Behavior in the Quebec Referendum

*Jon H. Pammett, Harold D. Clarke, Jane Jenson,
and Lawrence LeDuc*

By any standard, the Quebec referendum of May 1980 stands as a highly significant political event. The "meaning" of the result, which saw the referendum question rejected by 59.6 percent of the voters, is far from clear. Vital questions have been raised about the meaning of the event for future relations between Quebec and the rest of Canada, for divisions of powers and other constitutional matters, and for the fate of the Parti Québécois and Liberal party within Quebec. All of these subjects touch, one way or another, on the nature of the support for the Canadian political system that was displayed by voters in the referendum. This paper addresses the topic of political support in Quebec through an examination of data from interviews conducted at the time of the referendum and after the 1979 federal election with the Quebec sample of the National Election Study.[1]

The most influential conception of political support stems from the work of David Easton.[2] For Easton support is an input to the political

1. The 1979 National Election and Panel Study was conducted by the authors of this paper. The Quebec sample was interviewed immediately after the 1979 federal election and after the 1980 federal election. They were also contacted by telephone at the time of the referendum, half immediately before the vote and half immediately after. The number of respondents in the referendum wave of the study is 325. The National Election and Panel Study is supported by the Social Sciences and Humanities Research Council of Canada.

2. The most extensive formulation of his framework is found in David Easton, *A Systems Analysis of Political Life* (New York: Wiley, 1965). Easton considers that the only other body of theoretical work on support is that of Talcott Parsons. See David Easton, "Theoretical Approaches to Political Support," *Canadian Journal of Political Science* 9 (Sept. 1976): 431–48. For additional conceptual work, see William A. Gamson, *Power and Discontent* (Homewood, Ill.: Dorsey, 1968).

system directed at either the community, regime, or authorities level of that system. The concept of *community* defines the basic boundaries of those involved in the political system. Easton refers to it as "that aspect of a political system that consists of its members seen as a group of persons bound together by a political division of labor."[3] The *regime* as an object of political support refers to the structures of government, norms of procedure, power relationships, and underlying values which determine the manner in which government and politics are conducted.[4] The *authorities* are the occupants of the various regime roles at any given point in time.[5]

The nature of support directed toward these various levels of the political system is essentially different, according to Easton. Support for the authorities is primarily specific, related to their performance on the job and their production of satisfactory outputs.[6] Support for the regime and community levels, on the other hand, is more likely to be diffuse, "a reservoir of favorable attitudes or goodwill,"[7] which is not determined by evaluations of performance of the political system. Diffuse support may be based on perceptions of shared interests, feelings of legitimacy, or ideological convictions.[8] Changes in the amount of support for one level can obviously affect the others, though Easton sees a reduction in diffuse support for the political community as a final step. The one example of such a case he uses, however, is that of French Canada, where he perceives that a decline of support at the regime level resulting from dissatisfaction with the distribution of power in the Canadian political system has spilled over to the community level.[9] Thus, some support for the idea of a sovereign Quebec is based on regime-level discontent and could be mollified by regime-level changes, while some is the product of a lack of diffuse support at the community level and would remain unaffected by modifications of the structure and operation of the regime.

3. Easton, *A Systems Analysis of Political Life*, p. 117.
4. Ibid., pp. 190–211.
5. Ibid., pp. 212–29. See the division of attitudes toward the Canadian political system into these categories contained in Harold D. Clarke, Jane Jenson, Lawrence LeDuc, and Jon H. Pammett, *Political Choice in Canada* (Toronto: McGraw-Hill Ryerson, 1979), pp. 27–31.
6. The nature of specific support is outlined in David Easton, "A Re-Assessment of the Concept of Political Support," *British Journal of Political Science* 5 (1975):435–57.
7. Easton, *A Systems Analysis of Political Life*, p. 273.
8. Ibid., chaps. 18–21.
9. Ibid., p. 321.

In recent years a substantial amount of empirical work has been done in the field of political support, much of it concerned with measuring and assessing the relevance for support of attitudes such as political trust, efficacy, and alienation.[10] An important part of that literature is concerned with the distinction between such attitudes as indicators of political support at the levels of regime and authorities.[11] As an alternative investigative strategy, some writers regard the distinction between regime and authorities as too difficult to sustain methodologically, combine them, and distinguish that category from the community level.[12]

Studies of political support in Canada have focused primarily on Quebec and covered a number of different subjects. Analysis of survey data has shown that provincial partisan identification is correlated strongly with regime-level support in Quebec.[13] Further work has replicated this finding and determined that party identification is correlated with support at the community level as well. In addition, specific support, in terms of a view of the costs and benefits meted out by the federal system, is associated with diffuse support at "deeper" levels of the political system.[14] In another recent article, age is found to be a significant predictor of support at both the community and regime levels in Quebec.[15] These findings about political support in Quebec constitute a useful baseline from which we can proceed in this paper.

Politics in Quebec have always been characterized by nationalist movements, but these movements have differed considerably in the

10. A comprehensive summary of the literature is contained in Edward N. Muller and Thomas O. Jukam, "On the Meaning of Political Support," *American Political Science Review* 71 (1977):1561–95.

11. The Muller and Jukam article is a good example. See also Arthur H. Miller, "Political Issues and Trust in Government: 1964–1970," *American Political Science Review* 68 (1974): 951–72; and the ensuing comment by Jack Citrin.

12. John Fraser, "The Impact of Community and Regime Orientation on Choice of Political System," *Midwest Journal of Political Science* 14 (1970):413–33. Easton advises against this. See "A Re-Assessment."

13. Allan Kornberg, Harold D. Clarke, and Lawrence LeDuc, "Some Correlates of Regime Support in Canada," *British Journal of Political Science* 8 (1978):199–216. See also Jane Jenson and Peter Regenstrief, "Some Dimensions of Partisan Choice in Quebec, 1969," *Canadian Journal of Political Science* 3 (1970):308–17.

14. Allan Kornberg, Harold D. Clarke, and Marianne C. Stewart, "Federalism and Fragmentation: Political Support in Canada," *Journal of Politics* 41 (1979):889–906.

15. Allan Kornberg, Harold D. Clarke, and Marianne C. Stewart, "Public Support for Community and Regime in the Regions of Contemporary Canada," *American Review of Canadian Studies* 10 (1980):75–93.

amount of support they have denied to the Canadian political community and regime. From the early years of Confederation to the mid-twentieth century, the various manifestations of "French-Canadian nationalism" were not, for the most part, challenges to the political and economic project of the federalists.[16] The construction of a unified country from coast to coast to coast, the building of railways, the settling of hundreds of thousands of new immigrants, the industrialization of the center of the country, and the integration of this new country into the international economic order proceeded without interference from the cultural nationalists of Quebec. The movements had little reason to deny support to the federal project. They were almost exclusively culturally defined, emphasizing linguistic and religious preservation, and the state powers considered necessary for cultural survival were in the hands of the provincial government of Quebec.

The nature of the nationalist movement underwent a profound transformation in the post–World War II years. Industrialization and urbanization fundamentally altered the demographics of Quebec society, and these factors contributed to a secularization which challenged Church-promoted traditional nationalism. In its place came a new movement, one whose social base in the most modern sectors of the "new Quebec" (urban Montreal, the university-educated whose job expectations were in the large public and private bureaucracies) distinguished it from the old nationalism (which had its roots in rural and small-town Quebec, among the local notables and particularly the professions).[17] This new movement did pose a fundamental challenge to the federal system and the federal state, indeed to the very existence of the Canadian community as it was then defined. The movement's ideology was based on the use of the state, in this case a newly independent Quebec, for nationalist purposes. This ideology

16. See several of the articles in Ramsay Cook, ed., *French-Canadian Nationalism* (Toronto: Macmillan, 1969), esp. chap. 1 by Jean-C. Bonefant and Jean-C. Falardeau, and chap. 8 by Henri Bourassa; David Cameron, *Nationalism, Self-Determination and the Quebec Question* (Toronto: Macmillan, 1974), pp. 114–22; Marcel Rioux, *Quebec in Question* (Toronto: James Lewis and Samuel, 1971), chap. 4; Dale Posgate and Kenneth McRoberts, *Quebec: Social Change and Political Crisis*, 1st ed. (Toronto: McClelland and Stewart, 1976), pp. 65–70.

17. Hubert Guindon was one of the first analysts to identify these differences. See his "The Social Evolution of Quebec Reconsidered," in M. Rioux and Y. Martin, eds., *French-Canadian Society* (Toronto: McClelland and Stewart, 1964), pp. 137–61. See also Posgate and McRoberts, *Quebec: Social Change and Political Crisis*, chap. 6.

defined as the enemy any group or institution which could interfere
with the independently determined development strategy of a Québécois state. In line for particular attack, then, was the federal government within the Canadian federal system. The *indépendantiste*
program created a competition for the loyalties of the population of
Quebec between those who saw the federal system as best able to
meet the needs and demands of the Québécois, and those who could
see only a fully independent and newly sovereign state as able to do
so. Support for these alternative political communities became the
focus of the debate.

By 1960 the first organized nationalist group of this new type had
arisen. By the mid-1960s a fully developed political movement devoted to denying community-level support to the Canadian political
system and dedicated to the establishment of an independent sovereign state had been created. By 1968 much of that movement had coalesced into a well-organized political party, the Parti Québécois,[18]
which prepared to contest the 1970 provincial election with a substantial chance of becoming a major threat to the governing parties.

The strategy developed by the PQ in the late 1960s owed much to
the proposals for sovereignty-association that René Lévesque developed in his protracted divorce from the provincial Liberal party.[19]
This position took as its basis that independence for Quebec (sovereignty), followed by new arrangements for an economic common market (association) with the rest of Canada, was the only solution to the
century-long disadvantage the population of Quebec had labored under since Confederation. According to this analysis, constitutional revamping—regime-level change, such as that proposed by the Liberals and Union Nationale—was inadequate.[20] The strategy which
the PQ proposed was "Independence—then negotiation." The party
would win power, declare independence unilaterally, and then negotiate the details of the transfer and any continuing economic arrangements later, as an equal partner.[21] This strategy involved, then, a chal-

18. An account of this early period is contained in John Saywell, *The Rise of the Parti
Québécois, 1967–76* (Toronto: University of Toronto Press, 1977), prologue and chap. 1. See
also Henry Milner, *Politics in New Quebec* (Toronto: McClelland and Stewart, 1978), chap. 8.

19. These are outlined by René Lévesque in his *An Option for Quebec* (Toronto: McClelland
and Stewart, 1968) and *My Quebec* (Toronto: Methuen, 1979).

20. Saywell, *The Rise of the Parti Québécois*, pp. 15, 23.

21. Ibid., p. 16.

lenge to the Canadian political community as it had existed since
Confederation—two states were to exist where for more than one
hundred years there had been only one.

Sovereignty-association, by its very nature, raised all sorts of issues
about what kind of arrangement was being proposed, and engendered
considerable confusion. The use of the two words allowed interpretations emphasizing community-level change (sovereignty) or regime-
level change (association). As the PQ moved closer to power during
the 1970s the party was called upon, if only by its electorate, to clarify
its position. By the last moments of the 1973 electoral campaign, the
matter of a consultative referendum had become an additional important factor generating confusion. In early formulations, the referendum was to be held to ratify the new constitution of a sovereign
Quebec, to "implant sovereignty."[22] At the November 1974 Congress of the PQ, the party adopted a text developed by Claude Morin
which removed from the statutes of the party the concept of a fixed
timetable for transition to sovereignty-association and added the notion of further consultation with the population *before* any major constitutional changes would be undertaken.[23] This new strategy anticipated that a majority of the population of Quebec could be convinced
to support the *indépendantiste* position, but realized that considerable education would be required to accomplish it. Such an educational focus suggested that the PQ perceived that it was encountering
very heavy going in its efforts to mount a full challenge to the Canadian political community.

It was of great importance to the outcome of the 1976 election that
the PQ no longer proposed to use the election outcome as sufficient
justification for a declaration of sovereignty. The declaration that it
would put its plans for sovereignty-association to a referendum before
undertaking negotiations allowed it to shun discussion of its proposals
in this area during the election campaign and concentrate instead on
the economic and social record of the Liberals. This strategy was successful, despite the Liberals' campaign focus on the "anti-separatist"
theme.[24]

22. Ibid., pp. 77–79. Daniel Latouche et al., *Le process electoral au Quebec: 1970, 1973*
(Montreal: Hurtubise, 1976).
23. The text adopted is in Saywell, *The Rise of the Parti Québécois*, pp. 114–15. See also the
discussion in Andre Bernard, *Quebec: Elections 1976* (Montreal: Hurtubise, 1977), pp. 90ff;
Lévesque. *My Quebec*, chap. 4.
24. Bernard, *Quebec: Elections 1976*. For excellent analyses of the 1973 and 1976 elections,

The public's acceptance of the PQ election strategy of 1976 of deferring the question of sovereignty-association to a later referendum presaged a shift of the major focus of discussion of changes from the community to the regime level. By beginning with negotiations (a mandate for which the government unsuccessfully sought in the 1980 referendum) rather than a unilateral declaration of independence, the most likely result became some form of transformed federalism. As so many observers noted during the referendum campaign, it did not seem at all likely that the federal government would agree to negotiations which changed the political community to the extent of creating a sovereign state of Quebec. Since the federal government, and especially the federal Liberal party, had been vehement opponents of the position of the PQ, more than a remodeled federal system was unlikely to result even if the PQ won the referendum and the federal government agreed to enter into negotiations. The emphasis on the association aspect of sovereignty-association was an effort to deflect the discussion away from the theme of basic change in the Canadian political community and toward the interpretation that what was being proposed was a series of changes to the regime. After an initial reluctance to debate on these terms and an attempt to focus the discussion on the less popular concept of separatism, the provincial Liberal party organized its proposals around a "renewed federalism" and issued them in a Beige Paper containing various revised structures of power in a revamped federal system.

Part of the strategy of the Parti Québécois in attempting to fight the referendum as a regime-level question was that such a shift enhanced the possibility of strategic voting. By wording the referendum question so as to provide for a second referendum before any changes were implemented, they sought to reassure hesitant supporters and appeal to those who either wanted some enhanced provincial powers out of personal conviction or a feeling that some such change was needed to appease the nationalists. Thus, the PQ argued during the referendum campaign that those who agreed with the need for some reallocation of federal and provincial powers should support the "yes" side, giving the PQ a strong mandate to negotiate forcefully with the

see the articles by Maurice Pinard and Richard Hamilton, "The Independence Issue and the Polarization of the Electorate: The 1973 Quebec Election," *Canadian Journal of Political Science* 10 (1977):215–60; and "The Parti Québécois Comes to Power: An Analysis of the 1976 Quebec Election," *Canadian Journal of Political Science* 11 (1978):739–76.

federal government to bring about a reasonable change. It was further argued that if the "no" side prevailed, change would be difficult
to obtain, since the federal government might interpret such a result
as satisfaction with the status quo. Much of the campaign rhetoric of
the "no" side sought to reassure such voters that a "no" vote would be
interpreted as a desire for renewed federalism, meaning enhanced
provincial government powers.

The attempt to transform the referendum campaign and voting into
a regime-level support question could obviously not be completely
successful. For some part of the population, relations between Quebec and Canada would always be a question of community. Those
whose basic goal was the independence of Quebec would be voting
for sovereignty-association as a stepping-stone to that end. For others, the changes that were being proposed constituted "breaking up
the country," or separatism, and had to be resisted on those grounds.
Even those people not holding these beliefs could be expected to
ponder the question in terms of the effect of the referendum and the
proposed negotiations on the Canadian political community. One major factor enhancing the importance of community-level voting in the
referendum was the conviction of a large part of the Quebec population that the real goal of the PQ was not sovereignty-association, but
independence.[25]

As the referendum campaign began in earnest, yet another complicating factor entered the equation. The campaign was being conducted, not in the abstract, but by the political parties and leaders at
both federal and provincial levels of the Canadian system. Thus the
possibility was raised that the referendum would involve, not just
community and regime-level support questions, but the authorities
as well. It was the political parties which issued the White and Beige
papers, and which promoted the several sets of changes, which conducted the campaign debate in the Quebec National Assembly, which
mobilized the funds and conducted the advertising, and which were
covered daily in the media. The stamps of Messrs. Lévesque and Ryan

25. In a survey taken three weeks before the voting, the responses to the question, "What do
you think is the aim of the present government of Quebec?" were: to achieve [full] independence for Quebec—39 percent; to get a better place within Canada for Quebec—19 percent; to
achieve sovereignty for Quebec with an economic association with the rest of Canada—32 percent; don't know—10 percent. Source: Radio-Canada, *Les Québécois et la campagne référendaire*, (Services des recherches a la division des services français) May 9, 1980, p. III-19.

were on the proposals of the "yes" and "no" sides, and the personal appeal of Mr. Trudeau was utilized toward the end of the campaign. Thus, the probability that opinions and preferences on the referendum options would be linked to party and leader preferences at the authorities level became high indeed.[26]

Public Opinion about the Referendum Options

As the conflict between nationalists and federalists was transformed from one of dispute over community to one of regime reform, the result was considerable public confusion about both the nature of the issue and the meaning of the options being advanced. This confusion was clearly evident a year before the referendum in responses given during the 1979 Federal Election Study, when Quebec respondents were asked to answer open-ended questions about their understanding of the meaning of sovereignty-association and renewed federalism.[27]

Table 12.1 presents responses to the question asking for the meaning of sovereignty-association. It shows that only a very small number of respondents emphasized the concept of the equality of the two states, that the term meant a relationship of equals. However, a substantial proportion of respondents—about 40 percent of those who had a definition, and a quarter of the first mentions—chose to think of sovereignty-association in community-level terms, as either the independence of Quebec or separatism. Independence as a term has more positive connotations than separatism (Lévesque has always denied he is a "separatist"), but both are community-level readings of the meaning of sovereignty-association.

A somewhat smaller number of respondents—18 percent of all respondents, and 36 percent of those with a definition—gave a regime-level definition of the term as more control for Quebec in association

26. The extent of the partisanship that would be involved in the campaign appears to have taken some participants by surprise. See the comments by Daniel Latouche in Elliot J. Feldman, ed., *The Quebec Referendum: What Happened and What Next?* (Cambridge: University Consortium for Research on North America, 1980), p. 22.

27. The exact questions were: "The Quebec government would like to negotiate sovereignty-association with the rest of Canada. What do you usually think of when the term sovereignty-association is mentioned?" "Many people these days are talking about renewed federalism. What do you usually think of when the term renewed federalism is mentioned?"

Table 12.1. *The Meaning of Sovereignty-Association—1979*

	First mention	Two mentions[a]
Relationship of equals	2%	3%
Independence	11	16
Separation; separatism	15	24
More control for Quebec, with economic association	4	7
More control for Quebec, in association	14	28
More control for Quebec	7	13
General negative feeling	9	20
It has never been made clear	6	9
Other	6	15
No answer	25	—
(*N* =)	(753)	(565)

a. Missing data excluded.

with Canada, the kind of meaning that the Parti Québécois was seeking to give the term. These answers are far outweighed, however, not just by community-level definitions, but by those who failed to define the term. Table 12.1 shows that 9 percent of all respondents simply stated that they did not like sovereignty-association, 6 percent claimed it had never been made clear, and 25 percent failed to provide any response whatsoever regarding the system which they were going to be asked to pronounce upon in the following year. Nor is there much reason to believe that the public later clarified its understanding of the meaning of the term. A Radio-Canada poll in March 1980 asked Quebecers, in an open-ended question, to define what the Quebec government meant by sovereignty-association. At that time, 26 percent said they did not know, and 33 percent interpreted it (favorably or not) in community-level terms, as independence or self-determination for Quebec, or separation.[28] Another Radio-Canada survey, taken three weeks before the vote, showed substantial disagreement on several specific aspects of the sovereignty-association plan.[29]

28. Radio-Canada. *Une question de pays/A question of country* (Services des recherches à la division des services français), Apr. 25, 1980, p. 98.
29. In this survey, conducted between Apr. 26 and May 3, there was disagreement about whether, under sovereignty-association, Quebec would have its own money (32 percent yes, 52 percent no—even though the referendum question specifically stated there would be a common currency); Quebec would have its own army (43 percent yes, 41 percent no). Source: Radio-Canada, *Les Québécois et la question référendaire* (Services des recherches à la division des services français), May 9, 1980, p. III-18. Answers to the same questions, asked in an earlier

Table 12.2. *The Meaning of Renewed Federalism—1979*

	First mention	Two mentions[a]
Change the way things are done	12%	24%
The same old thing; a ploy to keep status quo	10	18
Change the constitution	14	19
Repatriate the constitution	3	5
Change the federal government	4	9
Strengthen the provinces	4	12
To deal with Quebec	3	10
To restore Canadian unity	2	5
It has never been made clear	4	7
Other	3	8
No answer	40	—
(N =)	(753)	(452)

a. Missing data excluded.

Renewed federalism, the federalists' counterproposal, fared even less well (table 12.2). One year before the referendum, 40 percent of Quebec respondents could provide no meaning for renewed federalism. In addition, a further 11 percent defined the option very generally, as a means of changing the way things are done, and 10 percent saw it as no change at all, simply as a ploy to perpetuate the status quo. Many of the other answers were very vague, and thus a substantial proportion of those who did attempt to define renewed federalism had nothing of substance to say about it as a constitutional option.

Additional evidence of substantial public uncertainty in 1979 is provided by a set of responses to the National Election Survey of that year which asked for *evaluations* of several constitutional options. As shown in the last column of table 12.3, when asked about their disposition toward renewed federalism, 37 percent were unable to give an evaluation. A similar number (34 percent) had no assessment of "special status." More striking, perhaps, is the 30 percent who had no evaluation of sovereignty-association. Only the options of "no change" and independence were evaluated by an overwhelming majority of respondents, with fewer than 10 percent having no opinion about them. Thus, both major proposals for changes in the regime were

poll in Feb. 1980, are very similar indicating that little clarification of the issues may have taken place during the campaign. For the earlier results, see Radio-Canada, *Les Québécois et la question référendaire* (Services des recherches à la division des services français), Mar. 7, 1980, p. 162.

Table 12.3. *Evaluations of Constitutional Options—1979–80*

Option	Very favorable	Somewhat favorable	Not very favorable	Not at all favorable		NA
No change						
1979	18%	18	24	40	(691)[a]	8%
						(753)[b]
1980	11%	18	18	53	(310)	5%
						(325)[b]
Renewed federalism						
1979	27%	33	22	18	(473)	37%
1980	32%	35	19	15	(301)	7%
Special status						
1979	16%	36	24	23	(500)	34%
1980	13%	39	26	22	(256)	21%
Sovereignty-association						
1979	19%	19	17	44	(529)	30%
1980	25%	22	16	38	(311)	4%
Independence						
1979	9%	9	13	69	(684)	9%
1980	12%	13	15	60	(314)	3%

a. Missing data excluded.
b. *N* with missing data included.

only imperfectly understood one year before the referendum, and many people were hesitant to express opinions about their worth.

Although public knowledge of the specifics of these proposals may not have improved much by the time of the vote, public uncertainty about their value did not continue. Table 12.3 shows that the number of respondents with no evaluation of renewed federalism fell from 37 percent in 1979 to 7 percent in May 1980. In the same months the percentage of people willing to assess sovereignty-association went from 70 percent to 96 percent. Special status, in contrast, not much discussed by the major actors, remained poorly evaluated. Clearly, the year of the campaign had a major effect on the development of positions on the principal options.

Not only did opinion crystallize, but it also changed. Table 12.3 shows that between 1979 and 1980 a stronger feeling developed among Québécois that some kind of change was needed. By May 1980, only 29 percent approved of the status quo, with renewed federalism, sovereignty-association, and independence all being favored by larger percentages than a year earlier. The impression left by an examination of the evaluations of these three options is that the mobilization for the referendum increased the desire for regime change generally. There remained, of course, disagreements about what form that change should take, with 45 percent of the population favoring sovereignty-association, and 67 percent, renewed federalism.

It is obvious from inspection of the above figures that not everyone perceived the necessity of choosing between sovereignty-association and renewed federalism. Indeed, the cross-tabulation of the two evaluations reveals a Tau b of "only" -0.46. In percentage terms, 22 percent of respondents were favorable to *both* options, while 8 percent were unfavorable to both. The remaining results show that 26 percent favored sovereignty-association but not renewed federalism, while 45 percent felt the opposite. If all those people who favored sovereignty-association had voted "yes" in the referendum, that side would have come much closer to winning than it did. As we will see later, however, many of the voting decisions were not made strictly on the basis of these regime-level options.

Table 12.3 shows the aggregate distribution of opinion on the options in 1979 and 1980. A good deal *more* movement than appears there is revealed when we look at the positions of individuals in the two years. Table 12.4 shows individual-level shifts in opinion from 1979 to 1980. Opinion on independence, a community-level option, was clearly the most stable, with fully 71 percent having exactly the same opinion of it in each poll. More than half of the sample (54 percent) claimed that they were "not at all favorable" to independence both times they were asked. People became substantially less favorable to the "no-change" option, reinforcing our earlier conclusion about the increased receptivity to change on the part of the Quebec population during the year prior to the referendum. In the case of both sovereignty-association and renewed federalism, more people shifted to a more favorable opinion than went the other way. While there was certainly some disgruntlement with the definition of the regime-level options (22 percent became less favorable to renewed federalism and 16 percent to sovereignty-association) the referendum campaign seems to have increased support for *both* of the competing options at the regime level. Given this trend, sovereignty-association was not able to narrow the popularity gap between it and renewed federalism.

One further regime-level factor remains to be introduced, since it

Table 12.4. *Constitutional Options: Opinion Stability and Change over the 1979–80 Period*

	Opinion			
Constitutional option	Same	More favorable	Less favorable	(N=)
No change	45%	17	37	(308)
Renewed federalism	42%	36	22	(219)
Special status	35%	31	35	(209)
Sovereignty-association	54%	30	16	(254)
Independence	71%	18	11	(305)

Note: Individuals are included in the category "same" if they have exactly the same evaluation of the option at both points in time.

will prove to be related to referendum voting. Among politicians, journalists, and academics alike, evaluations of the distributive and redistributive mechanisms of federalism have been the substance of never-ending disputes. Arguments about whether or not federalism is "profitable" are certainly not limited to Quebec; indeed a feeling of being unjustly treated by the operations of the federal system seems to exist everywhere in Canada.[30] In the context of the referendum battle, proponents of the status quo or some form of renewed federalism argued that the more drastic change associated with sovereignty-association would alter the cost/benefit ratio of federalism to Quebec's disadvantage, while those favoring sovereignty-association and independence maintained that the present cost/benefit ratio was not to Quebec's advantage anyway.

To investigate this point, we constructed a five-point federalism cost/benefit index,[31] utilizing the 1979 National Survey data. Inspection of scores on this index shows that in every region, including Quebec, a majority of respondents perceived inequities in current federal arrangements. Indeed, Quebecers were by no means the most dissatisfied—55 percent of Quebec respondents as compared to 57 percent,

30. See Clarke, Jenson, LeDuc, and Pammett, *Political Choice in Canada,* chap. 3, esp. pp. 81–85. See also Peter Leslie and Richard Simeon, "The Battle of the Balance Sheets," in R. Simeon, ed., *Must Canada Fail?* (Montreal: McGill-Queen's University Press, 1977), pp. 243–58; Andre Bernard, *What Does Quebec Want?* (Toronto: James Lorimer and Company, 1978), pp. 48–70.

31. The index was constructed from questions in the 1979 survey asking whether a respondent's own province or region paid more or fewer of the costs of governing Canada, and received its fair share, or less, of the benefits, and also from questions asking whether other provinces or regions were equitably or inequitably treated with regard to costs and benefits.

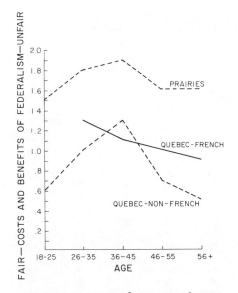

Figure 12.1. *Evaluations of Costs and Benefits of the Federal System by Age and Region, 1979*

61 percent, 70 percent, and 73 percent of those living in the Atlantic provinces, Ontario, the Prairies, and British Columbia, respectively, expressed at least some unhappiness with current federal arrangements. Similarly, Quebec's mean score on the index is 1.1, a figure equal to the means for the Atlantic provinces and Ontario, but somewhat less than those for the Prairies (1.6) or British Columbia (1.8).

Within Quebec, francophones judged the federal system more harshly than anglophones. Anglophone Quebecers, in fact, were more positive about the benefits of the system than were residents of any other region. Among francophones, evaluations of the federal system had a clearly defined monotonic relationship with age, younger Québécois being considerably more dissatisfied than those older (figure 12.1). At the same time, figure 12.1 shows that Quebecers, regardless of age or ethnicity, were *less* unhappy with present federal arrangements than were citizens in the Western provinces, where relatively high levels of dissatisfaction characterized all age groups.[32]

32. For the sake of clarity, only the data for the Prairies are shown in figure 12.1. Data for British Columbia are generally very similar.

Table 12.5. *Mean Levels of Affect for Leaders, Parties, and Political Communities by Evaluation of Costs and Benefits of the Federal System (thermometer scores)*

| | Costs and benefits of the federal system | | | | | | |
	System entirely fair 0	1	2	3	System highly unfair 4	P	eta
Ryan	53	52	37	34	19	0.001	0.35
Provincial Liberal party	62	61	46	43	33	0.001	0.37
Lévesque	54	51	65	74	75	0.001	0.31
Parti Québécois	51	45	61	67	70	0.001	0.30
Province of Quebec	82	86	87	87	86	NS	0.16
Canada	77	74	69	62	54	0.001	0.31
Trudeau	75	66	65	63	44	0.001	0.31
Federal Liberal party	70	64	61	56	38	0.001	0.37
Clark	38	38	37	37	42	NS	0.05
PC party	43	41	39	40	45	NS	0.07

Note: This table includes Quebec referendum respondents only.

Opinions about the costs and benefits of federalism in Quebec were correlated with orientations toward federal and provincial political authorities and the national political community as measured by thermometer scores (table 12.5). Thus, people believing the system operated unfairly gave substantially lower thermometer scores to Canada than did those believing the opposite.[33] Interestingly, however, feelings about the federal system were not related significantly to feelings about Quebec, which was highly regarded by all sides. Those who judged that the system operates unfairly manifested considerably lower levels of support for the federal Liberal party, and its leader, Mr. Trudeau, as well as the provincial Liberal party, and its leader, Mr. Ryan. In contrast, they were more favorably disposed to the Parti Québécois and Mr. Lévesque. Within Quebec, attitudes toward the Progressive Conservative party and Mr. Clark were not related to evaluations of the federal system.

Opinions on the constitutional options we have been referring to

33. All of the data in table 12.5 are mean thermometer scores. The thermometer scale used here is similar to that described in Clarke et al., *Political Choice in Canada*, pp. 406–7.

Table 12.6. *Preference for Constitutional Options by Provincial Party Identification (horizontal percentages)*

Party identification	Very unfavorable	Somewhat unfavorable	Somewhat favorable	Very favorable
No change				
Prov Lib 1979	32%	22	20	26
Prov PQ 1979	54%	27	13	6
	V=0.17[a]			
Prov Lib 1980	37%	19	27	17
Prov PQ 1980	73%	19	5	4
	V=0.24[a]			
Fed Lib 1979	35%	24	19	23
Renewed federalism				
Prov Lib 1979	8%	12	44	37
Prov PQ 1979	31%	35	21	13
	V=0.27[a]			
Prov Lib 1980	2%	11	39	49
Prov PQ 1980	30%	31	29	11
	V=0.32[a]			
Fed Lib 1979	9%	17	39	35
Sovereignty-association				
Prov Lib 1979	68%	17	11	4
Prov PQ 1979	9%	17	33	41
	V=0.36[a]			
Prov Lib 1980	63%	20	12	5
Prov PQ 1980	1%	9	35	55
	V=0.44[a]			
Fed Lib 1979	56%	19	16	9
Independence				
Prov Lib 1979	92%	6	2	1
Prov PQ 1979	28%	24	22	26
	V=0.37[a]			
Prov Lib 1980	88%	11	2	0
Prov PQ 1980	19%	23	30	28
	V=0.41[a]			
Fed Lib 1979	83%	9	4	4

a. Statistically significant at 0.001 level.

throughout this section were, with the exception of special status, strongly related to a major authorities-level support factor, party identification. Table 12.6 shows the relationships with the direction of federal and provincial partisanship in Quebec, in the latter case at two different times. Not unexpectedly, Parti Québécois identifiers were more favorable to sovereignty-association and independence than the Liberals.[34] It is interesting to note, however, that the differences between the parties' degree of approval of the options grew stronger between 1979 and 1980, as indicated by the higher V scores. Apparently, the parties' involvement in the referendum campaign polarized their supporters' attitudes toward both community- and regime-level options to a greater extent than had previously been the case.

We should not be surprised at the close correlation between support for the authorities- and the regime-level options displayed in table 12.6. In particular, approval of the sovereignty-association option, which we have interpreted as being a regime-level measure, reflects support for a regime option which has been vigorously promoted (and indeed was created) by the present political authorities in Quebec and formed the ground on which the referendum was fought. In fact, it may be argued that sovereignty-association as a regime-level concept has no meaning other than that given to it by the authorities before and during the campaign. However, the relationship between sovereignty-association and PQ partisanship, while strong, was not perfect. Even at the time of the referendum, there were still 10 percent of PQ identifiers who were unfavorable to the option, and another group whose support of sovereignty-association was only lukewarm.

Correlates of Referendum Voting

The extent of societal polarization in Quebec which took place at the time of the referendum is revealed by the fact that there were strong correlations between referendum voting and all of the variables we have been discussing so far, and some we have not mentioned. Attitudes toward the constitutional options, shown in table 12.7 (with the exception again of special status) were strongly related to the voting. This is true of options at the level of community support (no change, independence), as well as at the level of regime

---

34. Split identification tempers these relationships substantially. For example, of Parti Québécois identifiers who are federal Liberals, only 27 percent are very favorable to sovereignty-association, while 49 percent of Parti Québécois identifiers who are not federal Liberals are very favorable to it.

Table 12.7. *Referendum Vote by Opinion on Constitutional Options (table entries are percent voting "yes" or intending to vote "yes" in the referendum)*

	Opinion on options			
	Very unfavorable	Somewhat unfavorable	Somewhat favorable	Very favorable
No change	65	53	10	16
Renewed federalism	93	74	44	21
Sovereignty-association	3	31	77	95
Special status	43	56	54	51
Independence	18	75	93	97

support (renewed federalism, sovereignty-association). That attitudes about these options were not the complete explanation of the referendum outcome is suggested, however, by the number of people whose referendum votes were not in line with their constitutional preferences. For example, table 12.7 shows that almost a quarter (23 percent) of those who were "somewhat favorable" to sovereignty-association, and 5 percent of those who were "very favorable" to it, did not vote "yes." Conversely, some of those who were favorable to the status quo (e.g., 16 percent who were "very favorable" to the "no change" option) ended up voting for the "yes" side.

The referendum produced an almost complete correspondence between Parti Québécois identification and "yes" voting. The strongest zero-order correlations in table 12.8 are those of party identification itself, and variables associated with it, such as the thermometer rating of the Parti Québécois and René Lévesque.[35] Since party identification was correlated so highly with referendum voting, it may be seen in table 12.8 that a control for this variable substantially reduced the correlations between most of the other explanatory variables and referendum vote. Variables with strong correlations with referendum voting include demographic characteristics (age, language), community-level support (attitudes toward status quo and independence, thermometer

35. At the time of the referendum, the mean thermometer score for René Lévesque was 58.4 while that for Claude Ryan was 45.6; the Parti Québécois thermometer was 54.0 compared to the 54.9 mean score for the provincial Liberal party. For purposes of the correlational analyses, to account for the possibility that respondents may use the thermometer scale somewhat differently, *standardized* thermometer scores were computed using the mean and standard deviation of each respondent's thermometer ratings of several political objects.

Table 12.8. Correlates of Referendum Vote (Pearson's r)

	Zero order	First order partial controlling for party identification or PQ thermometer
Party identification	0.86	—
PQ thermometer	0.81	—
Lévesque thermometer	0.81	0.50
Ryan thermometer	−0.72	−0.34
Attitude to sovereignty-association	0.76	0.57
Quebec government thermometer	0.74	0.49
Liberal party thermometer	−0.74	−0.35
Canada thermometer	−0.72	−0.31
Canadian government thermometer	−0.66	−0.28
Attitude to independence	0.59	0.19
Attitude to renewed federalism	−0.48	−0.17
Attitude to status quo	−0.43	−0.26
Age	−0.41	−0.19
Language	0.32	0.14[a]
Quebec thermometer	0.12[a]	0.15[a]
Gender	−0.10[a]	0.00 (n.s.)
Attitude to special status	0.04 (n.s.)	0.01 (n.s.)

a. Significant at 0.05; all other coefficients significant at 0.01 or higher unless otherwise shown.

rating of Canada), regime-level support (attitudes toward sovereignty-association and renewed federalism), authorities-level support (party identification, thermometer ratings of the PQ, Liberals, René Lévesque), as well as the thermometer ratings of the Quebec and Canadian governments, which combine several levels of support.

An additional correlate of regime-level support with referendum voting can be seen if we reintroduce the measure of the costs and benefits of federalism, as seen by the respondents, referred to in the previous section. These results, reported in table 12.9, show that perceptions of the costs and benefits of federalism were strongly correlated with the vote—the percentage of respondents voting "yes" increasing monotonically from 31 percent of those persons who judged that the federal system operates fairly to 79 percent of those who were highly dissatisfied with the way the system works. Similarly, if the overall index is disaggregated into its separate "cost" and "benefit" components, both of these were associated with the direction of vote (V [costs] = 0.25; V [benefits] = 0.32).

Table 12.9. *Referendum Vote by Evaluation of Costs and Benefits of the Federal System*

	Costs and benefits of the federal system				
	System entirely fair 0	1	2	3	System highly unfair 4
Referendum vote					
yes	31%	40%	60%	75%	79%
no	69	60	40	25	21
(*N* =)	(107)	(64)	(55)	(32)	(23)
V=0.36, p≤0.001					

Multivariate Analyses of Referendum Voting

The number of significant correlates of the referendum vote, and the strength of the interrelationships among these variables, signal the need to employ multivariate techniques to assess the overall effects of several independent variables and make a more precise estimate of their relative impact. We are particularly interested in making a judgment about the impact on referendum voting of variables measuring political support at the community, regime, and authorities levels. Before applying more sophisticated statistical techniques to the data introduced so far, we can get an initial idea of the relative impact of political support at these levels considering answers to the question in the referendum survey which asked respondents "to take a moment to think over all the reasons why you have decided to vote (YES/NO) in the referendum and just briefly tell . . . . the things that are *most* important to you."[36]

Responses to this question about the most important reasons for voting as delineated by the respondents themselves emphasize the crucial importance of reasons associated with community-level concerns to the defeat of the referendum. Although reasons having to do with questions of community dominated the responses given by partisans of both sides, table 12.10 shows that they were particularly im-

36. This question, which is preceded by the statement, "Sometimes, in asking all these questions, researchers can lose track of what was *really* important to people," has been used in the national election studies since 1974. See Clarke et al., *Political Choice in Canada*, pp. 321–24.

Table 12.10. *"Most Important Reasons" for Referendum Vote*[a]

A. Percentages of "yes" and "no" voters citing various types of reasons		
	Voted yes	Voted no
Community	69	77
Regime	44	21
Authorities	26	18
B. Direction of vote by type of reason (in percentages)		
	Voted yes	Voted no
Mentions community	45	55
Mentions regime	66	34
Mentions authorities	56	44

a. Multiple responses.

portant to the "no" forces. Overall, 73 percent of respondents citing a reason specified a community-level reason, as opposed to 32 percent who cited one having to do with the regime, and 22 percent who mentioned the authorities.[37] And, as panel B of table 12.10 indicates, of those who mentioned a community-level reason, a majority voted "no." The people who made a choice for regime-related reasons were quite likely to vote "yes"; and the people who chose for authorities-related reasons were likely to vote "yes," but those reasons were cited as important by fewer than half the voters.

Aside from the question of their relative importance, it is important to note that attitudes of support at the community, regime, and authorities levels are cumulative, each having an independent effect on referendum voting choice. To this end, table 12.11 shows the percentages of respondents voting "yes" for various combinations of orientations toward the national political community, regime, and authorities. In this analysis, community support is measured using thermometer scale scores of affect for Canada, respondents being divided into those making positive, or neutral, or negative assessments. Atti-

37. References having more than a few cases which were coded as community, regime, or authorities are: *Community:* Separatism or independence; Need for a change, or fear of change; Desire to remain a Canadian; Search for a Québécois cultural identity; To maintain the French language; For the good of Quebec; Maintain Canada's culture. *Regime:* Sovereignty-association; Renewed federalism; Special status; To get more powers for the provincial government; To negotiate against status quo; Options are not clearly defined. *Authorities:* Lévesque; Economic conditions or issues; Parti Québécois; Federal election results.

Table 12.11. *Referendum Voting by Orientations toward the National Political Community, Regime, and Authorities*

	Community orientation			
	Neutral or negative		Positive	
	Authorities orientation		Authorities orientation	
Regime orientation	Neutral or negative	Positive	Neutral or negative	Positive
Negative	93%[a] (40)[b]	95% (20)	46% (46)	35% (68)
	a	b	c	d
Positive	90% (10)	55% (4)	36% (28)	18% (65)
	e	f	g	h

a. Percentage voting yes in referendum.
b. Number of voters in group.
Measures: Community orientation: Affect for Canada (thermometer); Regime orientation: Costs/benefits of federalism index; Authorities orientation: Affect for *national* authorities, Trudeau, Clark, Liberal party, Progressive Conservative party (thermometers).

tudes toward the regime are measured by the index of the costs and benefits of the federal system used previously in this paper. Support for the national political authorities is measured by dividing the sample into those having positive, or neutral, or negative mean thermometer scores for the national Liberal and Conservative parties and their leaders. Although table 12.11 illustrates our point using measures of national orientations, a parallel analysis using provincial-level measures yields similar results.

Inspection of the data in table 12.11 demonstrates that attitudes toward community, regime, and authorities all play roles in determining referendum voting choice. The effects of national community support appear to be the strongest. Considering respondents with negative or neutral feelings toward Canada, (cells *a*, *b*, *e*, *f* of the table), only when both regime and authorities orientations are positive does the percentage voting "yes" drop below 90 percent (to 55 percent, cell *f*). In contrast, when attitudes toward the national community are positive (cells *c*, *d*, *g*, and *h*), in no case do as many as 50 percent of the respondents vote "yes," even when they have negative feelings toward both the national authorities and the regime (cell *c*).

For every combination of community and authorites support, different evaluations of the regime have an impact on the voting. The effects of such differences in evaluation are small when both community and authorities support are negative (3 percent, cell *a* minus cell *e*), but considerably larger (mean difference = 22 percent) in other cases. As for support for the national authorities, the impact of positive orientations are noticeable in all instances except where both community and regime support are negative (cell *a* minus cell *b*). If people did not like Canada and thought the federal system was unfair, admiration for national authorities was not enough to make them vote "no" to the referendum.

For a more comprehensive multivariate analysis of the effects of orientations toward the community, regime, and authorities on electoral choice in the referendum, as well as the impact of various socioeconomic and demographic characteristics, a series of multiple regression analyses were performed. The first of these, reported in panel A of table 12.12, employed the national community, regime, and authorities support variables discussed with relation to table 12.11. Also included here were measures of ethnicity (French-other), socioeconomic status (Blishen score),[38] age, and gender, as well as an index measuring attitudes toward the two regime options (sovereignty-association—renewed federalism[39]) which dominated political debate during the referendum campaign.

The order of entry of predictors into the regressions was controlled to permit inferences regarding their unique effects. On the assumption that socioeconomic and demographic characteristics summarize long-term forces which influence attitudes toward various aspects of the political system, these variables were entered first. Next, support for the national community and the cost/benefit evaluations of the federal regime were entered, with their order of entry being reversed in separate analyses. The logic for this procedure[40] stems from the

38. See Bernard Blishen and Hugh McRoberts, "A Revised Socioeconomic Index for Occupations in Canada," *Canadian Review of Sociology and Anthropology* 13 (1976):71–80.

39. This index is computed by recoding responses to the sovereignty-association and renewed federalism options as follows: very favorable = +2, somewhat favorable = +1, somewhat unfavorable = −1, very unfavorable = −2, no opinion = 0. Scores on the former were subtracted from those on the latter.

40. This procedure is known as the analysis of commonalities. See Norman H. Nie, Sidney Verba, and John R. Petrocik, *The Changing American Voter* (Cambridge: Harvard University Press, 1976), p. 303, n. 8.

plausibility of two constrasting propositions. First, levels of community support may be at least partially specific, that is, a product of calculations regarding the costs and benefits of the existing political order for particular individuals and groups. Second, it is equally possible that evaluations of the operations of the regime reflect attitudes associated with deep-seated community sentiments and loyalties, in other words, diffuse support. Last to enter the regression equations were the variables measuring support for the national political authorities and opinions regarding the relative attractiveness of sovereignty-association and renewed federalism. Again, the regression analysis was performed twice with the order of entry of these variables being reversed, on the assumption that while feelings about national political authorities may have influenced opinions on the regime options, the reverse causal ordering is also plausible.

The result of the regressions (table 12.12, panel A) indicates that the measures of ethnicity, age, gender, and socioeconomic status account for 23 percent of the variance in referendum voting. An inspection of F values at this point in the analysis shows that the first three of these variables have statistically significant effects, while socioeconomic status does not. The next step in the analysis, namely the entry of the national community support and regime cost/benefit variables, reveals that the former has by far the larger unique effect, accounting for fully 25 percent of the variance. This finding is consistent with the importance of community-level reasons for voting suggested by responses to the open-ended "reasons for voting" question presented above (table 12.10). Last to enter the regression equations were the variables measuring support for the national political authorities and regime option preferences. Taken together, these account for an additional 12 percent of the variance in referendum voting. Of this, 8 percent is uniquely attributable to regime option preferences and 2 percent to feelings about the national authorities. Both of these increments in the explained variance were statistically significant.[41] In total, the regression analysis explains 67 percent of the variance in referendum voting.[42]

41. For a discussion of the test of significance used, see Gordon Hilton, *Intermediate Politometrics* (New York: Columbia University Press, 1976), p. 173. It is possible to study the effects of the community, regime, and authorities variables in more detail by constructing interaction terms.

42. Empirically, none of the three first-order interaction variables nor the second-order term

Table 12.12. *Summary of Results of Multiple Regression Analyses of Referendum Voting*

A. Regression using national authorities measure

Predictor variables	Variance explained (in percent)
Ethnicity, age, gender, socioeconomic status	23
Unique effects[a]—national community support	25
Unique effects—costs and benefits of federalism	2
Joint effects—community support, federalism	5
Unique effects—national authorities support	2
Unique effects—relative preference, regime options	8
Joint effects—authorities support, regime options	2
Total variance explained	67

B. Regression using provincial authorities measure

Predictor variables	Variance explained (in percent)
Ethnicity, age, gender, socioeconomic status	23
Unique effects—national community support	25
Unique effects—costs and benefits of federalism	2
Joint effects—community support, federalism	5
Unique effects—provincial authorities support	12
Unique effects—relative preference, regime options	1
Joint effects—authorities support, regime options	9
Total variance explained	77

a. As estimated by analysis of commonalities.

It is useful to replicate this analysis with a provincial authorities support measure (identification with the Parti Québécois versus identification with another party or no party) being substituted for support for national political authorities. This is done for two reasons. First, although support for the *national* authorities appears to be a relatively poor predictor of referendum vote, the substantial bivariate correlations between Parti Québécois identification and other relevant variables documented previously (table 12.8) indicate the potential importance of a *provincial*-level authorities measure. Second, and

―――――

makes statistically significant contributions to the variance explained over and above what can be explained by the main effects of these variables.

more specifically, the substitution of a measure of Parti Québécois partisanship enables us to investigate the extent to which identification with that party influenced referendum vote independently of the regime variable of sovereignty-association associated with it. The party's ability in 1976 to put together an electoral coalition broader than its original nationalist base, and its ability to pursue policies of concern to voters as the government of Quebec in the years since then, suggest that voter attitudes to the PQ may have been shaped by issues other than those connected with the referendum campaign. As a result, if the party had managed to increase support for itself by virtue of superior performance in office, it may have been able to persuade some of those skeptical about sovereignty-association to support this "Péquiste option" regardless of such reservations.[43]

The regression analysis employing PQ partisanship (table 12.12, panel B) explains 77 percent of the variance in referendum voting, 10 percent more than when support for the national political authorities was included. The analysis of commonalities reveals that 12 percent of the variance explained is *uniquely* attributable to PQ partisanship, and a further 9 percent is shared by this variable and the measure of preferred regime options. Only 1 percent of the variance explained is uniquely attributable to the latter variable. These results are consistent with the notion that support for the PQ had independent effects on referendum voting over and above feelings generated by the party's advocacy of sovereignty-association. Identification with the PQ has of course been shown to be strongly related to the variables of community and regime support. Despite the strength of these relationships, however, PQ partisanship explained (either uniquely or jointly) an additional 21 percent of the variance in referendum voting.

Conclusion

The most salient factors in the defeat of the referendum were the extent to which the question was treated as a matter of community

43. It is worth noting in this regard that identification with the PQ has increased over all waves of the panel. The percentages of the Quebec samples doing so, as percentages of all party identifiers, are: 1974—19 percent, 1979—35 percent, Feb. 1980—39 percent, May 1980—42

support by Quebec voters, and the propensity of these community-minded voters to vote "no." By breaking the theoretical conception of political support into the three component levels of the political system toward which it is directed, analyses suggest that the amount of community-level voting may have been crucial in preventing the referendum question from obtaining the support of a majority of Quebecers. By no means all of the community-level reasons for voting were displayed by "no" voters; these were very important in compiling the "yes" total as well. But they totally dominated the "no" voting.

The efforts, initially by the Parti Québécois and the "yes" forces, and ultimately by the Liberals and the "no" side as well, to discuss the referendum as a choice between regime-level options of sovereignty-association and renewed federalism were only partially successful. There remained a substantial amount of confusion about the exact meaning of these proposals, but most voters had adopted an opinion about them by the end of the campaign. However, multivariate analyses reveal that the unique contribution to the explanation of the referendum vote made by opinion on these regime-level options (or by another regime-level support measure, opinion on the distribution of the costs and benefits of the current federal system) was distinctly secondary to the contribution made by support at the level of the political community. To the extent to which voting was based on questions of regime-level support, however, it favored the Parti Québécois and the "yes" side.

We also have noted that authorities-level support as a motivation for voting favored the Parti Québécois. To the extent that the PQ was able to increase its support after coming to power, the referendum result was affected accordingly. The problem was that the party had much too far to go; although support for the PQ enhanced the probability of a "yes" vote, most of the variance in referendum voting remained a function of more basic attitudes toward the political system. Since opinions regarding sovereignty-association were changing only very slowly in the PQ's direction, the party could have succeeded in gaining majority support for its option only by establishing enormous

percent. Considering only francophones under the age of thirty, comparable percentages are: 40 percent, 62 percent, 64 percent, and 71 percent, respectively.

popularity among the Quebec electorate on grounds other than those associated with attitudes toward this option. It was perhaps impossible for the party to accomplish such a transformation given the configuration of social, political, and economic forces in Quebec. The party had certain advantages associated with being the government of the day, such as the timing of the referendum vote, control of debate in the National Assembly, and, to a certain extent, access to the mass media. These incumbency advantages were at least partially offset, however, by the party's self-imposed time constraint of holding the referendum during its first term in office, and possibly also by the more general problems associated with enhancing support while governing during a period of persistent economic difficulties.[44]

The amount of authorities-level support generated by the PQ's record in office, and the amount of regime-level support produced by the party's ability to persuade voters that sovereignty-association was a desirable way to change existing political structures, fell short of what was needed for a referendum victory in 1980. As a result, the community-level support factors dominated referendum voting, and here the "yes" forces were at a distinct disadvantage. As we have already seen, many voters were suspicious of the government's real intentions and felt that, despite the rhetoric, the proposal was still one for independence or separatism. There remained a substantial amount of genuine diffuse support for the Canadian political community and a basic reluctance to initiate a fundamental change in the nature of that community. The importance of support at the community level, and the secondary role of regime-level voting, brand as rather fanciful the postreferendum interpretations of the result as being a mandate for regime change along the lines of renewed federalism. Granted, opinions on the constitutional options indicate that the majority of the Quebec population would favor or at least accede to such change. However, given the fact that the referendum was voted

44. At present, little is known about the extent to which Canadians hold federal as opposed to provincial authorities responsible for societal or personal economic conditions. More generally, in the past half decade, a number of studies have explored linkages between economic trends, perceptions of economic well-being, and political support in western democracies. See, for example, Edward R. Tufte, *Political Control of the Economy* (Princeton: Princeton University Press, 1978); Richard Rose and Guy Peters, *Can Government Go Bankrupt?* (New York: Basic Books, 1978); James Alt, *The Politics of Economic Decline: Economic Management and Political Behavior in Britain Since 1964* (New York: Cambridge University Press, 1979); and Morris Fiorina, *Retrospective Voting in American Elections* (New Haven: Yale University Press, 1981).

voted down because of the lack of desire for fundamental alterations in the nature of the Canadian political community, even widespread support for some sort of revamped federalism should not be interpreted as necessarily threatening the continued viability of the community or even the basic contours of its regime.

The Quebec Referendum:
National or Provincial Event?

Joel Smith and Allan Kornberg

Modern states are a variable aspect of societal organization, and al-most any of their identifiable qualities are variables as well. The maintenance and sustenance of any state by its population typically entail both the discharge of routine obligations imposed by virtue of being in its territory (e.g., complying with accepted formal and infor-mal rules of conduct, paying taxes) and the provision of valued per-sonal resources during state crises (e.g., volunteer work in national emergencies, service in the armed forces during wartime). Although compliance is never universal, in most modern states levels of com-pliance generally are at least sufficient on a day-to-day basis. Presum-ably this circumstance depends on some adequate combination of three conditions—acceptance of the state's legitimacy in defining goals and means and in acting to attain these goals; voluntary com-pliance with the state's authoritative edicts; and the acceptance of coercive measures by the state when voluntary compliance does not suffice.[1] For reasons that need not concern us, overt coercion cannot be used extensively and continuously and, so, uncoerced conformity, presumably undergirded by a fund of positive feelings, is the main underpinning of the functioning state. Over time, however, public

1. The literature on these points is a vast one. See, inter alia, Hanna Pitkin, "Obligation and Consent I and II," *American Political Science Review* 59 (1965): 990–1000, and 60 (1966): 39–52; Roland Pennock and John W. Chapman, eds., *Nomos XII: Political and Legal Obligation* (New York: Atherton, 1970); John Rawls, *A Theory of Justice* (Cambridge: Harvard University Press, 1971); Richard Flathman, *Political Obligation* (New York, Atheneum, 1972); Richard Taylor, *Freedom, Anarchy and the Law: An Introduction to Political Philosophy* (Englewood Cliffs: Prentice-Hall, 1973); and Burton Zwiebach, *Civility and Disobedience* (Cambridge: Cambridge University Press, 1975).

compliance with the state's authoritative edicts will vary, and, therefore, it follows that the positive feelings just mentioned are dynamic, that they increase or decrease, are mobilized or quiescent. It is these variations, it can be argued, that are the crux of the study of support. If so, the holding of the May 1980 Quebec referendum on sovereignty-association indicates that Canada would appear to be an excellent site for an investigation of support.

Since Confederation, broadly based strong support for the Canadian state has been a rarity, while public debate over the rationale for a country so constituted and organized has been relatively frequent.[2] Periodically, incidents such as the execution of Louis Riel, the Manitoba schools controversy, the wartime election of 1917, and the conscription referendum of World War II have raised tensions between French- and English-speaking Canadians to a dangerous level. More recently, first ministers' conferences have provided relatively frequent opportunities for Canadians to be mobilized on behalf of or against competing federal and provincial proposals either to continue the present form of the state (federalism) or to loosen it by increasing the authority and autonomy of the constituent units (devolution).[3] Joined with these issues have been periodic heated debates over patriation and the content of a new Canadian constitution.[4]

Unfortunately, as was noted in the introduction to this volume, the study of support has been hampered by the functional and circular character of the concept.[5] However, one way of understanding support and its relation to political action and change is to examine it in the context of rare watershed political events[6]—those that have been

2. David Bell and Lorne Tepperman, *The Roots of Disunity: A Look at Canadian Political Culture* (Toronto: Macmillan, 1979). See also Violet Anderson, ed., *Problems in Canadian Unity* (Toronto: Thomas Nelson and Sons, 1938); and David Bercusion, *Canada and the Burden of Unity* (Toronto: Macmillan, 1977).

3. See Joel Smith and David Jackson, *Restructuring the Canadian State: Prospects for Three Political Scenarios* (Durham: Center for International Studies, Occasional Papers Series, No. 11, 1981).

4. See the discussions by Alan Cairns, including "Constitution-Making, Government Self-Interest, and the Problem of Legitimacy," in this book, chap. 14; "Recent Federalist Constitutional Proposals: A Review Essay," *Canadian Public Policy* 5 (1979):348–65; and "The Other Crisis of Canadian Federalism," *Canadian Public Administration* 22 (1979):175–95.

5. See, for example, David Easton, "A Re-Assessment of the Concept of Political Support," *British Journal of Political Science* 5 (1975):435–57, and "Theoretical Approaches to Political Support," *Canadian Journal of Political Science* (1976):431–48. See also the discussion of regime support in Allan Kornberg et al., "Some Correlates of Regime Support in Canada," *British Journal of Political Science* 8 (1978):199–216.

6. On the importance of focusing on critical political events in the study of support, see

widely anticipated because they have been made public and which promise significant changes in the character of the state. In such circumstances it is reasonable to assume that: (*a*) support may be mobilized; (*b*) the event's implications may be compelling enough to be understood by most people; and (*c*) the processes by which support shapes people's involvement in the event and which subsequently may cause support to be altered will be more apprehensible.

Despite its obvious significance, there were a number of reasons why the referendum may not have been the kind of watershed event around which a study of national regime support can profitably be organized. They include the following:

1. Participation in the event was limited to Quebec. Other Canadians could participate only indirectly or vicariously at best. Moreover, much of the commentary about the event was in French and could not be experienced concurrently and with precision by most English-speaking Canadians.
2. The referendum proposition did not mention either separation or independence. It only authorized the provincial government to enter into negotiations on sovereignty-association with the federal government, but it could not commit the latter government to participate. Moreover, Quebec government spokesmen emphasized throughout the campaign that any proposed changes that emerged from any negotiations were to be submitted for general approval in yet another referendum.
3. Quebecers' and francophones' concerns for their unique status and survival are longstanding and there has been a rather continuous agitation for separate and improved positions in the country. Hence, English Canadians may have been indifferent to this latest crescendo in Quebec nationalism.
4. More generally, specialists in public affairs tend to be aware of events that may escape the attention of members of the general public and/or to assign those events meanings and importance that they do not have for others.

For these reasons, it is mandatory in this first report of a major study of regime support in Canada to demonstrate that the referen-

Sidney Kraus, Dennis David, Gladys Engel Lang, and Kurt Lang, "Critical Events Analysis," in Steven H. Chafee, ed., *Political Communications: Issues and Strategies for Research* (Beverly Hills: Sage Publications, 1975).

dum did indeed carry a widely perceived threat of dismantling or seriously altering the regime, and, therefore, was the sort of proposition appropriate for study. In this paper, then, we will consider the extent to which average people in Quebec and elsewhere in Canada came to regard the referendum as a watershed event which could have significant consequences for the continuity of their country in its current form. We do so by addressing the following four specific questions:

1. What were the levels of awareness, interest, and knowledge both inside and outside Quebec before, during, and after the campaign and vote?
2. How did interested people perceive the meaning of the event and did those perceptions shift?
3. How did people perceive political objects for which we presumed that the event had significance? and
4. What were the levels of public support for key objects and did they change between pre- and postvoting day?

It will be argued that the data leave no doubt that the Quebec referendum did become a national event for most Canadians. Levels of public interest and participation[7] both inside and outside of Quebec were unusually high and large numbers of people regarded the outcome of the referendum as having important consequences for the entire country. Finally, with regard to the referendum's impact on the more general question of support, the data suggest that the problem of maintaining the Canadian political community and its principal institutions and processes is not rooted in a fatal absence of support for them but rather is grounded in a combination of provincial chauvinism and antipathies.

Research Design

As just observed, this is a first report of a major study of regime support in Canada. The issues raised in the total study required collection of a wide variety of information (e.g., through interviews with

---

7. It should be noted that innumerable questions about the sources of these perceptions and responses, the factors involved in the development of differential interest and participation, and the like are not addressed here. Nor do we presume to analyze the referendum outcome, even though our data do mirror the shifts in the fortunes of the competing groups very well.

media officials, content analyses of television, radio, and newspaper coverage of the referendum, and their presentation generally of the current and future positions of Quebec in Canadian society, etc.). The discussion in this paper is based on information derived from three waves of personal interviews variously oriented to the general issue of national integration and change with random samples of approximately 300 residents in each of three medium-sized Canadian cities. The first wave of interviews was conducted almost immediately after the referendum campaign formally began, the second approximately ten days before the actual voting, and the third, one week after the event.[8]

The role of the media and their impact were a major concern, and since they were, we decided not to conduct a national study but instead to center our investigation on local communities[9]—Trois Rivières, Quebec; Peterborough, Ontario; and Lethbridge, Alberta. All three have local newspapers and television stations, but a substantial portion of supralocal television and wire service coverage is the same in each community. Their relatively similar modest sizes also provide more manageable environments in which to examine the interaction between common stimuli and different community contexts as mediating factors in a study of the impact of a critical event on people's support for the national political community and regime. An

8. The core of each interview focused on respondents' interest in and perceptions of the referendum, the leaders on both sides, and the issue positions and involvement in the campaign of political parties and other key groups. We wanted to ascertain the effects not only of media exposure but also of personal relationships and other factors on respondents' information levels as well as on their evaluations of the credibility of the media, the completeness of their coverage, their accuracy, and the like. These issues were examined during each of the three waves, as were respondents' perceptions of the meaning of the outcome of the referendum both for Canada and for Quebec. Of course, Quebec respondents also were asked their vote intentions in the two prereferendum interviews and, in the postreferendum questioning, how they actually voted. Since the three waves of interviewing were administered during a relatively brief time span, many of the changes in control variables (e.g., occupations, education, address, age, household composition of respondents) that plague longitudinal studies are minor and can be ignored. Moreover, many of the problems involved in analyzing panel data also should not arise because we are not interested in using long-term secular trends to explain aggregate shifts in rates of change. Instead, our intention is to gear our analyses to two concerns: (1) the different ways in which people arrive at their final opinions and actions; and (2) the process of how people come to understand—if indeed they do—that they are taking a stand or witnessing an event that will bear directly on the kind of country in which they will be living in the foreseeable future.

9. The supralocal material electronic and print media provide is delivered through local affiliates, subject to local editing, and consumed by individuals in local settings. With rare exceptions, even unedited wire service stories or national newscasts generally come to individual consumers through locally identified media.

even more important consideration in their choice is the fact that these three communities are located in areas with varied political climates pertinent to the past, present, and future Canadian state.

Trois Rivières, of course, reflects Quebec's long tradition of cultural identity and uniqueness as well as its deeply ingrained sense of exploitation and internal colonial status. All Québécois certainly do not and did not agree on what the future status of their "nation" in the Canadian Confederation should be, but a substantial portion certainly believe that it is in order *to consider* a change as substantial as separation.[10] Peterborough, in contrast, represents the English-Canadian Ontario heartland, and although many Ontarians would strongly disagree, most of them would tend to view the present federal arrangement as proper. Moreover, they—and, even more, the residents of peripheral provinces—also have viewed that arrangement as a most efficacious device for sustaining Ontario's dominant position in the nation. Lethbridge is in a traditionally peripheral province where the federal arrangement long has been perceived as dominated by the central Toronto-Montreal-Ottawa core of the country, the so-called "Golden Triangle." Resentment over past and present core exploitation through the vehicle of federalism is longstanding and the province is recognized as being the present center of escalating separatist sentiments. Nonetheless, there is little sympathy for similar francophone concerns and complaints. Indeed, Albertans tend to identify Quebec with Ontario as part of the established exploitative

10. There also is an enormous body of literature on Quebec nationalism. See, inter alia, Michael Brunet, "The French Canadians' Search for a Fatherland," in Peter Russell, ed., *Nationalism in Canada* (Toronto: McGraw-Hill of Canada, 1966); Stephen Clarkson, "A Programme for Binational Development," in Russell, *Nationalism in Canada*; Daniel Johnson, "What Does Quebec Want?—1967," in J. Peter Meekison, ed., *Canadian Federalism: Myth or Reality* (Toronto: Methuen, 1971); Henry Milner and Sheilagh Hodgins Milner, *The Decolonization of Quebec: An Analysis of Left-Wing Nationalism* (Toronto: McClelland and Stewart, 1973); Carl J. Cuneo and James Curtis, "Quebec Separatism: Analyses of Determinants Within Social Class Levels," *Canadian Review of Sociology and Anthropology* 11 (1974): 1–29; Dale Posgate and Kenneth McRoberts, *Quebec: Social Change and Political Crisis* (Toronto: McClelland and Stewart, 1976); Symposium on "Conflict and Consensus in Canadian Confederation," *Canadian Public Policy* 3 (1977): 409–78; *The Canadian Review of Sociology and Anthropology* 15 (1978), special issue on Quebec; Rudy Y. Fenwick, "Communal Politics in Quebec: Ethnic Segmentation and Support for Political Independence Among French Québécois," unpublished dissertation, Duke University, 1978; Neil Nevitte, "New Nationalism and Religion: The Case of Quebec," unpublished doctoral dissertation, Department of Political Science, Duke University, 1978; Elliot J. Feldman and Neil Nevitte, eds., *The Future of North America: Canada, the United States, and Quebec Nationalism* (Cambridge: Center for International Affairs, Harvard University, 1979); and A. Milton Moore, "Fact and Fantasy in the Unity Debate," *Canadian Public Policy* 5 (1979): 206–22.

and controlling power center that has been frustrating their ambitions to capitalize on extensive local energy resources.[11] In addition, without going into detail, the provinces differ in ethnic makeup, party dominance at both the federal and provincial levels, economic base and resources, and so on. Such considerations obviously also were major factors in our choices.

Our confidence in the appropriateness of both the choice of research sites and the assumption that the referendum would provide a focus for systematically examining support was shaken rather severely by the results of public opinion surveys conducted by the CBC and released in March of 1979 and 1980.[12] These suggested that Canadians both in and outside of Quebec may not have been taking the referendum very seriously. Given these unexpected poll results (Americans should try to imagine public reactions to a similar referendum on sovereignty-association for, let us say, the Midwest), it seemed possible that the data from our panel study might show that the referendum was not the watershed event we had expected it to be. We turn, therefore, to the first of our questions. What *were* the levels of awareness, interest, and knowledge both inside and outside Quebec before, during, and after the campaign and vote?

Awareness of and Interest in the Referendum

Contrary to the counterindications of the early CBC polls, the data support our initial decision to use the referendum to study the emergence of understandings that may mobilize and alter citizens' feelings of regime support. Obviously there are community variations. On

11. The American reader can capture the flavor of these and other positions taken by spokesmen for the several provinces and regions in Donald V. Smiley, *Canada in Question: Federalism in the Seventies*, 2nd ed. (Toronto: McGraw-Hill Ryerson, 1976); Richard Simeon, ed., *Must Canada Fail?* (Montreal: McGill-Queen's University Press, 1977); Roger Gibbins, "Models of Nationalism: A Study of Political Ideologies in the Canadian West," *Canadian Journal of Political Science* 10 (1977):341–72; John Richards and Larry Pratt, *Prairie Capitalism: Power and Influence in the New West* (Toronto: McClelland and Stewart, 1979); Task Force on Canadian Unity (Pepin-Robarts Report), *A Future Together: Observations and Recommendations*, Vol. 1, *Coming to Terms: The Words of the Debate*, Vol. 2, *A Time to Speak: The Views of the Public* (Hull, Que.: Canadian Government Publishing Centre, 1979); and Harry H. Hiller, "From External Exploitation to Internal Manipulation: Staples, Power, and Socioeconomic Change in the New West," unpublished manuscript, University of Calgary, 1980.

12. Canadian Broadcasting Corporation, "Confederation/Referendum" (March 1979), detailed tabulations; Canadian Broadcasting Corporation, "A Question of Country" (April 1980), detailed tabulations.

balance, however, the data reveal extensive interest and awareness of the referendum, albeit with varied interpretations of its meaning. Although there is residual evidence of a positive relationship between ignorance of the referendum and distance from Quebec (as shown in the CBC polls), reports of awareness were overwhelming. Almost every member of the Trois Rivières sample (96 percent) and almost 90 percent of those of the other two (89 percent in Peterborough, 87 percent in Lethbridge) had heard of the referendum. Including those who claimed to know that there would be a proposition to negotiate a new status for the province, less than 10 percent of the sample members in any city said they knew nothing about the situation.

When those who claimed to have heard about the referendum were asked what was being proposed, however, differences magnified along lines of distance from Quebec. Whereas Quebecers volunteered most frequently (50 percent) and with some accuracy that the referendum sought authority for the provincial government to negotiate sovereignty-association with the Ottawa government, that proportion dropped slightly in Peterborough (46 percent) and sharply in Lethbridge (33 percent). The contrasting perception that separation and independence were being proposed was volunteered by only a little more than a quarter (28 percent) of the Trois Rivières respondents, but by almost half of those in both Peterborough (46 percent) and Lethbridge (50 percent). Even more noticeable is the shift in balance between the interpretations: the negotiation version predominating in Trois Rivières (by 22 percent), the two occurring with equal frequency in Peterborough, and the independent Quebec version dominating in Lethbridge (by 17 percent). Among the key contributory factors may be city differences in the quantity of information available, the greater precision in French coverage of details than in English-translated versions, the greater closeness and availabilty of Quebec coverage to Peterborough than to Lethbridge, different levels and types of personal interest, and different provincial interests invoked as contexts within which to give the referendum local pertinence and meaning.

Reports of having seen, read, or heard specific material that made an unusual impression on the person (presumably a factor in sustaining a person's knowledge and understanding) were much less frequent (43 percent in Lethbridge, 33 percent in each of the others).

Given their constant bombardment by referendum coverage in the media, it is not surprising that so many respondents felt at a loss to single out any particularly noteworthy items about the event. It should be noted that as the campaign wore on mentions of noteworthy items increased in Trois Rivières and Peterborough and declined sharply in Lethbridge. The precipitous decline of such reports in the latter city suggests either that residents there were so overwhelmed by the volume of material that they could no longer single out specific items, and/or that the quantity and constancy of the material bored and disinterested them.

Furthermore, at least at the time of the first round, there were clear communal differences in what respondents reported as noteworthy. Relatively speaking, non-Quebecers seemed fixated on predictions of the outcome and commentaries on its implications (44 percent in Peterborough and 45 percent in Lethbridge of those who cited noteworthy material). Quebecers, in contrast, hardly seemed to notice such material (5 percent). Given the extensive polling and commentary reported within and outside Quebec this probably does not reflect differences in the types of available material. Moreover, it also is pointless to speculate that such a sharp difference reflects a cultural variation between French and English. Instead, it seems reasonable that this may reflect Quebecers' need to find a basis for reaching a final decision on how to vote, in contrast to the others' interest in simply forming and sustaining attitudes about the event and the outcome they would prefer.

This possibility is consistent with some other differences in the material the respondents recall as noteworthy. Relative to other topics, Quebecers emphasized the debates on the wording of the question (13 percent) and the concept of sovereignty-association and its meaning (17 percent). The debates on the wording of the question involved proponents of the "oui" and "non" sides in arguments over the "real" meaning of the proposition and its implications. The discussions of the meaning of sovereignty-association, in contrast, focused on its implication for the future status of Quebec and its relations with the rest of Canada as well as on the obvious unavoidable implications of the mysterious new relationship for such personally relevant issues as who would pay for which government services and functions. Residents of Peterborough and Lethbridge, in contrast, emphasized material not only on the outcome—much of which was analogous to the copious speculative reporting about winners that precedes major sporting events—but also on the wording of the question (29 percent and 31 percent, respectively). The latter is not surprising in view of their unfamiliarity with the subtleties of Quebec politics and the tendency (noted above) to perceive the referendum as a decision on separation and independence. It is quite possible that the long and involved statement and its failure to mention separation or independence came to many non-Quebecers as a stunning surprise.

In addition to these indications of both general awareness of the forthcoming referendum and respondents' feelings that they were informed and comprehended the nature of the event, the data suggest that both Quebecers and other Canadians were considerably interested in the event. However, expressions of personal interest (44 percent) have a number of unexpected features. First, four out of each nine Quebecers (44 percent) expressed little or no interest at the inception of the campaign, and that proportion rose to half (50 percent) shortly before voting day. Second, in contrast, reported interest was much higher in both of the other cities and, furthermore, showed slight increases between the first (74 percent in Peterborough and 79 percent in Lethbridge) and the last week of the campaign (79 percent and 82 percent, respectively). Third, higher levels of interest, unlike information, increase with distance from Quebec. This last observation simply may reflect the fact that when most people are less informed (presumably because local conditions neither motivate nor provide a facilitating environment for becoming informed), higher interest may have been the precipitating factor for those who do become informed. Accordingly, the positive relationship between interest and distance is not considered further.

The more important issue is how to judge whether these reported levels of interest are high or low relative to what they might be. First, we simply note that in each case the predominant proportion of those who experienced a shift in interest in the very last days before the vote reported an *increase* (31 percent increase versus 9 percent decrease in Trois Rivières; 54 percent versus 4 percent in Peterborough; 53 percent versus 3 percent in Lethbridge). Therefore, we presume that whatever interest level existed shortly before voting day increased with the coming of the vote. Second, it may be that standards as to what *real* interest is vary among the three communities. Thus, with respect to the lower levels of interest reported in Trois Rivières, it should be noted that much higher proportions reported that they perceived the level of community interest to be higher (56 percent very interested, first wave; 65 percent, second wave; 61 percent, third wave) than residents of Peterborough and Lethbridge perceived those levels to be in their communities (16 percent, 13 percent, 24 percent; and 18 percent, 16 percent, 16 percent, respectively), a reversal that suggests such a difference in standards. At the very least, standards for high interest simply may be higher in Trois Rivières, where, for example, an unusually large proportion of interested residents (34 percent versus 16 percent in Peterborough and 13 percent in Lethbridge) claimed that they planned on doing something to influence the outcome. Moreover, high proportions of such people apparently followed through. Using a minimal level of activity—discussing the event with others—as a measure, we find that active interest is quite high in all three communities (45 percent—first wave, 57 percent—third wave, Trois Rivières; 77 percent and 64 percent, Peterborough; 76 percent and 62 percent, Lethbridge). Admittedly, talk is cheap, but in each case substantially higher proportions of residents had discussed the referendum than report that they often discuss federal (17 percent, 29 percent, and 33 percent, respectively) and provincial politics (23 percent, 30 percent, and 34 percent, respectively).[13] The proportions claiming to have been active in the campaign, although much lower than those for discussion, still are much higher than the 2–5 percent who report ever having engaged in various campaign activities previously (data not shown). Indeed, in view of the facts that they could not vote, had no direct access to meetings and campaign headquarters, and were not members of either the contesting provincial parties or the organizations created for the campaign, the levels of activity reported by the residents of Peterborough and Lethbridge were unusually high. For all these reasons we would conclude that levels of knowledge, awareness, and interest were high and that this applied throughout the country, at least as the country is represented by these communities.

13. See, for example, the various data cited by William Mishler, *Political Participation in Canada: Prospects for Democratic Citizenship* (Toronto: Macmillan, 1979).

Perceptions of the Meaning of the Referendum

In noting the emphasis in Peterborough and Lethbridge on referendum materials that speculated about the outcome, we surmised
that non-Quebecers may well have treated the event as entertainment, as a kind of athletic contest, and thus a matter of no real lasting
significance. This possibility raises a serious question as to whether,
in fact, most people anywhere saw the event as having wider significance for the country. To pursue this issue, in each of the first two
waves of interviews respondents were asked an open-ended question
as to what meaning they thought the two possible outcomes might have
for Canada. In the final wave they were asked for their assessments of
the meaning of the proposition's loss for Canada. As might be expected, many of the answers pertained more to the relationship with
Quebec than to the shape of the future Canadian state. Thus, remarks
outside of Quebec, like "Maybe they'll stop making so much trouble,"
or remarks in Trois Rivières like "They'll pay more attention to us"
were not uncommon. Because the substance of all the answers was
highly varied and not all directly pertinent for present purposes, we
simply classify them as being remarks about the future of the Canadian state, comments regarding other outcomes with no clear pertinence to Canada's future, or indications that the referendum really
did not impress the respondent as pertinent (e.g., declaring prior to
the question that the respondent did not see the referendum as holding any interest, explicitly declaring that there would be no changes,
regardless).

Using this classification, responses suggest that during the course
of the referendum campaign respondents increasingly developed an
awareness that the event would have considerable significance for the
country. In both Lethbridge and Peterborough the sense of pertinence increased and was directed more toward Canada's future as a
state than toward other things. Perceptions that the referendum
was a critical event for Canada were higher at each interview in those
cities than in Trois Rivières (see table 13.1). This is to be expected,
inasmuch as for so many Quebecers the referendum was defined as
an opportunity to change Quebec's status and realize its nationhood.
On balance, these data are consistent with the proposition that sub-

Table 13.1. Responses Volunteered as the Meaning of Referendum Vote Outcomes to Canada

	Trois Rivières			Peterborough			Lethbridge		
	Wave 1	Wave 2	Wave 3	Wave 1	Wave 2	Wave 3	Wave 1	Wave 2	Wave 3
If approved									
Changes for Canada	30%	a	b	48%	52%	b	47%	48%	b
Other results	16			11	9		10	10	
Not pertinent	54			41	39		43	42	
If disapproved									
Changes for Canada	27%	a	50%	49%	48%	68%	47%	45%	61%
Other results	12		34	3	9	10	5	11	16
Not pertinent	61		16	48	43	22	48	44	23

a. Insufficient responses owing to error in questionnaire.
b. Not pertinent.

stantial proportions of Canadians did perceive the referendum as an event having significant import for Canada's future.

Not surprisingly, most non-Quebecers did not want to see the proposition carry and were happy with the outcome.[14] Regardless of their feelings for Quebec (of which more shortly) and whether they wished Canada to change drastically in the future, they did want a Canada that includes Quebec. That they did not foresee resorting to force to keep Quebec in Confederation should the course of events lead to its independence (84.6 percent in Peterborough, 80.3 percent in Lethbridge) is quite consistent with the Canadian emphasis on due process and an orderly approach to problems. Indeed, the typically Canadian character of the whole situation is perhaps its most notable feature.[15] With regard to the ultimate significance of the referendum, the data reveal that substantial proportions (36.9 percent in Trois Rivières, 40.8 percent in Peterborough, 57.3 percent in Lethbridge) judged that other provinces would defect should Quebec take that step. Moreover, these were thoughtful judgments. The respondents named provinces (e.g., Newfoundland, Alberta, British Columbia) in which there have been mounting expressions of separatist sentiments and/or growing expressions of dissatisfaction with federalism as it currently functions. These concerns were greatest in Ontario, where, most observers would agree, the costs of decreasing central control would be greatest.

Finally, a cross-tabulation of people's feelings about the prospects for Quebec independence with their estimates as to whether other provinces would move toward independence if Quebec separated (although not marked by high relationships) revealed a general tendency in the three cities for expectations for Quebec's independence to be linked to similar expectations for other provinces. Although the experience of the referendum campaign does not seem to have had a substantial impact on aggregate feelings about whether Quebec will become independent at some future time (56.3 percent before the referendum versus 56.7 percent after it in Trois Rivières; 49.5 percent

14. Residents of Trois Rivières responded and acted in line with prevoting polls and the election outcome.

15. In how many other countries would a referendum seeking permission to negotiate a changed constitutional status be held by a duly elected incumbent government long known to have associated itself with separation and independence?

versus 41.3 percent in Peterborough; 44.5 percent versus 39.0 percent in Lethbridge estimate the chances of independence at 50–50 or more), sizable proportions of respondents expected at least some changes in the nature of Confederation (84.9 percent in Trois Rivières, 78 percent in Peterborough, 75.9 percent in Lethbridge). Moreover, of those that expected changes, most thought such changes would weaken the federal government (27.4 percent; 29.6 percent; 44.1 percent in the same order) or involve the departure of provinces (16.2 percent; 29.6 percent; 26.4 percent in the same order). In summary, then, although the data are not consistently clear, people who gave the referendum some thought felt that it had national relevance in that it foreshadowed (either by defection of provinces and/or the decline of federal power) significant alterations in the structure of the future Canadian state.

Images of the Political Objects Involved

The data we have reviewed derive from questions about Canada, Quebec, the federal government, and similar objects. When distributions and relationships in the three cities are compared, there is an implicit assumption that in their remarks people are responding to the same stimuli. However, our strategy in selecting these particular cities for study was premised on the possibility that their residents' views of some of the key actors and issues in the referendum event may have been substantially different. For this reason part of the second wave interview was given over to a number of semantic differentials which, it was hoped, would enable us to specify with somewhat greater precision what it was that people might have had in mind in answering our questions. In this section we shall discuss some community similarities and differences in conceptions of some of these key elements.

The semantic differential provides two types of data useful for our purposes: (1) average scores on a fixed seven-point scale for a descriptive continuum applicable to a concept and (2) any underlying constructs that may be reflected in the choices on these individual continua. With respect to the latter, if we were interested in quantitatively precise differences among the communities, we would pool the three samples and derive factors on which all respondents in all three communities could be scored. Here, however, we are interested primarily in whether the image structures in each community tend to be similar (i.e., do people have a coherent set of ideas about an object that makes sense in the context of that community, and, if they do, how similar are such images).

Given our long-term interest in using the referendum as a focal point for studying regime support rather than as a phenomenon in its own right, we begin by examining the semantic differential for Canada. Respondents were asked to indicate for each of fourteen different pairs of alternatives which most closely matched their feeling when "Canada" is mentioned. Examples of pairs, which were the poles of a seven-point scale, include "united-divided," "like-dislike," "weak-powerful," and "democratic-undemocratic." The dimensions for which the word pairs stand as poles are varied to include both substantive and evaluative dimensions. For validating purposes, the same options also were applied to the United States, with differences of a sort that indicate that the procedure is meaningful and reliable. For example, in all three communities respondents "like" both countries, but are more positive about Canada than the United States. Both countries tend to be viewed as equally free and democratic. Canada is slightly but consistently seen as more conservative and just, while the United States is seen as more united, powerful, energetic, and dynamic. Comparison of the means for each of the fourteen dimensions in the two non-Quebec cities reveals only slight differences between them. Both, however, vary considerably, although not qualitatively, from Trois Rivières. In the latter city, the mean for "liking" Canada, although clearly positive, is almost a full point lower. The Quebecers also see Canada as stronger, more dynamic and progressive, and not as humanitarian or democratic as do their countrymen in Peterborough and Lethbridge (see table 13.2).

The constructs that underlie these fourteen choices could well have foreshadowed the referendum vote outcome. Two factors accounted for almost half the variance (47.2 percent) in the matrix of correlations for Trois Rivières and both were loaded on liking Canada (see table 13.2). The first factor emphasized social attributes (e.g., just, equality, progressive, free, humanitarian, unprejudiced, democratic) and the second reflected a theme of capability (e.g., united, power-

Table 13.2. Semantic Differential for "Canada": Rotated Solution

	Trois Rivières				Peterborough						Lethbridge					
	X̄	Factor 1	Factor 2	Communality	X̄	Factor 1	Factor 2	Factor 3	Factor 4	Communality	X̄	Factor 1	Factor 2	Factor 3	Communality	
United (1)	3.31		−0.35	28.1%	3.73					—	3.74			−0.40	36.7%	(7) Divided
Weak (1)	5.02		0.42	27.6	4.25			0.43		32.4%	4.34			0.42	50.4	(7) Powerful
Just (1)	3.31	−0.45		48.7	3.00					38.3	3.15	0.46			—	(7) Unjust
Favoritism (1)	3.95	0.72		43.7	4.12	0.37				27.4	3.85			0.62	34.1	(7) Equality
Dynamic (1)	3.20		−0.46	55.9	4.25		−0.12	0.48		50.7	3.79	−0.69			57.5	(7) Stagnant
Progressive (1)	3.59	−0.45		39.9	4.48		−0.63			40.6	3.84	−0.66			38.8	(7) Conservative
Aggressive (1)	3.75		−0.53	19.7	4.99		−0.71			50.9	4.34	−0.84			56.2	(7) Passive
Restricted (1)	4.76	0.64		40.3	3.16	−0.43				34.6	4.71			0.43	32.2	(7) Free
Proud (1)	2.71		−0.70	45.9	4.25					45.9	2.86	−0.40			22.4	(7) Humble
Lazy (1)	5.09		0.62	51.6	2.87			0.47	−0.63	38.9	4.74	0.47			45.1	(7) Energetic
Humanitarian (1)	3.22	−0.47		41.0	4.21	0.57				44.8	2.77				—	(7) Calloused
Prejudiced (1)	4.03	0.56		24.8				0.41		18.7	3.87				—	(7) Unprejudiced
Democratic (1)	3.26	−0.38		22.1	2.84	0.81				60.7	2.74		0.67		55.1	(7) Undemocratic
Dislike (1)	5.28	0.42	0.33	47.8	6.09					—	6.25		−0.56		28.2	(7) Like
Eigen value	5.52	1.10			3.59	1.73	1.21	1.04			4.31	1.74	1.12			
Cumulated % of variance matrix	39.4	47.2			25.6	37.9	46.6	54.1			30.8	43.2	51.2			
Correlations	r₁₂=0.71				$r_{12}=-0.21$; $r_{13}=-0.35$; $r_{14}=-0.25$; $r_{23}=0.38$; $r_{24}=0.31$; $r_{34}=0.31$						$r_{12}=0.26$; $r_{13}=0.49$; $r_{23}=-0.42$					

ful, dynamic, aggressive, proud, energetic). Because of outlier effects, the factors in both Peterborough and Lethbridge are not so
clearly demarcated, although with two exceptions, they too suggest
positive images. For example, the second factor in Peterborough is
loaded heavily on dynamic, progressive, and aggressive. Furthermore, a composite of the second, third, and fourth factors for Peterborough appears to be very much like a composite of the two Trois
Rivières factors. In both cities those factors are positively correlated.
The first factor in Peterborough, however, contrasts with these results, being comprised of undemocratic, calloused, restricted, and
unjust. However, further examination shows this to be a statistical artifact. The means for these dimensions indicate that most people in
Peterborough view Canada as highly democratic, humanitarian, free,
and just. That they do implies that the factor reflects the impact of a
small group of people who *oppose* the dominant view and make a
stereotypical but consistent set of negative choices on these dimensions. A similar phenomenon also occurs in the "Alberta" semantic
differential for Lethbridge, as well as in the second factor for "Canada" in that same sample. In that case the only two items loading
were "undemocratic" and "dislike." The first factor in Lethbridge,
however, (with the addition of progressive), was exactly the same as
the capability (second) factor in Trois Rivières. *Essentially, then, except for small groups of strident, dissatisfied people, the images of
Canada are largely positive and built in various combinations around
themes of social justice and energetic dynamism.*

Even more surprising than the generally positive vein in which
Canada is viewed in Quebec, as well as elsewhere, is the imagery
conveyed by the federal system of government. For this concept the
Quebecers' perspective is summarized by two factors, both very positive in character. Moreover, the means also are positive. The symbolic protagonist in the referendum campaign was characterized first
as "important," "unified," "effective," "necessary," "trustworthy,"
"strong," "near," and "like." This factor, with its positive emphasis
on essentiality and dependability, accounts for almost half (48.1 percent) the variance in the matrix. The second factor puts slightly more
emphasis on positive aspects of the social role of the federal system
(democratic, unifies, effective, and works in the public interest) and
accounts for slightly more than another 10 percent of the variance in

Table 13.3. Semantic Differential for the "Federal System of Government": Rotated Solution

	Trois Rivières				Peterborough					Lethbridge				
	X̄	Factor 1	Factor 2	Commu-nality	X̄	Factor 1	Factor 2	Factor 3	Commu-nality	X̄	Factor 1	Factor 2	Commu-nality	
Important (1)	2.76	−0.50		48.3%	2.46	0.55			—	2.31			—	(7) Not Important
Don't like (1)	4.63	0.75		48.3	4.62				40.4	4.48			—	(7) Like
Democratic (1)	3.22		−0.50	35.8	3.15			−0.73	48.0	3.08	−0.48		40.6	(7) Undemocratic
Unifies (1)	3.51	−0.45	−0.37	55.8	3.39			−0.59	42.3	3.49	−0.65		38.4	(7) Divides
Effective (1)	3.31	−0.55	−0.38	71.9	3.67		0.41		49.9	3.54	−0.71		52.8	(7) Ineffective
Unnecessary (1)	4.97	0.64		34.8	5.59	0.54			22.6	5.78		0.70	39.1	(7) Necessary
Works in the public interest (1)	3.53		−0.66	31.2	4.25			−0.46	20.1	4.01	−0.51	0.51	25.8	(7) Works for special interests
Untrustworthy (1)	4.68	0.77		51.0	4.31	0.57			44.2	4.27			49.2	(7) Trustworthy
Strong (1)	3.05	−0.55		39.5	3.70		0.72		49.9	3.58	−0.57		32.4	(7) Weak
Near (1)	3.62	−0.71		56.9	4.24			−0.46	22.2	4.69	−0.52		30.3	(7) Distant
Eigen Value		4.81	1.04			3.08	1.24	1.06			3.77	1.09		
Cumulated % of variance matrix		48.1	58.5			30.8	43.1	53.7			37.7	48.6		
Correlation		$r_{12}=0.66$				$r_{12}=-0.36$; $r_{13}=0.54$; $r_{23}=-0.38$					$r_{12}=0.57$			

Table 13.4. Semantic Differentials for "Alberta," "Ontario," and "Quebec": Rotated Solutions

(1)	Trois Rivières $\bar{X}$	Factor 1	Factor 2	Factor 3	Communality	Peterborough $\bar{X}$	Factor 1	Factor 2	Factor 3	Communality	Lethbridge $\bar{X}$	Factor 1	Factor 2	Factor 3	Communality	(7)
Alberta																
More powerful than other provinces (1)	4.28	-0.82			67.1%	3.11			0.76	60.9%	3.13		-0.50		29.3%	(7) Like other provinces
Unproductive (1)	5.54	-0.80	-0.61		46.7	5.84		-0.81	0.50	63.0	6.12			0.66	51.1	(7) Productive
More important than other provinces (1)	4.76				63.6	4.64				22.5	4.43		-0.68		47.6	(7) As important as other provinces
Taker (1)	3.90			-0.39	33.1	3.47	-0.36			24.3	5.05	-0.66			53.6	(7) Giver
Cooperates with Ottawa (1)	3.84			-0.47	26.4	4.77	0.55			28.0	3.88	0.57			29.6	(7) Doesn't cooperate with Ottawa
Rich (1)	3.15		0.72		61.4	2.40			0.30	37.0	2.20		-0.34	-0.40	28.0	(7) Average
Only care about themselves (1)	3.74		0.35	-0.63	51.4	3.37	-0.75			65.3	5.02	-0.64			49.9	(7) Cares about country
Like (1)	3.59		0.24	0.65	47.1	3.21	0.50	0.30		28.1	1.61	0.20		-0.31	18.8	(7) Dislike
Eigen value		2.45	1.67	1.27			2.40	1.38	1.16			2.27	1.56	1.03		
Cumulated % of variance matrix		30.7	51.5	67.4			30.0	47.3	61.8			28.3	47.8	60.8		
Correlations		$r_{12}=-0.13$; $r_{13}=0.30$; $r_{23}=-0.04$					$r_{12}=0.01$; $r_{13}=0.26$; $r_{23}=-0.09$					$r_{12}=0.06$; $r_{13}=-0.35$; $r_{23}=0.07$				
Ontario																
More powerful than other provinces (1)	4.30	-0.85			75.4%	3.30	0.59			37.3%	3.15		-0.77		61.7%	(7) Like other provinces
Unproductive (1)	5.29		-0.52		36.9	5.46		0.50		32.2	5.37				—	(7) Productive
More important than other provinces (1)	4.66	-0.85			67.8	4.70	0.59			35.9	4.62		-0.54		28.3	(7) As important as other provinces

[illegible] (1)																cooperate with Ottawa
Rich (1)	3.27		0.65		49.3	3.48	0.65			50.7	3.10		−0.64		40.4	(7) Average
Only care about themselves (1)	3.79			0.75	58.4	5.14	0.31	0.51		38.8	3.92	−0.75			61.8	(7) Cares about the country
Like (1)	3.72		0.25	−0.76	54.6	2.29		−0.48		24.2	3.37	0.67	−0.21		43.9	(7) Dislike
Eigen value		2.64	1.65	1.26			2.03	1.74	1.06			2.09	1.87			
Cumulated % of variance matrix		33.0	53.6	69.4			25.4	47.2	60.5			26.1	49.5			
Correlations		$r_{12}=-0.19$; $r_{13}=-0.40$; $r_{23}=0.13$					$r_{12}=-0.11$; $r_{13}=-0.12$; $r_{23}=0.26$					$r_{12}=0.20$				
Quebec																
More powerful than other provinces (1)	4.45	−0.78			62.3%	4.18		−0.67		52.2%	3.75		0.71		50.7%	(7) Like other provinces
Unproductive (1)	5.59		0.60		38.5	4.47			−0.70	52.2	4.32			0.79	63.7	(7) Productive
More important than other provinces (2)	4.81	−0.77			59.9	4.95		−0.68		47.0	4.80		0.28		62.1	(7) As important as other provinces
Taker (1)	4.35			0.41	21.4	2.99	−0.61			39.4	2.60	−0.58			34.8	(7) Giver
Cooperates with Ottawa (1)	4.33			−0.49	31.5	5.41	0.33			14.7	5.41	0.46			30.3	(7) Doesn't cooperate with Ottawa
Rich (1)	3.44		−0.55		32.2	4.64		−0.44		22.9	4.57		0.63		45.5	(7) Average
Only care about themselves (1)	3.91			0.66	41.8	2.82	−0.74			54.5	2.53	−0.78			61.7	(7) Cares about the country
Like (1)	2.08		−0.48		24.3	3.82	0.44		0.15	23.2	4.20	0.59	−0.30	−0.25	38.0	(7) Dislike
Eigen value		1.88	1.64	1.34			2.01	1.65	1.11			2.37	1.78	1.19		
Cumulated % of variance matrix		23.4	44.0	60.7			25.1	45.8	59.7			29.6	51.8	66.7		
Correlations		$r_{12}=0.05$; $r_{13}=0.06$; $r_{23}=0.18$					$r_{12}=0.14$; $r_{13}=0.16$; $r_{23}=0.19$					$r_{12}=-0.20$; $r_{13}=-0.15$; $r_{23}=0.02$				

the matrix. Both are highly related ($r = 0.66$). The first factor on the "federal system" for Peterborough reflects a sense of security (like, necessary, trustworthy)—almost the ways in which a child might think of a security blanket. The second factor, in contrast, reflects dissatisfaction with the system, weakness and ineffectiveness: ironically, precisely the sort of qualities that might have been expected to be revealed among Québécois. The third factor, with the substitution of nearness for effectiveness, reproduced the social value factor that was second in Trois Rivières. The first factor in Lethbridge is strongly positive and emphasizes the integrative, equalitarian features of the system (democratic, unifies, effective, in the public interest, strong), mediated with a dash of symbolic affect (near). The second factor mirrors the first (security) factor in Peterborough without the affect (see table 13.3).

If people in such diverse parts of the country perceive it and its style of governmental organization so positively—the means on the items tend to be more similar than different—where are the seeds of current Canadian national discord and disunity? Perspective on this issue is provided by the semantic differential results on conceptions of the provinces in which the three cities are located. Here are reflected some possible bases for the present rancor and discord. The means are particularly revealing. On the "giver-taker" dimension, each city's residents see their own province as a giver and both of the other provinces as takers. The same pattern applies to the "only care about themselves—care about the country" dimension. Each sample sees its province as altruistic and the other two as self-centered. It is no wonder that residents of each city like their own province considerably more than they like either of the others. Although the structure of these factors is not pertinent to this discussion, it is worth mentioning that, in each case, factors pertaining to other provinces were weighted on the dislike side. No love is being lost among these three.

A particularly pertinent pattern in the means is the difference between the Quebec sample and the other two. Quebecers see the others as much more powerful than the others see themselves or one another. Even more striking is the tendency of Ontario and Alberta residents to see Quebec as more powerful, less productive, much more of a taker, more uncooperative with Ottawa, less wealthy, and much less concerned for the country than do the residents of Trois

Rivières. Given such differences in perspective, it is hard to imagine that there could have been a satisfactory outcome to negotiations between Ottawa and Quebec had the referendum passed and negotiations been undertaken (see table 13.4).

These results suggest that at a general level residents of each city had the same Canada in mind when they addressed themselves to the referendum and its consequences. They even had similar conceptions of the federal system. Although not reviewed here, however, they had very conflicting images of the Parti Québécois and this did not ease relationships. Most important, though, are the sharp differences in their conceptions of each other's provinces.[16] These images are associated with strong feelings of like and dislike and reflect a genuine sense of inequity, injustice, and distrust. Moreover, the feelings are mutual. In that sense too the referendum tapped a national situation.

Political Support Before and After the Vote

In order to estimate support for political objects we asked respondents prior to the vote to rate a number of different Canadian political actors and institutions on a thermometer scale. After the referendum, five items most intimately involved in the referendum were measured again. We consider here only the thermometer scores for Canada, Parliament, and the federal government. This material was examined for each community sample as a whole and for various pertinent subgroups within each (e.g., sex, age, actual vote in Quebec and patterns of campaign interest in the others, federal and provincial political party preferences). Although there are community-provincial variations, a number of general trends are apparent. (1) The referendum seems to have had little impact on the aggregate level of feelings of support. (2) Support for Canada is much stronger than support for either the federal government or Parliament. (3) Party identifications, response to the referendum, and age are the factors most consis-

16. Data supporting this generalization are contained in Allan Kornberg, Harold D. Clarke, and Marianne Stewart, "Federalism and Fragmentation: Political Support in Canada," *Journal of Politics* 41 (1979):889–906. Their analysis is based on data derived from a 1974 national election study. A report of the public's perceptions of the provinces, using 1979 national election data, that replicates their findings is contained in Allan Kornberg, William Mishler, and Harold Clarke, *Representative Democracy in the Provinces* (Scarborough: Prentice-Hall, 1982), chap. 2.

tently related to differences in support. We shall take each of these points in turn.

Despite the relatively small sample sizes for the subgroups, few before and after correlations of support scores are above 0.6. In contrast, somewhat more of them are less than 0.2. Feelings for Canada tend to be most stable in Trois Rivières; those for Parliament and the federal government are most stable in Peterborough. Because the concept of support refers to something relatively stable and deep-seated, under ordinary circumstances we would expect it to change slowly and that for the few weeks between interviews the correlation scores for the same item would be quite high. However, had the campaign been traumatic and its outcome stimulated the patriotism of some, there could have been unsystematic changes in scores that would have produced lower correlations. Neither alternative fits these data. The coefficients tend to be low, rarely reaching a level at which half the variance is being explained, but when they are low, the "after" mean is not consistently higher than the "before." In one graphic case—that of younger sample members in Peterborough—the means before and after are equal and the correlation is only 0.60. These correlations may indicate either that feelings of support are less stable than surmised, or that they are so homogeneous and stable that all that is being correlated are small, random measurement errors.[17]

Although they are lower in Trois Rivières than in the other two cities, the mean levels of support for Canada tend to be very much higher than those for either Parliament or the federal government. The comparatively lesser support for Parliament and the federal government, even in Peterborough, may suggest a widespread readiness for structural change in the federal system, but with a commitment to maintain the national framework. Even this is speculative, however. Finally, politics make a difference. Provincial Liberals in Trois Rivières rate Canada at almost the same high level as do Canadians in the other two cities. So did "non" voters. As another example, in Ontario and Alberta federal party identification has a substantial impact on

17. It is difficult to evaluate these possibilities without a study designed for that purpose. There is a slight, but inconsistent, tendency for the correlations to be lower when the variances are lower. More consistent is the tendency of correlations to be high in Peterborough and low in Lethbridge. Comparison with correlation coefficients and standard deviations for comparable thermometers for Canada and the federal system taken for a panel during the 1979 and 1980 postelection studies show our correlations to be higher and the standard deviations to be comparable in Trois Rivières and lower in the other cities.

levels of support for governmental institutions. Thus, even though respondents had been asked to express sentiment for certain structures and not for their incumbents, there may have been a carryover influence anyway. In both cases, identifiers with the incumbent federal Liberals felt more positive than did supporters of competing parties. Moreover, support for each of the objects increases slightly but consistently with age. However, because of period differences, it may not be legitimate to argue that as the youth age they will acquire orientations similar to those of older people.

The differences in average scores (before and after means for Canada are 72.3 and 71.4 in Trois Rivières, 86.9 and 85.5 in Peterborough, and 85.1 and 86.0 in Lethbridge—83.4 in the national panel of the 1980 postelection survey) among the three research sites tend to conform to differences among the positions of the provinces in Confederation.[18] This suggests that we are tapping nationally relevant phenomena in this effort to measure support. The small shifts in averages for Canada between pre- and postvoting day, however, suggest that the referendum had relatively little immediate impact on national sentiments. Understandably, as a reflection of credible performance and postvote euphoria, there were more positive feelings for Parliament in both anglophone cities and for the federal government in Trois Rivières and Lethbridge after voting day. However, until we are able to examine the individual cases to determine who shifted how, these data cannot be interpreted with more clarity or confidence. It would seem, though, that insofar as our other data have indicated that the referendum was a national event, its principal relevance may have been to externalize and reinforce existing feelings and concerns rather than to cause major shifts in response to the realization of how close the country had come to a potentially cataclysmic change.

Discussion and Conclusion

The various data examined here leave no doubt that the Quebec referendum did become a national event for most Canadians. Early indications of people's unawareness and ennui, which were contained

18. See Alan Cairns's chapter 14 in this book for a concise description of these positions.

in the national polls and suggested in our private conversations with media and public officials, apparently were not sustained when the campaign moved into gear with the first step in a process that still might conclude in the departure of almost a third of the country. Levels of interest and participation both inside and outside Quebec were unusually high. The numbers of respondents in both Peterborough and Lethbridge who voluntarily reported sending postcards and signing petitions was an unusual contrast with ordinary campaign participation patterns in both Canadian and American elections. So, too, were the large numbers of respondents in all three cities who, after voting day, saw the event as having meaningful substantive significance for both Canada and Quebec. The strong Anglo North American tendency to discount electoral politics as devoid of real meaning had abated for the referendum—at least according to our respondents.

We might then ask what these data portend for our primary goal of studying regime support. First we should note that despite the hue and cry about disunity and Canada's future as a nation, there seems to be a deep reservoir of support for both Canada and its federal system.[19] Had Quebec's incumbent political leaders realized how deep those sentiments are, even in Quebec, they might have tried other tactics or invented ways to avoid a decision at that point. In any case, from the perspective of these data, the "non" victory is understandable.

Do the data suggest any new perspectives on regime support? The meaningfulness of our thoughts on this issue, as well as the validity of our previous comments, depend, of course, on only a preliminary analysis, which for now, at least, we accept. It seems reasonable to suggest that regime support may have different implications for nations with different types of regimes. Thus, even though Canada and the United States are both democracies governed through structures legitimated by general elections for which there is almost universal eligiblity, comparable levels of regime support need not necessarily have the same consequences for the state. In the United States, differences in people's feelings about or ignorance of the other forty-nine states normally make little difference for the country at a national

19. Similar conclusions are drawn by Kornberg and Stewart in chapter 3 of this volume on regime support and national identity employing 1979 national election study data.

level. In Canada, however, differences in people's feelings about the several provinces apparently make a great deal of difference. According to our data, *the problems that presently beset Canadian federalism may arise not from the absence of support for the country or its federal system, but from the combination of domestic provincial chauvinism and other provincial antipathies.* In each of our samples, residents admire their own province and disparage the others. Because the Canadian system invites provincial residents to expect (and their party leaders to try to arrange) special statuses and conditions in their federal relations, each province translates those feelings first into pressure and then into conflict with the federal level as it tries to respond to its particular vision of interprovincial conditions and the forces that have created and sustained them.

The responses in each sample on the semantic differentials for the three provinces on the "giver-taker" and "like-dislike" dimensions provide trenchant testimonials to the situation. Each sees itself as altruistic but exploited by others and disliking them for it. The result is a cacophony of conflicting, particularistic demands that probably cannot be satisfied fully by any federal government, regardless of its partisan composition. Indeed, a federal government would require more than the proverbial wisdom of Solomon to be able to satisfy the claims of each province while simultaneously trying to affect attitudinal changes which would facilitate the development of more positive feelings for one another. This seems to imply, then, that in a political system like that of Canada, support is a key factor in the survival and welfare of the state. However, the pertinent aspect is not so much support for the country and its regime as it is the *interaction* between support at the national political community-regime levels and support for other key units (e.g., provinces) that have negotiable relationships with the state. As long as Quebec or any other province can attempt to decide its future unilaterally, and in response primarily to feelings about itself in the context of its sentiments toward other provinces and its perception of their sentiments toward it, support for Canada and its federal system may be only a necessary but not sufficient condition for understanding the problems and the future of the Canadian state.

Constitution-Making, Government Self-Interest, and the Problem of Legitimacy

Alan C. Cairns

Constitutional Malaise and the Dominance of Governments

The leading actors in the process of constitutional renewal in Canada are the eleven governments of the federal system. Each government seeks not some abstract goal of legitimacy for the system as a whole, but a version of legitimacy designed to serve *its* present and future interests. Each government seeks security and influence for itself, built on the insecurity of others if necessary. This is most clearly the case with the amending formula where the desired position is a veto over the removal of what one possesses, and flexibility with respect to what one hopes to achieve.

No single actor, not even the federal prime minister, views it as his major task or prime responsibility to accord a generous place for the ambitions of others within his own objectives for constitutional change. The clear-sighted pursuit of self-interest is the governing consideration. There are, of course, communities of interests, and alliances built on them, which reduce the anarchy that otherwise would prevail. Further, there is a continuing Canadianism, based on sentiment and utility behind even the staunchest advocate of provincial goals, even, it is now clear, in Quebec. Similarly, the pursuit of central government ambitions to enhance the future role of Ottawa is not indifferent to the inescapable reality of federalism in Canada. Neither Ottawa nor any provincial government seeks the total displacement of

I wish to thank Keith Banting, David Elkins, and John Hayes for detailed criticisms of an earlier version of this paper.

the other governments by aspiring to, for the former, a unitary state, or for the latter, independence. What they all seek, including post-referendum Quebec, is a constitutionally guaranteed improvement in their position.

To put the preceding in different language, it is evident that Ottawa speaks for a more developed Canadianism than is compatible with provincial ambitions, and that the provinces espouse a more complete provincialism than is compatible with the ideal federal system as seen from Ottawa. The political pressures that derive from the separate systems of governmental power over which they preside push the Canadianism of Ottawa and the provincialism of the contending provincial governments further apart at the conference table than they are in the psyches of individual Canadians. No participant is responsible for taking an overall perspective, for rising above the limitations of a particular government connection, and attempting to maximize the satisfaction of all the participating governments. Finally, there is no evidence of an 'invisible hand' at work capable of extracting the optimum constitutional product from elites' competitive pursuit of conflicting self-interests.

The domination of the constitutional reform process by governments represents the high point of executive federalism and challenges its utility for attaining consensus. The breakdown of the most extensive effort at constitutional renewal in Canadian history, in the summer of 1980, underlines the difficulties faced by this intergovernmental process in facilitating agreement. Four weeks of ministerial discussions in the summer of 1980, followed by the First Ministers' Conference in September, confirmed what was apparent from other evidence. No self-evident new equilibrium has emerged which it is the straightforward task of constitutional draftsmen to embody in a document for the future. This is partly because the existing system, for all of its imperfections, still functions. It is for all governments, then, a fallback position, against which proposed constitutional changes can be measured. Its comforting existence allows a slackening of effort when the possibilities of success seem remote. This was evident in the lull in federal government constitutional initiatives in the early 1970s after the failure of the Victoria Charter to get unanimous agreement.

Paradoxically, the existence of the status quo as an acceptable fallback position also helps explain the aggressiveness of provincial demands at the 1980 conferences and their general reluctance to make major concessions. The extreme nature of their demands, as measured by the limited probability of their attainment, reflected an interim preference for the status quo over any major compromise. This was particularly so for Quebec for whom an engineered failure that could be blamed on Ottawa was the very acme of success. (That some provinces may subsequently have had second thoughts, given the postconference unilateral action of Trudeau, described below, is another matter.) While a similar judgment can logically be made of the federal government's position—that a failure that could be blamed on the provinces was not without its attractions—there is a crucial difference. Ottawa, unlike the provinces, had, as we now see, the possibility of a partial escape valve in unilateral action. To the extent that Ontario shared in the federal government objectives, which had been clearly revealed in a leaked federal strategy document,[1] that province, via the proxy of Ottawa, also had an enlarged capacity to maneuver.

The norms governing constitutional conferences severely limit the possibilities of far-reaching reform. Neither the federal government, any single provincial government, nor even the combination of ten provincial governments has the power and authority to impose its preferences on the others. The overriding political reality of this process of executive federalism is its domination by governments, dissatisfied in different ways and in different degrees with the status quo, but insufficiently so to generate a conviction that the crisis requires major self-sacrifice. These governments seek agreement under an inhibiting convention of unanimity—variously viewed as an unbreakable rule or an unattainable aspiration which might have to be discarded in unspecified circumstances.

The acceleration of the constitutional activity of every government since the Confederation of Tomorrow Conference called by Premier Robarts of Ontario in 1967 has produced a heightened appreciation of the interests at stake in constitutional change, and a consolidation of each government's position. The long exploration of constitutional futures since the mid-1960s has contributed more to the elaboration of self-interested definitions of what each government seeks from con-

1. "Report to Cabinet on Constitutional Discussions," summer 1980, and "The Outlook for the First Ministers Conference and Beyond," Ministers' Eyes Only, August 30, 1980.

stitutional renewal than to a widespread disposition to altruism. Governments increasingly arrive at the constitutional bargaining table well-briefed, with carefully prepared proposals. As the September 1980 First Ministers' Conference revealed, there has been an impressive improvement in the quality of constitutional advocacy and understanding at the provincial level. While this produced a more stimulating adversary process it did not facilitate the reaching of agreement.

The range of issues on the constitutional table has grown dramatically from the restricted agenda considered at the Victoria Conference in 1971 to the much lengthier, and more contentious list at the 1980 constitutional conference. The enlargement of the agenda is both cause and effect of an increase in the number of governments seeking major change. The limited agenda of the Victoria Conference ence in 1971 to the much lengthier and more contentious list at the 1980 constitutional conference. The enlargement of the agenda is

Constitutional discussions from 1968–71 were primarily a vehicle for an Ottawa-Quebec confrontation, with the other governments shifting from spectator to semiparticipant roles as the occasion required. In that less demanding climate of constitutional discussion, several governments participated only in a desultory fashion. For Premier Ross Thatcher of Saskatchewan constitutional reform was the 101st item on his list of 100 priorities. By 1980, however, the resource issue in the three westernmost provinces, the growing assertiveness of Newfoundland over fisheries and offshore resources, and the reaction of Ontario to various perceived threats to its economic and political power made the simple question "What does Quebec want?" no longer adequate to uncover the tensions constitutional renewal should alleviate.

The escalation of provincial demands outside Quebec was also fostered by the curious hiatus between the election of the Parti Québécois in November 1976, and the Quebec referendum in May 1980. During this period, after an initial lull, a veritable frenzy of constitutional soul-searching occurred. Initially a reaction to the PQ victory, much of this constitutional effort developed a life of its own as the Péquiste government remained on the sidelines, assiduously seeking the perfect time and the perfect question for the carefully controlled exercise in plebiscitarianism to which it was committed.

The spiritual absence of the PQ government from the official and unofficial discussions its election had precipitated encouraged the provincial governments of English-speaking Canada to ignore Quebec in their constitutional proposals. After all, the Quebec government had declared its total lack of interest in the small change of constitutional reform when the big prize of sovereignty-association seemed tantalizingly within reach. Further, the Quebec provincial Liberals were in disarray for some time after their crushing 1976 defeat. They were incapable of projecting a clear federalist alternative to Lévesque. Thus while numerous private conferences and reports, along with the Pepin-Robarts Task Force on Canadian Unity, treated the Quebec question as primary, the provincial governments of English Canada tended to accord it a distinctly secondary status while they got on with the more important task of protecting and advancing their own interests.

Concurrent with this phenomenon, two orientations to a federal system in disequilibrium attained prominence. On the one hand, the recognition that an old, loved political system was in danger of breakup could elicit a rush of patriotism in defense of the country. On the other hand, the behavior of the Quebec government could well be viewed as an instructive lesson in the politics of total self-interest. Here was a duly elected government of a province, functioning as a normal government while simultaneously working unremittingly to sever its historic political relationship with the rest of Canada. A provincial government, whose citizens sent MPs to Ottawa and paid federal taxes and received federal benefits in return, devoted its considerable resources to eliminating Canadian identity within its borders. Residents of Quebec were henceforth to become solely and exclusively Québécois. The possible consequences for the rest of Canada of this attempted transformation of a province into a country were of negligible concern to the government of Quebec.

The PQ example opened up the language and subject matter of political debate. Options and possibilities hitherto unexamined moved out of a vaguely taboo category into the public forum of open discussion and calculation. The demise of Canada was no longer out of the question. Challenges to the central role of the federal government, already well under way in response to the developing provincialism feeding on a variety of centrifugal forces, were given further legitimacy and came to be almost normal provincial government behavior.

Given this transformation in the climate of federal-provincial controversy, it was not surprising that by the time the Quebec referendum had been defeated, and serious constitutional bargaining com-
menced in the summer of 1980, the governments of British Columbia,
Alberta, Saskatchewan, Newfoundland, and Ontario were no longer
on the sidelines, but had become actively involved, espousing explicit interests of their own. The three Maritime provinces, and
Manitoba, if perhaps less possessed of an elaborate list of concrete demands, were much more conscious of the interests at stake than they
had hitherto been. Further, the decisive defeat of the watered-down
PQ referendum question produced a chastened, reactive Quebec
delegation, lacking a mandate, without a developed position on constitutional change within federalism, and in any case with little enthusiasm for the aggressive pursuit of the transformed federal system
it had consistently claimed was neither possible nor desirable of
attainment. Had the referendum question passed, or had Claude
Ryan's Liberals replaced the PQ at the bargaining table, a strong, dynamic Quebec presence in the constitutional discussions would almost
certainly have heightened the Quebec-Ottawa confrontation and reduced the salience of the extensive demands from other provinces. An
additional historical might-have-been would also have had a marked
effect —the retention of power by Mr. Clark, with his definition of
Canada as a community of communities, and a much more flexible, less
centralist version of federalism than that of the Liberals. With the return of Mr. Trudeau, however, the highly developed philosophy of
federalism which he has consistently adhered to since 1965 once again
pervaded Ottawa's strategy and objectives.

The intensity of conflict to which the above factors contributed was
exacerbated by the transformation of Canadian federalism in the 1970s
from a system of *cooperative* federalism, to a new system for which a
covering label has not been coined, but which is more conflict-ridden
and seemingly incapable of attaining equilibrium. The basic factors in
the disappearance of the cooperative federalism characteristic of the
conditional grant era have been outlined elsewhere, and do not require extensive discussion here. In the 1960s and 1970s the constitution lost much of its capacity to regulate the behavior of the key government actors. As the constitutional settlement of 1967 appeared
destined for the graveyard, governments responded by paying less
and less heed to the canons of civility and respect for traditional con-

stitutional boundaries to which they had previously adhered. Between Quebec and Ottawa, especially after the PQ victory, a form of intergovernmental guerrilla warfare developed in which each side sought to discredit, embarrass, and undermine the other. The carefully staged walkout at intergovernmental conferences by Premier Lévesque, the fierce Ottawa-Quebec battle over the Chrétien sales tax reduction in 1978, the Quebec government support of Social Credit in the 1979 federal election in an attempt to unseat Trudeau, the propaganda war of the balance sheets as Ottawa sought to undermine sovereignty-association and the PQ sought to prove that Canadian federalism systematically exploited the Québécois, were all manifestations of the escalating intensity of the Quebec-Ottawa conflict and of a profound constitutional malaise.

There is some reason to believe that the depth of the Quebec-Ottawa differences on constitutional matters strained the loyalties of civil servants in both jurisdictions, particularly federalists in Quebec City and Péquistes in Ottawa. This led to a higher-than-average incidence of leaked documents and the underground transmission of strategy and policy information to the other side, particularly it seems from the federal to the Quebec side. (Movement of information in the other direction, I am told, is more likely to be communicated orally, in part because of the lesser degree of bureaucratization and formality in the policy process of the smaller Quebec bureaucracy.)

Intergovernmental conflict spilled over into the courts in the 1970s as governments sought to bolster their political base and bargaining positions with supporting judicial decisions. The prominent theses of the late 1950s and the 1960s that the courts had been retired and replaced by more political methods of resolving intergovernmental disputes proved premature. Resort to the courts and the threat of resort became widespread. A series of major court battles involving Saskatchewan, Manitoba, and Quebec undermined the appearance of impartiality of the Supreme Court, and encouraged several provinces to place it on the constitutional agenda as an institution requiring reform in the direction of greater sensitivity to provincial interests. This enhancement of the judicial role enlarged the pool of aggrieved losers and raised questions about the Supreme Court's composition, the methods of selecting its members, and related matters. Resultant provincial attacks on the court as an instrument of federal domination parallel earlier attacks by Ottawa on the Judicial Committee of the Privy Council as an arbiter from whom impartiality could not be automatically expected.

The reassertion of a major Supreme Court role in constitutional adjudication reflects the diminished capacity of more explicitly political processes to resolve intergovernmental differences which, in turn, is due to the increasingly higher stakes involved. That six provinces concerted their strategy in 1980–81 for a series of court challenges to the federal government's constitutional initiative, which followed the failure of the September 1980 First Ministers' Conference, is illustrative of this political failure. Resort to the courts in areas of intense political controversy reveals the gravity of the Canadian constitutional breakdown, heightens the Supreme Court's visibility, and simultaneously threatens to sap the court's legitimacy.

The Governmental Takeover of Society: The Competition among Nation-Building, Province-Building, and Quebec Nation-Building

The tensions and acrimonious federal-provincial disagreements of the past decade are the surface manifestations of a profound change in government-society relations which inexorably drives the eleven governments of the system into ever more competitive relationships.

Nation-building has been long and lovingly described by English-Canadian historians as the raison d'être of the central government, manifested initially in the creation of a national community and a national economy in defiance of parochial provincial interests, and later in the movement from colony to nation as Ottawa incrementally eroded the British role in Canadian affairs. The fostering and nurturing of a single Canadian nation and of the national government that served it were built on the erosion of imperial power and the relative enfeeblement of provincial power. For the English-Canadian intelligentsia which emerged out of the Great Depression of the 1930s nation-building served as an adequate description and guide to the present and the future. For a heady decade after World War II their vision seemed vindicated as the federal government enjoyed a pleasing dominance. In a brief interlude between the twilight of Empire and the later resurgence of provincial governments, Ottawa enlarged the Canadian domain by the addition of Newfoundland, abolished appeals to the Judicial Committee of the Privy Council, gave itself a limited capacity for constitutional amendment, performed competently as a national government, and played a leadership role in international affairs as a peace-keeping middle power.

By the mid-1960s, however, a new drive and a new label, province-building, indicated that provincial governments were no longer content to play the subsidiary, peripheral role of minor actors to which the nation-building definition of the country confined them. The battles between Ottawa and W. A. C. Bennett of British Columbia, a vigorous province-builder since assuming office in 1952, over his hydroelectric development of the Peace and Columbia rivers, and the Quebec-Ottawa pension battle of the Lesage-Pearson years revealed the coexistence of competing elite ambitions in federal and provincial governments. The forces of centralization and Ottawa dominance no longer automatically carried the day.

With the growth of a positive province-centred Quebec nationalism, no longer content with protecting the past, Quebec nation-building emerged as a third fundamental process of socioeconomic transformation under state aegis. As the Quebec Legislative Assembly became the National Assembly, as the province of Quebec was rechristened the state of Quebec, and as French Canadians within Quebec provincial boundaries were redefined as Québécois, it became evident that province-building was an insufficiently precise label to capture the essence of the objectives that Quebec elites had for their people. Hence, to the general process of province-building and the Ottawa-led process of nation-building was added a third category, which overlapped the other two, and the future of which either within or without federalism is yet to be decided: Quebec nation-building.

The competitive, elite-led processes of nation-building, province-building, and Quebec nation-building manifest themselves in a general drift of power and decision making from the market to government. Both levels of government are active and entrepreneurial in attempting to implement competing federal and provincial visions of desirable futures. Both therefore intervene vigorously in the overlapping societies and economies under their jurisdiction in the pursuit of divergent grand designs.

In a unitary state the decline of the market results in a straight-forward displacement of private by public decision making. In a federal system with strong governments at both levels the result is much more complex. What was hitherto handled by the processes of markets and by nonpolitical decision makers, for whom the federal division of powers was irrelevant, is not only politicized but federalized as well. Federal and provincial jurisdictional differences penetrate to ever deeper and more profound levels of citizen existence. The sphere of society outside the political, and therefore outside the federal system, experiences constant shrinkage. This federalization from above, which tends to demarcate citizen activity as federal or provincial, reflects the penetrative dynamics of nation-building, province-building, and Quebec nation-building. Sophisticated interventions in society and economy in the service of the competing isms of Canadian nationalism, various provincialisms, and Quebec nationalism displace the market, extend the political, and necessarily generate inter-governmental conflict. The simultaneous success of both levels of government in enhancing their own authority multiplies the potential for federal-provincial clashes ranging from incompatible regulatory details to the most basic issues of public policy.[2]

Inevitably, the existing constitution is embroiled in and victimized by intergovernmental power struggles it cannot tame. Equally inevitably, constitutional change is pressed into service by political elites for its potential contribution to the goal of nation-building, province-building, or Quebec nation-building. Constitutional change, ostensibly sought for the elevation of the citizenry, is covetously pursued in the service of elite ambitions. The idea of the constitution as rules of the game is displaced by the unsavory reality of the constitution as weapon.

The Search for Positional Advantage in a New Constitution

The constitutional revision process is dominated by the spokesmen for these three elite-led drives to transform the societies, economies,

2. This paragraph and the preceding one are taken with minor changes from the author's "The Constitutional, Legal, and Historical Background," a chapter in Howard R. Penniman, ed., *Canada at the Polls, 1979 and 1980* (Washington: American Enterprise Institute, 1981), pp. 1–23.

and identities under their respective jurisdictions. They bring to their common task contending ambitions whose possible attainment they seek to enhance by appropriate constitutional change. They recognize that, as did its predecessor, a future constitution will evolve. They seek, therefore, to position themselves so that they will benefit from rather than be damaged by future constitutional evolution which they cannot predict.

Government elites do not view constitution-making as a process aiming to produce a constitution which will be a mirror image of an existing distribution of socioeconomic forces struggling to find constitutional expression. They certainly do not see themselves as disinterested agents of demands welling up from below—from the societies they profess to serve. On the contrary, the definitions of the public interest they seek to entrench in a new constitutional document are unabashedly their own interpretations which, with remarkable consistency, are designed to produce changes beneficial to their own governments. They do not wish to have the existing distribution of government power and influence, which has grown up around the present constitution, reflected in a new document. They seek not to enshrine the present, but to carve out a future improvement in their constitutional position. They recognize the creative role of constitutions, the bias that is implicit in all constitutional arrangements. They seek to have that creativity, that bias, work for them rather than against them. Each government recognizes that the other governments are driven by self-interest. In the Darwinian process of constitutional change each government fears that altruism will be a destructive act, for itself, for its successors, and for the future it seeks for the people partially under its jurisdiction. Concern for others, therefore, is carefully controlled. Such concern is positively stimulated by a desire not to destroy the overall system, but, barring that unlikely eventuality, it remains subservient to the dominant goal of enhancing one's position.

Government Self-Interest and the Sequence of Constitutional Change

The search for positional advantage in a new constitution is logically preceded by a search for positional advantage in the process of seeking a new constitution. Although this manifests itself in many ways, its most typical expression is with respect to the sequencing of the constitutional review process itself. Since 1968, the federal government has consistently and continually tried to impose a sequence of constitutional change under which the division of powers would only be attended to after prior constitutional change had strengthened Ottawa's bargaining position. Specifically, as the first step, Ottawa has attempted (*a*) to strengthen the national community by means of an entrenched Charter of Rights and the protection of official language minorities, and (*b*) to make such central government institutions as the Senate and Supreme Court more representative of, or sensitive to, regional/provincial interests. When these goals were achieved, a strengthened central government, based on a reinvigorated national community, and with a heightened claim to represent and speak for provincial interests, would be ready to undertake constitutional discussions over the division of powers. The Quebec government, against whom this strategy was originally devised, with a tenacity and consistency the equal of Ottawa, has preached the necessity of reversing the sequence, or at least of dealing with the totality of constitutional change in one package. The other provinces with somewhat less tenacity, and with the partial exception of British Columbia, have leaned more to the sequence suggested by Quebec than that of Ottawa. They do not forget Trudeau's initial lack of enthusiasm for constitutional discussions, and they have feared, not without justification, that Ottawa's eagerness for constitutional review might flag after its own major objectives had been attained.

Unilateralism: An Escape from the Constraints of Executive Federalism—The Search for the Ultimate Positional Advantage

The strategy of the government actors seeking desirable constitutional change is profoundly influenced by their differential capacity for unilateral action. Unilateralism is a means to enhance the possibility of attaining desirable constitutional outcomes for the government claiming to possess it, and in defiance of opposition from other governments. As the possession of a unilateral capacity is basically restricted to the central government, the debate over unilateralism

takes the form of a controversy between Ottawa and some or all provinces over the extent of federal unilateral powers and over the constitutional propriety of their use. The opponents of federal unilateralism fight for the preservation of the executive federalism process on
which their constitutional bargaining power is based.

Ottawa has, of course, unilateral control over those matters covered by the domestic amending procedure contained in the 1949(2)
amendment, itself an example of earlier federal government unilateralism. Further, only Ottawa has access to the British Parliament
to make requests for amendments on matters not under the direct
amending control of the federal parliament as a result of 1949(2). In
both cases there are disputes at the margin over what is properly
included in these two categories. With respect to the former, the constitutionality of a unilateral central government initiative with respect
to Senate reform was recently denied by the Supreme Court of Canada, thus seriously reducing federal government maneuverability in
the reform of central government institutions. The official federal
position had been that all matters contained in Bill C-60 for immediate action, including Senate reform, were entirely within the amending authority of Ottawa alone, without the necessity of recourse to
Westminster, and without requiring provincial agreement. That attempted federal unilateralism failed.

At the time of this writing another version of federal unilateralism,
based on the privileged federal government access to the United
Kingdom Parliament, and contained in a Resolution of the Senate and
House of Commons to be forwarded to the United Kingdom Parliament for passage, seeks to patriate the British North America Act,
and incorporate an amending formula, a Charter of Rights and Freedoms, and a Statement of Equalization in the revised Canadian constitution.[3] The constitutionality of this, too, is being challenged by
provincial governments. Both the Canadian courts and the British
Parliament are being utilized by those who deny the constitutionality
of the federal initiative.

Inevitably, the federal government seeks a broad definition of its

3. In addition to extensive modifications of the Charter in the Joint Committee of the Senate
and the House of Commons, important provisions were added to the Resolution dealing with
aboriginal rights, and provincial jurisdiction over natural resources. The amended version, as
recommended to Parliament, is contained in "Minutes of Proceedings and Evidence of the Special Joint Committee of the Senate and of the House of Commons on the Constitution of Canada," Issue No. 57, February 13, 1981.

capacity for unilateralism, and the provinces a narrow definition, both with respect to the federal utilization of the amending authority domiciled in Canada under exclusive federal jurisdiction as a result of the 1949(2) amendment, and for constitutional amendments that still have to be passed by the United Kingdom Parliament. For the latter, the crucial question is whether a discretion exists for Westminster to look behind the federal request and to reject a request that does not respect Canadian constitutional law or tradition. The controversy within Canada over the Westminster role neatly captures the self-interested flavor of constitutional reasoning when tensions are high. Those provinces opposed to the federal government submission to Westminster view Britain as a trustee of the integrity of the Canadian federal system, and specifically as a trustee of provincial rights against federal usurpation. To these provinces there is a real British discretion, which should be exercised in rejection of the federal package. The federal government, by contrast, claims that relevant precedents and Canadian independence require an automatic, positive British response to its constitutional package. Both sides emotively label the behavior of their opponents as colonial.

These federal and provincial differences of opinion over the scope of unilateral federal powers reflect the fundamental axiom of the politics of constitutional bargaining—minimize the resources available to your opponents, and maximize those under your own control. The politics of consitutional change, like Leo Durocher's approach to baseball, is governed by the maxim "Nice guys finish last."

In strict constitutional terms no province possesses a unilateral capacity over any aspect of the amendment procedure likely to advance its cause. The provincial governments' control over their own constitutions under 92(1) is essentially irrelevant to any provincial constitutional reform objectives.

Recent Parti Québécois strategy, however, seeking sovereignty-association and employing a referendum as a resource, was a shrewd attempt to create a justification for unilateral action in pursuit of a goal with minimal support in the rest of the country. Unlike federal unilateralism, based on a privileged constitutional position, the unilateralism of the PQ government was to be justified by the expressed will of the people in a referendum. In essence, the Quebec strategy aimed at elaborating a provincial right to self-determination in the absence of an explicit constitutional provision establishing such a right.

Although the goal of winning a referendum failed, and with it the possibility of using a referendum success as a legitimating device to press the claims of Quebec to sovereignty-association, the Quebec effort is instructive for students of Canadian federalism. The Quebec government had considerable success in defining the breakup of Canada as a question to be answered unilaterally by the Quebec population. Although there were "outside" interventions in the referendum campaign, it is undeniable that the rest of Canada was largely reduced to the role of spectator. Significantly, the discussion outside Quebec focused more on the practical question of the attainability of economic association with the rest of Canada, than on the constitutional question of the right of Quebec to attain sovereignty, if such turned out to be the wish of its people.

The legitimacy of this kind of exercise in attempted unilateralism was accepted by the Pepin-Robarts Report, with some qualifications, and by various leading politicians. There was an almost overwhelming assumption that any resort to force in defiance of the clearly expressed wishes of the Quebec electorate, and in defense of the existing constitutional order, was unthinkable. This was a testament not only to the civility and tolerance of the Canadian political tradition, but also to the success of the Quebec government in having its attempted unilateralism viewed as legitimate. After the referendum defeat, the Quebec government, in the 1980 intergovernmental constitutional discussions, tried, without success, to have a right of self-determination written into the revised constitution to provide sanction for future unilateralism. Although glimmerings of separatism are not entirely absent outside of Quebec, by and large the other nine provinces lack the will and the broad public support to play the brinksmanship politics undertaken by the Parti Québécois. Their search for positional advantage, accordingly, eschews unilateralism, occurs within the framework of executive federalism, and presupposes the continuation of the federal regime.

Constitutional Positions: An Overview

The following section provides a general overview of the major tendencies in provincialist versions of federalism. Next are two sections which examine the constitutional goals of British Columbia and Alberta, two of the most clearly expressed provincial versions of positional advantage sought in a revised constitution. A subsequent section discusses the competing versions of positional advantage of the main political contenders in Quebec, the sovereignty-association of the PQ outside the federal system, and the Ryan Liberal position of a strengthened Quebec in a revamped federal system. The material on Quebec is followed by a section which deals with the federal attempt to exploit its unilateral powers by imposing an amending formula which will greatly enhance its future capacity to achieve desirable constitutional change. These examples leave little doubt of the pervasive impact of self-interest on the determination of government objectives for constitutional change. Admittedly, the governments selected for study are those in which self-interest is most patently evident. Possibly, a detailed analysis of the conduct and goals of the remaining governments, which is precluded here by space limitations, would fundamentally undermine the overriding hypothesis of this paper. My own expectation, based on some examination, is that the general picture, while perhaps modified in detail, would survive the addition of more cases.

Provincialist Versions of Federalism

Provincialist versions of federalism reflect the diverse interests of ten provinces, and the more detached analyses of academics and publicists in both language communities. Accordingly, no single provincialist version has universal support. In fact, much of the federal government's bargaining strength in constitutional matters derives from interprovincial differences and disagreements on the desirable direction of constitutional change. Nevertheless, as legal entities the provinces share many things in common, and they confront the same federal government at the bargaining table. Further, they are all affected by the same prevailing intellectual and political trends in thinking about federalism, and they interact intimately with each other. Accordingly, there are various recurrent themes which characterize contemporary provincialist thought.

Perhaps the most powerful tendency is the widely asserted need to erode or restrict the central government role in provincial affairs. In 1867 the central government was given a battery of weapons to inject

a national presence and outlook into provincial arenas through disallowance, reservation, and declaratory power, and other instruments
of intervention. Contemporary provincialist thought completely re-
pudiates the major premise of 1867 that the flow of intergovernmental influence in the federal system should spring from a central government capacity to make provincial governments more amenable to
Ottawa's leadership. Thus there is general agreement that many of
the key centralizing aspects of the 1867 settlement, which induced
K. C. Wheare to call Canada a quasi-federal system, are anachro-
nisms. The elimination of disallowance and reservation, and in some
proposals the transference from Ottawa to the provinces of the power
to appoint Lieutenant Governors, are advocated as desirable and necessary responses to the growth of the provinces to maturity. A measure of constitutionally guaranteed provincial control over the federal
declaratory power, the emergency power, and the spending power
has also been standard in provincial proposals for the federalism of
the future. This desire to reduce federal government "interference"
in provincial affairs is accompanied by a hostility to the concept of
"levels of government," with its unacceptable assumption, capable of
justifying Ottawa's paternalism, that there are senior and junior levels. To the provinces all governments are now senior governments,
with the exception of local governments firmly kept under direct provincial control.

As the second century of Confederation unfolds, numerous provincialist analyses of our constitutional ailments make clear that yesterday's leader and the led are to change places. Accordingly, the federal
role in provincial affairs is to be replaced by a provincial role in federal affairs. The guiding assumption here is that the wielding of national power must be tempered by provincial realities, as defined by
provincial governments—a reversal of the historic assumption that
the wielding of provincial power must be tempered by national realities, as defined by Ottawa. "National policy making," in the words of
the British Columbia brief to the Special Senate Committee on the
Constitution, "ought not to be the private preserve of the national
government."[4] From this perspective, the task of constitution-making
is defined as accommodating and placating provincial governments

4. Rafe Mair, Chairman, British Columbia Cabinet Committee on Confederation, in *Proceedings of the Special Senate Committee on the Constitution* (September 28, 1978), 9:13.

and the territorial diversities they represent by giving those governments an increased impact and influence on central government decision making.

Alternatively, constitutional reform should proceed by allocating increased jurisdiction to the provinces, and relatively diminishing the role of Ottawa in the federal system. Provincialist thought dances back and forth between these contrasting ways of restructuring the federal system, sometimes as in the Ryan proposals demanding significant movement in both directions at once. While these two orientations—more power to the provincial governments at home or an enhanced provincial government role at Ottawa—differ profoundly in their overall vision of federalism, they are united by the common assumption that the roles and responsibilities of provincial governments must grow, and federal powers must be reduced or controlled.

These provincial approaches to constitutional reform are justified not only by the growing competence and maturity of provincial governments, but by a supporting definition of Canada as composed of limited identities and provincial communities. Thus, the Pepin-Robarts Report noted the various ways in which regionalism could be defined, but quickly focused on the provinces and the northern territories as "the basic building blocks of Canadian society and the logical units on which to focus a discussion of Canadian regionalism," because "provincial political institutions are the primary frameworks through which regional populations can organize and express themselves, and their existence serves in turn to develop the social networks and interests based on them, thus reinforcing the provincial focus of regionalism."[5] This line of analysis sometimes slides into an implicit denial that Canada is more than the sum of its parts. The stress of Pepin-Robarts on duality and regionalism, coupled with its less than positive references to Canadianism or to the central government, viewed by many citizens as "a remote, shambling bureaucracy that exacts tribute from its subjects and gives little in return,"[6] is symptomatic of this tendency to downgrade the federal government and the Canadian community in province-centered views of Canadian federalism.

5. The Task Force on Canadian Unity, *A Future Together: Observations and Recommendations* (Ottawa: Minister of Supply and Services, 1979), pp. 26–27.
6. Ibid., p. 16.

The following sections, dealing with the constitutional proposals of British Columbia, Alberta, the Parti Québécois government of Quebec, and the Quebec Liberal party will illustrate more fully several specific and different orientations to constitutional change.

The Search for Positional Advantage

British Columbia.[7] The constitutional goals of British Columbia cogently illustrate how governments have responded to the possibilities of major constitutional change by attempting to enhance their strategic leverage in a future constitution. Quebec, the precipitant of the search for constitutional renewal, receives negligible attention in a package of constitutional proposals directed to British Columbia interests.

Since the election of Bill Bennett's Social Credit government in 1975, the provincial cabinet has worked diligently to develop a coherent position on constitutional change far surpassing in quality and scope the work of its predecessors. To a considerable extent this reflects the desire of the incumbent government to foster an image of British Columbia as a serious, hard-working performer on the national scene, in marked contrast both to the Barrett NDP government it succeeded and the first Social Credit government of W. A. C. Bennett from 1952–72.

The British Columbia proposals are couched in terms of Canadianism and of a desire to improve the functioning of the federal system, including specific recommendations to improve intergovernmental relations. They proceed from an analysis that the major weakness of the existing system is the insensitivity of Ottawa to the regions of the country, an insensitivity produced by inappropriate institutions. Accordingly, British Columbia's recommendations focus more on transforming the institutions of the central government to generate a greater sensitivity to provincial concerns than on a devolution of more jurisdictional authority to the provinces.[8] In that sense

7. Province of British Columbia, *British Columbia's Constitutional Proposals, Presented to the First Ministers' Conference on the Constitution, October, 1978* (Victoria, B.C.: Queen's Printer, 1978).

8. The government's position paper on "The Distribution of Legislative Powers" goes little

they can be viewed as a salvage operation to prevent the erosion of Ottawa's power, which is to be saved by transforming the nature of its exercise. The specifics of the proposals, presented in nine booklets published in 1978, however, make it clear that not only will all provincial governments have new and impressive responsibilities in Ottawa, but the relative position of British Columbia compared to other provinces is to be significantly enhanced.

Official and unofficial constitutional analysis in Quebec has long stressed a dualist, two-nation definition of Canada, in an obvious attempt to improve the relative status of Quebec. In the same way, Social Credit cabinet members in recent years have assiduously advocated a five-region Canada, with the government of British Columbia, as the spokesman for the new fifth region, elevated from the status of one province in ten to one region in five. The claim for recognition as a fifth region is based on the economic and ethnic distinctiveness of the province from the three Prairie provinces, its mountainous terrain and maritime orientation, and on the rapid population growth which has made it the third largest province in Canada. Constitutionally, the claim is represented as a natural development of the precedent when the fourth Western region was created for Senate representation in 1915, with representation equal to that of each of the three original regions. Recognition of British Columbia's fifth region status is thus presented not as a departure, but as building on existing precedents.

Although the pursuit of status is not irrelevant to the British Columbia government, its primary objective is to increase the influence of British Columbia on a variety of fronts. The general claim for recognition as a fifth region is integrated with the specific claim that all regions should be assured of representation on the Supreme Court, thus precluding the recurrence of situations in which for long periods British Columbia has been without a member on the court. While such a judicial appointment is not to be viewed as a representative or delegate of the province or its government, it is clearly hoped and assumed that a justice from British Columbia would help assure a sensitivity to the concerns of the province, and a sympathetic understanding of its idiosyncracies in Supreme Court decision making.

---

beyond the provision of a preliminary taxonomy. Mention is made of a forthcoming major study of the division of powers, but this has not yet appeared.

Under the proposed British Columbia amendment formula, recognition as a fifth region also entails the giving of a veto to the province over constitutional amendments. This would extricate the province from the no longer acceptable Victoria formula of 1971, which the first Social Credit government had supported, and by which the province, as one of four provinces in a Western region, could have had amendments passed against its wishes. The British Columbia amendment veto is based not on a principled defense of provincial government sovereignty, which would have given a veto to all provinces, but on the attempted replacement of a four-region Canada by a five-region Canada, three of which are provinces. By getting itself classified as a region, British Columbia, along with Ontario and Quebec, would receive a veto. By grouping seven other provinces in two regions—Western and Atlantic—British Columbia would benefit from the flexibility of an amendment procedure built on the insecurity of seven other governments.[9]

The centerpiece of the British Columbia proposals, however, is not the securing of a permanent member of the Supreme Court, or a permanent veto on amendments affecting provincial government powers and rights, but a revised second chamber, with equal membership from each of the five regions, to represent provincial government concerns at the center. The proposed British Columbia entitlement of one-fifth of the Senate members is to be appointed by the provincial government. Although this new second chamber is to continue to perform the traditional review functions of the existing Senate with respect to legislation passing the House of Commons, its major function from the provincial government perspective is to be a ratifying or vetoing body with respect to certain federal initiatives which significantly impinge on provincial jurisdiction—federal laws to be administered by the provinces, the declaratory power under 92(10)(c), and the use of the federal spending power in areas of provincial jurisdiction. The new body would also have the power to approve or withhold its approval of appointments to the Supreme Court and to certain key federal boards, agencies, and commissions whose functions

9. The preferred forum for aggregating regional votes on constitutional amendments was the reformed Senate proposed by British Columbia. This, however, was incidental rather than essential to the amendment formula. In the absence of the appropriate Senate reform, approval or rejection of amendments would be the task of provincial legislatures.

are deemed to be of special significance to the provinces. For these responsibilities the provincial government appointments are to be instructed delegates. The leading member of each provincial delegation, a provincial cabinet minister, would cast a bloc vote reflecting provincial government interests. In performing the traditional function of legislative review the members would be free agents, endowed only with a suspensive veto.

Behind the drive for a particular kind of Senate reform there is a concerted attempt to overcome what the government views as fundamental deficiencies in British Columbia representation in Ottawa. The existing distribution of Senate seats is clearly unacceptable, as British Columbia with six senators is outnumbered by Nova Scotia and New Brunswick with ten senators each, and much smaller populations. There is little redress available in the House of Commons where representation by population ensures that for the foreseeable future the province cannot play more than a supporting role to the big battalions from Ontario and Quebec. From the vantage point of Victoria, the British Columbia weakness in Ottawa is compounded by the fact that since 1952 the provincial government has been controlled by Social Credit and the NDP, both of which are weak national parties likely to influence federal policies only in times of coalition or minority governments. Isolation from national power in Ottawa is especially pronounced for Social Credit, which has not elected a federal member from the province since 1965. From the perspective of the British Columbia Social Credit government the political environment at Ottawa, and particularly the partisan makeup of the MPs and cabinet ministers from the province, has not been such as to induce a feeling of powerful friends at court in the national capital. The strategy to overcome these representational deficiencies is relatively straightforward. Give the Senate more power, particularly in areas of special importance to the provinces; increase British Columbia representation in the Senate from 6 in 102 to 12 in 60, proportionately, a more than threefold increase; place the appointing power in the hands of provincial governments; and turn the appointees into instructed delegates on a predefined list of federal policy areas of special concern to the provinces.

The achievement of these objectives, even without the significant increase in provincial jurisdiction in the fields of fisheries, offshore resources, and communications sought by the province in the 1980 constitutional talks, would dramatically transform Canadian federalism to the advantage of British Columbia. Dressed in its new regional garments British Columbia would be one of only three provinces with an amendment veto, and with a constitutional requirement of a Supreme Court judge, leaving seven other provinces behind as second-class provinces in the Atlantic region and in the truncated Western region. As a region British Columbia clearly would become a first-class province. Further, it would have the same representation in a more powerful Senate as Ontario with more than three times the population of British Columbia, and as Quebec with more than twice the province's population.

Although there would be undoubted and striking benefits to British Columbia in constitutional recognition of its claims, the provincial government has been engaged in a very high-risk strategy. Its chances of success depend on the willingness of the federal government to accede to a decisive new role for provincial governments at the center, within Parliament itself, and on the willingness of the three other provinces in the Western region to see British Columbia singled out for preferential treatment. This is a proposition especially galling to Alberta with a population only slightly less than British Columbia and some possibility of passing its western neighbor in the not too distant future.

More generally, although the increase in the powers of the Senate and the proposed changes in its membership would increase the influence in Ottawa of what has come to be called "outer Canada" at the expense of central Canada, British Columbia would be the major provincial beneficiary of the change. Assuming equal provincial representation in a new Western region, the provinces of Alberta, Saskatchewan, and Manitoba would experience an infinitesimal increase in their membership share of a revised Senate; Quebec and Ontario would drop from slightly under one-quarter to one-fifth; and the four Atlantic provinces would experience a major reduction of almost one-third of their entitlement, from just under 30 percent to one-fifth of Senate members. The more than threefold increase in British Columbia membership would be at the expense of Ontario, Quebec, and the four Atlantic provinces, while the general increase in provincial government power at the center, from which all provincial governments would benefit, would be at the expense of the central government.

There are other difficulties in the British Columbia position. In a sense the provincial government played its cards too early. It presented an integrated, comprehensive position on constitutional reform with much fanfare and publicity in the autumn of 1978, but made few changes in its basic position in the next two years. Further, although intellectually there is a certain attractiveness in the coherence of the British Columbia position in which so much revolves around the twin and related goals of Senate reform and regional recognition, the very tightness of the constitutional package created certain problems. As nearly everything was related to everything else, it inhibited bargaining by the government; and so deeply were provincial spokesmen wedded to the position they had so laboriously hammered out, and the principles they had publicly espoused, that the development of a fallback position in the intensive bargaining culminating in the First Ministers' Conference of September 1980 was somewhat hampered. Clarity, consistency, and publicity in the pursuit of constitutional objectives are not necessarily bargaining assets.

Alberta. A Canadian federal system built to British Columbia specifications, with its significantly expanded role for provincial governments on the national stage, would be a major departure from the status quo. In marked contrast to the outward-looking expansiveness of the British Columbia proposals, the defensive and inward-looking Alberta position is based on a very different version of self-interest.[10] Its aim is to protect the government and the people of the province from changes they oppose, not to increase the influence of the province on the national scene. Accordingly, the very core of the British Columbia position, a restructured Senate appointed by provincial governments, is strongly opposed by the Alberta government, which much prefers the direct confrontation between elected heads of government at First Ministers' Conferences.[11] The only element of intrastate

10. Government of Alberta, *Harmony in Diversity: A New Federalism for Canada* (Edmonton: 1978).
11. This was the official Alberta position up to and including the September 1980 First Minis-

federalism[12] advocated is the peripheral demand that 40 percent of the members of the designated national boards and agencies, such as the National Energy Board and the Canadian Wheat Board, should be appointed by provincial governments, thus making their operation more sensitive to provincial perspectives.

Alberta is not indifferent to an expansion of provincial jurisdiction. In 1978 Premier Lougheed proudly asserted that his province had "presented the strongest proposition for the strengthening of provincial governments in Canada," with proposals which "include an over-all shift of responsibility to the governments that can do the best for the people: the provincial governments."[13] Specifically, the 1978 position paper *Harmony in Diversity* recommended giving the provinces access to indirect taxes with the exception of customs and import duties, that communications and transportation be included as concurrent powers, and that seacoast and inland fisheries and culture be concurrent powers with provincial paramountcy. In addition, jurisdiction over offshore minerals should be given to the provinces, and the established provincial role in certain areas of international relations should be constitutionally confirmed. In their cumulative effect, these proposed changes, all of which favored the provinces, are not trivial. Nevertheless, they are clearly secondary to the major thrust of the Alberta proposals, to render impossible any diminution of the rights, proprietary interests, or jurisdiction of the province without the specific consent of its government.

The Alberta position is based on the proposition that provincial ownership of resources is "one of the fundamental cornerstones of Confederation," "a fundamental principle of Confederation, because if there is a cutting away of that basic concept of provincial ownership

---

ters' Conference. Premier Lougheed subsequently reconsidered the Alberta position and is now in favor of "some national institution to bring into focus our various regional interests." "Excerpts of Premier Lougheed's Address to the Canada West Foundation Conference, Banff, Alberta, Saturday, November 29, 1980" (mimeo.), p. 7.

12. The concept of intrastate federalism was first introduced into Canadian constitutional thinking by Donald Smiley in his article, "The Structural Problem of Canadian Federalism," *Canadian Public Administration* 14 (Fall 1971). It refers to the accommodation of regional diversities within the institutions of the central government, and is contrasted, as an ideal type, with interstate federalism in which regional diversities find their outlet primarily or exclusively through provincial or state governments.

13. *Alberta Hansard*, November 3, 1978, pp. 1702, 1705.

of resources, we really do violence to the whole fabric of this federation."[14] Thus the first specific recommendation of the Alberta government is to strengthen those sections of the B.N.A. Act protecting provincial ownership and control of natural resources; and the second recommends clarification of the constitution to reaffirm provincial authority to tax and collect royalties from the sale and management of natural resources.

Given this focus of concern and the desire for maximum security of possession, the Victoria Charter amending formula, which was supported by the Social Credit predecessors of the Lougheed Conservative regime, is unequivocally rejected. The government's position on an amending formula is based not on a desirable flexibility so that Alberta could obtain future amendments to its liking, but on a single-minded search for security to prevent the imposition of amendments that it opposes. Hence the opposition to the Victoria Charter which, by reducing Alberta to one of four provinces in the Western region, raised the possibility of a constitutional amendment being passed against Alberta's wishes. Whereas British Columbia sought to extricate itself from the Western region by becoming its own region, and then advocating regional equality, such a strategy is unavailable to Alberta with its smaller population, and with far from obvious claims to distinctiveness from its prairie neighbors. To Alberta, the regional equality of either the Victoria Charter or of the British Columbia proposals is simply a selfish device of the large provinces, posing as regions, to produce provincial inequality. Alberta, therefore, seeks to replace regional equality with provincial equality as the base point for an amendment formula.

The proposed Alberta amending formula, as summarized by the Alberta Minister of Federal and Intergovernmental Affairs, is based on

the fundamental principle that all provinces have equal constitutional status. Accordingly, it is designed to give all provinces an equal say in amendments and to ensure that any amendment affecting existing rights, proprietary interests and jurisdiction of a province may not be imposed on any province opposed to that particular amendment . . . . no one province has a veto un-

14. Peter Lougheed, "Notes for Opening Statement First Ministers' Conference on Energy, Ottawa—November 12, 1979" (mimeo.), p. 7; Lou Hyndman, *Alberta Hansard*, October 25, 1978, p. 1524.

der this formula. There are no first and second-class provinces under the Alberta formula. Only the Parliament of Canada has a veto.[15]

The specter of unanimity with its consequent rigidity, which is raised by the principle of provincial equality, is neatly avoided by a relatively flexible amending formula—the support of the federal government and the legislative assemblies of two-thirds of the provinces with more than 50 percent of the population. The dangers of flexibility are then sidestepped by an ingenious provision allowing up to three provinces to opt out if the proposed amendment affects (*a*) the powers of the legislature of a province to make laws, (*b*) the rights or privileges granted or secured by the constitution of Canada to the legislature or the government of a province, (*c*) the assets or property of a province, or (*d*) the natural resources of a province.[16]

The battery of measures aiming at provincial protection also includes provisos for the repeal of the federal government powers of disallowance and reservation, the limitation of the federal emergency power to prevent federal encroachment on provincial jurisdiction, and the placing of constitutional limitations on the federal spending power. Of particular importance in the present climate of federal-provincial tension and controversy over energy and resources is the proposition that the federal declaratory power, to declare a work within provincial borders to be for the general advantage of Canada or of two or more provinces, could only be applied with the consent of the affected province in which the work is situated. This requirement would transform a centralizing instrumentality of the constitution into an innocuous mechanism of cooperative federalism. The protection against the use of the declaratory power given to Ontario and Quebec by their votes in the House of Commons is to be achieved for Alberta by constitutional guarantees. Alberta seeks to replace the unequal distribution of protection deriving from the inequalities of political power with an equality of protection grounded in the constitution. The devising of ground rules to control power, natural to a minority, runs like a thread through the Alberta constitutional package.

15. Dick Johnston, Minister of Federal and Intergovernmental Affairs, Alberta, public letter to all members of the House of Commons and senators, December 4, 1980.
16. "Alberta Proposal: Amending Formula for the Canadian Constitution Presented by Premier Lougheed to the First Ministers' Conference on the Constitution, February 5, 1979, Ottawa" (mimeo).

The goal of eliminating or minimizing threats to the security of the province in its possession of jurisdiction and resources also requires a fundamental transformation of the Supreme Court. From the Alberta perspective the Supreme Court, domiciled in Ottawa, with federally appointed members, and not entrenched in the constitution, displays an unacceptable centralizing bias in its constitutional decisions. Lougheed is not happy with having "constitutional political matters resolved by a centralist court," and he views "the Laskin court [as] out of touch with the realities of Canadian aspirations in the regions."[17] The solution is the creation of a separate seven-member constitutional court, representative of the diversities of the country, whose members in particular cases would be randomly drawn from a panel of superior court judges of forty to fifty members. Panel members are to be selected by a complicated process of provincial nomination and federal selection.

The purpose of this particular recommendation, viewed as crucial by the Alberta government, is to ensure that the unavoidable element of discretion in constitutional adjudication has a major provincial component. This provincial orientation would result from the provincial role in the determination of the membership of the constitutional panel, and from the fact that the judges would continue to reside in the various provincial communities rather than in the "hothouse atmosphere" of Ottawa,[18] where the environment allegedly conditions judges against provincial interests. A related provincializing tendency was the expectation that about half of the cases would be heard outside Ottawa. It would be almost impossible for such a court either to play a leadership role in constitutional change, or to develop a coherent, enduring policy orientation to its judicial task. Little judicial specialization would be developed as the judges who heard a particular case were to be ineligible for reselection until all other panel members had heard a constitutional case. Given the Alberta suspicion of judicial power these shortcomings are considered advantageous. The proposals for judicial reform fitted neatly and coherently into the overall Alberta pursuit of the maximum security and protection compatible with continued membership in the federal system.

17. "Excerpts from the Opening Remarks by Premier Lougheed to the Canadian Institute of Chartered Accountants—September 28, 1978" (mimeo.), p. 7.
18. Lou Hyndman, *Alberta Hansard*, Oct. 25, 1978, p. 1524.

However the novelty of the proposals precluded their serious consideration in subsequent constitutional discussions.

To a limited extent the overall Alberta position is based on the traditional grass-roots argument that local control produces local sensitivity. A philosophical opposition to centralization is supported by an interpretation of the contemporary constitutional and political malaise as a product of overcentralization, which generates alienation and frustration on the peripheries as an inevitable reaction. More particularly, however, the constitutional search for fortress Alberta is a reaction to a hostile political environment in which political power at the national level is concentrated in Ontario and Quebec. In Lougheed's analysis, the federal government attitude to Alberta, particularly under the Liberals, is conditioned by the fact that

they have no seats to lose . . . secondly, they realize that in Ottawa they have to cater to Ontario or Quebec—in practical terms—to stay in office. However, this select group cannot accept that other provincial governments in other parts of Canada could be allowed to become moderately independent and not subservient to them for their discretionary grants. So—Alberta, in the interests of their vision of Canada—this upstart province—cannot be allowed to get into that position. A position that would perhaps spread to Newfoundland and others. The only answer from their point of view is to club us into submission.[19]

The search for new ground rules for Confederation, and for iron-clad protection, is the Alberta government's response to its numerical weakness when faced with the political power of central Canada. The intergovernmental energy battles of the last decade have produced a profound sense of insecurity and persecution in the provincial government which inevitably manifests itself in the concurrent search for constitutional renewal. The provincial government nurses a deep sense of grievance that its extensive contributions to the Canadian economy through less-than-market prices for oil and gas are insufficiently appreciated. Provincial efforts to obtain a price closer to the world price have been thwarted by a central government that Alberta considers to be dominated by the shortsighted interests of consumers, particularly in Ontario, to the long-run detriment of energy self-sufficiency.

19. "Excerpts of Premier Lougheed's Speech to the Edmonton Chamber of Commerce—Edmonton—November 19, 1980" (mimeo.), p. 6.

Alberta's feelings of impotence and isolation are compounded by political tendencies in the Western region itself. Historically, all of the remaining Western provinces have been governed by the NDP. The party currently holds power in Saskatchewan and Manitoba and is an important political force in British Columbia. The NDP's ideology is anathema from Lougheed's free enterprise perspective, and the possibility of NDP governments in all of the other Western provinces strengthens Alberta opposition to the amending criteria of the Victoria Charter. These criteria, based on regions, are essentially repeated in the federal constitutional package for Westminister. If Alberta could not extricate itself from regional amending criteria, the oil sands and resources of the province could then be removed from Alberta's jurisdiction, despite its opposition, at the behest of the future NDP governments of the region, under the influence of a party philosophy which Lougheed describes as asserting "that the central government must be dominant in Canada in order to assure the most effective state control."[20] Even the neighbors cannot be trusted.

The feelings of insecurity and persecution at the base of Lougheed's constitutional prescriptions cannot be divorced from the political history of the province and the traditions and memories built on that history. Historically, only in the six years from 1905 to 1911, and in the brief interlude of Joe Clark's Conservative government, has the provincial government been of the same party as the power holders in Ottawa. For half a century, from 1921 to 1971, the province was governed by the United Farmers of Alberta and Social Credit, parties with only a weak presence on the national scene. Further, the political movements behind these governments reflected an alienation from, and a challenge to, what was viewed as an imperialistic and intertwined economic and political establishment in central Canada. In the early years of Social Credit, the courts, the federally appointed lieutenant governor, and the unilateral federal disallowance power were successfully employed on behalf of that establishment to thwart the reform objectives of Aberhart. In addition, Alberta, along with the two other Prairie provinces, was deprived of control of its own natural resources until 1930. The resources were kept in federal

20. Peter Lougheed, "Speech on Motion Concerning Patriation of Canadian Constitution," Province of Alberta, 18th Legislature, Second Session, Nov. 1, 1976 (reprint), p. 6. See also Premier Lougheed, *Alberta Hansard*, Nov. 3, 1978, pp. 1702–5.

hands for, in a disturbingly evocative phrase, "the purposes of the Dominion." The Natural Resources Transfer Agreement of 1930, which transferred the resources of Alberta, became a symbol of a hard-won equality of status, now once again challenged half a century later by federal policies which threaten provincial resource control.

Given these historical and contemporary indications of central government and majoritarian insensitivity, constitutional change is viewed by the Alberta government as an opportunity to blunt the weapons of the enemy, and to strengthen constitutional bulwarks against the ever-present threat of usurpation of the rightful heritage of Albertans. The protection which a minority cannot find in numerical strength and by the free exercise of its political power is to be rooted in constitutional guarantees. The only answer is a strong, completely secure province, immune from the wiles of the federal foe. In the words of Lougheed:

The only way that there can be a fair deal for the citizens of the outlying parts of Canada is for the elected provincial governments of these parts to be sufficiently strong to offset the political power in the House of Commons of the populated centres. That strength can only flow from the provinces' jurisdiction over the management of their own economic destinies and the development of the natural resources owned by the provinces.[21]

Quebec. The Quebec search for positional advantage is not like the others. It is not simply a response to the placing of constitutional issues on the federal-provincial agenda by someone else. It is based on a profound historic sense of the linguistic and cultural distinctiveness of a minority deeply concerned for its own future in an English-speaking North America. What is new in Quebec is not the obsession with constitutional matters, but the means and ends of collective action. Until about 1960 the goal was a fortress Quebec with its traditional values protected from outside incursions by the bastion of provincial autonomy. This made Quebec a staunch defender of federalism. Its chief complaint was the lack of respect that system received in English Canada. However, in the last two decades the original Confederation settlement has lost its attractiveness. It is no longer seen as an adequate vehicle for the advancement and nourishment of Quebec society.

21. Opening statement by the Honorable Peter Lougheed, Federal-Provincial Conference of First Ministers, Ottawa, Oct. 30–Nov. 1, 1978, p. 5.

With the defeat of the Bourassa Liberals in 1976 the Parti Québé-cois option of sovereignty-association temporarily monopolized the provincial debate on Quebec's future.[22] As the Liberals regrouped in 1978 under their new leader, Claude Ryan, an explicit federalist alter-native emerged.[23] Both the PQ and Liberal positions were based on the premise that a distinctive French society existed in Quebec—a society which was inadequately served by available constitutional ar-rangements. Both sought to transform the constitutional and institu-tional provisions governing relations between Quebecers and other Canadians to the advantage of the former. Both parties asserted the right of Quebec to self-determination.[24] Both saw a role for the people via referenda in the constitutional renewal process.[25]

Only in Quebec, at least until the 1980 PQ referendum defeat, has the provincial citizenry faced a fundamental constitutional choice generated by contenders for provincial government power. Some-what paradoxically, neither of the Quebec options has reached the federal-provincial bargaining table, the PQ sovereignty-association position because of the referendum defeat, and the Ryan option be-cause the Liberals remain in opposition, and much of the Ryan pack-age is unattractive to the federal Liberals.

The Parti Québécois' repudiation of Canadian federalism and em-brace of sovereignty-association rests on a series of related and linked propositions which constantly recur in Péquiste advocacy:

1. Canada is composed of two distinct nations concealed "behind the fiction of ten provinces,"[26]
2. Political power in ethnically/nationally divided states is an instru-

22. See Gouvernement du Québec, *Québec-Canada: A New Deal* (Québec:Éditeur Officiel, 1979) for the official prereferendum position of the government. Maurice Lamontagne's *The Double Deal* (Montreal: Optimum Publishing Co, 1980) is a powerful critique by a prominent French Canadian federalist and Liberal senator.

23. The Liberal position was developed in two documents, Quebec Liberal Party, *Choose Québec and Canada* (Montreal, 1979), and the Constitutional Committee of the Quebec Liberal Party, *A New Canadian Federation* (Montréal, 1980). For an insightful comparison of the constitu-tional proposals of the Lévesque government and the Ryan Liberal party see Gerard Bergeron, "Lecture du Livre Blanc et du Livre Beige Selon une Perspective 'Super-Fédéraliste'," *Canadian Public Policy* (Summer 1980).

24. Quebec Liberal Party, *A New Canadian Federation*, p. 10.

25. However, the referendum idea was more tentative for the Liberals and less central to the constitution-making process than was the case for the Parti Québécois. For the Liberals see *A New Canadian Federation*, p. 133.

26. "An Address Given by Mr. René Lévesque, Prime Minister of Quebec, before the Mem-bers of the Assemblée Nationale, 'We are Quebeckers,'" (Paris, November 2, 1977), p. 13.

IV. Crises

ment of the ethnic majority, of English Canada in the Canadian case. This is true both at the central government level, and even more emphatically at the provincial level. The rapid decline of French language and culture outside Quebec and of the Quebec share of the total Canadian population, predicted by demographic projections, will further weaken French-Canadian influence in Ottawa and in the English provinces. Based on present trends Quebec will have less than one-quarter of House of Commons seats by the end of the century.

3. The only government directly and wholeheartedly responsive to francophone interests is the Quebec provincial government which, in Lévesque's negative description, uses "the powers that the federal system deigns to grant us."[27]

4. English Canadians are inveterate centralists. Their every success aggravates the minority status of Québécois by diminishing the jurisdictional importance of the only government French Canadians control. There is no possibility of a major devolution of power to the provinces. It is striking that the government white paper, *Québec-Canada: A New Deal*, systematically ignores or denies the regionalism of English Canada which so impressed the Task Force on Canadian Unity. Equally striking is the Péquiste assessment of the original Confederation settlement as essentially centralist, and their explicit denial that Confederation was a pact. The political necessity of blackening the origin and development of Canadian federalism leads the PQ to accept the hitherto politically odious Donald Creighton centralist interpretation of Confederation, and consequently to repudiate the hitherto standard French-Canadian interpretation, most fully elaborated in the Tremblay Report.

5. In the modern world the goal of a flourishing national culture requires a powerful state as a means, a state whose citizenry is not divided by a competing allegiance to a government controlled by others.

Three conclusions logically follow from the above propositions:

1. The English-speaking minority in Quebec, about one-fifth of the population, is anomalous. The political logic of ethnic self-interest,

27. Ibid., p. 11.

which explains the insensitivity of English Canada at Ottawa, must be equally expected to dictate an insensitivity by the francophone Quebec government to ethnic, linguistic minorities within Quebec. Parti Québécois literature, not least *Québec-Canada: A New Deal*, abundantly illustrates the point. As a Quebec Liberal party pamphlet puts it, not unfairly: "the White Paper does not hesitate to distort reality by referring to the people of Quebec as though they were composed solely of Francophones."[28] The overwhelming appeal of this document of political mobilization is directed to the francophone majority. Those who are asked to seize the future are the descendants of the noble 60,000 left behind after the skirmish between Wolfe and Montcalm. The concept of Québécois, which theoretically applies to all Quebecers, is, in this emotional appeal to found a new state, restricted with rare exceptions to the ethnic-linguistic majority. This is not accidental. It logically follows from an analysis which posits nation and ethnicity as the prime motive forces of political action.

2. The concept of a French Canada extending beyond Quebec is a snare and a delusion. The interests and future evolution of francophones inside and outside Quebec must diverge. The former have a government, a potential independent state, at their disposal. The latter, lacking this necessary support, have no long-run hope.

3. Since power in Ottawa, based on the self-interest of the ethnic-linguistic majority, must be wielded on behalf of English Canada, it is in reality unavailable to French-Canadian Quebecers. Accordingly, the only way to make all government power available to the francophone majority in Quebec is to strip Ottawa of jurisdiction over Quebec and transform the province into a sovereign state. Or, to reverse the argument: "The fact that it is impossible, in the present federal framework, for Québec to become a nation, constitutes the very basis of the Canada-Québec political problem."[29]

In the real world of political calculation the search for majority support in a referendum required the Parti Québécois to cater to the

28. Quebec Liberal Party, *The White Paper on Sovereignty-Association: A House of Cards* (Montreal: n.d.), p. 5.
29. *Québec-Canada: A New Deal*, p. 42.

conservatism of the Quebec electorate. Thus, in the referendum campaign sovereignty was indissolubly linked with the idea of an economic association with Canada. In a further concession to the perceived unwillingness of the population to take risks for purely nationalist goals, the referendum question reassuringly committed the government to another referendum for approval or rejection of whatever change in political status resulted from negotiations.

The institutional infrastructure of the proposed Quebec-Canada association was given only a rudimentary description in *Québec-Canada: A New Deal*, the official White Paper on constitutional goals. In a document of 109 pages only four pages are devoted to a cursory, almost casual, description of the four major bodies proposed to oversee the monetary union.[30] The bulk of the remainder of the White Paper, a political document directed more at the Quebec electorate than to the proposed partners in association, is devoted to consciousness raising.

The four major bodies described below were to be the instruments of a monetary union, "defined as the area formed by sovereign states within which goods, people, and capital flow freely, this zone on the one hand being linked to [the] rest of the world by a single trade and tariff policy and, on the other hand, possessing a single currency and hence the same monetary policy."[31] A Community Council, a commission of experts, a Court of Justice, and a monetary authority were to be established by a Treaty of Community Association, which would have international status, and would "bind the parties in a manner and for a term to be determined."[32] The Community Council made up of ministers from Quebec and Canada, acting on instructions, and with a rotating chairmanship, would have "decision-making powers on matters entrusted to it by the treaty of association, and decisions pertaining to fundamental issues will require the agreement of both Quebec and Canada."[33] A commission of experts, drawn from the two countries, would act as a general secretariat of the community, with special responsibility for negotiating international agreements pertaining to customs and trade, which "will then be approved and

30. Ibid., pp. 61–64.
31. Ibid., p. 53.
32. Ibid., p. 57.
33. Ibid., p. 62.

signed by the council of the community."[34] A Court of Justice, with
equal numbers of judges from the two states, and a chairman jointly
chosen would have "exclusive jurisdiction over the interpretation and
implementation of the treaty of association; its decisions will be final
and binding to both parties."[35] A monetary authority, with seats allocated to each party on the board of directors "proportional to the relative size of each economy,"[36] and with a governor alternately selected
by each government, would control the creation of money, exchange
rate policies, and would have certain powers over the two central
banks of the two new states and the chartered banks. Conflicts over
monetary or exchange policy would be resolved by the community
council.

The core of the official PQ position was an unequivocal increase in
the influence of the government of Quebec over its own population,
and in its relations with the governments of the Canada it had left.
Sovereignty-association would have exalted the Québécois identity at
the expense of the Canadian identity. The latter would have been reduced to a historical memory only marginally sustained by the monetary union. Of special importance to the Quebec government, no
competing government would have had direct contact with the Quebec people. Loyalty conflicts born of divided jurisdiction would be
ended.

The principle of equality behind the drive to independence
was also to pervade the institutional infrastructure of the proposed
Quebec-Canada arrangements. The Community Council, and by implication the commission of experts which served it as a secretariat,
were to be governed by a double veto and no deadlock-breaking
mechanism. Although the composition of the board of directors of the
monetary authority was tempered by the concession to proportionality, the most important executive officer, the governor, was to be selected by each government in alternation. As noted, disputes in the
monetary authority would go to the community council with its double veto, based on the principle of equality. The overall effect of the
sovereignty-association proposals would have given the government
of Quebec no rival within its own borders, and a very large measure

34. Ibid.
35. Ibid.
36. Ibid.

of equality in the proposed agencies of the association with Canada. Further, should the economic association not prove beneficial to the government or people of Quebec, it could be repudiated.[37]

The counterpart of the attractions seen by the PQ in its version of sovereignty-association was the almost totally negative reaction of the proposed partners on the other side.[38] The institutional arrangements were more faithful to the principle of equality than to the requirements for reaching decisions. The political sequence of a referendum to be followed by negotiations produced constitutional proposals attuned to the political requirements of the former, at the expense of any serious concerns for the success of the latter. Or it may have been simply indicative of either a blinding self-interest or a nationalist intoxication that proposals so little directed to the interests of the other nine provinces and the central government should have been put forth in apparent seriousness. In any case, it is a mystery what the other ten governments, still living within the complexities of federalism in the residual state of Canada, would find appealing in a proposal for equality of veto power from a prospective partner outnumbered three to one by the population of the Canada it had left behind. The proposed institutional arrangements were almost guaranteed to ensure rejection outside Quebec.

Further, the PQ proposals overlooked the realignment of economic forces and interests in a Canada without Quebec. In a united federal Canada the Western provinces are compelled to accept the tariff and other policies of special benefit to the economic heartland in Ontario and Quebec. However, barring an unprecedented act of altruism, there was no reason for western Canada to cater to the tariff interests of a sovereign Quebec, let alone to allow a sovereign Quebec more power, as an equal partner, over tariff and other economic policies than it already enjoyed in the existing system. The Péquiste proposals ignored the elementary consideration that the distribution of advantages and disadvantages in the economic union they wished to maintain could only be sustained by the preservation of the politi-

37. Peter Leslie, *Equal to Equal: Economic Association and the Canadian Common Market* (Kingston: Institute of Intergovernmental Relations, 1979), Institute Discussion Papers No. 6, p. 2.

38. For many of the reasons for this negative response see Donald V. Smiley, *The Association Dimension of Sovereignty-Association: A Response to the Quebec White Paper* (Kingston: Institute of Intergovernmental Relations, 1980), Institute Discussion Papers No. 8.

cal system they sought to destroy. Although some of the declared unwillingness of government leaders outside of Quebec to negotiate sovereignty-association was undoubtedly designed to influence the referendum vote, that unwillingness essentially reflected realistic calculations of gains and losses, both economic and political. Indeed, the PQ dilemma was that the independent Quebec that the Quebec electorate would not support was preferable by far in much of English Canada to the sovereignty-association proposal.

The referendum result has, at least temporarily, reduced the practical importance of the PQ proposals. The collective trauma of the referendum exercise is unlikely to be repeated in the near future. Further, it is not at all clear that the sovereignty-association proposed by the PQ, even if completely implemented on Péquiste terms, would have significantly enhanced the security and linguistic prospects of the French-speaking Québécois population. That, however, is a different issue. For the purpose of this analysis the central point is simply that the government of Quebec under Lévesque differed from the other governments more in degree than in kind in its uninhibited pursuit of what it saw as self-interest for itself and its people.

The dialectics of political competition within Quebec in the buildup to the referendum required the provincial Liberals to construct an alternative to the Péquiste sovereignty-association option. The Liberal position was presented in two documents, *Choose Québec and Canada*, published in February 1979, and *A New Canadian Federation*, published a year later in January 1980. *Choose Québec and Canada*, a declaration of principles, was the strongest defense of federalism heard in Quebec for decades. The PQ monopoly of the antifederalist side induced the Liberals to make a virtue of necessity and vigorously defend the historical record of federalism and the general appropriateness of federalism for Quebec. Somewhat unexpectedly, this Liberal defense of federalism and Canada, which continued throughout the referendum campaign, elicited a remarkably positive, emotional response from the electorate. The referendum to extract Quebec from the evils of federalism was the occasion, for the first time in decades, for Quebec politicians to receive public acclaim for openly and vigorously defending and praising the virtues of Canada and the federal system, past and prospective. The Ryan position, however, was far from being a defense of the status quo. Its fundamental theme was the transformation of the federal system in the interests of the provinces, especially Quebec. *A New Canadian Federation* proposed very extensive reforms, which if implemented would have greatly increased the powers of all provincial governments. Not only would provincial governments have more jurisdiction, but they would also play a new and prominent role at Ottawa.

A New Canadian Federation moves back and forth between its major focus on the role of provincial governments and a minor theme of duality. The latter required the affirmation of "the fundamental equality of the two founding peoples"[39] to be manifested in a bundle of language rights, including a constitutional right for French, English, and indigenous peoples to be educated at primary and secondary levels in their mother tongue in their province of residence. Duality was also to be expressed, along with regionalism, in the composition of crucial federal agencies and Crown corporations. The Chief Justice of the Supreme Court was to be chosen in turn from Quebec and the other provinces, and the court itself was to have a dualist constitutional bench with half of its judges from Quebec, presided over by the Chief Justice. In a constitutional case, a dualist bench was to be constituted on the request of "the central government, . . . any provincial government or individual."[40] This clearly meant that the government of Quebec could have any constitutional case removed from the Supreme Court and transferred to the Dualist Bench where, if the Chief Justice is counted, half of the time there would be a majority of judges from Quebec. Also, as noted below, there was to be a Dualist Committee of the proposed Federal Council with special responsibilities in the sensitive areas of federal legislation, policy, and practice concerning language and culture.

For Trudeau, the recognition of duality in federal government institutions, in the Official Languages Act, and in provincial education systems is part of a larger strategy to strengthen the central government and reduce the pressures for concessions to Quebec. For Ryan and Quebec Liberals, by contrast, duality not only requires the constitutional changes suggested in the preceding paragraph, but also "the granting to Quebec of guarantees capable of facilitating the protection and the affirmation of its distinct personality . . . guaran-

39. Quebec Liberal Party, *A New Canadian Federation*, p. 22.
40. Ibid., p. 59.

tees . . . not [to] be narrowly confined to cultural policy."[41] Duality thus would require not only a response in Ottawa and the provinces of English Canada to the francophone population dispersed across the country, but also a recognition that "Quebec is the political expression of French Canada, and her role is that of a mother country for those in Canada who speak French."[42] Decentralization of power to Quebec would thereby be a necessary component of duality, and since the Ryan proposals eschew special status, the other nine provinces would be the beneficiaries of this aversion to an official recognition of asymmetry, and the federal government its victim.

A new Canadian federation fashioned after the Ryan proposals would scarcely have been recognizable to the Fathers of Confederation, or to students and practitioners of the federalism of the 1970s. The provinces were to have powers to allow them to be "the primary level of government responsible for the development of their own territories and human resources."[43] The government of Quebec was to be treated "not only as the government of a province but also, and above all, as having the primary responsibility at the political level for the cultural self-realization and affirmation of that distinct society, of that original national community which has its principal home in Quebec and important extensions in the other Canadian provinces."[44]

Powers to be transferred from the Parliament of Canada to provincial legislatures included federal powers pertaining to marriage and divorce, contributory pensions, offshore mineral resources, responsibility "for the training, retraining, and placement of manpower,"[45] penitentiaries and parole systems, and many others. The provinces were also to be given the right to raise money by any means of taxation. In an attempt to give provincial governments a leverage on the future, the residual power was to be transferred from Ottawa to the provinces. Various unilateral powers were to be abolished, or to require provincial approval before being exercised. These changes were based on the principle of nonsubordination, "an essential element in the establishment of a genuine federal system."[46] They included abo-

41. Ibid., p. 22.
42. Ibid., p. 15.
43. Ibid., p. 63.
44. Ibid., p. 15.
45. Ibid., p. 86.
46. Ibid., p. 73.

lition of the federal power to legislate for peace, order, and good government, of the declaratory power, of the federal power to disallow provincial acts, and of the capacity of the lieutenant governor to reserve provincial acts. The same desire to restrict federal intervention in provincial affairs was behind the recommendation that provinces were to have authority to appoint lieutenant governors in the future and to make appointments of all superior court judges in the provincial court systems.

The most profound alteration in Canadian federalism, however, would have come not from the changes in the division of powers, but from Ryan's proposed new Federal Council, "conceived as a special intergovernmental institution and not as a legislative assembly controlled by the central government."[47] This body would "allow the provinces, which have become senior governments, to participate directly in the government of the federation itself."[48] The council was to be composed entirely of appointees of provincial governments, 25 percent from the province of Quebec, who would act as instructed delegates. The head of each provincial delegation would be the premier or his representative. Nonvoting federal representatives would be allowed to put forward federal views.

In this new Federal Council provincial approval by a two-thirds majority would be required for the federal use of the emergency power, the spending power in fields of provincial jurisdiction, and for any programs of a cultural nature outside federal jurisdiction. Approval of an unspecified majority of the Federal Council would be required for the ratification of appointments of Supreme Court judges and the chief justice, the president and chief executive officers of "major central government bodies such as the Bank of Canada, the National Energy Board and of Crown Corporations such as Canadian National Railways and Air Canada,"[49] for the intergovernmental delegation of power, for treaties in fields of provincial jurisdiction, for legislation relating to interprovincial or international marketing plans for agricultural products, and for all legislation relating to the budgets or funding of "existing federal research bodies in the areas of social science and medical science."[50]

47. Ibid., p. 52.
48. Ibid.
49. Ibid., p. 53.
50. Ibid., p. 78.

The proposed new Federal Council was also to be given a roaming advisory power to offer its opinion on a broad range of matters which fall under exclusive central government jurisdiction "but which have an important impact on the whole federation."[51] Such matters include monetary policy, regional development, transportation, harmonization of federal and provincial fiscal and budgetary policies, equalization payments, and generally "on any federal proposal affecting the provinces or regions which it deemed to be sufficiently important."[52] In its most extensive sense this advisory role would amount to a permanent, free-wheeling, highly visible inquisition by provincial government delegates of virtually any and all of Ottawa's policies.

In addition, there would be a permanent Dualist Committee of the Federal Council with an equal number of English- and French-speaking delegates, with about 80 percent of the latter coming from Quebec. This committee would have power to ratify "federal laws and other initiatives which pertain to the status and use of the official languages."[53] It would also ratify appointments of "presidents and Chief Executive Officers of culturally oriented federal agencies and Crown corporations such as the Official Languages Commission and the Canadian Broadcasting Corporation. In addition . . . . the dualist committee would have a precise mandate to ensure that the Civil Service reflects Canadian dualism at all levels."[54] This recommendation, if seriously implemented and rigorously executed, would give important executive power over the federal bureaucracy to provincial governments, particularly the government of Quebec, which would control at least 40 percent of the Dualist Committee membership.

The particulars of the Ryan proposals, sampled in the preceding paragraphs, are less important for our purposes than is the general picture of a revised Canadian federalism which they reveal. Overall, the Ryan proposals would free the provinces from certain unilateral powers of Ottawa, while subjecting Ottawa to checks by provincial governments in the Federal Council. The provinces are clearly identified as the primary actors in Canadian federalism, a reflection of the primacy the report accords to the regional communities of English-

51. Ibid., p. 53.
52. Ibid., p. 54.
53. Ibid.
54. Ibid.

speaking Canada and the national French-Canadian community in its Quebec homeland.

The Beige Paper of the Quebec Liberal party displays a systematic bias in favor of the provinces generally, and Quebec specifically. A province- and Quebec-centered view of the desirable direction of change in a renewed federalism governs the proposed new division of powers, the systematic reduction of unilateral federal government intervention in provincial affairs, and a systematic enhancement of provincial government powers of intervention and veto in the affairs of the central government.

The relative enhancement of the powers of the Quebec government both in its own jurisdiction and on the national scene envisaged by the Ryan proposals is extensive. All provinces, but particularly Quebec, would gain an impressive new role in Ottawa on the provincial-government-dominated Federal Council. The Dualist Committee, in which the Quebec government would control at least 40 percent of the members, would give Quebec a supplementary influence beyond that available to the provincial governments of English Canada. The government of Quebec would gain power and influence compared to every other government of the system. A Quebec government fully exploiting its enlarged powers of provincial jurisdiction, wielding one-quarter of the powers of the Federal Council, and nearly half the powers of the Dualist Committee, would rival Ottawa as the most powerful government in the system. In its new role as an influential actor on the national scene, Quebec's decisions would affect the whole country. The Ryan proposals are crafted to make the Quebec prime minister a serious rival to the federal prime minister as the most powerful political leader in Canada. The proposals diminish the power of the latter over Quebec, and increase the power of the former over the whole country.

In three areas the Quebec Liberal party proposals are directly or indirectly supportive of the national community, the central government, or both. The recommendation for a Charter of Rights and Liberties enshrined in the constitution and binding on both levels of government displays a concern for the equal treatment of Canadians regardless of province of domicile. The recommendation for a study of proportional representation, designed to find ways to improve the representative character of national parties is based on a desire to en-

hance the legitimacy of the central government. The recommendation for a constitutional clause guaranteeing the free circulation of
goods and capital, subject to certain reservations, is a response to
the tendencies for provincial governments to balkanize the Canadian
economy in the interest of local producers.

In spite of the above, the overwhelming impression left by the
Beige Paper is of a methodical attempt to rearrange Canadian federalism in the interest of the provincial government which its authors
hope to control. The Ryan proposals would fundamentally tilt the future evolution of the federal system in favor of the provincial governments, particularly that of Quebec. After the federal system has been
restructured to Quebec's advantage, the proposed amending formula,
which provides that all provinces which have previously had 25 percent of the Canadian population will possess a veto, would protect in
perpetuity a Quebec with its shrinking population from a commensu-
rate diminution of its power and influence.

The Federal Search for Positional Advantage[55]

The search for positional advantage receives a classic expression in
the federal government's Proposed Resolution Respecting the Constitution of Canada. This proposal was Ottawa's response to the breakdown of the September First Ministers' Conference. The federal resolution, it must be emphasized, was not designed for discussion and
modification at a First Ministers' Conference. It is a government resolution presented to Parliament in its capacity as representative of all
Canadians in all regions.

The substitution of Parliament for the First Ministers' Conference
is more than a short-run expedient to modify, for one time only, the
procedures for constitutional change in Canada. It is part of a more
general and fundamental effort to give a new political definition to
Canada in which the federal government, Parliament, and the Cana-

---

55. The first version of the amending formula presented to the Joint Committee is contained
in Government of Canada, *The Canadian Constitution 1980: Proposed Resolution respecting
the Constitution of Canada*. The revised version, as amended by the Joint Committee and presented to Parliament, is in *Minutes of Proceedings and Evidence of the Special Joint Committee
of the Senate and of the House of Commons on the Constitution of Canada* 57 (February 13,
1981).

dian people enjoy increased status and constitutional significance at the expense of the provinces, and particularly of provincial governments. This was strikingly illustrated in the Joint Committee hearings, the major effect of which was to toughen a charter originally designed to go some way to placate provincial government sensitivities at the expense of the citizenry it was supposed to protect. The political process before the Joint Commitee set the civil rights activists against the provincial governments, resulting in a revised charter much more congenial to the former and much more repugnant to the latter, especially to the dissenting provinces. The Charter, as is noted in the next section, above and beyond its function in protecting citizen rights, has centralizing consequences of major benefit to Ottawa.

To put it differently, the political process by which the Resolution wends its way through Parliament partakes of the same orientation to federalism as is found in the contents of the Resolution. Both the parliamentary political process to give legitimacy to the Resolution, and the objectives of the Resolution, particularly in the proposed amending formula, and less directly in the Charter, represent a central government effort to align the Canadian people and Ottawa in a direct political and constitutional relationship to the disadvantage of provincial governments and provincial communities. The entire Resolution is highly instructive of how the federal government is attempting to exploit its unilateral access to the United Kingdom Parliament to its own benefit. The provisions dealing with the amendment of the constitution are particularly revealing of the permanent leverage that Ottawa seeks to entrench for itself in the new constitution.

In its Resolution, as originally presented to Parliament and the Joint Committee, the federal government proposed a modified version of the Victoria Charter amending formula. The proposal indicated the procedures and criteria by which the provinces could propose an alternative formula, and, should the provinces succeed in this endeavor, gave the federal government the option of offering yet another unspecified formula. A referendum was specified as the device by which the people could choose between the federal and provincial amending formula proposals. Every single facet of this complex proposal reveals the federal government's drive to strengthen its hand in the formula to govern future amendments.

1. The federal amending proposal, based on the relatively flexible 1971 Victoria Charter proposals, was clearly more favorable to Ottawa than any formula likely to emerge from a contemporary First Ministers' Conference. Provincial positions in the 1980 constitutional talks fluctuated between an inhibiting requirement for unanimity and the more flexible procedure devised by Alberta[56] which, by the end of the conference, had considerable provincial support. From the federal perspective the very desirable flexibility of the Alberta proposal was more than nullified by the opting out provisions which raised the specter of a checkerboard Canada. By contrast, the federal proposal, with vetoes only given to Ontario, Quebec, and Ottawa, and with the four Western provinces and the four Atlantic provinces treated as regions whose support required only the approval of two provinces with more than half the regional population, was more flexible than the unanimity rule sought by some provinces, and was devoid of the fragmented application of amendments possible under the Alberta proposal. The provincial advocates of the Alberta proposal were prepared for Canada to pay the price of a checkerboard fragmentation in order to avoid the situation where an amendment might apply to a province against its will. Advocates of the federal proposal, by contrast, could view with equanimity a situation in which, for the sake of a desirable constitutional uniformity, and in conformity with normal federal system practices, amendments could be imposed on particular provinces without their consent.

2. In a major modification of the earlier Victoria Charter formula the federal proposals gave Ottawa the power to employ a referendum as an alternative to obtaining agreement of the requisite provincial governments. Such a referendum would pass if it obtained a national majority, and a majority in those provinces, the support of whose governments would have constituted provincial approval of the proposed amendment. The referendum alternative to the agreement of governments for proposed amendments would decisively enhance the maneuverability of Ottawa in pursuit of desired amendments. Only Ottawa could activate the referendum process and go directly to the people, and it could do so without making any effort to seek provincial government approval first. The reverse possibility of bypassing the

56. See above.

federal government's opposition to amendments which receive the support of the requisite provincial governments was not to be open to the provinces.

Ottawa's resort to the referendum procedure might not, of course, succeed. Further, it is probable that if Ottawa were to use referenda there would be several provincial governments equally interested in a positive outcome. Nevertheless, it is clear that although some provincial governments might also be winners, only Ottawa had the guarantee of not losing jurisdiction it wishes to retain. The crucial consideration is the evident enhancement of the federal government's discretion and the potential diminution of provincial government input into the determination of the success or failure of proposed future amendments. This is part of a larger federal strategic response to centrifugal pressures, the attempt to weaken the ties between provincial governments and their electorates, and to mobilize the latter into a national constituency, to the inevitable long-run advantage of Ottawa.

3. The proposal by which provincial governments could have an alternative amending formula placed before the Canadian electorate was designed to inhibit the emergence of an amending formula less favorable to Ottawa. The requirement that such an alternative must have the agreement of eight provinces with 80 percent of the population gave Ontario and Quebec a veto on any amending formula less favorable to their interests. Since it is not likely that the other eight provinces can develop an alternative more favorable to Ontario and Quebec than the existing federal proposal, their agreement is unlikely to be given. Ottawa has adroitly employed a divide-and-rule strategy to render almost impossible the emergence of a formula less advantageous to itself than the one in the federal resolution.

4. Should this federal strategy be unexpectedly foiled by the appearance of a provincial alternative, the referendum decision on which an amending formula is to be included in the constitution is to be by a simple majority, a necessary consequence of the desire to obtain a clear-cut decision between two competing options. In a federal system, the political logic of majoritarianism is centralizing.

5. Finally, as an ultimate safeguard, Ottawa has reserved to itself the option of proposing an alternative to the modified version of the Victoria Charter formula should the provinces come up with a for-

mula of their own. Thus the federal government confronts the provinces with the threat that the referendum choice, to be decided by a simple voting majority, may include a federal government alternative even less attractive to the provincial governments than the updated Victoria Charter version. This possibility further constrains the already highly restricted provincial maneuverability in the search for an alternative amending formula.

As a straight exercise in manipulative strategy to enhance its role in the determination of future constitutional amendments, the federal proposals could scarcely be bettered. Success in its efforts would be a major victory for Ottawa, overwhelmingly so in the symbolic sense, significantly so in the psychological sense of transforming the climate of intergovernmental debates, and practically so to an important if indeterminate extent in actual constitutional change via the amendment route in the future.

The preceding discussion refers to the Proposed Resolution for a Joint Address as originally proposed. In response to provincial criticisms of the advantage given to Ottawa, the federal government made several concessions so that the Resolution, as recommended to Parliament, moved some way toward satisfying provincial objections.[57]

1. The original requirement for the submission of an alternative amendment procedure by the provinces to the Canadian people was marginally changed from eight provinces with 80 percent of the population to seven provinces with 80 percent of the population. Since this change did not affect the major roadblock for the provinces, the 80 percent requirement, it is inconsequential.

2. Of somewhat more significance was the concession to Prince Edward Island whereby the consent of the Atlantic region, either by governments or by referendum, was changed from any two provinces with at least 50 percent of the regional population to any two or more Atlantic provinces regardless of population. While this change was obviously advantageous to Prince Edward Island—and it was, incidentally, supported by the governments of Nova Scotia and New Brunswick—it was also beneficial to the federal government in that it

57. See *Minutes of Proceedings and Evidence of the Special Joint Committee of the Senate and of the House of Commons on the Constitution of Canada* 57 (February 13, 1981).

further enhanced the flexibility of the overall amendment formula, whether by the route of agreement of governments or of the people. Since Ottawa retained its own veto, this flexibility could only be to its advantage.

3. The revised Joint Resolution also contained new provisions for a three-man Referendum Rules Commission, chaired by the Chief Electoral Officer, with one federal nominee and one member who would be the nominee of the governments of a majority of the provinces.[58] The Commission is empowered to recommend rules to Parliament for the holding of referenda. The final decision, however, remains with Parliament. The Rules Commission would operate both with respect to the initial choice of alternative amending formulae which might be placed before the Canadian people, and with respect to referenda subsequently held under the general amending formula proposed by Ottawa.

4. The revised federal resolution also requires a delay of twelve months after a resolution authorizing a proposed amendment has passed the Senate and the House of Commons before a proclamation authorizing a referendum can be issued. This was a response to the objections of Premier Blakeney, and others, against the possibility of the federal government holding an instant referendum.

There were several other minor changes in the amendment proposals. On the whole however, the federal government concessions did not seriously reduce the advantages it had given itself in the original proposal—specifically, the maintenance of the modified Victoria Charter formula falling short of unanimity, the maintenance of the referendum option, the preservation of the federal monopoly to initiate referenda, and the continuing absence of a requirement for any provincial government support before proceeding with a referendum. While similar advantages exist for the national governments of other federal systems, they have not hitherto existed for Ottawa in the Canadian case.[59]

58. Clause 50(2)(c)(ii) provides alternative procedures if the governments of a majority of the provinces do not recommend a candidate in the appropriate time period.

59. The government introduced a last-minute amendment, just before the resolution was forwarded to the Supreme Court for determination of its constitutionality, in which it removed the 50 percent population requirement for amendment approval by the Western region. This change, making the treatment of the Western and the Atlantic regions the same, was to the advantage of Saskatchewan and Alberta, the two smallest Western provinces, and to Ottawa.

Trudeau's Philosophy of Federalism and the Goals of Ottawa

It is impossible to divorce the objectives and strategy of the federal government from the particular philosophy of federalism espoused by Pierre Elliott Trudeau. Since 1967, when Trudeau became minister of justice, Ottawa's conception of appropriate constitutional change has consistently been informed by his vision of federalism. The Trudeau vision directly confronts powerful tendencies in Canadian federalism. The dualism and regionalism which the Pepin-Robarts Report saw as at "the heart of the Confederation crisis,"[60] and to which it asserted there must be a positive response if the country is to survive, are not so much responded to and accommodated by Trudeau's preferred reforms as contained, deflected, undermined, and attacked. To Trudeau both the pervasive centrifugal pressures created by the growing powers of the provinces and inward-looking, Quebec-focused French-Canadian nationalism are incompatible with the survival of Canadian federalism. For Trudeau, Quebec nationalism is equally incompatible with the preservation of toleration and civil liberties in an independent Quebec.

The tenacity with which Trudeau has pursued his vision is sustained by his philosophy of countervailing powers. In areas of fundamental concern he does not see his duty as being flexible and accommodative of trends he dislikes. On the contrary, he searches for counterweights to turn back the tide. The desired Trudeau constitution, therefore, is most emphatically not one which acts as a mirror to the times. Trudeau's response to the two dominant forces of dualism and regionalism which, as Pepin-Robarts noted, are lined up behind provincial governments, is to strengthen the central government and build up a transcending Canadian community looking to Ottawa for leadership and protection.

Trudeau's political philosophy displays a profound hostility to having the boundaries of political systems coincide with the boundaries of nationality. Since he assumed office his developing analysis has come to include an opposition to provincial governments fostering provincial cultures and provincial economies for which they may then

60. Task Force on Canadian Unity, *A Future Together*, p. 36.

claim exclusive positions as spokesmen, in defiance of an overriding Canadianism. The francophone Quebecer in a united Canada, seen by Claude Morin as a partial man torn between the conflicting demands of allegiance to Quebec City and Ottawa, and by Lévesque as a fragmented half-man, is positively viewed by Trudeau. He sees the divided political system and the divided psyche, which sustain each other, as guarantors of the health of the system and of the freedom of the individual.

Federal constitutional objectives and the strategy for their attainment faithfully reflect this philosophy. It is federal strategy to stress and even bolster heterogeneity *within* provinces. Constantly to remind the government of Quebec of the presence of a sizable nonfrancophone minority is to deny Lévesque the title of spokesman for an ethnic nation. The protection of the official language minority in Quebec facilitates the movement of anglophones to that province, or at least slows the exodus, and thus contributes to the maintenance of linguistic duality. It thus forces the PQ to grapple with the troubling ambiguity of the concept of Québécois which fluctuates between encompassing the entire Quebec citizenry, and a restricted and more passionate definition limited to the francophone majority. To push aggressively for the extension of French-language rights outside of Quebec, particularly in education, is to remind the governments of English Canada that they too must live with, and respect, at least a limited degree of linguistic duality in their own backyard. The extension of the provincial melting pot to the official language minority is unCanadian.

The little-appreciated purpose of the House of Federation proposals in Bill C-60 was to render visible the partisan heterogeneity within provinces such that the twenty-four Quebec seats in the proposed House, for example, would have been filled by six different parties, two of which would have had their membership selected by both the federal and Quebec legislatures. Where critics saw an indescribable and unpalatable smorgasbord in such a House of the Federation, the federal government positively gloried in the heterogeneity such a body would display, with "the multiplicity of federal and provincial parties represented in the new chamber, all of whom will have different allegiances and objectives."[61] This would be a useful contri-

61. Government of Canada, *Constitutional Reform: House of the Federation* (Ottawa: Canadian Unity Information Office, 1978), p. 19.

bution to the erosion of provincial government claims to speak for a monolithic provincial citizenry.

In addition to stressing and fostering heterogeneity within provinces, it is basic federal strategy to stress communities of interest that cross provincial boundaries. This is most clearly the case with the Trudeau goal of keeping alive by appropriate policies the reality of a French fact from coast to coast, thus directly challenging the more restricted concept of a French Canada confined to Quebec, relabeled Québécois, and looking to the provincial state for salvation. In practical terms the federal goal of facilitating francophone migration from Quebec to other provinces reduces the political control of the Quebec government over its population and is designed to strengthen the Canadian identity.

The federal position paper on "Powers over the Economy,"[62] released at the summer 1980 constitutional conference, was directly aimed at provincial government policies which limit the free flow of goods, persons, capital, and professional services across provincial boundaries. Although much of the reasoning in this paper was based on the economic consequences for Canada of restricting an already small domestic market, it was also based on the supposition that major reductions in the utility of a Canadian identity work against Canadian unity and chip away at the psychological base of central government power and authority. One suspects that for Trudeau the practical economic consequences were less important than his principled objection to tendencies to provincial autarchy in which government-created provincial economies coincided with provincial boundaries.

The counterpart of this assault on an exclusive provincialism is an attempt to develop and sustain an overriding, all-encompassing Canadian community. The effort to strengthen francophone communities outside Quebec, and to a lesser extent the anglophone community in Quebec, is designed to keep alive their links with confreres in other provinces. As a seminal by-product it is also designed to stimulate allegiance to a national political system that protects them through its constitution, which enshrines their rights, and which provides for their enforcement by a Supreme Court located in the na-

62. Government of Canada, "Powers over the Economy: Securing the Canadian Economic Union in the Constitution," July 9, 1980 (mimeo.), document 830-81/036; subsequently published as a pamphlet. Honorable Jean Chrétien, *Securing the Canadian Economic Union in the Constitution* (Ottawa: Minister of Supply and Services, 1980).

tional capital. Federalism, according to Trudeau, "is ultimately bound
to fail if the nationalism it cultivates is unable to generate a national
image which has immensely more appeal than the regional ones."[63]

From this nation-building perspective, the Charter of Rights, in
the many versions it has undergone since it first appeared on the constitutional agenda in 1968, has been too often seen in terms of citizen-
state relations, and too seldom seen in terms of its contribution to
building a Canadian community. The Trudeau description of such
rights as part of a people's package which adds to the powers of neither
federal nor provincial governments, but instead impartially hedges the
exercise of power by both, is only a partial truth. From a more enlarged perspective the rights it creates are Canadian rights, and the
community it fosters is a national community. Such a Charter does
not allow a citizen to challenge a federal exercise of power as infring-
ing on the rights of an Albertan. It allows a citizen of Canada to challenge the exercise of power by the government of Alberta on the
grounds of its infringement of his rights as a Canadian. That such a
right can also be used against the federal government does not alter
the fact that the identity that is fostered and the community that is
vitalized by the exercise of such rights is the Canadian identity and
the Canadian community. Rights entrenched in the Canadian constitution, and enforced coast to coast by a highly visible national Supreme
Court, nourish a single Canada-wide community, which inevitably will
be employed as a resource by a future prime minister in the never-
ending power struggle between federal and provincial governments.
Such a Charter of Rights is many things, not least being an instrument
of nationalism to Canadianize the psyche of the citizenry.[64]

While several aspects of the Charter provide special collective
rights to the official language groups, its more fundamental orientation is an allocation of rights to individuals undifferentiated by ethnic
or linguistic origins or practice. In this sense the Charter raises the
status of the Third Force in Canada. Along with patriation itself,
doubtless particularly attractive to immigrants whose mother country

63. Pierre Elliott Trudeau, *Federalism and the French Canadians* (Toronto: Macmillan,
1968), p. 193.

64. The extent to which this suggested consequence of the Charter is being deliberately
sought by Ottawa is unclear. The various officials questioned on the matter give contradictory
answers. Some agree and some deny that this is a clear federal objective consciously pursued.

is not Great Britain, the Charter has a special attractiveness to members of nonfounding ethnic groups, more likely in fact and in self-perception to be the victims of discrimination. It is at least plausible that the Charter, therefore, will be particularly successful in strengthening the already high positive identifications with the central government among Canadians of other than French or British background.

In various ways the Trudeau Charter sustains a conception of Canadianism which weakens links between citizens and provincial governments. Its stress on individual rights cuts across provincial communities and reinforces citizen involvement in the transcending national community. The limited stress on official language minority rights in education, where numbers warrant, contributes at the level of individuals and families to mobility across provincial boundaries, and thus supports the interprovincial occupational mobility protected elsewhere in the Charter. More generally, Trudeau's ideal federal system would greatly reduce the psychic and economic costs of mobility across provincial boundaries, loosen psychological attachments to particular provinces, and significantly erode the capacity of provincial governments to foster diversities coincident with provincial boundaries.

Competing Versions of Intrastate Federalism

The definition of Canada as a community of communities, or as a country of limited identities, tends to give legitimacy to a strong role for provincial governments—these viewed as being closer to the allegedly dominant realities of contemporary Canadian existence. From a provincialist perspective there are, as already noted, two very different constitutional responses capable of accommodating the developing and intertwined realities of assertive regional communities and the provincial governments which both respond to and shape them. The simplest response is old-fashioned decentralization, the transfer of power from the government farthest removed from the regional communities which constitute Canada to provincial governments in direct contact with such communities. This approach, in fact, probably remains the most widely held of all constitutional views at the provincial government level. However, it has enjoyed only a limited visibility throughout the last decade and a half of constitutional controversy because of the considerable federal success in keeping the division of powers off the constitutional reform agenda.

The alternative provincialist response also focuses on the enhancement of provincial government power, but not by devolution of additional jurisdictional responsibilities to the provinces. Rather, the solution is to restructure the central government to produce a greater federal sensitivity to the wishes of provincial governments. This orientation, labeled intrastate federalism by Donald Smiley,[65] informs the constitutional proposals of British Columbia, the Task Force on Canadian Unity, Canada West, the Canadian Bar Association, and the Quebec Liberal party.

This version of constitutional change is almost the direct antithesis of the Confederation settlement. In 1867 the lines of intergovernmental influence flowed from Ottawa to the provinces, giving the former a clear constitutional capacity to strike down legislation entirely within provincial competence. The contemporary provincialist version reverses the original pattern and gives to provincial governments an equally clear capacity, subject to varying majority requirements, to control and veto federal legislation in key areas.

From the perspective of those who advocate a provincialist version of intrastate federalism, the problem of the federal government is not, as Trudeau would have it, a deficient Canadianism, but insensitivity to the regionalism of Canada and to the provincial governments which speak for it. A sensitized Ottawa thus requires provincial government input at the center. The reconstruction of central government institutions to generate this increased sensitivity variously includes some provincial input into the appointment of Supreme Court judges and some Supreme Court reconstruction on dualist lines. A further element of necessary change requires a provincial role in the appointment process for key federal boards and commissions whose functions, although entirely within federal jurisdiction, have a major impact on the societies and economies of the provinces. The centerpiece of intrastate federalism, however, is invariably a revised Senate, appointed in whole or in part by provincial govern-

65. Smiley, "Structural Problems of Canadian Federalism."

ments and with specified ratification powers concerning clearly identified areas of federal policy and legislation.[66]

Psychologically, the creation of such a second chamber would have
a profound effect on the political image of the country. It would give
provincial government delegates—in the British Columbia proposals
the provincial delegation was to be headed by a cabinet minister,
and on certain occasions the premier himself would be present—a
constitutionally guaranteed visibility on the national stage. This in
turn would almost certainly contribute to a view of the country in
which national interests would be less differentiated from provincial
than is now the case. To provincialize national institutions at the center is also to bring national and provincial identities closer together in
the psyche of the citizen and probably to elevate the latter at the expense of the former.

The contribution of self-interest to policy prescription is clearly
revealed by the fact that in the hands of federal officials a similar
definition of the problem produces recommendations designed to
strengthen Ottawa at the expense of provincial governments. This
centralist version rests on the same underlying premise as the provincialist version, namely that the central government is weakened to
the extent that it does not provide an outlet for provincial and regional interests at the center. In the Bill C-60 paper on the House of
the Federation it was admitted that the Senate, the Cabinet, and the
House of Commons all failed publicly to represent and advocate regional interests. Although federal-provincial conferences had played a
helpful role in reconciling regional and national interests, they had
several drawbacks. Their frequent failure to produce agreement or
any clear outcome

leaves an impression of continual discord between governments which can
exaggerate the degree of division within the country. The federal institutions
of government, because they do not contain an effective regional forum, lose
political authority. The result has tended to reinforce some of the centrifugal
tendencies which have always been present in the Canadian Federation and
which weaken our sense of unity.[67]

However, the centralist version of intrastate federalism refuses to
accept that provincial governments, necessarily recognized as the le-

66. See the discussion of the British Columbia Senate proposals, above.
67. Government of Canada, *Constitutional Reform: House of the Federation*, pp. 4–5.

gitimate expression of provincial interests with respect to areas of provincial jurisdiction, should play the same role with respect to aspects of federal jurisdiction. Although Ottawa has considered, and on occasion proposed, a provincial government role with respect to Senate appointments, a more consistent federal tendency has been to look to other than provincial governments for regional input, and not to confine the search to reform of the second chamber. Trudeau's belated interest in some form of proportional representation to give the Liberals spokesmen from western Canada and the Conservatives spokesmen from Quebec is the most recent indication of this orientation in federalist thought. The official languages policy was an earlier attempt to strengthen the image and reality of Ottawa as a government sensitive to francophone interests both inside and outside Quebec. The destruction of the anglophone image of the central government at which this policy was directed was intended to frustrate the exclusive alignment of Quebec francophone interests behind the provincial government. The consistent federal pursuit of constitutionally entrenched official language minority rights, especially in education, has been similarly motivated. In Bill C-60 this federalist strategy was extended to the other provinces in the ill-fated House of the Federation, a body explicitly designed to check the growing provincial government role in the representation of provincial interests at the center, but not of course to eliminate executive federalism for the conduct of intergovernmental business. Ottawa was prepared to pay the price of a possibly more recalcitrant second chamber in the pursuit of a federal system more to its liking.

The centralist and provincialist versions of intrastate federalism clearly reveal the pervasive influence of governmental self-interest which colors the search for remedies to a commonly agreed structural deficiency in the Canadian federal system. The tendency of the centralist version of intrastate federalism is to strengthen the central government at the expense of provincial governments. The provincialist version is designed to extend provincial government power into the national arena in areas hitherto considered of exclusive federal government jurisdiction.

The Electorate and the People: Tools for Manipulation

The domination of the constitutional review process by governments, and the corollary that the interests most likely to be articulated are those of the participating *governments*, will not surprise students of Canadian federalism. What is surprising is the developing tendency for governments, in reaching out for new bargaining resources to help attain desirable constitutional outcomes, to involve the citizenry at large. This has led to more talk of referenda and plebiscites in the last ten years than in the preceding century.

It is characteristic of the elite domination of the constitutional process in Canada that the activation of the electorate is unfailingly at the discretion of governments. The idea that the people, on their own initiative, could require a referendum has been conspicuously absent from official proposals. In the Quebec case, the timing, the wording of the referendum question, and the nature of the referendum process were controlled by the provincial government. The open, honest debate on the future of Quebec which the government had promised after its 1976 victory did not occur. The influence of Claude Morin, the Mackenzie King of Quebec politics, was evident in a complex question devised after extensive polling, and in a campaign characterized by obfuscation and a constant softening and fudging of the government position. The government, indeed, kept its discretion to the very last minute with its constant allusions to the fundamental difference between an arithmetical majority, and a relevant majority based on the francophone community alone.

The use of the "people" as a resource has not been confined to Quebec. Throughout the long, drawn-out constitutional negotiations over the summer of 1980, the federal government brilliantly deployed a "people vs. powers" definition of the interests of the competing government participants. What it sought was a "people's package" in contrast to the provincial governments' alleged pursuit of narrow governmental self-interest. This undeniably put the provinces on the defensive as they struggled to justify their claims as being no less in the public interest than those being pursued by Ottawa. That the federal government, aided by extensive advertising, was also able to create a strong impression that the people were on its side hovered constantly over the conference proceedings to the marked distress of the provincial governments.

Federal government exploitation of the citizenry as a resource is equally evident as a justification for the unilateralism of the proposed Resolution for the United Kingdom Parliament dealing with patriation, a Charter of Rights, an amending formula, and other matters. This package is portrayed as a matter of honor, as the federal government's response to the vague commitment for renewed federalism given by Ottawa to the Quebec people in the referendum campaign. Not only did the referendum fail to further Parti Québécois constitutional objectives, but by a profound irony Trudeau has turned the referendum on its head. From his own participation and that of other federalists he has extracted from the victory of the "no" forces a mandate to implement the precise reforms of Canadian federalism he has been pursuing for more than a decade. The appeal to the people is carried a stage further by the federal government in its proposed amending formula: referenda will become part of the regular procedures available for constitutional amendment, capable of being used by Ottawa to bypass provincial governments. As already noted, this aspect of the proposed amending formula, and the likely manner of its utilization, will tend to increase the capacity of Ottawa to get its way in future amendment controversies with provincial governments.

For Trudeau, as for Lévesque, appeals to the people and claims of their support are obviously straightforward devices to assist in the attainment of particular constitutional goals. In both cases, the direct appeal to the people is a strategy to bypass the connection between citizens and a competing government in the other jurisdiction. Thus, the Quebec government tried to use its referendum legislation to exclude the federal government as an independent actor in a campaign for the declared objective of removing the federal government from participation in Quebec affairs. While the federal government's referendum options in its amending formula do not eliminate a role for provincial governments in the battle for public support, the contest is to be waged on a nationwide basis in response to a referendum question, the initiation and wording of which, ultimately, given the restricted role of the Referendum Rules Commission, are to be at Ottawa's discretion.

Equally, important, however, is the fact that both Lévesque and

Trudeau wish to mobilize their respective peoples. For Lévesque the referendum appeal to the Quebec electorate, an introspective exercise in collective consciousness raising, was a stratagem to advance Quebec nationalism. For Trudeau, the Joint Committee hearings and, more explicitly, the future use of referenda are devices to strengthen his claim that the new constitution and future amendments to it are based on the popular will rather than on the preferences of provincial governments. Should he succeed in forging his alliance between the national government and the Canadian people the compact theory of Confederation will be left to the musings of historians. In other words, the elites who seek out the people via the referendum mechanism, aim not only at the attainment of specific objectives, but also at the more long-range goal of adding substance and purpose to the community under their jurisdiction. Referenda are devices not only to give voice to popular sentiments but also to create and recreate a political community by the symbolism attached to participation in a dramatic political act. In the last analysis, the strengthening of community by governments is a way of strengthening the governments which claim to speak for them.

In the contemporary Canadian case, resort to the people is a weapon in intergovernmental warfare. Not surprisingly, it is viewed as a threat by the governments that do not control the referendum process in particular circumstances. Thus the referendum aspects of Trudeau's proposed amending formula are vehemently opposed by the governments of provinces denied an individual veto, either for themselves or for their people, in a process of popular consultation which the federal government can initiate subject to only limited constraints. In the words of Brian Peckford, premier of Newfoundland: "The power of our provincial legislature is threatened. There is only power for people and the federal government—people means referendum—referendum means majority—majority means we're out in the cold."[68]

It is typically Canadian, if somewhat saddening, that there is virtually no popular discussion of the merits and weaknesses of popular participation in the proposed Liberal amending formula. The controversy about popular participation is conducted almost entirely by

68. "Province Wide Address by the Honourable A. Brian Peckford to the People of Newfoundland and Labrador, October 20, 1980," p. 11.

governments. The bringing in of the people reflects no grass-roots populism struggling for expression, but an elite manipulation in the service of government objectives. The citizens of the eleven jurisdictions in their electoral roles, and as the substance behind the public opinion claimed to be supportive of particular constitutional objectives, are viewed by governments as resources. They are to be selectively employed where helpful, selectively ignored where not helpful, and in general to be restricted to clearly defined supporting roles when a government's interest can be served by their mobilization. From a democratic perspective, it is some consolation that the process of manipulation from above may occasionally backfire.

Concluding Reflections

The coexistence of the procedures and norms of executive federalism with the existing distribution of political forces tends toward stalemate in the search for constitutional renewal, drives governments to reach deeper into their societies for political support, and encourages the only government with a possible capacity for constitutional unilateralism to respond to temptation in the manner of Oscar Wilde, by succumbing. More specifically, the preceding analysis suggests the following points:

1. The adversary logic of executive federalism induces provincial governments to pursue an exaggerated provincialism and the federal government to pursue an exaggerated Canadianism. The resultant government positions across the bargaining table are more incompatible with each other than are the federal and provincial orientations of the citizenry for whom governments profess to speak.

2. There is no visible equilibrium position present in the existing constitution, nor in the conflicting government demands seeking recognition in a new constitution. Although the last two decades have often been described as a period of provincial government assertiveness and federal government retreat, that description is misleading as a guide to the relative strength and ambitions of the contending forces. Not only do the provinces disagree among themselves, but the federal government under Trudeau is far from being a spent force, reconciled to a major reduction in its overall role in the federal sys-

tem. At the moment it is struggling to recover the initiative not only in the constitutional arena but also in the energy field.

The British tradition of parliamentary supremacy and the self-interest of provincial political elites work against general provincial acceptance of the basic federal demands. The Charter of Rights is broadly viewed as outside the British-Canadian tradition, as a measure which, under the guise of giving rights to the people, in effect gives powers to the courts, with a consequent encroachment on provincial parliamentary supremacy. Equally unpalatable to the provinces, with few exceptions, is the federal demand for constitutional sanctions to maintain an economic union by restricting provinces' powers to balkanize the Canadian market. The federal government, by contrast, resists the provincial definition of Canada which, with many shadings, accords provincial governments, economies, and societies priority, and which, in its extreme versions, views the central government as a disposable superstructure.

3. The unanimity convention gives all provinces a veto, increases their bargaining power, works against agreement, and thus reinforces the constitutional status quo.

4. The existing constitution, for all its deficiencies, still represents for many governments a more acceptable fallback position than any compromise likely to emerge from the bargaining process of executive federalism. This too works against agreement on major change.

5. The federal and most provincial governments have grandiose ambitions for the societies and economies under their control. The stakes of constitutional change, therefore, are very high. Constitutional change in the era of the positive state is much more difficult to achieve than in an era when the responsibilities of government are severely limited.

6. The sophisticated understanding of the constitutional matters developed over the past decade and a half has made political elites unusually aware that all constitutions represent a mobilization of bias capable of advantaging or disadvantaging their governments as the new constitution evolves. This recognition hampers agreement by making all too clear the possible long-run consequences of winning and losing. By a perverse logic, the recognition of the creative role of constitutions contributes to the maintenance of the status quo.

7. The turbulence which has afflicted the Canadian polity, econ-

omy, and society in the past two decades has generated a sense of nostalgia for the constitutional certainties of the past and superficial hopes for their reassertion in the future. However, implicit in the behavior of contemporary political leaders is a growing appreciation that yesterday's constitutional certainties were based on a far more stable and predictable society and economy, both national and international, than future generations will face. Put differently, their inability to predict the new social and economic forces a revised constitution will encounter in a world they cannot foresee generates a profound unease about its unpredictable future effects on their own goals. For the political leaders of any single government a new constitutional text begins to look less like a desired goal than a potential threat, unless its provisions are built to the specifications of that government and tailored to give it maximum leverage in tomorrow's world. Each government is thus driven to seek a degree of mastery, composed of a specific mix of rigidities and flexibilities, which is inherently unattainable for all. Given these considerations the failure of the constitutional conferences of the summer of 1980 is no occasion for surprise.

8. There is no external power, as there was in 1864–67, capable of applying pressure to obtain an agreement that the actors cannot voluntarily achieve.

9. The increasing recognition of the preceding considerations produces a search for alternatives to executive federalism as the vehicle for achieving constitutional renewal. The limited, if growing, support for a constituent assembly is based on a perceived incapacity of the existing system of executive federalism to produce results, and on the recognition that the dominance of government interests at the bargaining table distorts the process unacceptably. The constituent assembly idea, however, founders on the self-interest of governments it is designed to overcome. In the absence of a constitutional breakdown far more serious than the present situation there is no possibility governments will give up the powers of constitution-making they now possess.

10. The only alternative available, unilateralism, was unsuccessfully pursued by the Parti Québécois. The unilateralism of Trudeau in the proposed Resolution for the British Parliament has a greater chance of success. The Resolution is designed not only to break the

present deadlock, but by its proposed amending formula falling short of unanimity, and with the escape valve of referenda, it seeks a future flexibility to prevent a repetition of past rigidities and stalemates. That the overall unilateral federal package is to the long-run advantage of Ottawa is not a matter for surprise. The incumbent prime minister profoundly believes that the salvation of Canadian federalism necessitates a strengthened Ottawa and a strengthened Canadian community to which his proposed reforms will contribute. To have found the right time, via a completely unexpected return to power, to further his deeply held view of the public interest is the very definition of heaven for this consummate politician. Pierre Elliott Trudeau has long and patiently awaited the opportunity to implant his vision of Canada on the fragmented country he inherited.

Postscript: December 15, 1981

The perils of academic commentary on ongoing events are compounded when publication takes place some time after the original presentation. This paper, initially presented in November 1980, was slightly updated but not significantly revised in the spring of 1981. This belated postscript was written in partial response to the dramatic developments that have produced a constitutional package very different from the federal government proposals forwarded to the Supreme Court in April 1981. Those proposals were the product of a tortuous political process, including lengthy hearings before a Special Joint Committee of the Senate and the House of Commons, followed by an acrimonious debate in the House of Commons which was only ended by the Liberal government's reluctant agreement to allow the Supreme Court to judge the constitutionality of its proposed course of action. By the time the federal proposals reached the Supreme Court, the Manitoba, Newfoundland, and Quebec Courts of Appeal had already delivered three separate judgments, with contradictory findings.

Just prior to the commencement of the Supreme Court hearings, the eight dissenting provinces—all but Ontario and New Brunswick— proposed an alternative constitutional package. It was restricted to patriation and an amending formula patterned on the earlier Alberta

amending proposals[69] that had received considerable provincial support in the intergovernmental meetings in the summer of 1980. This
Constitutional Accord, as it was called, contrasted markedly with the
federal package supported by Ontario and New Brunswick. It contained no charter of rights, and its amending procedures included no
referendum role for the people. Given its genesis in provincial intergovernmental meetings from which the two provinces sympathetic to
the federal position were excluded, and given the perceived political
necessity of keeping Quebec in the provincial "gang of eight," the
Constitutional Accord, not surprisingly, reflected a provincialist vision of Canada.

The Accord, which allowed up to three provinces to opt out of
amendments "derogating from the legislative powers, the proprietary
rights, or any other rights or privileges of the Legislature or government of a province," and which required the federal government
to "provide reasonable compensation to the governments of such
provinces" was immediately and curtly rejected by the federal government as a recipe for a checkerboard Canada and incremental
separatism.

From the time the Supreme Court hearings ended in early May to
the announcement of its decision on September 28, the constitutional crisis receded from public view. In an impressive display of
self-discipline stretching over nearly five months the court preserved
the confidentiality of its internal proceedings and of its pending decision with total success. Consequently, the complexity of its decision, delivered in the unique setting of televised proceedings, was
unexpected.

By a 7–2 margin the court upheld the legality of the federal proposal, but by a 6–3 margin asserted that in terms of convention it
was unconstitutional as it lacked sufficient provincial support. "The
federal principle," according to the majority opinion on convention,
"cannot be reconciled with a state of affairs where the modification of
provincial legislative powers could be obtained by the unilateral action of the federal authorities."

Although the Supreme Court decision clearly damaged the legitimacy of the proposed federal government submission to Westmin-

---

69. See above for the Alberta amending formula.

ster, and thus provided ammunition to the dissenting provinces, its finding that federal action would be legal allowed Ottawa to revive its threat to proceed unilaterally. Further, by its very deliberate refusal to support the position argued by seven of the eight dissenting provinces, that convention required unanimous provincial consent, the Supreme Court changed the dynamics of intergovernmental bargaining in the very fluid situation created by its decision. The possibility of intergovernmental agreement was markedly enhanced by the court's elimination of the power of one or two recalcitrant provinces to block agreement, or to insist on major concessions as a price of their adhesion. In the judicious phrase that "at least a substantial measure of provincial consent is required," the court made it clear that the agreement of two provinces was insufficient, and the agreement of ten was not necessary.

Although both sides, predictably, claimed victory in public, the major impact of the court decision was to nudge the eleven governments back to the bargaining table. After a month of competitive bluffing, posturing, and jockeying for position, federal and provincial representatives reassembled for constitutional discussions within the framework of the new mix of law and convention fashioned for them by the Supreme Court. After a four-day process simultaneously fascinating in its unpredictability and unedifying in the blatancy of its horsetrading, an agreement was hammered out between Ottawa and nine of the provincial governments, Quebec alone refusing to sign.

The compromise package which emerged was built around provincial acceptance of a modified charter, and the acceptance by Ottawa, Ontario, and New Brunswick of a slightly modified version of the amending formula contained in the Constitutional Accord of the eight provinces opposed to the original federal government package. The major charter modification was the introduction of an override capacity for Parliament or a provincial legislature to declare that an act, in whole or in part, "shall operate notwithstanding" those sections of the charter dealing with Fundamental Freedoms, Legal Rights, Equality Rights and, in part, notwithstanding a section which "guaranteed equally to male and female persons" the rights and freedoms in the charter. Provincial agreement to the charter was obtained not only by the availability of an override capacity which partially placated the devotees of parliamentary supremacy, but also by the reluctant and grudging federal acceptance of an amending formula which Ottawa had consistently satirized since its introduction into constitutional discussions by Alberta several years earlier. Federal acceptance of this amending formula, with its possibilities of a constitutional checkerboard which Ottawa feared, was made conditional on the deletion of a clause in the original provincial Constitutional Accord requiring "reasonable [financial] compensation" for provinces opting out of constitutional amendments. Presumably the federal objective was to diminish the incentive to opt out, and thus to increase the probability of the nationwide application of future amendments.[70]

Both sides had undeniably made significant concessions, especially with respect to the charter. While the introduction of an override was unquestionably a basic federal concession, it did not emasculate the charter. The override did not apply to Democratic Rights, Mobility Rights, and Minority Language Educational Rights, and its application was hedged in by the condition that each declaration of an override would expire at the end of five years, unless reenacted. Provincial government opponents of the charter had made extensive concessions to the Trudeau vision of Canada.

Somewhat surprisingly, this solemn agreement of ten of eleven governments was not the end of this phase of constitution-making. The agreement had to be put into suitable language, and then returned to Parliament for final passage before submission to Westminster. As the recognition sank in that in closed intergovernmental bargaining many of the rights fashioned and refined in the Special Joint Committee and in the House of Commons had been diluted, a blizzard of angry protest emerged, particularly from women's groups and from various aboriginal organizations. The former were furious that the clause guaranteeing the charter's rights and freedoms "equally to male and female persons" had been subject to an override by eleven male first ministers in secret sessions. The latter were angry that a clause by which "the aboriginal and treaty rights of the aboriginal peoples of Canada are thereby recognized and affirmed" had been completely deleted.

In both cases the symbolism of what had been done made a greater contribution to mobilizing women and native peoples than did the practical consequences of the changes, which were far from clear. In

---

70. Compensation resulting from political negotiations was, of course, not precluded.

any case, orchestrated political pressure without parallel in Canadian history completely overwhelmed the provincial premiers responsible for the changes. They were compelled to agree to the removal of the applicability of the override to the equal guarantee of the rights and freedoms of the charter to men and women, and to the reinstatement of the aboriginal rights clause.[71]

Given the general, albeit fluctuating, government domination of the constitutional reform process throughout Canadian history, this successful assault on executive federalism by organizations of women and aboriginal peoples was in itself an event of great constitutional significance. Admittedly, both groups were overtly encouraged by the federal government and opposition parties. Further, an alliance between "the people" and Ottawa against the provincial governments has been a longstanding objective of Trudeau. Nevertheless, this dramatic display of grass-roots mobilization was an early indication and portent of fundamental change in the practices and values of Canadian democracy which the Charter of Rights would inexorably bring in its wake.

The major and serious shortcoming of the agreement transmitted to Westminster after receiving formal parliamentary approval was the nonparticipation of the government of Quebec. The process of constitutional renewal, which received its prime impetus from events in Quebec, concluded its first phase amid bitter assertions from the Parti Québécois government that the constitutional package was a product of English-speaking imperialism, one more confirmation of the incapacity of the federal system to respond sympathetically to the duality of Canada. In an action aimed at the history books, Quebec flags on public buildings were flown at half-mast to coincide with the conclusion of debate in the House of Commons.

In an attempt to erode the rationale for the nonparticipation of the Quebec government the federal Liberal government, partly in response to pressures from its own Quebec caucus, introduced several modifications to the Resolution for Joint Address to Her Majesty the Queen,[72] to no avail. In a last desperate attempt to frustrate the im-

---

71. The reinstated clause, modified by the addition of "existing," reads as follows: "The existing aboriginal and treaty rights of the aboriginal peoples of Canada are hereby recognized and affirmed."

72. A section was added requiring Canada to "provide reasonable compensation" to a province that opts out of an amendment "that transfers provincial legislative powers relating to education or other cultural matters from provincial Legislatures to Parliament."

plementation of the constitutional package the Quebec government asked the Quebec Court of Appeal to rule whether the consent of Quebec was, by convention, constitutionally necessary for an amendment which would reduce the lawmaking authority of the Quebec legislature. The struggle between rival definitions of Canada showed no sign of ending.

The "mother tongue" language clause that gave citizens of Canada "whose first language learned and still understood is that of the English or French linguistic minority population of the province in which they reside . . . . the right to have their children receive primary and secondary school instruction in that language in that province" was changed so that it would only apply to Quebec when the legislative assembly or government of Quebec so approved.

Index: Persons

Index: Subjects

454   *Political Support in Canada*

Constitution (*continued*)
  proposals for, 394–95, 398, 403–10, 425, 443–44, 446; British Columbia proposals for, 394–95, 398–403, 405, 434–35; conferences on, 381–86, 402, 425, 431, 437, 442, 445; Parti Québécois proposals for, 398, 410–17, 447; Quebec Liberal party proposals for, 398, 411, 417–23, 434, 439
Corporatism, 295, 298
Cost-benefit analysis, 5, 8, 17, 33, 116, 261, 288, 290, 325, 336
Culture: Canadian, 245, 404, 418, 420–21, 429; cleavages within, 13, 49, 175, 177; media content, 157–58; Québécois, 295, 297–98, 301, 303, 305, 308–20, 326, 355, 359, 361, 410, 412, 418–19

Decentralization, 15, 148–49, 217–19, 222, 232, 242, 244–45, 302, 366, 395–96, 403, 408, 419, 433
Defense, 271, 275
Deferential polity, 118
Devolution, 354, 398, 412, 434
Disaffection, 8, 13–14, 16, 35, 61, 144, 247, 254; in Quebec, 9, 35
Discrimination, 52–53, 56–57, 70, 433
Disfranchisement, 55–56, 60
Disunity, 48
Dominance: definition of, 50; theories of, 10, 49–51, 57, 62, 68–72
Doukhobours, 54

Education, 5, 36–37, 216, 235, 237, 244–45, 249–50, 321; and cognition, political, 108–9; confessional, 313; and continental socialization, 104–5, 110, 113–14; and language instruction, 418, 430, 433, 446; and self-concept, 76, 79, 81, 87, 98; U.S. influence on, 113–14; as variable in analysis, 81. *See also* Schools
Efficacy: measurement of, 28, 31–32, 38–39, 79, 82, 93, 99, 117–18, 121, 252, 258–59, 263–64, 268, 325; perceived, 9–10, 39–40, 47–48; as variable in analysis, 82
Elections, 8, 13, 191–94, 207; abstaining from, 202–3; Elections Act, 173; electoral imperatives, 21; and the media, 13, 130, 134, 154–70 passim; provincial issues in, 18; reform of, 173
Employment, 281, 288, 319
Energy, 5, 155, 249, 262–63, 288, 359, 406, 408, 441
Environment, Department of, 259; and economic development, 255–57, 259–61, 263–65, 267–69; Environment Week, 260;

grants, 261, 264; ministries of, 258–60, 265, 267
Environmental Assessment Act, 260–61
Environmental issues, 16, 254–56, 258–63, 265–69, 288; interest in, 256, 261–62, 268; and interest groups, 254–58, 260–68
Environmental Protection Act, 260
Established Program Financing, 249
Ethics and politics, 132; and socialization, 105, 121
Ethnicity, 40, 78, 80, 87, 89, 91, 105, 108, 175, 187, 202, 346–47, 359, 399, 432–33; and divisions among groups, 12, 14, 71, 170, 411–13; and elections, 155; and self-concept, 80, 81, 87, 89, 91; as variable in analysis, 81
Europe, Canadian relations with, 278–79, 283
Exports, 42, 275, 277
Expulsions/Evacuations, 59, 62–66

Fairness doctrine, 13, 125, 144; fairness theory, 28–29, 32–33, 37–38, 48
Federal Council, 420–22
Federal-provincial relations, 15–16, 21, 73, 99, 145, 163–65, 222, 226, 231–32, 234, 237, 396–97, 435; conflicts, 15, 20, 194, 204, 206, 217–18, 225, 238, 240–41, 244–45, 249, 354, 379, 385, 387, 389, 392–93, 406; distribution of power, 9, 156, 242–45, 300, 318, 391, 396–98, 410, 420
Federalism, 7, 78, 87, 90, 171–72, 177, 205–6, 220–21, 244, 249, 329, 331, 336–38, 354, 358, 366, 379–80, 384–86, 388, 394–97, 402, 410–12, 416–17, 419–24, 437, 443; cooperative, 15, 218–20, 385, 406; cost-benefit index of, 336–38, 342, 345–47, 350; efficiency of, 239–40; executive, 249, 381–82, 391–92, 394, 436, 440–42, 447; fiscal, 250–51, intrastate, 403–4, 433–36; intrastate, centralist, 435–36; intrastate, provincial, 434–36; and the media, 143; provincialist, 394–97; renewed, 19, 304, 329–31, 333–36, 341–42, 346–47, 350–52, 422, 438; revised, 23, 241, 421; Trudeau's philosophy of, 385, 429–33, 436, 438–39, 443, 446
Foreign investment, 271, 273–90; Foreign Investment Review Act, 276–78; policies, 17, 273–74; policies of Foreign Investment Review Agency (FIRA), 276, 278, 282, 284, 290; and the United States, 17, 271, 273–74, 277–78, 280, 282–90
Foreign policy, 271, 275, 278, 281–83, 285,

• Contributors •

E. Donald Briggs is professor of political science at the University of Windsor. Currently he is working on the role of the media in Canadian elections.

Alan C. Cairns is professor of political science at the University of British Columbia. He is the author of numerous articles on Canadian politics.

Harold D. Clarke is professor of political science and department head, Virginia Polytechnic Institute and State University. He is co-author of *Political Choice in Canada, Citizen Politicians—Canada,* and *Representative Democracy in the Canadian Provinces,* and co-editor of a special issue of *Legislative Studies Quarterly.* His articles have appeared in journals such the *American Journal of Political Science,* the *British Journal of Political Science,* the *Canadian Journal of Political Science,* and *Comparative Politics.*

Ronald S. Dick worked for many years in the educational media. Specializing in international and political affairs, he made some forty documentary films for the National Film Board of Canada, including the series *Commonwealth of Nations* and *Struggle for a Border,* the latter a visual history of Canadian-American relations to 1871. He also acted as director of research for NFB English productions from 1970 to 1977.

David Falcone is associate professor of health administration at Duke University. He formerly taught at Carleton University in Ottawa. He has written a number of chapters for books and has published articles in *Comparative Politics,* the *Journal of Politics, Round Table, Current History,* the *Policy Studies Journal,* the *Journal of Community Health,* and the *Journal of Health Politics, Policy, and Law* of which he is associate editor.

François-Pierre Gingras is associate professor and chairman of the department of political science at the University of Ottawa. He is the author of numerous articles and papers on Quebec politics and na- tionalist movements, including chapters in D. J. Bellamy, J. H. Pam- mett, and D. C. Rowat, eds., *Political Parties in Canada*; R. Pelletier, ed., *Partis politiques au Québec*; E. Cloutier and D. Latouche, eds., *Le système politique québécois*. A contributor to *Cahiers interna- tionaux de sociologie*, he also edited a special issue on ethnic relations of the *International Review of Modern Sociology*.

Jane Jenson is associate professor of political science at Carleton University. She is coauthor of *Political Choice in Canada; Crisis, Challenge and Change: Party and Class in Canada*; and *Canadian Politics: An Introduction to Systematic Analysis*. Her articles have ap- peared in journals such as the *Canadian Journal of Political Science* and *Comparative Politics*.

Allan Kornberg is professor and chairman of the department of po- litical science at Duke University and editor of the *Journal of Politics*. He is author of *Canadian Legislative Behavior*, coauthor of *Influence in Parliament: Canada, Citizen Politicians–Canada*, and *Representa- tive Democracy in the Canadian Provinces*, and editor of *Legislatures in Developmental Perspective* and *Legislatures in Comparative Per- spective*. His articles have appeared in journals such as the *American Political Science Review*, the *British Journal of Political Science*, and the *Canadian Journal of Political Science*.

Ronald G. Landes is associate professor of political science at Saint Mary's University, Halifax, Canada. He has published articles on po- litical socialization and political behavior in such journals as *Parlia- mentary Affairs*, *Publius*, *The Journal of Commonwealth and Com- parative Politics*, and *The International Journal of Comparative Soci- ology*. His book, *The Canadian Polity: A Comparative Introduction*, was published by Prentice-Hall of Canada in 1983.

Lawrence LeDuc is professor of political science at the University of Windsor. He is coauthor of *Political Choice in Canada* and co- principal investigator of the 1974, 1979, 1980 National Election and

Quebec referendum panel studies. His articles have appeared in *Comparative Politics, Comparative Political Studies,* the *Canadian Journal of Political Science,* the *British Journal of Political Science, International Perspectives, Public Opinion Quarterly,* and the *European Journal of Political Research.*

J. Alex Murray is Dean of the School of Business at Wilfrid Laurier University. His research interests have focused on the impact of multinational business on the nation state.

Neil Nevitte is associate professor of political science at the University of Calgary. He is coeditor of *The Future of North America: Canada, the United States and Quebec Nationalism* and author of a number of articles on electoral behavior and nationalism.

Douglas C. Nord is assistant professor of political science at the University of Minnesota, Duluth. He has published in the *American Review of Canadian Studies* and is currently engaged in a study of the foreign policy implications of transboundary environmental pollution between the United States and Canada.

Jon Pammett is associate professor of political science at Carleton University. His publications include articles in the *Canadian Journal of Political Science* and *Comparative Politics.* Also, he is coeditor of *The Provincial Political Systems* and *Foundations of Political Culture: Political Socialization in Canada,* and coauthor of *Political Choice in Canada.*

Ronald Rogowski is professor of political science at the University of California, Los Angeles. He is the author of *Rational Legitimacy: A Theory of Political Support* and has published articles in journals such as the *American Political Science Review* and *World Politics.*

Walter I. Romanow is professor of communication studies at the University of Windsor and Dean of the Faculty of Social Science.

Mildred A. Schwartz is professor of sociology at the University of Illinois at Chicago Circle. She is author of *The Environment for*

Policy-Making in Canada and the United States, Politics and Territory, and *Public Opinion and Canadian Identity,* and coauthor of *Canadian Political Parties: Origin, Character, Impact* and *Political Parties and the Canadian Social Structure,* as well as numerous articles on Canadian society and politics.

Joel Smith is professor of sociology at Duke University. He is coauthor of *Citizen Politicans—Canada, Restructuring the Canadian State,* and *Ecology and Demography,* and coeditor of *Legislatures in Development.* He has written numerous articles for sociological and political science journals in both Canada and the United States.

Walter C. Soderlund is professor of political science at the University of Windsor. In addition to coauthoring *Canadian Confederation: A Decision-Making Analysis,* he has published articles in such journals as the *Canadian Journal of Political Science, Comparative Politics, Journalism Quarterly,* and *Gazette.*

Marianne C. Stewart is a doctoral candidate in political science at Duke University and a visiting assistant professor of political science at Hollins College. She has published in the *American Journal of Political Science,* the *Journal of Politics,* and the *American Review of Canadian Studies.* She currently is assistant editor of the *Journal of Politics* and is engaged in a study of the determinants of political support in Canada.

Rick Van Loon is professor of political science at the University of Ottawa and formerly was Assistant Deputy Minister, Income Support and Transfer Payments in the Ministry of State for Social Development of the Government of Canada. He was for several years a member of the faculty at Carleton University in the department of political science and the school of public administration. His recent publications have dealt with federal-provincial shared-cost programs and public sector financial management policy processes. He also is coauthor of *The Canadian Political System: Environment, Structure, and Process.*

Ronald H. Wagenberg is professor of political science at the University of Windsor. He is coauthor of *Introduction to Canadian Poli-*

tics and *Canadian Confederation: A Decision-Making Analysis,* as well as a number of articles in various journals.

Geoffrey R. Weller is associate professor and chairman of the department of political studies at Lakehead University. He has contributed chapters to various books and he has published articles on health policy and the Canadian north in journals such as the *Canadian Journal of Political Science, Canadian Public Administration,* the *Journal of Canadian Studies, Inuit Studies,* and the *Journal of Health Politics, Policy and Law.*

John Wilson is professor of political science at the University of Waterloo. He is the author of a number of articles on various aspects of Canadian national and provincial politics which have appeared in the *Canadian Journal of Political Science* and the *Journal of Canadian Studies.*